MW01166390

NJINGA

Breaking the Cycle in Africa   22,040km 20 countries 299 days

KATE LEEMING

*An Official Activity for the United Nations
Decade of Education for Sustainable
Development*

Copyright © 2014 Kate Leeming
Maps by Tandem Design (tandemdesign.com.au)

Published by Vivid Publishing
P.O. Box 948, Fremantle
Western Australia 6959
www.vividpublishing.com.au

National Library of Australia cataloguing-in-publication data:
Author: Leeming, Kate, 1967- author.
Title: Njinga : breaking the cycle in Africa : 22,040km 20 countries 299 days / Kate Leeming.
ISBN: 9781925171297 (paperback)
Subjects: Leeming, Kate, 1967-
            Breaking the Cycle (Cycling expedition) (2010)
            Cycling--Senegal
            Cycling--Somalia.
            Bicycle touring--Senegal
            Bicycle touring--Somalia.
Dewey Number: 796.6

Printed in China. All rights reserved. No part of this publication may be reproduced, stored in a retrieval system or transmitted in any form or by any means, electronic, mechanical, photocopying, recording or otherwise, without the prior written permission of the copyright owner.

**To order further copies or to contact the author,
please visit www.kateleeming.com**

Acknowledgements

Creating, performing and documenting the Breaking the Cycle Expedition would not have been possible without the dedicated support of family, friends and associates, businesses and organisations, all of whom have generously donated their time, energy, expertise and funds. Due to the scale of the expedition and associated projects, it is not possible to list all the committed supporters who helped make this project happen. In particular, I sincerely thank the following:

Expedition sponsors

Nando's, Ausenco, Coca-Cola South Pacific, Coca-Cola Amatil, Restons Solicitors, Ericsson, Range Resources, EMC2 , Ascend Sports (MGC Nutritionals), Furnace Engineering, NKWE Platinum, Continental Coal, Globe Metals and Mining, Bassari Resources, Tailored Consulting, 2XU, Wilderness Wear, The North Face, SRAM, Davidson Branding, Swisse Vitamins, CycleWorks (Boxhill), DMC Mining, Gryphon Minerals, Avonlea Minerals, Link Pumps, Mineral Deposits Ltd, Schwalbe, Allegro Bikes, Centricity, Noah's Rule, NGM Resources, Equip, Trumpet PR, Clinique

Arthur St Hill, Henry Turnbull, Lorna and Ted Leeming, John and Anne Link, Kip Curren, Anne and Peter Stanley, Philip Barker and Diane Rennard, Chittimas Ketvoravit, Owen and Annabel Guest, Michael and Angela Rodd, Mark Sayer, Bryce and Christine Courtenay, Richard and Emma Allen, Carla and Rowan Story, Charles Wright, Glenn Brockwell, Prue and Bob Atkins, Paul Schneider and Margarita Silva, Peter Au and Sandy Lai, Paul and Penny Montgomery, Andrew Lindsay, Don Hawkins, Mark Miller, Merrin Mackay, Ian and Elizabeth Ritchard, Geof Fethers, James Guest, Greg and Leonie Moran, Mackinnon family (Ken, Andrew, Richard), John Bailey, Gavan Griffith, Margaret Cameron, Rob Teese, Jonathan and Judith Sear, Michael MacAleavey, Peter Harman, John Deniz, Roger Speers, Troy Dillon, Robert French

Additional support in Africa: SGS Laboratories, Sundance Resources, African Energy Resources

Expedition supporters

Robert Swan, Tamara DiMattina, Lizzie Brown, Jane Leeming, David Cook, Mark Mackay, Victor Susman, Anton Whitehead, Brendan O'Brien, Jacinta Cavalot, Jeremy Howard, Evelyn Yee, Brendon Sinclair, Anthony Ferguson, Rob Eva, Vladimir and Pauline Markov, Simone Hewett, David Tasker, Linda Fairbrother, Richard Allen, Craig Williams, Philip Endersbee, Brigitte Claney, the Royal Melbourne Tennis Club, Peter Gilmore, Georgia Costello, David Lloyd Jones, Richard Simpson, Frank Filippelli, Jonathan Howell, Ruaraidh Gunn, Chris Chapman, Paul Tabley, Tim Johnson, Julian Snow, Documentary Australia Foundation, Greg Yeoman, Claudio von Planta, Judith Stuhrenberg.

Team

Expedition support: John Davidson (support leader), Daniel Harman, Simon Vernon
Camera operators: Zdenek Kratky, Patrick MacAleavey, Stuart Kershaw

In Africa

Alex Mackenzie, Limane Diouf, Papa Moussa Bâ, Seyid Ould Seyid, Governor Rana, community of Oualata, Bado Fermin, Dr Bocary Kaya, Severin Omar, Isabelle Guirma, Francoise Kabore, Oumarou Koala, Mamadou Alichina (Ali), Professor Boubacar Yamba, Peter and Sally Cunningham, Limane Feldou, Martin Buinlem, Valentine Alobwede, Samuel Londo, Thomas Ngala, Robin Longley, Nerice Nixon, Henri Okemba, Inspector Évariste, Pierre Oba, Adrian Fick, Moira Alberts, Friedrich Alpers, Kyaramacan Association (Tienie, Vasco and Jack), Tim Budge, Benjamin Phiri, Kristin Tweardy, Dave Neiswander, Gatera and Mami Rudasingwa, Donald Ndahiro, Jeanette Mukabalisa, Helen Brown, David Ssemwogerere, John Tembo, Claude Auberson, Christian Kemp-Griffin, Innocent Mwesigye, MaryJane Johnson, Patricia Nightingale, Andrew Nightingale, Matt O'Brien, Brother Barry, Rose Mbithe, Phaustine Ambasisi, Suzie Grant, Valerie Browning, Ismael Ali Gardo, Omer Jama, Issa Farah, Anne-Marie Treweeke, Abdiwali Hersi Nur, Dr Abdirahman M Mohamud (Farole), the Puntland government and security forces, Yassin Mussa Boqor, Mayor and community of Hafun, African Express Airways, Singapore Airlines

Book

Simone Yeo, Jason Swiney, Amy Hayball and Lesley O'Byrne (Tandem Design), Susan Powell, Bron Sibree, Charles Wright, Dick Friend, Russel Howcroft, Valerie Browning, Claire Soveny.

Any factual errors in this book are entirely mine. Unless otherwise indicated, all photographs were taken by myself. Where another person has used my camera, I have marked the image with the photographer's initials.

Partner organisations

UNESCO

Victorian Department of Education and Early Childhood Development

Plan International Australia

World Bicycle Relief

Edun Live

Millennium Promise

500 Supporters' Group

Afar Pastoralist Development Association

HUG (Help Us Grow)

Taakulo Somaliland Community

Aspermont Pty Ltd (resource media partner; MiningNews.net and Resource Stocks)

Additional organisations

Tidène (Niger)

Serving In Mission (Niger)

Integrated Rural Development and Nature Conservation (IRDNC) (Namibia)

Kenana Knitters (Kenya)

To my godson and nephew,
Austin Leeming
A thoughtful and enquiring young mind

Encouraging the next generation to explore to find their passion

The better road to Timbuktu (JD)

Contents

FOREWORD

Valerie Browning AM

Valerie on the steps of her Barbara May Maternity
Hospital (under construction), Mille, Ethiopia

My first sighting of Kate Leeming was in Ethiopia's arid north-east, 70 kilometres from my organisation's field office/base. I couldn't help but be impressed by her sense of timing. We'd made an appointment by email, and meeting it required her to ride about 1500 kilometres from Kenya across almost the entire length of Ethiopia and here she was cycling into town on the very minute we'd set for the rendezvous.

Twenty years living with the nomadic Afar people means that any encounter with a fellow-Australian fires me with electrical joy, but this was something special. This enigma of a woman had achieved so much, and she would go on to complete the 22,040-kilometre bike ride she had planned across the widest part of the African continent – from Senegal in the west to Somalia's Puntland in the east (dodging al-Shabaab extremists on the final leg of this epic journey). She crossed an astonishing total of twenty African countries and met up with 'real' people in all of them as she pushed those pedals around with grinding determination. Kate sampled the stunning diversity of landscapes and people that had intrigued her for so long in a way that could not have been experienced from the seat of a car, a bus ride or, least of all, from airport to airport.

Kate and I hugged on meeting as if we were – as many Afar thought – long-lost relatives. It being close to sunset when she arrived, we scooped her and her bike into our organisation's vehicle and captured her for a couple of days, first taking her back to our implementing base in Logia. That evening,

Kate (along with her support team) joined in with the inaugural Afar youth conference before she slept the night in our household of roughly twenty-five people. We hung off her every word about her adventure, blown away by her insurmountable courage and seeming disregard for danger. Kate conveyed her impressions of the intricately diverse needs, and the solutions, of the communities she had dropped into along her trail. As well as the struggle for education we knew about, they also battled for healthcare, work, economic security, adequate shelter and other factors vital for human development.

My personal encounter with Kate revealed that I had found a soul-mate, a fellow-believer in the urgency and importance of bridging understanding between African communities and her current and my previous homeland, Australia and other Western countries. We were on the same wavelength immediately. Through my marriage to an Afar leader, Ismael Ali Gardo, I have lived an amazing life of high privilege, unprotected from the rawness that poverty brings. I've learnt the treasures of community life, far from the polished, almost sterile, individualism that now structures people's lives in the 'developed' world. Unlike myself, Kate had not lived for two decades far from any semblance of Western life but she instinctively knew where the Afar, who have not had the same chance of education, are coming from.

As she pedalled on her unbroken line across Africa, Kate brushed with death as the local people encounter it; she sat among communities and shared food – and then ended up with diarrhoea – and she was exposed to the pain, and the humour, of disempowered people who long for the same opportunities to learn as have Australians. Not only the words of *Njinga* but also the hundreds of images tell of her meaningful encounters with the inhabitants of this world who still do not have the chances they deserve.

'Njinga' means 'bicycle' in Nyanja, a Zambian language. I think it is significant that it also refers to a seventeenth-century Angolan heroine, a strong, courageous, compassionate woman who resisted Portuguese colonists for four decades and who was known as Queen *Njinga*.

We cannot all do what Kate did but one great thing that we can do is to allow ourselves to be drawn by her infectious enthusiasm into knowing, appreciating and sharing something of the cultures of Africa and into facing the need of human beings for simple justice.

Kate Leeming has become one of the African continent's best ambassadors. I invite you through *Njinga* to be led away from the presumptions of the 'developed' world in relation to this great continent. Allow yourself the freedom to share with her and myself in standing beside the youth who are emerging as Africa's hope.

Kate has inspired me to continue day in day out trying to achieve the justice of development for the Afar people against the odds. Here, resource exploitation is fast becoming the name of the game, when it is the resources that could be used to foster people who are struggling, and Western governments are bowing out of the tedious struggle to bring safety to motherhood, dignity of self through employment and education for all. As 2015, the 'achievement year' for the Millennium Development Goals fast approaches, we are closer but still a long way from reaching targets such as universal access to primary education. There is much to do.

I will probably not come back and live in Australia. Kate struggles on to be the voice of the voiceless from Australia. You too can take your place among those eager to see a better-balanced world. Enjoy this magic read as I have. Meet the communities of this other world, and resolve to do something about the indifference that so often stunts our vision.

Introduction

A HEART TO HEART

A wonky door in Oualata, Mauritania, a
sister town of Timbuktu

I first heard the expression 'From here to Timbuktu' from my grandmother, who only ever travelled out
of her home state, Western Australia, once in her lifetime, and that was to visit relatives in the east of the
country. I doubt whether she knew where Timbuktu was. For most of us, the familiar phrase refers to
somewhere inaccessible or an unimaginable distance away. Many people even believe Timbuktu to be
a fictitious place, rather than the legendary town it actually is on the edge of the Sahara Desert in Mali,
West Africa. But I had long identified it in my world atlas as a place I wanted to visit some day.

Growing up, I had very limited exposure to what was commonly referred to as the 'Dark Continent.'
Apart from basic geography, little was taught about Africa at my Australian school, and with the exception
of one fellow-student, I had no exposure to black African people. My impressions of Africa were almost
entirely formed by images in the media – film and television, magazines, newsprint and radio. Through
these I fell for its natural beauty. Nature programs and magazines such as *National Geographic* further
revealed its vast landscapes of savannah, desert, jungle and mountains and its indigenous mega fauna
(elephants, giraffes, rhinoceroses, hippopotami...), big cats and great apes. The same sources featured

stories about minority groups of people such as the Maasai of Kenya and Tanzania or the San of southern Africa. I enjoyed these too, even if they were not representative of the majority of African people.

The story which inspired me most in primary school was that of paleoanthropologist Mary Leakey unearthing the first jawbone of an early hominid, 'Nutcracker Man,' at Olduvai Gorge in 1959. Her team's subsequent discoveries of 'Handy Man' and the Laetoli footprints infused me with a deep curiosity about Africa as the 'Cradle of Humankind.' The account of one woman's discovery was kindling to fire in my adventurous soul.

As an eleven-year-old I was, of course, unaware that many of these messages and images were laden with stereotypes. Africa was typically portrayed as a culturally monolithic country rather than a diverse, dynamic continent of fifty-four nations, each a melting pot of sometimes hundreds of different languages and cultures. Colonial days were usually glorified and African people painted as primitive, uncivilised, inferior and without history prior to European influences. The Africa I learned about was perceived to be a dangerous place, where violence was endemic and problems unsolvable. The most indelible images of the continent were of famine and starvation or conflict.

Then came the Live Aid concerts in 1985. I was eighteen at the time, in my first year at university and with an awakening social conscience. For me Live Aid was like a siren with flashing red lights. In the end, the initiative raised almost $US200 million for victims of the 1984 Ethiopian famine and thousands of lives were saved as a result. Its most lasting value was the broad-scale awareness that it brought to an estimated audience of nearly two billion people. People like me. But at the time, I found it difficult to relate to what I was seeing. I lived a world away, growing up on a farm 130 kilometres north-east of Perth, the most geographically isolated major city on the planet. I had little experience of other cultures, my comfortable existence revolving around family, sporting successes, study and an active social life. So while I was aghast at the images of starving children and motivated by the messages delivered by international stars, it was difficult to fully empathise with issues so remote from my own life.

In early 1990, just as the world celebrated the release of Nelson Mandela and the dismantling of apartheid in South Africa, I started my first mini cycle tour in Ireland and, soon after, a series of longer journeys through Europe. Initially I did not understand what could be achieved on a bike, but travelling under my own steam really appealed to my sense of adventure. On a bike I felt free – free to feel the sun on my back, wind in my face, rain on my shoulders and bumps in the road. I could smell the organic farm scents and the salty Atlantic breeze. I could hear the birds singing, dogs barking and the wind rustling through the trees. Even food tasted better, and using up so much energy, I needed to consume quite a lot. I loved bringing the lines on a map to life; from the red lines of busy highways to the white lines of peaceful country lanes, from the blue lines of rivers to the brown contour lines denoting mountains, and from the border lines of a country or region to coastlines of an island or a continent.

I found this mode of transport enabled me to delve into the heart of a land and its cultures, something that doesn't happen so easily when one is cocooned in a vehicle. A cyclist poses no threat and is usually not considered to be wealthy (or they wouldn't be riding a bike). Travelling by bike tends to break down social barriers; it encourages the best in local hospitality. Putting my trust and faith in people was usually reciprocated in spades – these new friends appreciated the effort made to see their neck of the woods. Because it engenders such a close connection between people and land, travelling by bicycle gives an unrivalled sense of place, an awareness of how it all fits together. For me this was the nub.

Travelling this way also gives a very personal, grounded perspective. You have to explore and push your own boundaries both physically and mentally. Arctic frost nip, bracing Celtic winds and sleet and stifling Mediterranean heat all toughened me up. Plenty of testing demons were out there if I allowed myself to be overcome, from demon drivers to the demons in my head. There was the raw backside, nagging headwinds, dehydration, insatiable hunger, debilitating fatigue and rare but unnerving encounters with opportunists trying to take advantage. No-one could do the work for me and so counteracting such problems built resolve. I learned that there was always a way if I just kept turning the pedals, stayed alert and focused on the positives. By the end of each day, week, month and journey, by sticking at it through thick and thin, the intrinsic rewards were deep satisfaction, greater inner strength and feeling an invincible level of fitness. Every region travelled becomes a small part of me. Memories are vivid, even after twenty years. I can not only identify every photograph I've taken on tour, but also the story behind each one; how I was feeling, what the weather was like, who I spoke to, whether I had a puncture just before the stop, the mountain I had just climbed...

Every journey is a learning process. The 15,000 kilometres I cycled through Europe from Spain to Turkey to the Nord Kapp, Norway, the most northerly tip of the continent, was like doing an undergraduate degree in the university of life. I had discovered my passion, but realised that there was a far greater value to these journeys than personal satisfaction. In all of my 'postgraduate studies' since, I have attempted to generate a two-way relationship. In return for being enriched by the experience, I always try to create a benefit for the people or countries that I choose to travel through. The purpose of my first major expedition, the 1993 Trans-Siberian Cycle Expedition, a 13,400-kilometre, five-month journey from St Petersburg to Vladivostok, was to aid the children of Chernobyl. The Great Australian Cycle Expedition (known as the GRACE Expedition) of 2004-05 promoted the importance of education for sustainable development. That 25,000-kilometre, nine-and-a-half-month journey included 7000 kilometres on remote desert tracks, the most challenging section being the Canning Stock Route that crosses almost 1000 sand dunes and four deserts. The project, which included an education program, was selected as an 'official activity' for the United Nations Decade of Education for Sustainable Development (2005-14).

I've always been attracted to the idea of travelling through Africa. But I previously hadn't had the confidence or belief that I could successfully pull off a journey there, perhaps due to the many misconceptions about the continent that were conveyed during my upbringing. Now, fuelled by the success of my past expeditions, I turned to Africa. I knew that it must be possible to travel through it by bike because Cape Town to Cairo is a well-worn trail and cycling down the west coast from Morocco south, while less usual, is still attempted by a few every year.

The route I chose evolved out of personal interests and sensitivities developed from previous experiences and influences. Much of the land that I had cycled through in Australia was either desert or marginal pastoral country on the edge of the desert. Given my own background of growing up on a wheat and sheep farm, I was interested in land use, particularly in these fragile environments that are susceptible to desertification. My eye was drawn to the Sahel, an eco-region approximately 300 kilometres wide at the base of the Sahara Desert. 'Sahel' means 'shoreline of the desert' in Arabic. As a former teacher I had a keen interest in the importance of education, and when I studied a world map showing levels of illiteracy, the standout zone for me was again the Sahel. It appeared that not just Africa's but the world's lowest levels of education were generally concentrated along a band of countries spanning Africa, where people eke out an existence on the dry, infertile environment of the Sahel. The climate, which in recent decades has become drier and more prone to extremes, magnifies the problems.

My original plan had been to cycle across Africa from west to east between its widest points, thus following a route where the geography and the education-related issues intersected. When I researched further, it became obvious that high illiteracy was inextricably linked to the incidence of poverty. In order to understand why these countries have such inadequate education, I needed to explore all of the key issues relating to extreme poverty, economic, political, social and environmental.

The journey also had to be a continuous line starting from the most westerly tip of the African continent, Pointe des Almadies, just west of Dakar, Senegal, and finishing at the most easterly landmark at Cape Hafun, Puntland, Somalia. The underlying concept to not break the line was to demonstrate (metaphorically at least) that everything is connected; every issue, every culture – including my own. I wanted to create a positive and constructive grassroots story that linked non-Africans to Africans to help dispel some of the many misconceptions about the continent and its issues. From a competitive adventurer's point of view too, cycling an unbroken line was important because I could find no record of anyone completing the journey previously – at least not to the tip of Cape Hafun. Not missing even a kilometre was also essential for my personal discipline. Without this goal it would be easy to miss a section, perhaps through the inevitable hard times or when negotiating with troublesome authorities. For the sake of my own psyche the continuous line was paramount.

I settled on a purpose that I wholeheartedly believed in after years of thought and research and as a culmination of experiences and lessons learned from previous expeditions. In order to undertake and sustain a project of such magnitude, motivation must come from the heart first. This project would take over my life. I would need to devote about five years to organise the expedition, complete the journey and document it post-expedition. The commitment meant resigning from work (again), stepping out of my comfort zone and channelling all my physical and mental energy. I basically had to live it. The core question to answer was 'why?'. I had to be sure of my reasons for doing this to endure the anticipated hardships. I had to back up 'why' with 'how' and 'what' to sell the project to others: future team-mates, potential partners, sponsors, educators, the media and supporters. Compared to previous expeditions, the Breaking the Cycle Expedition, as I called it, was going to be my PhD. And all my thinking, questioning and research culminated in this mission statement which I published on the Breaking the Cycle in Africa website (www.btcycle.com):

> *The purpose of the project is to learn firsthand about the causes and consequences*
> *of extreme poverty and, through the story of the expedition that unfolds, educate*
> *and inspire actions which will assist in making communities more sustainable and*
> *resilient to the issues. Essentially this is about giving a 'leg-up' rather than a 'handout.'*

Organising this expedition and associated projects was incredibly complicated – the most difficult, multifaceted lead-up I have experienced. I realised that the subject matter was vast and complex and that it would be difficult to make sense of it all by simply pedalling through a region. The point of cycling was to gain a grounded perspective of the countries and geographies, and a taste of the cultures, I would be exposed to. To understand issues related to chronic poverty and put them into a perspective for others to comprehend, I planned to seed the story by visiting various projects along the route. Local and international experts would add the weight of their experiences and knowledge about each aspect.

If each continent on Earth could be represented by an organ of the human body, then Africa, even by virtue of its shape and location, would be the heart. And if the heart-shaped continent's roads could represent its own coronary blood vessels, then cycling along them is akin to the flow of oxygenated blood bringing them to life – pumping through the major arteries (highways) to the capillaries (minor roads) and cells. I could not wait to see Africa come 'alive,' feel its heartbeat.

From what I had already learned, Africa's heart could be in better condition and I was keen to find out what can and is being done to 'improve its health.' Firstly, I planned to look at modern Africa's 'congenital heart diseases': inherent disorders such as slavery, the long-term effects of colonialism and post-independence despotic rulers. Next was to find out what is being done to dissolve the 'clots' of conflict and war, lower the 'cholesterol' of corruption and repair any 'leaky valves' by improving transparency and governance. I had arranged to visit projects that reduce the likelihood of an 'environment-induced cardiac arrest'; schemes that are halting desertification, protecting diversity and preventing loss of habitats. I wanted to see how communities were adopting a 'heart-safe diet' by means of developing agriculture, increasing food security and improving access to clean drinking water and sanitation. To stay healthy and resilient, a heart must maintain a fitness regime. I planned to focus on initiatives that build 'heart capacity,' such as the education of primary students and future leaders, projects that empower women and improve health across the board. Finally, a healthy heart needs to have fit, elastic external blood vessels to transport the life-giving blood around the body. On my journey, I had questions to ask about aid effectiveness, the outcomes of debt cancellation, how countries can develop trade and be competitive, what is being done to attract foreign and local investment and the benefits of improved infrastructure and communications.

In 2000 the 189 member states of the United Nations set a blueprint, the Millennium Development Goals (MDGs), to end extreme poverty. The eight goals reflect an understanding of the many interconnected factors that contribute to acute poverty and include time-bound measurable targets to address the issues. The MDGs are the world's shared framework for development, to be achieved by 2015. They are applicable for every nation, developed and developing, because poverty is not uniform and it exists in every society to some degree. For Africa, the continent where poverty is most prevalent, the MDGs are like the prescription to improve 'heart health.' At the time they were set, these goals were considered ambitious and only

Millennium Development Goals

1. Reduce extreme poverty and hunger by half

2. Achieve universal primary education

3. Promote gender equality and empower women

4. Reduce child mortality by two-thirds

5. Reduce maternal mortality by three-quarters

6. Combat HIV/AIDS, malaria and other diseases

7. Ensure environmental development

8. Develop a global partnership for development

achievable, as Kofi Annan (UN Secretary-General 1997-2006) put it, 'if we break with business as usual.'

By the time the expedition was ready to go, I had built into the itinerary a way of at least touching on each of these key issues that conspire, in any number of combinations, to keep people trapped in a cycle of extreme poverty. With the aim of understanding them from as many different angles as possible I had formed partnerships with ten different organisations ranging from small grassroots enterprises to global operations. As with my previous 2004-05 expedition, The Great Australian Cycle (GRACE) Expedition, UNESCO selected the project as an 'official activity' for their Decade of Education for Sustainable Development (DESD, 2005-14) stating that the project 'is quite timely and helps in promoting a new vision of a more just and sustainable world.'

The Victorian Department of Education and Early Childhood Development (DEECD) came on board as the key educational partner, creating a custom-designed education program with the objectives of 'deepening students' awareness and understandings of African cultures, geography, environmental sustainability and the causes and effects of extreme poverty.' With educational input from Plan International, the end result was an e-learning program that far exceeded the scope of my original proposal. The department created three interdisciplinary units from three 'fertile' questions designed to be applicable to many aspects of the expedition and to be undertaken at any point during the journey. The units were:

How am I connected to Africa?
How does where I live affect who I am?
Why should I care about poverty?

A special networking website was designed for teachers and interested followers to collaborate and share their ideas, resources, experiences and enthusiasm. While the program was originally tailored for Australian middle school students, UNESCO helped to publicise the project internationally, further diversifying and enriching the learning platform.

I was excited about what was being produced: the fertile questions the DEECD had identified, when it came down to it, were the very questions I wanted to answer for myself. My generation certainly never had access to this kind of learning. This further fuelled my motivation.

✳

Forming a team of people with the appropriate credentials and commitment was a key challenge. This time I planned to make a documentary film in order to fully realise the potential of the story and the educational purpose of the expedition. To successfully record the journey I therefore needed to find an independent camera operator. I also needed a support vehicle and driver. While cycling unsupported is a more intimate way of travelling that has, in the past, allowed me to slip quietly through the net, having a support vehicle changes the nature of the travel experience. On the positive side, it allows greater flexibility to divert off the route at times to visit projects and other sites of interest. Using vehicle support means the team is less dependent on the immediate environment as more water, food and fuel can be bought at major centres, stored and carried further distances. It also means there is space for a few more luxuries than can normally be lugged in four bicycle panniers. The downsides are that a group is a more visible target for thieves and corrupt customs officials, there is more likelihood of mechanical breakdown and accidents, and hiring a driver and vehicle more than doubles the cost of the expedition.

The success of the Breaking the Cycle Expedition was going to be largely dependent on my finding the right person to provide and coordinate support. Almost a year before the journey was due to start,

I was connected with John Davidson, a veteran leader of many seasons of overland trips for Exodus, a British adventure travel company. More recently, he had been specialising in providing appropriate support for one-off expeditions like mine. When not on expedition, John works as a farmer in East Lothian, Scotland. John was vastly experienced in African conditions, especially in the Sahara. I hoped his presence would become the perfect foil for my lack of African experience.

I also wanted to find a cyclist to accompany me for the bulk of the journey. Locating someone with the relevant experience and ability who was able to commit for any length of time was difficult. It would be better to have no one than the wrong person. I connected with Daniel Harman, a young Brit, after reading his blog. With a seemingly insatiable passion for travel, this twenty-four-year-old carpenter had already ticked off an impressive list of destinations. The previous year he'd cycled 11,000 kilometres from his hometown on the English south coast to Sierra Leone, raising money for the British organisation FARM-Africa. He had originally planned to cycle through to South Africa but had not done so, for personal reasons; however he intended to regroup and complete the journey. I could gauge his adventurous spirit and the positive intent from his writing and contacted him. Initially he committed to cycling with me as far as Namibia, from where he would continue his journey south as planned, but after about three months of communications, six months before the expedition was due to start, he decided to come the whole way.

I felt that in John and Daniel I had found team-mates with shared passion and enthusiasm for Africa and for the cause of the expedition. I believed that we would make a balanced core group with complementary strengths and skills. On the flip side, we were strangers. I endeavoured to communicate with them regularly but we would not meet in person until two weeks before the start when I travelled to the UK. Our relationship was built on trust: I had to trust that they would honour their commitment and they had to trust that I would pull everything together and on time – the budget, equipment, partners, education program and logistics.

John had to ensure that his vehicle was prepared and kitted out for the rigours of the journey. He arranged for his friend and colleague Simon Vernon, another experienced overland tour driver and Land Rover mechanic by trade, to relieve him for the two months that he would have to leave the expedition for farm commitments. As a meticulous character and mechanic, Simon proved to be a vital part of the team, ensuring the vehicle was ready for action. When he wasn't driving in Africa Simon acted as a backup expert for the expedition in the UK. It didn't matter how good Daniel or I were at cycling if, because of the way this expedition was set up, the vehicle broke down or the drivers faltered, we could go no farther. This was to be a team effort.

Patrick MacAleavey, a recent graduate of the Bachelor of Creative Arts (Film and Television) course at Deakin University in Melbourne, saw joining the expedition as an opportunity to fast-track his film-making career. I had previously helped Paddy with one of his university projects and, when searching for someone appropriate to come with us, put the idea to him. He had excelled at his studies and was proactive in developing his business. He had travelled overseas before, although not to developing countries, which meant that he was uninitiated in the rigorous, testing conditions he would soon be exposed to. What he lacked in experience, however, I thought he would make up for with enthusiasm: I believed he would rise to the opportunity. Once he committed to the project three months prior to the start, he worked hard to set up the filming side with an appropriate standard of camera equipment, and began to document the final weeks of the organisational phase. I was impressed with his effort and tried to bring him up to speed with what to expect.

One of the most important issues that I needed to convince my team-mates and supporters about was security. Had I conformed to the travel warnings set by the Department of Foreign Affairs and Trade (they were the same on all major national websites – Australian, British, US, Canadian and French), then I would have skipped many countries, or zones in certain countries, that were essential to get through to maintain the continuous line. I didn't ignore the warnings but I developed my own inside connections with trustworthy sources to ensure we had the best chance of passing through safely. John provided a few contacts he had made with Tuareg organisations in Niger and Mali during a previous journey, and some expedition partners were helpful with information about the specific regions where they were active. One of the most effective strategies I developed for security and logistics was to approach Australian resource companies with interests in Africa. They always had the most up-to-date security information and were well-connected to the government of the country in which they were operating. Initially I targeted companies working in Senegal, Cameroon, the Republic of Congo and Puntland, Somalia, but by the time I was ready to go, there were eleven different companies involved. While I heard many murmurs implying that I would be lucky to make it through to the finish, my attitude to organising the project was that we would be unlucky not to get there safely.

Although the missions were set, the planned route was continually being shaped by the locations of projects I arranged to visit and by security obstacles. As usual, I planned for the maximum itinerary possible, on the understanding that the course could be adapted to account for the ever-changing and unpredictable circumstances that were likely to surface. If all went to plan, we would travel through at least twenty different countries and over 22,000 kilometres in ten months. Of course, the journey had to be kept to a continuous line if humanly possible. This all had to be timed with the seasons – to pass along the base of the Sahara Desert during the coolest months and minimise the amount of time travelling through the tropical Wet. Given that the route involved crossing the Equator twice, it was not possible to avoid all the Rainy seasons completely. This all meant that to make it work, the only time to start was October 2009, otherwise I would have to wait another year.

The process of developing and organising the Breaking the Cycle Expedition resembled the life-cycle of a cyclone or hurricane. It starts off as a weak, low depression out to sea and gradually builds momentum, becoming more powerful and more intense and sapping more energy as it nears land. All of the vision and ideology, fitness, plans, partners, team-mates, education program, logistics, branding and publicity would be to no avail unless I could raise an estimated budget of $AUD200,000. And there was a recession going on. As is always the case, few sponsors commit until the pressure of time forces them to make a decision – and no one wants to be first. With four months to go, everything was progressing in the right direction but it was all moving too slowly. The intensity had to be ramped up further. Without the efforts of my long-time mentor Robert Swan OBE, the first person in history to have walked to both the North and South poles, and other friends and colleagues, I may not have made it to the start line. Miraculously it all came together. In the final two weeks I pulled in the last $AUD40,000. Talk about stress. This cyclone had morphed into a perfect storm.

When giving media interviews I tried to appear calm, focused and in control, but in reality there was a hurricane in my head too. Responses from the general public to my pending journey could be categorised into two distinct streams. On the surface, many well-wishers voiced their support while there was a negative undercurrent from those who expressed concerns and deep-rooted Afro-pessimism. These responses mirrored the misconceptions portrayed in some media and beyond.

'Africa's problems are too big to solve', 'Why should we care about their problems when we have our own in Australia?', 'Why don't Africans want to help themselves?', 'Donating aid is like throwing money down a bottomless pit', 'Nothing will ever change, so why bother?'.

I had received the same reactions during the course of the organisational phase from a broad demographical cross-section – the media only reflect society's view of itself and these reactions confirmed it. These attitudes and misconceptions served to galvanise my spirit and reinforce the importance of the messages I was sending out. If I was to travel to Africa with these stereotypical images ingrained in my thoughts, I would always travel in fear. Fear attracts fear, and then I definitely wouldn't make it.

The preparation for such an enormous undertaking was never going to be perfect. I could always do something more but I had to be content with the lot that we had. All of the basic systems were in place. We were slightly short on funds and the education program needed better promotion. After all the best intentions, my physical preparation amounted to more like a de-training program. I had tested myself, especially my permanently injured right knee, to determine that I was up to it. I wasn't totally unfit, but in the last few months my time had been limited to mostly intensive gym workouts as I had been working four days a week while putting everything together, quite often surviving on a few hours of sleep. I knew that I was capable but I would have to rely on my natural fitness for the first few weeks until I was up to speed.

The knee, which had deteriorated since my previous expedition, was my biggest fitness concern as it had not fully recovered from my competing back-to-back in the women's real tennis British Open and World Championships in 2007. I had since then made many sacrifices as a real tennis professional to ensure that I preserved the knee for the expedition. Cycling is the best exercise I can do for it but it was impossible to determine how the knee would go day after day, month after month, for ten months. My management plan involved injections of Synvisc (temporary artificial cartilage substitute) prior to setting off, taking an anti-inflammatory every morning on cycling days and ensuring I cycled with the most efficient technique. I had been developing specific strength with regular clinical Pilates sessions. The main issue was to control any swelling.

In the final few days I ran solely on adrenalin, my emotions on a knife-edge. I had to ensure we had all the equipment and clothing, flights were organised, 180 kilograms of baggage, insurance, documents ready – the checklist was extensive. Vladimir from Cycle Works delivered the boxed bikes the night before we were due to leave and the last of the t-shirts were packed, still warm from the screen printers, about an hour before Paddy and I left for London.

✳

The two weeks spent in the UK served as the metamorphic stage of the expedition: meeting the team, pulling all the ends together and making the final preparations before spreading our wings and heading for Dakar. After the long build-up, there was an air of excitement when all five team members finally came together for the first time on Simon's parents' farm, just south of Birmingham. Dan, Paddy and I drove up from London in the loaded hire van to meet John, who had just arrived from Scotland after finishing harvest. Simon was already hard at work giving John's Land Rover a thorough mechanical overhaul in preparation for the journey. The old red Defender not only looked the perfect vehicle for the job, it possessed a personality all of its own. The engine idled with a deep, reassuring throaty voice while the exterior had a real presence – it had muscles. Being an older model, it was not going to be as desirable to bandits as would a shiny new Land Cruiser. The Defender fitted with the understated image that I wanted the expedition to have, and John liked the simplicity of the mechanics, which he said would be much easier to maintain than those of a newer vehicle.

With a day and a half together to sort out operations, there was barely time to get to know each other … but there would be plenty of time for that during the journey. We were quickly down to business. I found it reassuring to finally be with four other committed individuals all working for this common goal. Our gear was soon spread over the floor of Simon's tidy workshop. Dan couldn't wait to try out his new bike for the first time. John and I had to formalise our business partnership as that was central to the running of the expedition. From the start, it was apparent that John was a no-fuss, straight-down-the-line kind of guy. I could work with that.

As quickly as all the equipment was laid out, sorted and assembled, it was packed away again. The day after Dan, Paddy and I returned to London, John and Simon embarked on their first challenge – a ten-day, 5000-kilometre drive from the UK, through Spain, Morocco, Western Sahara and Mauritania to Senegal. They hoped to make it all the way to Dakar in time for the start on 21 October although it was going to be tight. Our contingency plan was that they meet us in St Louis – Dan and I would start from Dakar and cycle the 250 kilometres up to St Louis with the support of Bassari Resources, a Senegalese-based sponsor.

London is far better connected to Africa than Melbourne and so finding the remaining specific equipment, sorting out communications, flights and visas was much easier from there. Five days before we were due to start pedalling, we wrapped everything up and boarded our Dakar-bound flight.

✳

It all started surprisingly well as we disembarked from the plane into the stifling heat and humidity of early evening. We met up with Bigué, who had been sent by our sponsor to see us through the airport safely. But as we headed for Customs we hit a wall of chaos. 'Helpers' and opportunists swarmed like moths to a flame and I suddenly had visions of all the equipment that I had carefully selected and earned from sponsors vanishing into the darkness. Somehow, along with all our gear, we ended up in the right place, were bundled into two vehicles, and off.

A monument to the liberation from slavery, Île de Gorée

Being driven around Dakar's chaotic streets during the first few days, I tried to imagine how we were going to cope with the random traffic on bicycles. It was the tail-end of the Wet season and regular downpours filled gaping potholes and caused storm drains to block. Trapped in the constant traffic jams we sweltered in the clammy conditions, made worse because we were reluctant to wind down the windows for fear of allowing mosquitoes in. Faced with such an unfamiliar, testing set of circumstances, without local support we would not have been able to turn everything around in five days: obtain visas for Mali and Mauritania, acclimatise, make all sorts of final preparations and see something of Dakar. A priority was to visit Île de Gorée, a principal depot and transportation point for the 300-year-long transatlantic slave trade that ended in the mid-1800s.

John and Simon kept us posted with news of their progress on the drive from the UK to Senegal. And the news was good. They had surpassed their target of reaching St Louis and were on their way, braving the bedlam of Dakar, to join us. They would be weary from the effort but I was pleased that we would start the expedition together and on time.

We had discovered that the most westerly extremity of Pointe des Almadies is a pile of rocks that can only be accessed by walking through privately-owned restaurant grounds. As the business would be closed in the morning when we wanted to leave we visited at sunset on the eve of our departure. To our dismay, the gate to the walkway was locked and the manager would not give us permission to open it. Determined to reach this landmark, we scaled the fence like fugitives, bikes and all. Once safely ensconced on the rocky outcrop, there was just enough time to pause and take it all in. Here I was, finally standing on the most westerly tip of the continent, the intense organisational phase over, the team poised and ready to go, students waiting to receive news of the story as it happened. I felt an immense sense of achievement even to get this far. I couldn't wait to start pedalling the next day. How would the journey unfold? Would I make it to the most easterly point? Somalia seemed a world away. In the life-cycle of the expedition hurricane, this was the eye of the storm, a brief moment of tranquillity and reflection on a beautiful, calm evening.

A brief moment of tranquillity. Standing at Pointe des Almadies, the most westerly tip of the African continent (PM)

This journey promised to be a test of my heart in so many ways; physically, emotionally, spiritually. In a very obvious sense, it was going to be tough pedalling on average six to eight hours a day over every type of terrain and exposed to the full range of weather conditions. I was looking for the positives – for initiatives and ideas that are contributing to peace and prosperity, protecting diversity and beauty and instilling hope and optimism. On the other hand, I knew I would be confronted with some challenging situations where compassion and empathy would tear at the heart strings. But I was ready for my heart-to-heart with the African continent.

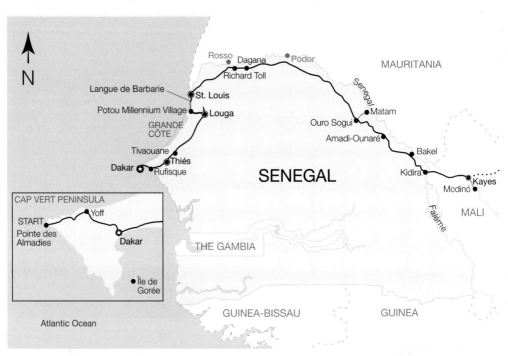

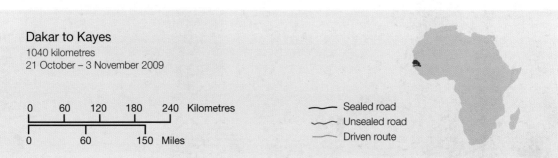

Dakar to Kayes
1040 kilometres
21 October – 3 November 2009

0	60	120	180	240	Kilometres

0		60		150	Miles

——— Sealed road
∼∼∼∼ Unsealed road
········· Driven route

1

BREAKING THE CYCLIST INTO AFRICA

Dakar to Kayes (Senegal)

Ready to go. With (from left) Daniel, John and Paddy at the most westerly point (SV)

The twenty-first of October was upon us and finally the moment of truth – we were ready to go. The team and a small band of well-wishers gathered at the most westerly point of the continent. Organising the expedition had been incredibly intense. In reaching the start line, I felt so knackered and choked with pride, it could well have been the finish line. I didn't have much to say except that our first task was to get through Dakar's traffic – alive.

The first few kilometres from Pointe des Almadies to Yoff were sedate compared with what was to follow. There was little time to get used to handling our brand-new laden bikes and find a rhythm before the leafy green avenue evolved into a chaotic scramble where road rules are non-existent. The freeway forms a mad bottleneck: the main artery in and out for the six million people who live in Dakar and the surrounding Cap Vert peninsula.

I took the menagerie of vehicles that we shared the road with as representative of the diversity of West Africa's economic capital. At one extreme, shiny new 4WDs and trucks hauling container loads from the busy port represented the new Dakar surging ahead with international investment. At the other extreme, donkey carts that carried the wares of the local market sellers, or the entire belongings of the owner, kept well to the right of the lanes, straddling the gutter. The bulk of the traffic that occupied the centre of the spectrum consisted of 'bush taxis' and other older vehicles, often Europe's throwaways, poorly maintained and usually held together by wire and packing tape. Noisy exhausts spewed poisonous cocktails of chemicals into the humid, smoggy atmosphere. Our faces blackened and clothes filthy, we had to remain alert or we would not live long enough to worry about any long-term effects of the pollution.

These conditions continued for about 50 kilometres until we passed through the old French port of Rufisque. Away from the city we could breathe again and, thankfully, the pace of life slowed. The testing heat, humidity and road conditions along with exhaustion from my perfect 'de-training' programme – lack of sleep, illness and stress – took their toll. By lunch, I was feeling cooked, whereas Dan, who had few of the organisational worries, was eighteen years younger and had been cycling regularly, seemed bright and full of energy.

Our aim for the first two days of travel, from the modern capital, Dakar, to the first colonial capital, St Louis, was to establish how we could best work as a team. We'd all come from such different backgrounds and had varying amounts of experience. While organising the expedition I had endeavoured to keep my team members updated with everything as it developed but now we had to ensure that we really were on the same page. And all this while we were learning, adapting and moulding our routines to the transient environment around us to reach common goals.

As I passed a roadside market in Rufisque, a young lad began sprinting alongside me at a very decent pace – I clocked him at around 20 kilometres an hour for a couple of hundred metres. Eventually the would-be Usain Bolt eased up, still smiling and waving me on enthusiastically. Leaving Rufisque and the urban congestion behind, we passed through tranquil countryside, lush at the end of the Rainy season and adorned with stands of majestic baobabs. It was a wonderful feeling to be finally cycling through 'romantic' Africa, absorbing the ever-changing scenery and friendliness. By the time I arrived in Tivaouane at the end of the day, not only were my leg muscles aching but my smile muscles also.

My sponsors in Dakar had prearranged a place for the team to stay in Tivaouane, but on arrival we could not raise our hosts by phone and so there was no-one to direct us where to go. Fortunately we were put in touch with Moussa, the brother of our St Louis connection. Without hesitation, Moussa invited us to his home. He escorted us through the unlit back streets of town – the centre for the Tijāniyyah Brotherhood, the most significant religious order in Senegal. We were a much larger team than I was used to travelling with; in the past, cycling unsupported, one or two cyclists being invited in to someone's home was simple but as a group of five with a vehicle to keep secure, we were a more imposing ensemble. Still, this did not seem to faze Moussa's family who offered immediate, uncompromising hospitality. We rested on cushions set up outside while the women swung into action to prepare a meal.

It was clear that our team not only came from a diversity of backgrounds but also ranged in temperament. At one extreme, Dan was proving to be so laid-back he fell asleep waiting for dinner whereas I, even though tired, was still wound up like a spring. Not wishing to miss any of the experience, I remained wide awake. We had more than survived our first day; starting in the chaos of Dakar amongst familiar faces and finishing 109 kilometres later in the home of welcoming strangers, privy to a very different culture in an historic religious town. Following the meal, Moussa's family vacated their tiny one-bedroom house for the night. They insisted that I slept on their only bed – a king-sized four-poster where the whole family would normally have lain. The boys crammed into the living room. Moussa's family bunked in with their cousins across the courtyard.

The precious little sleep I had was interrupted by the first call to prayer at 4.00 a.m. It was still dark when the second set of prayers at 6.00 a.m. served as the alarm clock. In order to get some distance done before the heat kicked in, we had to set off early. But moving at speed was an optimistic concept for me, still not recovered from the first day. Having cycled through West Africa the year before, Dan was familiar with what to expect in Senegal. For breakfast he led me to a roadside cafe for his usual power food – eggs.

Eggs were available everywhere, regularly whisked into an omelette, combined with onion and some Maggi flavour enhancers and fried in recycled cooking oil before being served in a baguette. The bread, a positive legacy of the French colonial era, served to soak up the excessive grease. All this was usually washed down with coffee so sweet it was difficult to drink. The calories were soon burned up as we rolled through the town that, like me, was struggling to warm up and get out of first gear for the day.

Girls at Leona market

From the leafy environs of Tivaouane, the N2 (Route Nationale No. 2) cut a path across a harsher landscape, where large baobabs were gradually replaced by spiky acacias and sparse green vegetation coverage. At the midday break, where we sought the dappled shade of a thorn tree, a less romantic view of West Africa's environment became apparent. I stood up and nearly blinded myself on the toothpick-sized thorns, also the cause of Dan's first puncture. We were entering the realms of the Sahel region.

My lack of condition, along with decreasing amounts of protection from the elements, contrived by afternoon to send me into a state of heat exhaustion. Our thermometer topped out at 38 degrees Celsius in the shade but the heat which radiated from the highway would have been enough to fry one of those pale-yoked eggs we'd consumed earlier. I recognised the signs of heat exhaustion from my Australian expedition: my heart-rate crept up and I felt hot, tired, breathless and light-headed. I had to stop and cool down: trying to push through when the core body temperature is above its normal range is not only dangerous, it takes a long time to recover. The team really pulled together to support me. At my worst I had to rest about every five kilometres, whenever my heart started to race, rehydrating while John soaked a towel to cover my head. When I pushed on it was at a reduced pace, just concentrating on keeping the pedals turning. I always knew that starting the expedition would physically be a case of biting the bullet but this was an extreme baptism of fire. 'This will only get easier,' I thought, trying not to dwell on the fact that there was still another ten months to go – if all went to plan. Gradually I was able to do longer stints, until at last light we reached Louga, our target for day two, 104 kilometres from Tivaouane.

✳

We had to reach the St Louis region in time to visit our first assignment, the Millennium Village Project at Potou, about 50 kilometres south of the city. These villages are innovative model projects which have been set up in hunger 'hotspots' in marginal regions across sub-Saharan Africa. The purpose overall is to achieve the Millennium Development Goals (MDGs) in these vulnerable rural communities by 2015, using a budget defined by the financial pledges of donor nations and national resources. I was interested to see how international policies and monetary commitments from the world's richest countries could be put into practice at grassroots level, so that they are relevant and sustainable in rural Africa.

The Millennium Village Project operates in a range of agricultural and ecological zones, representing a variety of challenges to income, food production, disease ecology, infrastructure, and health system development. A partnership of Millennium Promise (an international non-government organisation and expedition partner), the Earth Institute at Columbia University (United States) and the United Nations Development Program (UNDP), the project benefits about half-a-million people in ten countries. To ensure that they are not isolated islands, each scheme also requires input and finance from its national and local governments. New ideas and lessons learned are shared amongst the web of projects across the continent.

An artist's impression of Potou at the entrance to the Millennium Village

I hadn't planned to hook up with a Millennium Village Project until Mali, but when Amadou Niang, the director of the program for West and Central Africa, suggested we stop by Potou on the way to St Louis, I thought it a good opportunity to be introduced to the MDGs. While from a Western perspective, the eight MDGs appear to be a clearly defined, simple set of targets and guidelines to alleviate extreme poverty, the path to achieving them is not straightforward. There is no single formula, no 'one size fits all': each culture, community and situation meld together to give rise to an individual fingerprint of complex circumstances. Our guides, local experts, explained that the key decisions are made by the community, with help and advice from national and international partners. The problems are tackled together to ensure long-term, culturally-specific change.

Daouda, the project facilitator, Djiby, the economist, Moustapha, the health coordinator and Ousmane, the agricultural technician, gave us a snapshot of some of the projects addressing the main issues. Potou is not a single village, rather it is a cluster of six principal settlements. Daouda, the best translator, explained that their efforts were focused at a local level, village by village.

Before the project began in 2006 there was only one small hospital for the 30,000 people who live there; now there were six, meaning that all women can give birth in a hospital rather than at home. The head nurse told us that 80 per cent of the patients at her clinic were treated for malaria, the biggest killer in this region. I was surprised to learn that Senegal, unlike many countries of central, southern and eastern Africa, has almost no HIV/AIDS. The Senegalese government had initiated preventative programs in the mid-1980s, much earlier than most other countries. Community and religious leaders,

Muslim and Christian, were educated; high-risk groups such as sex workers were targeted and the communities were taught about the need for wearing condoms for casual sex (usage went from virtually zero to 70 per cent). The government ensured that the country had a safe blood supply and reduced the incidence of mother-to-child transmission of HIV. An on-going awareness campaign and support program has enabled Senegal to stabilise the incidence of HIV/AIDS to less than 1 per cent, as opposed to the other extreme in Swaziland in southern Africa. There, one-quarter of the population – and half of those in their twenties – has HIV, resulting in the very fabric of society being threatened. The Senegalese commitment to their ABCs – which in AIDS

Looking to a brighter future. All children in Potou have access to a primary education (JD)

education means Abstinence, Be faithful, use a Condom – brought me hope. It is an example of how, with foresight and appropriate planning, it is possible to prevent or turn around seemingly devastating problems.

Next we were taken to see ABCs of the more standard kind, at one of the new primary schools. Since the inception of the project, the number of primary schools in the region had been doubled, giving all children access to a primary education (in keeping with MDG 2 – achieve universal primary education). The project is not only about building infrastructure: teacher training is provided as well as school uniforms, equipment and facilities. Our group was welcomed into a couple of the packed classes

Trying my best to communicate with a class of Year 4 students (JD)

where youthful exuberance appeared to be bursting out of its louvred windows. With a poor command of each others' languages, communication embraced all sorts of animated gestures to compensate for our inadequate attempts at 'Franglais.' To the bright-eyed group of Year 4 students I stood in front of, my performance must have looked more like a comical game of charades.

The citizens of the Potou region had experienced poor food security in the past because Potou is set on an infertile coastal plain with an arid landscape. In an agriculture-based community like this, as in the rest of sub-Saharan Africa, securing growth in agriculture is more than twice as effective in reducing poverty compared to growth in the other main sectors. Priorities here had been given to developing agriculture and fishing. One well-organised farmer showed us his garden where he grew onions, tomatoes, aubergines, pineapples and the stable crop, groundnuts (peanuts). He could produce much more now that he was using better seed varieties and fertilisers. Proudly he pointed out his new drip irrigation system that delivers a consistent water supply, enabling him to stagger the growing seasons so he could produce food all year round.

A pirogue donated to the Potou fishermen

Down on the Grande Plage, the fishermen's fleet of colourfully decorated pirogues had been restored and added to. It was amazing to see what had been achieved in just three years of the project. Daouda explained that we had seen the fruits of Phase One, which was all about stabilising Potou's basic needs. Progressive emphasis was now being placed on operational and financial management.

With our tour over, there was a little time to amble along the fittingly named Grande Plage that extends all the way down to Dakar. A salty mist being whisked off the foaming whitecaps blended seamlessly with the transient white sands into the southern horizon. The beach was virtually deserted as the fishermen had done their work for the day. Watching the surf roll in I suddenly felt overwhelmed by a sense of just how far I had to go – both in distance and on my voyage of understanding. I may have been shattered from the pre-start organisational phase and physical stresses of the first two days of cycling but I was excited to be there. This was the start of the real purpose of the journey. I had to pinch myself.

❈

Just to the north of Potou, the Senegal River, which defines the country's northern border with Mauritania, enters the Atlantic Ocean. For the final 25 kilometres of its westward course, the river is separated from the ocean by a narrow sandy peninsula, the Langue de Barbarie. It was here, on a strategic island called Ndar, between the isthmus and the mainland, that the French chose to build St Louis, their first settlement in West Africa. Over the 350 years since, the city, which now has a population of 200,000, has spread to include the Langue de Barbarie and the mainland.

Rather than stay in the crowded urban hustle and bustle, John suggested we stop at the Zebrabar about 20 kilometres south. He knew of the peaceful sanctuary from a previous expedition which he had supported. Set within the Langue de Barbarie National Park, a bird watcher's paradise, and near to where the Senegal River enters the ocean, the Zebrabar's bungalows and campsite accommodation provide an idyllic place for travellers to re-energise. There we could pause, spread out and prepare for the next stage – heading into the more remote West African interior.

A view across the Langue de Barbarie in St Louis to the Atlantic Ocean

Compared with boisterous, pressured Dakar, St Louis was a breath of fresh Atlantic air, wafting an alluring yet antiquated charm. The streets and buildings on the island have a kind of faded elegance which begged further exploration, inside and out. At the Hôtel de Ville, one of the better-preserved structures, the deputy mayor, Mr Cissé, officially welcomed us. Inside, we wandered the protected warren of corridors and rooms which housed collections of images of the city's history: upstanding leaders and politicians who had controlled the French colonies of Senegal and Mauritania, high society, scenes reflecting the town and port in its heyday. Nearby, on the walls of the council chambers at the Gouvernance (Governor's Palace) hung more images depicting three centuries of political and economic power, bolstered by the trade of slaves, gold, ivory and gum arabic. There we were formally greeted by representatives of the regional government. Outside, apart from some of these most important buildings, much of the crumbling architecture appeared as though it had not been touched for fifty years – which was the case. After independence in 1960, when Dakar became the capital, St Louis was dispossessed of its power base and its economy has struggled to recover.

But there was an air of optimism. Beneath the face of diplomacy at our two meetings the message was as upbeat as the city's world renowned jazz festival. The government officials explained how they were transforming the St Louis region, with future plans revolving around attracting more investment and tourism. Independently, the deputy mayor and the councillors acknowledged their region's strengths and weaknesses and talked of how they were implementing strategies to deal with their issues. The secretary to the regional president spoke of plans to promote the region as an economic entity, develop human resources and improve living conditions, seek regional integration, improve social cohesion and security and promote local governance. The whole city being listed as a world heritage site has contributed to reviving a distinctive urban culture (that includes the jazz festival) and the economy.

An extreme makeover for St Louis. One of the workmen renovating the Lycée Cheikh Omar Foutiyou Tall, formerly the Lycée Faidherbe

Limam Diouf, the high-powered businessman who arranged the day, was keen to show us the community projects he had initiated. He took us to see the micro-loans bank he was building to give people in small business, mostly women, opportunities to secure their financial future. Proud locals consider St Louis as the birthplace of Senegalese *teranga*, the local Wolof word for hospitability. We were indeed shown plenty of *teranga*. After a traditional lunch of home-cooked *yassa poulet* (chilli chicken with onions, olives and lemon juice), the tour of the city resumed. Mr Diouf, who had driven from Dakar to organise our visit, returned to the capital for work.

The baton was handed to Papa Moussa Bâ, Premier Conseiller Nationale and close friend of the president of Senegal. Before the journey, I'd had small badges made with the expedition name and logo printed on them which I presented as a token of appreciation to people who contributed to the journey. Here I gave these out liberally. I noted that when the recipient pinned the badge on upside down it was a sure sign that either they could not read English or that their eyesight was very poor. When I handed a badge to Papa Moussa Bâ, it was obvious that communication was going to be a challenge. Papa Moussa's eminence, however, seemed to give us rock star status. Everywhere we were driven, through the old town and across to the Langue de Barbarie, locals would peer inside the vehicle, wave to Papa Moussa and greet us as celebrities. Even the police waved us through. When I gave Papa Moussa the badge, he

Papa Moussa Bâ (in blue) with some of his old friends

presented me with his business card. Even after he had gone, we quickly learned that simply showing his card and mentioning his name was a passport to negotiating tedious police checkpoints without a hitch. We milked this for as long as possible.

Papa Moussa Bâ's card was very useful over the next couple of days, as we oscillated between the Zebrabar and St Louis, and battled with a fluctuating internet system which seemed to not work anywhere in town most of the time. Film-maker Paddy was having trouble with the technical equipment and required more time to sort it out. As we'd already stayed two extra days and losing more time would eat into the schedule too much, Dan and I prepared to set off unsupported. John's role was just as much to support Paddy as it was the cyclists. Paddy's inexperience required plenty of patience and understanding from all of us but especially from John, who spent the most time with him. Simon, who had accompanied John on the long drive down to Senegal to support the start of the expedition, returned to the UK. We would not see him again until Cameroon, four months down the track.

❋

Our plan was to follow the course of the Senegal River from its mouth just near the Zebrabar, 800 kilometres inland to Kayes, Mali. French slavers and colonists had used the river as their main route into West Africa. Large boats could sail through as far as Kayes in the Rainy season. The settlers built various fortifications and ports along the course – such as at Richard Toll, Podor, Matam, Bakel and Kayes – to protect and service their exploits.

After one last, unsuccessful try to update my website, Dan and I set off past the famous Hôtel de la Poste and over the Pont Faidherbe. The bridge, which spans half a kilometre over the Senegal River, is an iconic symbol of St Louis, named after the governor who was responsible for much of its development. Opened in 1865, the bridge made a big difference to the fortunes of the colony, flailing as Dakar's importance rose. After learning about the state of the region and seeing some of the plans for its future development in action, it seemed only fitting that the current Pont Faidherbe, completed in 1897 by Gustav Eiffel (who also built the Eiffel Tower), was under renovation. Its surface was an uneven pavement of metal planks, many of which had upwardly curling sharp edges, bowing and splintering under the constant stresses. Traffic was congested so to move forward I cycled straight down the middle, often into the path of oncoming vehicles, ducking back to the right side to avoid collisions. The passage was narrow, so everyone had to give and take.

Mainland St Louis contains most of the population and industry. We worked our way through the busy streets, eventually merging back on to the N2, heading north towards Rosso on the Mauritanian border. The more village-like the environment, the more frequently we would exchange greetings. In the fringes of St Louis and villages which the highway bisected beyond, people would wave and call out 'Bonjour,' 'Ça va?,' 'Toubab.' At first I did not understand what they meant by *toubab*, but then Dan, who had been through the experience the previous year, explained that this was their word for white person. In Australia or the UK, to call someone the equivalent translation in English would be unacceptable but in Senegal and West Africa referring to white people as *toubabs* is not considered derogatory. It's just the way it is. After the trial of the first couple of days of pedalling, I was feeling much stronger. Certainly I was still a way from full fitness, but leaving St Louis and heading across the flat salty marshlands, I felt far less stressed and much freer.

Near to the river and the Mauritanian border, the countryside was degraded. Vast barren plains supported just a few goats, and there was no cultivation. The only notable places of habitation were some long-established refugee camps dotted amidst the completely bleak landscape. Dan refilled his water bottles from one of their wells closer to the road. Given that Senegal is recognised as one of the most stable and economically successful countries in the Sahel region, these clusters of semi-permanent dwellings were not something I was expecting during this part of the journey. In 1989, a two-year conflict now known as the Mauritania-Senegal Border War erupted over grazing rights. The dispute had begun when Mauritanian Moorish border guards fired at and killed two Senegalese peasants, resulting in people on the Senegalese southern bank rioting. In Senegal, where many storekeepers were Mauritanian, shops were looted and most Mauritanians expelled to Mauritania. In Mauritania, lynch mobs and police brutality ended in the forced exile of tens of thousands of southerners to Senegal, despite most of them having no links to the country. After two decades, roughly 20,000 of these Mauritanian refugees remain in Senegal in camps such as those we passed and along the Senegal River. It struck me that a whole generation lives in these oppressive conditions not knowing where home is.

Nearing Rosso, the highway followed a saline-looking ephemeral tributary that fed into the reedy wetlands of the Senegal River floodplain. Here, about 100 kilometres from St Louis, we turned east off the main highway towards Richard Toll. The road was flanked by small-time agriculture which seemed insignificant against the surrounding backdrop of large-scale commercial sugar cane plantations. Richard Toll was originally a colonial administrative centre and governor's retreat, productive and in convenient proximity to the West African capital. In street-side stalls there and in towns further east we noted, amongst many imports, bags of onions from the Netherlands. Even without the packaging they were easy to spot from their uniform size and shape and unblemished skins. Apart from the dreadful waste of energy used to transport the vegetables, I could not understand why the Senegalese should be making their favorite *yassa poulet* from expensive Dutch onions when so much appeared to be grown on the floodplains around them.

The road tracked the outer margin of the floodplain, which is so broad we rarely caught sight of the meandering river. Between Richard Toll and Dagana, the thin tarmac strip divided two zones. On the north side lay a prosperous green belt with mature trees and vegetable gardens. To the south, marginal tinder-dry grazing land was constantly being nibbled at by goats and cattle. Considering that we were travelling at the end of a very wet season, the grass cover should have been at its maximum density. I tried to picture how bare the land would become over the next few months.

The day rapidly turned evil. Leaving Dagana, just 20 kilometres from Richard Toll, there was little to impede the gritty headwinds, fan-forced straight off the Sahara to the north and east. In order to avoid a repeat of day two of the expedition, Dan and I found some shade to rest under, out the heat of the day. I noticed that the ground was packed hard, probably due to the large numbers of hoofed grazing animals – goats especially. It looked as though there was unsustainable pressure being put on the land.

Mid-afternoon, just as we were preparing to leave, two women appeared from the bush and handed us a large bowl of rice and fish – or should I say fish bones – and a basin of water. They smiled shyly, said nothing and returned to their mud and thatched houses about 500 metres back. The rice had a fair amount of sand in it, but as we thought it may have been perceived as offensive had we wasted even a morsel, we (especially Dan) did our best to demolish the offering. When we walked over to return the empty bowls we found the women and many young children also sitting out the heat. As these graziers did not even speak French, just their local language, Wolof, communication was awkward. We shook hands – they were definitely hard-working hands – and as we returned to the bikes with a full complement of water bottles it dawned on me that there was no well around where they lived. I was not only touched by the generosity of these people in sharing their food and water, but it was humbling to think that the water they gave would have been carried to their homes over a significant distance in the first place. This was an example of Senegalese *teranga* at its purest.

Continuing east, there was a change in demographics, with a higher proportion of nomadic herdsmen driving their stock beside the road. Every so often we would have to wait as they moved their cattle across it. Sometimes I would carefully weave my way through a large herd but I had to be careful of the horns: the animals were docile but with their great bulk, it would only take one swish of their head and I could be gored by massive horns, two or three feet long. The herdsmen were mostly Moorish, and dressed traditionally in turbans, robes, long shorts and sometimes knee-high socks. Less traditional were the mobile phones usually strapped around their necks. Tall and thin, these people of Arabic origin are referred to as 'white Moors,' just one facet of the ethnic melange inhabiting the realms of the Senegal River.

The fragility of the environment means that the river is the lifeline for all those who live north and south of the border. Its annual natural flooding cycle is essential to life in the arid region. Traditional landowners rely on the seasonal rhythm, cultivating crops on the floodplain after the waters, delivered during the Rainy season, flush life back into the land. While the river provided a convenient geographical demarcation for the French to divide Senegal and Mauritania, traditional land users, such as the Moors, Wolof, Soninké and Fulani, depended on cultivating on either side, according to the seasons. Sometimes they lived on one bank and farmed on the other, or raised cattle and shared land with a relative on the opposite side of the river. Land tenure rights were complex as they were also tied into the caste systems that are an integral part of each of the traditional cultures. To improve food security after droughts in the early 1970s, local producers set up small-time irrigation systems to supplement what was grown during the Dry season by established 'flood-recession' farming methods. On balance, understandings of land tenure seemed to work and were retained.

Keenly aware of the resource value of West Africa's second largest river, the governments of Senegal, Mauritania, Mali and Guinea, which make up the river catchment area, banded together to form the Senegal River Development Organisation, or OMVS (Organisation pour la Mise en Valeur du Fleuve Sénégal) with the intention of boosting food security, expecially through the poor seasons. The three main aims of the organisation are to provide water for large-scale irrigation programs, to make the Senegal River navigable between St Louis and Kayes all year round, and to create a hydro-electric scheme. Without consultation with the long-established land tenants, the flow of the river was altered by constructing two dams, including one in Mali impeding the Bafing – the Senegal River's principal tributary. The private sector was encouraged to irrigate sizeable farms for monocultures – mainly rice – and peasants were expected to adapt and retrain to become employees of the irrigation industry. (And

The sun sets over another spiky camp spot not far from the village of Pete

focusing on monocultures meant there was greater reliance on importing foods, maybe even Dutch onions.) Those who stuck to flood-recession farming sometimes had their crops washed away when water from the dam was released without warning. Sandy soils weren't capable of supporting two crops a year and yields declined due to soil depletion, salinisation and pollution. It was a combination of these conditions which led to growing tension and frustration between cultures and boiled over in the Mauritania-Senegal Border War.

Finding campsites off the road meant not only negotiating the bush thick with thorns but also burrs. These burrs were horribly familiar. They were introduced to my part of the world, Western Australia, from South Africa in the 1830s as the vegetable known as Cape spinach. There they are a ecological disaster: not only do they compete with crops and pastures, one weed can produce more than 1000 three-pronged spiky burrs. In Australia these burrs, *emex australis*, are more commonly known as doublegees, three-cornered jacks, bindis, devil's eggs or centurions, depending on which state you are in. In the Sahel region the same burrs are just as much a curse. I awoke from my second night of camping lying directly on the hard ground with my sleeping mat pierced in countless places. The tiny holes became detectable by pouring water over the mat and watching for bubbles, although I never managed to repair all of the leaks. Having wheeled our bikes cross-country to our campsite, the morning light revealed that our tyres were encrusted with literally hundreds of doublegees. The second annoyance for the morning involved manually extracting the blighters one by one before repairing several punctures. We set off carrying our bikes for about a kilometre back to the road.

The first two weeks were meant to be about 'breaking the cyclist into Africa' – becoming acclimatised to the conditions and finding a rhythm – but by the fourth day out of St Louis, I was nearly broken. We were averaging just over 100 kilometres a day, which is what I had planned for the first section, but the dry heat and nagging headwinds gnawed at my resolve. I was running on empty. Dan helped by draughting me for some sections, meaning that I cycled close to his tail so that he took the wind resistance. At Thilogne, where we stopped for lunch outside a small cafe, my mouth was so parched that I had difficulty swallowing my customary omelette baguette. There was the usual swarm of inquisitive kids hanging around and Dan and John challenged some of them to a game of table football, a very popular game in these parts. When I slipped a youngster the last half of my sandwich, it was like throwing a chip to a flock of seagulls – it nearly caused a riot. He and his mates were obviously hungry. As they tried to get their hands on the food, I realised I should be more discreet in similar situations in the future.

Senegal River at Matam

If we didn't venture off the main road we would not see the river again until we reached Kayes. We diverted to Matam, a major port on the river, 10 kilometres off the main drag. It seems that the poorest people tend to congregate near the river's edge. Here kids tried to salvage what they could from picking over the rubbish which had been tipped down the river bank. Small children were labouring hard, carrying large buckets of what looked like sludge on their heads – I could hear one of them straining as he emptied his load. Others were fishing or washing in the polluted waters. A motorised pirogue ferried a full load of passengers across to the other side – Mauritania. Life struggles on.

With the natural flow of the river being altered artificially, the reduction in seasonal flooding has led to increased waterborne diseases, diarrhoea and malaria. The pollution we saw would have been at its greatest levels around the urban area but natural flooding would normally have flushed many of the pollutants away. Other ecological downsides include a degradation of fisheries, increased salinity and more erosion of the river's banks. One fellow told us he sat there all day waiting to fill a three-litre container with the tiny bait fish he skilfully caught using a hand line. Patience, persistence, optimism...

The Matam Department of the St Louis Region, if anything, appeared worse off. The road surface, quite acceptable to that point, deteriorated into potholes which at times were so bad most drivers found it quicker to drive in donkey cart tracks alongside. We slalomed around most of the holes but when the surface was reduced to random islands of bitumen, we too moved off to the side. Setting off from Ouro

Sogui, John had a job catching us as he could not drive much faster than we could cycle.

At the last break of day eleven, we rested up in a café on the edge of a small village named Amadi Ounaré. Sometimes the most random moments can become the most pivotal. I struck up a conversation with a teacher, Babacol Gaye, and his friend Hussain, who could both speak some English. They were both very interested in the purpose of the expedition, particularly about the emphasis on the importance of education and development assistance. Babacol thought that one of the biggest problems for their country was that it was losing its best students

Some hard-working boys at Matam

overseas. Rather than staying to be a part of Senegal's development, the brightest sparks were being lured by the promise of more money and better opportunities in the larger cities and in Western countries. Reversing the brain drain was, he claimed, more important than attracting so-called development aid, which both men felt was holding the country back and preventing its people from standing up for themselves.

I suddenly felt very conscious that some of the things I was saying may have sounded a little condescending – talking about issues that I may have studied but of which I had no experience. I explained that this was a voyage of discovery; I was cycling across the continent to try to understand more about the different psyches and cultures and I had found that travelling by this means provided a great opportunity to relate at the level of the people. This journey was an attempt to see Africa more through African eyes; of course, I would never be African, but some things were starting to get under my skin. Babacol and Hussain pointed out that only Westerners would consider doing what I was doing: cycling through Africa is something no African would ever contemplate as 'they would not be rich enough to do it.' I had trouble convincing them that I was not materially wealthy by Western standards, and that I had spent the best part of two years putting the project together and finding backers. I explained that I had put everything on the line personally to do this – given up my job and invested all I had into it because I believed in the cause. They didn't think someone from Senegal would ever try to do that.

Our conversation was food for thought. As I set off to cycle through my favourite time of day – late afternoon – my mind churned over. They were right – I could only do this journey because I lived in a particular set of circumstances which enabled me to dream this up. I wasn't wealthy in terms of owning a house or having a fat bank account but I did have a decent education and a stable upbringing. I had choices which they didn't have. Was my view of what many African nations need to break away from chronic poverty different from what most African people believe they need to do? Even with all the best intentions, we are products of our respective environments and can only see things in relation to how we see ourselves.

As we headed out of the St Louis Region and towards Bakel, the scenery made a welcome change from gentle undulations to some more distinctive iron-based hills locally known as the 'little mountains.'

Cycling through typical countryside near Kayes

Villages appeared more prosperous and the road conditions improved. Bakel itself was more kempt and contained more services and light industry. Even the fort 'guarding' the river, one of Faidherbe's legacies, had been restored. Bakel is located just downstream from where the Falémé, the last of the three main tributaries, merges with the Senegal River. For more than a century it has been the site where the river's flow has been measured. To the states of the Senegal Basin, irrigation is considered the motor of development, and as a government centre Bakel has benefited. On the other hand, it is also the site where the conflict began which led to the Border War in 1989.

The final 68 kilometres down to Kidira and the Mali border was my favourite stint in Senegal, with scenery not too unlike the Kimberley region in Western Australia. We were back in baobab territory, having turned south and below the latitude of Dakar. At Kidira we connected with the main N1 road east and the Dakar-Bamako train line – a 1200-kilometre colonial engineering feat built with convict labour. With almost 1000 kilometres done, we crossed the Falémé River and no man's land before being stamped into country number two. The road to Kayes from Kidira is the main highway – and apart from a few washouts, was top-notch. For most of the journey to date we had been travelling through grazing land, but for the last 100 kilometres to Kayes the road was flanked by natural bushland with giant baobabs.

Kayes (pronounced *Kai*) received its name from the local Soninké word, *karré*, describing a low, humid place that floods in the Rainy season. Encountering the mighty Senegal River for the last time,

A busy street outside the Kayes market

this appeared to be an apt description. As a result of the end of the extended Wet season, the river was still high and many were taking advantage of the flow over the old causeway to wash taxis, carts, themselves and their clothes. Kayes, now a pleasant, easy-going regional hub by African city standards, was the first capital of the French Sudan, modern-day Mali.

While in Kayes we arranged to see the first colonial outpost in the West African interior at Médine, about 15 kilometres east of the capital. Built by Governor Faidherbe in 1855, the fort and buildings, which were being restored by the Mali government, sit high on a strategic position above the river. Steamships could travel all the way from St Louis to there in the Rainy season but upstream from that point was only navigable by pirogue. It was here that slaves and materials such as ivory, gold, cloth and gum were traded. From Médine, Faidherbe plotted the extension of the French empire farther into the interior to Niger. Governor Faidherbe's achievements in St Louis and Médine made symbolic bookends to the first stage of the journey.

In choosing to take this route along the Senegal River, I expected to see some of the colonial remnants such as the river ports between St Louis and Kayes that served early European exploitation of people and resources. I wanted to emphasise some of the effects of the so-called 'Scramble for Africa,' during which over the space of a few years, the whole of the continent was carved into pieces and divvied out amongst the rich European nations for the purpose of exploitation, to suppress slavery (which by then was outlawed in Europe) and to 'civilise' the populations. The thirteen European powers that divided up Africa at a conference in Berlin in 1884-85, paid no attention to local culture or ethnic groups, with the result that people from the same tribe were left on opposite sides of European-imposed borders.

Looking out to prosperous fields from the veranda of the derelict train station at Médine; crumbling over time along with the effects of colonialism

Independence offered West Africans greater freedom but could not conceal the fact that colonialism had created fragile economies based on cash crops prone to huge price fluctuations, and that few Africans were equipped to deal with such crises. Ethnic tensions created by these artificial boundaries and divide-and-rule policies manifested as border disputes (such as the Mauritania-Senegal Border War), military coups d'état and civil wars.

From what I had seen, the effects of colonialism were diminishing. Old colonial ties had mostly frayed away, perishing over time so that just a few tenuous strands remain. Senegal has broken free of its past because of the determination of its leaders and the will of communities to take charge of their future. Like most African nations, Senegal is undergoing an economic boom, its economy forging ahead at between 4 and 5 per cent per annum, whereas their old colonial power France, along with most of Europe, has stagnated. I hoped that, as the benefits eventually filter down to the poorer rural communities, there will no longer be 'Dutch onions' for sale in the streets.

Stage one of the expedition served to be a microcosm of what we should expect for the journey ahead. We'd had a taste of what the Millennium Development Goals were about at Potou and got a feel for life on the road. The team was generally pulling together well as we got to know each other. We were starting to find a rhythm.

Total distance: 1040 kilometres

SAHARA DESERT

MAURITANIA

• Oualata

• Ayoûn el-Atroûs

Seli hi yas
Telia (sud)

Timbedra

• Nema

• Koumbi Saleh

• Gogui

• Nioro du Sahel

• Nara

• Sokolo

• Dioko

• Sandaré

MALI

Kayes

• Niono

SENEGAL

Bakoy

Bafing

Senegal

Falémé

Niger

• Ségou

Bamako

GUINEA

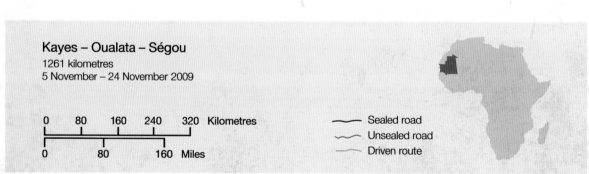

Kayes – Oualata – Ségou
1261 kilometres
5 November – 24 November 2009

| 0 | 80 | 160 | 240 | 320 | Kilometres |

| 0 | 80 | 160 | Miles |

——— Sealed road
- - - Unsealed road
——— Driven route

16

2

A DETOUR INTO WEST AFRICA'S DIVERSE CULTURAL HERITAGE

Kayes to Ségou (western Mali and Mauritania)

Young Fulani women and children brighten the drab Sahel landscape

In Kayes, although the internet was temperamental, I finally had an opportunity to respond to some of the questions and comments from students, mostly Year 6 Australians, who were participating in the education program. Many comments were messages of encouragement and support, however some queries I took as an indication of eleven-year-olds' images of Africa, poverty, cycling and philanthropy.

There were the thoughtful:

'I'm very sad that sometimes people in poverty are enslaved. I thought enslaving was just a myth...'

'I understand how you want to help other people and I'm sure you will understand how I want to help the [African] animals...'

There were the standard:

'What types of animals are you going to see on your bike ride?'

'I hope when you are riding you don't fall off and hurt yourself.'

'Are you really a good bike rider?'

'How much training did you do?'

'Watch out for lions and other animals...'

There were the searching questions that were way too big to answer effectively:

'Have you got any ideas for me of how I can help do something for my community, school, country or world?'

And there were words of wisdom:

'Good luck and strive for accuracy.'

'People who eat gritty rice have "true grit"...'

We could definitely learn from each other. I am always searching for accuracy and I knew the next leg would require plenty of true grit.

Fully laden, Dan and I set off, prepared to spend a couple of days on our own. We paused to buy a few bits and pieces and could not resist capturing images of the bustling market set amongst the ramshackle old colonial buildings. People were so preoccupied pushing their carts and balancing extraordinary loads on their heads that our presence barely attracted more than an inquisitive glance. While our bags were heavier than usual, they were small fry compared to what some were pushing.

Farewelling the river also signified the beginning of stage two of the expedition, leaving behind the French colonial route into West Africa. It would have been simple to continue along the direct road to Bamako, Mali's present-day capital, but I had very much wanted to include the ancient town of Oualata in south-east Mauritania in the story and considered it an important 700-kilometre detour.

Kayes is nicknamed the 'pressure cooker of Africa' due to its extreme heat (annual mean maximum daily temperature is 35 degrees Celsius). Pushing beyond the old French capital's limits and the crumbling iron-rich mountains which constitute the town's crucible, I was finally able to release some

Baobab pods

of my own steam. I had been so busy that I did not feel as rested as I would have hoped and Dan and I were setting off unsupported because Paddy needed another day to download an application – a task he could have initiated the previous day. We couldn't afford to lose more time. The team was becoming increasingly concerned about the attitude and disorganisation of our cameraman. I had to begin the next stage after precious little sleep, frustrated by the extra burden that John, Dan and I had to absorb. I was troubled by the potential for this friction to affect our morale and teamwork.

The region receives enough flooding rains to support magnificent stands of baobab trees and good grass cover for the abundant herds of cattle and goats. Over the course of our day, these woodlands graduated into the vast open plains of a mini-Monument Valley. Eventually the road conformed to the river's curves. The watercourse meandered through the reeds as if tired from millennia of work sculpting the spectacular escarpments and buttes which towered above. In the late afternoon light the landscape was inspirational.

The far-western pocket of Mali receives few tourists and I found it refreshing to roll into villages where locals were obviously less used to travellers. People would still wave and shout out 'Toubab' but we could sit and enjoy a *café au lait* and observe village life without too many hassles. Just occasionally I'd catch someone's shy, distant gaze.

In case this is sounding over-idyllic, I must explain that we were sipping the West African reincarnation of a *café au lait* – or simply a 'Carnation' of *café au lait* – a concoction made with a generous slurp of sweetened condensed milk and half a teaspoon of Nescafe coffee, whisked with hot water to make a froth and sometimes even further sweetened by spoonfuls of sugar. The drink is really an essence of what is practically available. There are often no refrigerators (or at least no power to run them) so milk is from a tin. Coffee is expensive for someone who lives off a couple of dollars a day, therefore it is used frugally, and while water may come free it often has to be carried some distance by hand. It takes a little getting used to but the drink is the perfect refreshment in this environment and I learned to appreciate it. The sugar hit ensured instant energy and after two cups I would be totally wired and ready for action.

Starting the second day out from Kayes, any extra shots of energy were welcome. Dan and I were faced with our first significant climb over the ancient range. It was only a few hundred metres elevation but in the context of the flat Sahel region, where the road altitude ranges little more than 300 metres at any point, this felt like a decent pass. We were enjoying cycling on a relatively new bitumen road towards Nioro du Sahel, along the main modern trade route leading to south-east Mauritania. The realigned course bypasses the original villages, luring away transitory trade and with it some of their livelihoods. Travelling along the new highways can be faster but is rather sterile in comparison with the original roads. To experience some of the unspoilt Africa and its rural innocence it is important to venture away from the busy highways. In planning the journey I aimed to strike a balance, because to only follow secondary roads would blow out the expedition schedule to well over ten months.

The old road to Nioro via Dioka was an absolute gem. Out of Sandaré, the track was so little used it was difficult to find. There were trails diverging in many different directions. The road had clearly not been touched since the new highway was laid. On the other hand, it was more stimulating to focus on negotiating overgrown paths, full of potential hazards – sandy washouts, sections of sharp slate stones and thorn trees – than avoiding speeding, dangerously overloaded juggernauts. Amazingly, every twenty or so kilometres, the intertwining tracks converged to lead into the next village.

After Dioko, where the landscape was more savannah-like, we started passing nomads wandering along the roadside, driving their goats and cattle to new pastures. The women were exquisitely dressed, wearing gold decorations in their hair and vividly coloured clothes. They really brightened the drab landscape with their own brand of glamour.

A little later, as we rested under a now-much-rarer giant baobab tree for lunch, a group of these stunning young Fulani women and children approached. The Fulani are known for having a huge respect for beauty. The largest nomadic group in the world, they inhabit the shoreline of the Sahara Desert, and have a four-tiered caste system in their proud culture: nobility, merchants, blacksmiths and the descendants of slaves. Judging by the intricate tattoo markings and decorative bling worn by the girls, my guess was that these young women and children were of Fulani nobility. The gold earrings and jewellery adorning the wealthiest may have been wedding gifts from their husbands, who usually have to sell off several cows to afford them. But Fulani women remain financially independent from their husbands, so gold and jewellery is often passed down from mothers to daughters.

The Fulani were extremely shy and particularly nervous of my team-mates. Every time the boys moved, the group ran off. They didn't seem so intimidated by me though. When I stood up and they didn't bolt I casually walked over to my bike which was balanced against the baobab and pulled out my camera. I first snapped a shot of Dan, so they could see that it was a harmless process. I then moved over to the nomads while gesturing and pointing to the screen on my camera, indicating that I wanted to show it to them. They gathered around. Their open-eyed expressions were of childlike intrigue – as if they had just seen magic. Then the most senior girl, a young mother who was probably sixteen or seventeen, signalled that she would like me to take a photo of her. I had broken the ice. They all wanted their pictures taken and then crowded around to marvel at the images.

Sahelian glamour – one of the young Fulani mothers

The younger girls were fascinated by my skin and hair, which I allowed them to feel. Then the older girl noticed my two-toned cycling suntan. She laughed with disbelief at the line made by my cycle shorts, and especially at the colour of my pasty white skin under the shorts. 'How could this be?' she must have thought as she innocently lifted up my t-shirt to see what shade I was underneath and whether I was made the same as them.

A woman elder ventured over from the tent dwellings a few hundred metres away to check out the situation. I shook her hand warmly and she appeared satisfied. The excitement over, I rejoined the picnic.

Later the girls noticed us pouring tea and were now bold enough to ask if they could try it. Knowing that our version of tea was not what they were accustomed to, Dan poured half a cup of stronger-than-usual black tea, stirred in a few teaspoons of sugar and gave it to the oldest girl to try. She inspected the brew and swirled it around the plastic mug as if it was a fine wine. As she tasted it she screwed up her face in disgust and spat it out as if it was a poison. It probably wasn't sweet enough for her palate; Dan added more sugar but the brew still did not meet her expectations. In her culture, tea drinking serves a very significant social function. The strong sugary green mint tea that they call *atay* would normally be served in an espresso-sized glass and drunk several times a day. Serving tea is an important way of welcoming someone: if strangers visit they will always be offered tea and dates. No wonder the girl seemed disappointed at our haphazard method of serving what must have tasted to her like dishwater. The messages would have been been confusing.

The last part of the track was very sandy, with old, rough cobblestones sometimes our best option. We took the opportunity to stock up on a few essentials in Nioro. This principal gateway town into south-east Mauritania is an important trading post with a good market. In particular we looked for some fresh produce because Mauritania isn't noted for growing much.

Dan was fighting off a cold and feeling low on energy, so we decided to draught to share the load;

A very special exchange. The young woman holding her baby led the group

cycling ten minutes in front, then ten minutes behind. It takes a fair amount of concentration to sit about a metre behind someone's back wheel but I was pleased to be able to help Dan out and return the favour. He had been a big support during the first week when I was struggling. Apart from the usual wind resistance, it was a treat gliding along the new highway. The Gogui border crossing was straightforward and we didn't lose too much time.

Once we'd set up camp out of view from the road, John decided he needed some exercise and took Dan's bike for a spin. Being early evening, he had hoped to slip through villages without being noticed; it had become tiresome having people shout at us all day long, wherever we went. He returned after dark, unable to believe it – just when he thought he had sneaked through the last village anonymously, a lone child's voice from the dark had called out 'Toubab'. 'There's no escape,' he exclaimed.

As we headed north towards Ayoûn el-Atroûs the grazing land became so denuded that sand drifts had enveloped the road in places. Off the main piste the grassland was either thick with doublegees and thorns or sandy, making the tempting idea of taking a shortcut to Timbedra on the main road out of the question – well, almost.

Our maps showed a smaller track which would save us approximately 40 kilometres, so John and Dan did a short recce in the vehicle to see what the track was like. I was suffering from my first severe bout of diarrhoea, and feeling washed out, I rested under the filtered shade of a thorny acacia. It was an uncomfortable, sweaty siesta. The temperature hovered around the mid to high thirties but it felt even hotter in my condition. The sunlight found ways of piercing the shelter and I sensed that the heat was serving to incubate whatever was fizzing and gurgling in my alimentary tract.

John and Dan returned, surmising that the track beyond the sandy roadside village would be cyclable, so we had a go. Unfortunately it was soft all the way and trying to find alternate paths away from the wheel tracks meant more sand and burrs. While puncture-threatening doublegees and thorn tree debris were primary concerns, it was the tiny burrs, called *initi* in Mauritania and commonly known as *cram-cram* throughout the Sahel region, that caused constant discomfort and annoyance. Microfilaments coating each tiny spine ensure that the burrs adhere to clothing and sometimes skin like a torturous Velcro; when attempting to remove them barbs snap off embedding themselves into clothing and fingertips. My socks soon resembled a hedgehog. At one stage, while weaving through the bushes, I slid in a sand trap and landed heavily. There was no major damage done. But one side of me was a prickly mass of *cram-crams*.

Exhausted and fast running out of daylight, we were welcomed into a small village called Seli hi yas Telia (sud). I had been a little concerned about how I, in particular, was going to be received in the conservative Islamic State of Mauritania. I had asked Seyid, my main Mauritanian contact (whom we were to meet the next day), and he had advised that, as I was cycling, people would understand that I was *sportif* and for that reason accept, or at least tolerate, my attire. However, in this remote village backwater where our unannounced arrival drew plenty of attention, I was still a little unsure. But I needn't have worried. A young man named Mohammed promptly stepped forward and assumed the role of main communicator and guide. He was home on a family visit but now worked in the capital Nouakchott, so he was more familiar with Western influences. As he escorted us through the village to the vacant house and fenced compound where we were to be accommodated, Mohammed offered to help push my loaded bike over the sand. His flowing *dara'a* (Mauritanian robe), however, kept becoming tangled in the spokes and drive train and I felt a bit guilty that I caused him to spoil his pristine white outfit. Ever the

A typical home in Seli hi yas Telia (sud)

gentleman, he persisted without complaint. I guess the *dara'a* is not made for cycling!

Our hosts, a select gathering of elders and community members (including Mohammed and his two brothers), could not do enough to make us feel welcome. Respect and hospitality were unconditional. I was soon led away to a neighbour's washroom and generously provided with two full buckets of water to wash. I had noted that water appeared to be quite scarce in these parts and so I took care to only use what I needed. I emerged clean and covered up, leaving the two buckets almost full so the contents could be put to more important use.

We set up our 'outdoor living room' on the concrete pad beside the one-roomed house to make the most of the cool, clear evening. Our hosts laid decorative foam mats and cushions on the ground in readiness for the tea ceremony. Similarly to the Fulani, and in fact across the breadth of the Saharan and Sahelian cultures, the traditional Mauritanian tea ceremony is very important. Firstly a sugarless infusion is skilfully poured from teapot to glass from a great height and then from glass to glass to create the all-important foam. The foam is retained and the sugarless tea discarded. Then three foaming brews are served in turn; the first is said to be strong like birth, the second is extra sweet like love and the third is for life. After that, the tea just seemed to keep coming.

I was feeling very delicate due to my gastric condition and so when the fresh goat's milk was offered, I had to politely refuse. Local unpasteurised milk is always guaranteed to stir the system up. Next the hosts presented their staple fare, which was couscous – three different types, fine, medium and ground into a paste. The idea was to combine these with milk to make a mixture – which to me tasted a bit like soggy Weet-Bix – and to drink more glasses of sweet strong tea. Communication was a challenge as the elders spoke Arabic, but between us we managed using various props and gestures.

The womenfolk tended to be very shy and generally left communications to the men. We did manage to converse with the French teacher, though, when she joined us later. The village, she told us, was home to approximately 300 people who

Village mosque and central common

lived in 70 houses and owned 500 cows, 150 sheep and 200 goats. The primary school had three classes and four teachers – one French teacher and three Arabic teachers. The main problem for the community is water. Their groundwater aquifers are drying up – the well is already 30 metres deep. Apart from this issue the villagers said they felt content, and there seemed to be no perception of being poor. We spent a captivating evening with these people and slept outside beneath the stars on their floor cushions.

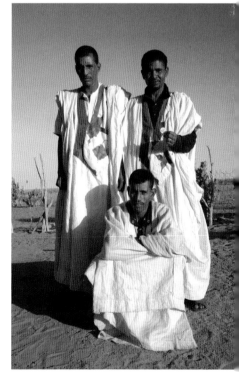

But I had a rotten night. Predictably, my system had reacted violently to the milk and couscous. By the early hours of the morning, I'd made several emergency forays into the bush. After that, I lay still in my sleeping bag, wide-awake. Watching the stars became all-night theatre as they gradually lost their sparkle and faded to grey with the encroachment of the pre-dawn twilight. By then some of the villagers were already up and about. In the gloom they appeared as ghosts 'floating' over the sandy ground in their *dara'as*. Beyond our fenced compound they moved their animals out from their pens to graze or lugged yellow containers of water from the well. Of our team, John was up first as usual, setting up the cooker to make porridge. I lay in a few more minutes, trying to summon up a modicum of energy. We had a tight schedule to keep in Mauritania and could not afford to miss any days. I had to press on so it was best not to dwell on my physical condition. There was little I could do except keep fluids up, try to ignore how I felt and go steady: difficult through the sandy terrain. Dan repaired yet another puncture before Mohammed set us on the right path to complete the shortcut.

Brothers Ahmed (left), Mohammed and Ellie (front), Seli hi yas Telia (sud)

✳

The road we picked up on heading to Nema was built in 2006 as the 'Road of Hope' but is now more commonly known as the 'Road to Nowhere'. It is the only tarmac strip running across Mauritania joining Nouakchott on the coast to Nema, approximately 1200 kilometres away. Long and straight, it reminded me a little of cycling across the open spaces of the Nullarbor Plain, complete with headwind! The small villages are a little closer together in Mauritania though. They have a different layout and atmosphere from those in Mali and even to the close-knit community of Seli hi yas Telia (sud) where we had stayed the previous night. I did feel uneasy cycling through some of these conservative Islamic villages. Sensing the inhabitants would be less understanding about my *sportif* attire, I did not hang around to let them think about it too much.

The position of Mauritania straddles the Arab and sub-Saharan African worlds. The country has a culture more closely aligned with Arabic nations to the north but has many development issues which are more similar to other Sahelian nations. Mauritania is classified as a Maghreb state. These are the countries of north-western Africa bordered by the Sahara Desert, Mediterranean Sea and the Atlas Mountains. Other Maghreb countries include Morocco, Algeria, Tunisia, Libya and the disputed state of Western Sahara.

In researching the journey through south-east Mauritania I'd heard that there were some serious security concerns. Through my broad network of connections, I was put in touch with Seyid Ould Seyid, a well-known Mauritanian journalist, writer and fixer. I employed Seyid to accompany us for at least six days to act as interpreter, organise our visit to Oualata and steer us away from trouble. Since Dakar I had been communicating with him regularly to coordinate all the details, including our rendezvous. We were going to meet at the village of Timbedra, 100 kilometres from Nema, but as we were running half a day behind schedule, Seyid arranged a lift to meet us on the road. And so on the 'Road to Nowhere,' in the middle of nowhere, as I was just setting off, head down after a break, a car travelling from the opposite direction slowed up and a strange voice called out my name. It was, of course, Seyid. A dynamic fellow, his positive energy, enthusiasm and constant quest to investigate were infectious. As he worked for Mauritanian television, radio, newspapers and internet sites, he was always looking for a story to send back to his editors. He has also worked for Al Jazeera, CNN and USA Today. In fact, Seyid was a journalistic machine, pumping out news items from the first day of travelling with us.

To ensure our safety, he had connected with government officials and the gendarmerie, letting them know what we were doing and that we would create some positive publicity both within and outside of Mauritania. As two journalists had been arrested the previous day for reporting from the region without permission, from this point we were under the protective wing of the gendarmerie and had to be counted at every roadside checkpoint. That night, rather than adopting our usual technique of camping out of sight of the road, we were forced to sleep beneath an open-sided shelter at one of these regular stations, 60 kilometres before Timbedra. Under their watch, we had to abide by their rules.

Our first main meeting was with the governor of the Hodh Ech Chargui Region of which Nema is the capital. In Nema we were escorted straight to the governor's residence by the local police. Having been on the road for seven days straight we were looking decidedly shabby. The team may have appeared like authentic adventurers but I certainly felt rather self-conscious being formally received by the local officialdom as a truly scruffy representative of Australia. I hadn't seen myself in a mirror for a while and the notion that I might have had a filthy face plagued my thoughts. Certainly our hosts acted as if they were not fazed by our appearance and accepted that I was wearing cycling attire. The welcoming tea may have been served from a more ornate teapot this time, but the meaning was equally as genuine. I did notice, however, that all the images Seyid captured for Mauritanian media were taken of my waist up.

Feeling a little scruffy and under-dressed while being received by Governor Rana (DH)

Since 1978, Mauritania has undergone ten military coups d'état, each overthrowing a democratically elected government. Following the most recent coup by General Mohammed Ould Abdel Aziz in 2008, his regime was isolated by the international community and punished by diplomatic sanctions and the cancellation of some aid projects. The pressure eventually led Abdel Aziz to organise new presidential elections earlier in 2009 which he, of course, won and international support was restored (after the previous president formally resigned under protest).

The newly elected regional governor, Mohammed Rana, was particularly keen to emphasise that the country is now a democracy and exuded a real air of optimism. The elections were a fresh start; an opportunity to move forward, improve infrastructure, promote international relations and encourage tourism. He explained that his government had plans to build an international airport to encourage visitors to the remote region of which Oualata was the trump card. Impressed that we had made a 700-kilometre diversion to include the World Heritage Site on our itinerary, he proceeded to give us an overview of the ancient town and what his government intended to do to preserve it as a living historical place. Having Seyid there to translate and direct diplomatic proceedings was invaluable. Governor Rana gave his guarantee that we would be looked after in his country.

Initial impressions of Nema confirmed how the 'Road to Nowhere' received its name. The rugged, dusty frontier town of about 60,000 people has an army barracks with security milling around everywhere and little to recommend it. There is certainly no infrastructure to support international tourism that the non-existent airport may one day bring.

At the governor's insistence, we were accompanied by an armed escort to Oualata, 120 kilometres north of Nema on an extremely rough and sandy road. We'd discovered that Mauritanians are incredibly hospitable people but the borders to the north with Algeria in particular are impossible to police. With the extreme terrorist group al-Qaida in the Islamic Maghreb (AQIM) known to have infiltrated into this region, the new government was not taking any risks. (AQIM is largely an Algerian terrorist group which has aligned itself with al-Qaida.)

❖

We decided to drive to Oualata rather than cycle so we could spend more quality time there. As this was a diversion away from my main route, I was not breaking the continuous line of the journey. The first two-thirds or so of the track was similar to the Nioro road – quite cyclable. The last 30-40 kilometres were a

The view from the mayor's office. The lower slopes of Oualata are succumbing to the desert

different story, with deep sand but not really any defined sand ridges; if I'd ridden this would have taken an extra day to push through. However, despite the obvious difficulties of the route and my weakened condition, I regretted not cycling at least one way. For me, driving does not give the same connectedness to the land as getting there under my own steam. Still, we needed the extra time and my body needed to recover, so it was the right decision.

The vast desolate expanses certainly gave a sense of isolation. Oualata is so cut off that, in Mauritania, being sent to the prison there is the equivalent to being sent to Siberia in Soviet times. Surrounded by desert and hundreds of kilometres from anywhere, there is no escape. The first president of Mauritania, Moktar Ould Daddah, who is often referred to as the father of the nation and who led the country to independence from France in 1960, was toppled in 1978 in the first military coup and incarcerated in Oualata as a political prisoner.

Baba, the deputy mayor, welcomes us to Oualata

Some of the deposed leaders from the subsequent coups were also sent to Oualata.

The old town is nestled on the rocky slopes of the Dhar Tichitt-Oualata escarpment, the steep incline forming a natural terracing. The high ridges flank a broad valley. On the far side of the valley, pink sands spill around the sandstone breakaways and the odd thorn tree. Through the shimmering midday heat haze and dust, a herd of camels congregated around the life-giving well in the valley, waiting to be watered. By law, all buildings in Oualata must be designed and constructed in the traditional way, with stones and ochre-brown coloured clay and dung rendering. Among them, the ruins of the old town, approximately 600 years old, sit the highest. Some newer government buildings conforming to the architectural regulations lie just above the valley floor, protected from the encroaching sands by substantial walls. Our journey ended at the mayor's office, halfway up on the hillside. Here we were greeted as official guests by the deputy mayor and other commune officials. We stayed in their adjacent guest house and were treated with a seemingly constant flow of communal meals, local specialities and, of course, Mauritanian tea.

Civilisation in this area dates to about 4000 years ago when the region was a much greener, more productive place. The remains of about 400 Neolithic settlements of the Dhar Tichitt-Oualata culture have been found in the rocky promontories nearby. These agro-pastoral people settled in the region to escape the expanding Sahara, grazing animals and domesticating bullrush millet to grow as their staple crop. Their stone settlements are probably the oldest in the west of the African continent. As the land dried out, these people were replaced by a few oasis-dwellers until traders ventured by camel across the desert. Oualata then evolved due to its prime geographical location as the southern terminus of two important Saharan trade routes and became a crossroad of civilisations. The trade route that traversed the Sahara to North Africa and southern Spain was travelled by Arabs, Berbers

The well in the valley floor still serves the camel trains that circulate between Oualata and Timbuktu, about 300 kilometres to the east

and members of sub-Saharan cultures such as the Soninké, all of whom have left their cultural imprint. Originally called Birou by the Soninké people, Oualata (also spelled Walata) received its name from the Berber word meaning 'shady place.' The original town, buried deep beneath the valley floor, was built in the eleventh century.

Salt was the main commodity traded: caravans would bring it to a site a few kilometres from the town and from there it was taken to be processed in Oualata. Salt caravans still exist, constantly travelling the 300 or so kilometres from Timbuktu, which is directly east. Timbuktu soon superseded Oualata as the centre for trade, which diminished the town's importance as an economic centre.

We were fortunate to see two of these caravans as they arrived for their pit stop to unload, water their camels, reload and set off. Those who work the route today are descendants of those who transported goods centuries ago: the business is kept in the family. Many other products were also traded – gold, cloth, kola nuts, metals, food, spices, religious manuscripts and educational texts. The level of education in Oualata back in the eleventh century is believed to be at least as advanced as in Europe at that time. The town's deputy mayor, Baba, is directly descended from one of the four original families of Oualata. His

The next generation of cameleers. Working the camel trains is family business

ancestors migrated across the Sahara from Iraq, bringing their education with them. Our other hosts, such as Cidina, cultural advisor and maths teacher, and Cidi Ould Merzong, general secretary of the commune and a history and civic education teacher, have similar stories. Cidina lived with his young wife, Zahra, in the home of his great-great-great- grandfather where he showed us 500-year-old books from his family library.

The city became an intellectual focus for Islam during the seventeenth and eighteenth centuries, when it was a refuge for Muslim sages. Spiritual leaders had sought a safe haven in Oualata while Timbuktu was under attack from the Tuareg and then the Moroccans. At that time Oualata had six Qu'ranic schools where leading doctors of Islamic law gave classes. The tradition of education still exists today, although times are changing. Seyid took me to the ageing Gdnou Square to visit the Sheikh, the religious leader and traditional teacher of the madrasa. In this, the traditional school of the desert, he is in charge of teaching long-established subjects such as Islamic law, religion, languages, literature and the history of ancient civilisations such as Greek and Roman. The learning process is for all stages of life from childhood to old age. In their culture, lifelong learning gives dignity and constant study is considered desirable. The most special moment came when the Sheikh, rekindling the ancient lineage of his ancestors, recited for us some verses now only read in Oualata and Andalucía (Spain).

The Sheikh recites verses now only read in Oualata and Andalucía (Spain)

The learned Sheikh acts like a barometer of society, in tune with Oualata's culture, past and present. He attributes colonialism as the main destructive force of Oualata's past civilisation, and views globalisation as a threat to its present way of life, outside

The only car in town. Some adaptations for moving with the times are more appropriate than others (JD)

influences fanning desires which draw away the younger generations. He explained that he was trying to adapt to keep education relevant and the community alive, believing it essential to balance modern subjects such as information technology with his traditional classes, to move forward while preserving the time-honoured culture. Many students are learning English and French with the hope that this will bring them opportunities outside of Oualata. A whole generation, he told us, is draining away from the community and with this trend the future of the town fades. The Sheikh was pragmatic, encouraging the younger generation to at least try to visit their town on holidays rather than disappear forever.

One of my major motives for travelling to Oualata was to see the library; a key reason why UNESCO designated Oualata as a World Heritage Site – as a place to be conserved for its cultural and historical importance. The library stores manuscripts from seven private family collections, the principal collection belonging to the Abderrahman family. The only surviving family member, Afe Mint Abderrahman, is in charge of the 1077 documents covering a broad range of subjects, including a comprehensive record of Saharan society. The library houses only about 30 per cent of the historic books in the town, the remainder being kept in private family libraries (such as Cidina's). The main library has made a second room available to store more documents should other families choose to display their books in an environment more conducive to preservation. While its international significance has been recognised, the cost of repairing, maintaining and preserving the documents, some up to 600 years old, is far beyond the means of the family or the commune. Expertise in cataloguing, creating microfiches and facsimiles, and preserving the library building is not available either. The main help has come from a Spanish cooperation through the NGO Món-3, and that ended in 2007.

Afe Mint Abderrahman presides over documents belonging to her family, kept in Oualata's main library

Over the generations, the people of Oualata have developed their own distinctive culture that is found nowhere else. Seyid explained that in ancient times this was known as the Azaire civilisation, and that it evolved over centuries of relative isolation from a unique fusion of Berber, Arab and African cultures. Some words of the age-old Azaire language are still used today and can only be understood by descendants of the Azaire people. The families of Oualata are still grouped by kinship in different tribes or *qaba'il*; these form a hierarchical pyramid in which men and women find their place according to their social

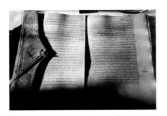

More resources and expertise are required to preserve, catalogue and display the books

and economic standing. Historically, traditional Oualata society was divided into free men (*ahrar*), traders, herdsmen and intellectuals, and their slaves. These days the Harratin, descendants of the slave class, make up approximately two-thirds of Oualata's current population of three thousand.

Being a Westerner, when I thought of slavery in Africa, I thought of the European and transatlantic slave trades and their shameful contributions to the history books. In Dakar we toured Île de Gorée, one of the many infamous ports where families were separated and herded onto ships to leave their homelands forever. While this is a disturbing monument, in Mauritania I learned that my focus needed to be more on the abolition of modern-day slavery.

Sadly, slavery is a major problem all over the world, in both developed and developing countries, and an inherent issue in a number of countries on my route. Mauritania is reportedly the country with the largest portion of its society still in domestic slavery – approximately 600,000 people, or 20 per cent of the population, according to

Mauritanian NGO, S.O.S. Esclaves Mauritanie – and the Harratin are the group most affected. The government, which banned the practice in 1905, 1961 and again in 1981 and only made it a punishable criminal offence in 2007, goes to great lengths to deny the problem, prohibiting the word 'slave' from use by the media, and threatening foreign journalists with arrest and deportation if they investigate the issue. Given that our hosts were not from the slave caste and, as community leaders, were bound to give the official government line about modern-day slavery, it was not possible for us to find out many specifics in Oualata, and Seyid had to be careful what he reported.

While the various regimes have been a major hindrance to fighting slavery, the inherent problem is that the issue has existed in Mauritania for hundreds of years and is deeply ingrained within society across the country. The very trade routes which were responsible for the development of cities like Oualata also acted as the tentacles allowing slavery to take hold. The Arab and Berber people who first crossed the desert to trade also sought to impose their religion on the sun-worshipping indigenous Harratin. When the local people resisted, they were enslaved. The slave trade in this part of the world evolved into centuries

A Harratin woman. The poorest class w are reportedly the descendants of slave the Harratin make up two-thirds of Oua population

of chattel slavery – and that has not ended.

The Harratin are traditionally owned by the Bidane, or 'white Moors', the minority ruling Arab-Berber elite. Individuals are born into slavery, their 'slave caste' is ascribed at birth. The various castes simply grow up in this society and live with a strong mutual dependence. Some of the slaves are treated well by their masters, others are abused. Those in slavery are devoid of all fundamental human rights, are owned and controlled by their masters and treated as their property. They are forced to work for their masters throughout their lives and are not paid for their labour. They do what their masters tell them or they are threatened and abused.

Slaves undergo a form of indoctrination underpinned by hundreds of years of tradition. They accept their position because they believe that if they do not obey their masters, they will not go to paradise. Raised in a social and religious system that every day reinforces this idea, slaves cannot revolt because they would lose everything. Those who do manage to escape face an uncertain future as they often have no education and few prospects of employment. Many slaves 'taste freedom' and return to their masters, begging for forgiveness. So even if the government enforces the law and provides education and

Baba's tour. Streets and alleyways have inbuilt shelters to protect from the harsh elements

Relocating on higher ground. The forces of erosion are at work before the building is complete

more support to former slaves and the Bidanes alike, the issue is so deep-rooted it will take many years to free the society from both its physical and psychological shackles.

❄

Baba, the deputy mayor, escorted us through the ancient streets of which he is clearly so proud. The enchanting labyrinth of narrow alleyways and buildings is a cultural heirloom of the past six centuries or so. Set highest on the hillside, many of the buildings that constitute the oldest quarter have not been maintained and instead left *au natural* to crumble back to earth. Amidst the rubble, family homes have been fastidiously cared for and finished off with a fresh adobe layer decorated with beautiful traditional artwork. Other walls were pocked and cracked, in dire need of superficial refurbishment using a mixture of mud, cow dung, water and pigment. Everything about the architectural design of the town is intended to protect the inhabitants from the intense sun and wind that are relentless all year round: thick insulating walls encapsulate a central courtyard in each dwelling, and the narrow winding streets provide shade and shelter from the wind and sand storms.

Buildings at the base of the town are being systematically consumed by the encroaching desert. One of our hosts, Cidi, explained that shifting sands have forced his family to relocate to higher ground twice so far in his lifetime. Constructing houses in the traditional way is certainly a labour-intensive 90-day process. Cidi took us to meet a team of workmen building a house:

A fresh renovation (JD)

31

'Times Square'

pouring mud over an insulating layer of straw on the roof, laying bricks and rendering stone walls. The men were exposed to the elements, receiving a sand-blasting in the heat of the day. In a never-ending cycle, it appeared that the forces of erosion were at work even before the building is completed.

Each of the town's narrow lanes converges at a small square or *rihab* which contains the all-important well. After translating details about the history of the most historical square, Seyid surmised that this was Oualata's 'Times Square' due to its significance, central location and what its wonky doors must have witnessed over the past 500 years. The weathering and scars on some of these doors, like the age rings of an ancient tree trunk, could tell many a tale.

The legendary Moroccan explorer, Ibn Battuta, passed through Oualata in 1352. Battuta's journeys lasted for a period of nearly thirty years and covered almost the entirety of the known Islamic world and beyond, extending from North Africa, West Africa, Southern Europe and Eastern Europe, to the Middle East, Indian subcontinent, Central Asia, South-east Asia and China, an area easily surpassing that of his predecessors and his near-contemporary Marco Polo. When Battuta arrived in Oualata, the main city and *rihabs* like 'Times Square' would have been under construction. He recorded only a brief description of the town itself:

Oualata's tradition and religion dictate that the town's doors should remain closed. What stories could this door tell?

My stay at Iwalatan (Oualata) lasted about fifty days; and I was shown honour and entertained by its inhabitants. It is an excessively hot place, and boasts a few small date-palms, in the shade of which they sow watermelons. Its water comes from underground waterbeds at that point, and there is plenty of mutton to be had. The garments of its inhabitants, most of whom belong to the Massufa tribe, are of fine Egyptian fabrics. Their women are of surpassing beauty, and are shown more respect than the men...

Oualata's streets are as quiet as the desert surrounds. The children appeared to be shy. Those plucky enough shadowed us around while playing their version of hide and seek; poking their smiling faces around a corner or vanishing amongst the ruins. While we too received great hospitality, Oualata's doors form a physical and metaphorical barrier, segregating families, and especially women, from the outside world. Battuta recorded that he was astonished by the great respect and independence that women enjoyed in the fourteenth century (relative to other cities in that era), but these days their tradition and religion dictate that doors are always closed. Women must stay in the home and may only go out in the daytime accompanied by a family member. It is considered disrespectful for a woman to be out on her own; she may be suspected of prostitution and rejected by her family or community.

Vatma explains that there is no water to grow the seedlings

I became inspired to visit Oualata a few years ago after reading a photo-story in the *Geographical* magazine. A venture which particularly interested me was the Women's Farming Project, an initiative set up by a cooperative between the Mauritanian and Spanish governments. I was impressed to see images of women from sixty of the poorest Harratin families in the town working in a newly created market garden – locally referred to as the Oualata 'Garden of Eden.' Each woman was given her own plot of which she took ownership, growing vegetables from seedlings in the nursery for her family with any excess traded for extra income. The article reported that the women were happy, empowered by a sense of purpose. I was struck by the lushness – the garden was an oasis of date palms, fruit trees and rows of vegetables. There were solar panels and a generator to drive the water pump. Given that in the magazine this all looked like a

xplains that the tanks are empty and that no one can fix the pump (DH)

paradise in the desert, I was shocked on arrival to see that everything was dead, bone dry and the women out of work. When I asked why, Cidi, the commune secretary, replied that there was no water. Why? The pump is broken. Why can't you fix the pump, it's just a simple part missing? I couldn't really get a direct answer other than they couldn't get any help. I didn't understand because these are well-educated people, leaders of the town. It was only after our tour, when I spoke to Seyid who had been doing some detective work, that I was able to find out the real story.

The farming project was set up in 1994 and run for ten years by the joint government venture, costing roughly six million Euros. It had four specific objectives aimed at benefiting the town as a whole. The first, to preserve the library and protect the manuscripts, received two years of support. The second was to develop the women's farming project, 'El Michtela' (Farming Laboratory), which received eight years of support. The third and fourth, to develop health facilities and the local grazing industry, received no assistance at all.

The Spanish organisation Món-3 took over the market gardening project, adding some tourist chalets as an extra form of income and contributing to some building and library restoration for the next two years. In 2007, the Mauritanian government's Ministry of Culture reclaimed responsibility under its National Institution for Protection of Old Cities of Mauritania.

What Seyid found out later explains what went wrong. Alongside the project, people were being given handouts of food parcels and other basics every two weeks. This created a culture of dependency. Secondly, all skilled jobs were given to foreign hired help from Spain and Morocco. There was no skills transfer and no education about management of such a project, so that when a relatively minor problem occurred such as the pump breaking down, the whole system failed – no water, no industry. This is a disheartening example of ineffective development aid, particularly common in the 1980s and early 1990s.

After the project tour and subsequent discussions with Seyid, I surmised that 'fixing the pump' in this case required far more than attending to a minor mechanical failure: that's just the short-term emergency.

All the women have the basic gardening skills to produce food but even though our hosts, community leaders, are products of a culture with centuries of learning tradition, there is a desperate need to empower them with managerial, operational and organisational skills. While their isolation is an issue, in modern times, especially with the internet, this can be overcome. Poverty is a problem too and more funds are required to restart the initiatives, but it would be money wasted if the whole project is not made sustainable and run by the citizens of Oualata. Of course, doing so is not simple and it would

Decorations in the mayor's office

require much negotiation and time to rebuild trust in foreigners offering help. Cidi and Baba affirmed that many have promised much to Oualata and not delivered. Seyid had had difficulty negotiating for us to see the library, for example, because the leaders say that they have been let down a few times. There was a lack of trust by some officials.

I was shown a few other bright lights: small businesses looking for connections but not sure how to go about it. In the course of this, I was introduced to Fatimetou Zahra Moulaye Ely, president of the Women's Cooperative for the Restoration of the Oualata Murals and Handicrafts. Women, many belonging to the cooperative, are responsible for all the distinctive artwork throughout the town. Their designs, mostly applied by finger painting, are generally filigrees symbolising different aspects of femininity, such as bellies and breasts. Besides the wall murals they produce fine ceramics and make their own colourful cloth, which they sell to tourists. Together with several *auberges* (inns), these small enterprises rely heavily on tourism. But although these people are traders by nature I don't think tourists will be flooding there in the near future. Outside of winter – December, January, February – the climate is too inhospitable for most. With bandits infiltrating occasionally across the porous Algerian border, the

police are vigilant in protecting locals and visitors. This doesn't help the tourist industry as it only takes one negative incident report to deter even intrepid travellers.

The three-and-a-half day stay in Oualata was so jam-packed with a steady flow of hospitality, sightseeing and learning – visiting the Sheikh, library, 'Garden of Eden,' camel trains, museum and finding out about the complex history, culture and contemporary issues – that I barely had time to breathe. One of the best ways to absorb some of the atmosphere was, I found, to simply wander alone through the ancient alleyways, over the sand and rubble, and up the hill to gain a panoramic view of the landscape. At dusk, everything was calm with a beautiful golden glow across the valley. The wind had died down and the cooler evening air was refreshing. Goats that had been grazing on the escarpment all day were walked back to their pens for the night. Satellite dishes that had sprung up like mushrooms from the roof terraces in recent years contrasted sharply against a backdrop of ruins and decorative courtyards. One last call to prayer floated out from the central mosque and over the millenarian town, then all was quiet. I tried to put everything into some sort of perspective in readiness to move on. Oualata appears to be clinging to its culture as its buildings cling to the hillside, continually relocating to higher ground to escape the encroaching sands. Will Oualata survive both the ravages of desertification and the exodus of its next generation? Will the ancient books and traditions of this living, breathing museum be preserved? I believe it is all possible if they could only learn how to 'fix the pump.'

Of course we would have loved to stay longer in Oualata but then we would never finish the journey in the time-frame I had set, and I had to always be aware of the big picture. I certainly didn't feel like moving though, as I could not shake off my illness. The way to deal with diarrhoea is to fast for a day or so and starve it. While cycling, this had been impossible and in Oualata the hospitality was such that great plates of food, including local specialties, were served several times a day. Not wishing to offend, I could not refuse at least a small amount. On the final evening, day ten of the problem, this all reached a crescendo – my body simply pushed the eject button. I couldn't even keep water inside me. Back in Nema, John found some antibiotics which set me on the right path.

*

After Oualata, Seyid volunteered to stay with us to ensure we travelled through his country safely. Thanks to him we were able to experience a part of the world that few people get to see and understand so much more about its culture and issues in a very short space of time. It was his proposal to alter our plans, return to Timbedra and take a more interesting, little-travelled shortcut across the border to Nara in Mali. The added attraction was that we would be able to visit the ruins of Koumbi Saleh, the once all-powerful capital of the ancient Ghanaian empire. In taking the more direct route, we also hoped to make up time as we had fallen a few days behind schedule.

While I had been looking forward to moving again, starting off was a real trial. The gastro episode had knocked the stuffing out of me – to put it politely. I was on the mend but had eaten nothing the day before. To add to this, we were not permitted to start cycling until the heat of the day. The local gendarmerie had been assigned to protect us through the Timbedra region and we were made to wait until 11.00 a.m. for our security escort to be ready. On the outskirts of town, the track degraded to a few sandy wheel ruts. I had assumed that we would be following a minor road that joined Timbebra to Nara, as shown on our large-scale Michelin map but, in reality, a single path does not exist. The road depicted was merely an average of the many small tracks – and in turn these gave birth to a confusing puzzle of alternate routes between villages. There were no directional sign posts and no signs to name the towns.

Of the first 21 kilometres I travelled only two of them were of harder-packed dirt which ran over a claypan; the rest was terribly disheartening. By the time we skirted the perimeter of a field of sand dunes, there was nothing left in my tank. The midday sun penetrated to my core as I leaned my whole body weight into the handlebars and pushed forlornly into a searing headwind over the hot, fluid sand. My spirits sank to rock bottom and I started to doubt everything. I knew the only way through at that point was to keep the head down and not stop. I considered cycling cross-country but off-piste the over-grazed ground was covered in thorns and burrs. It was tempting but I did not wish to risk getting punctures. I had brought fatter tyres to use in the sand but as they were not as puncture-resistant as the road tyres we could not use them on this terrain.

By lunch I was exhausted, overheated, and feeling very negative about the 'shortcut.' There was no indication as to whether the track would improve, no-one knew how far it was to the border and I seriously doubted whether we had made the right choice. I even suggested we retrace our tracks down the main road all the way back to Nioro in Mali and then continue along the tarmac to Bamako and Ségou. John pointed out that this would effectively take two days to travel by car. I didn't trust the local advice and didn't think the effort and lost time could justify the visit to the ancient capital, which we knew had not been preserved. Some nomads kindly offered us shade under their tent – without walls it had perfect ventilation. Over a couple of hours I was able to recover and eventually agreed to keep going.

The track bisected a sea of partially stabilised sand dunes

Dan was doing much better than I. He had been cycling in the grass all morning, while I slogged it out in the sand. I followed his lead in the afternoon and we both trail-blazed through the often long grass, giving the thorn bushes a wide berth. By doing this we used a lot less energy and could travel faster. In fact, I incurred the sole puncture for the day in the last few kilometres we did in the dark trying to reach a village. We only managed 37 kilometres on day one out of Timbedra! The chief of the village welcomed us and proposed to kill a goat in our honour. Seyid accepted his offer, but the rest of us just needed simple food and sleep. I was off any local fare for a few days to try and regain my health.

For the next two days, Dan and I cycled almost exclusively cross-country, bisecting a sea of old, partially grass-covered sand ridges. We discovered that there were fewer burrs in the long grass, even though moving forward was frustratingly tedious and slow. Travelling mostly on our own, we'd often come to unnamed intersections where the tracks forked and spend ages deliberating over which option to take. Then Dan marked the track by either drawing arrows in the sand or making pointers using sticks – or both – in the hope that John would pick up the route we chose.

To the locals we may as well have been from outer space. At one village, when Seyid asked a woman whether she had seen two cyclists pass by, she replied that she had seen a man and a woman moving through the grass with their legs going round and round but she didn't know whether that is what he called 'cycling.' She would have never seen a bicycle before! No one cycles in these parts. Many villagers were unable to give directions, or at least certainly not accurate bearings to the border. They would know how to reach the neighbouring villages but as they never needed to travel to the border, they had no idea how to get there. It was very easy to become lost – and we did lose each other several times.

To villagers in this remote region, I may as well been from outer space

✻

If we did not know where to look for Koumbi Saleh, it would have been easy to cycle straight past. There were no signs and nothing immediately spectacular to see. About a kilometre from the main ruins we noticed some piles of shale which would have once constituted a city gate. They would have been transported a long way as the ancient Ghanaian capital is set in a broad plain with a totally different

Watering cattle at Koumbi Maré

geology. This fact alone is evidence of the power of the empire and its rulers. To develop into a city of 30,000 people as Koumbi Saleh did must have taken a huge labour force to move millions of stones from distant quarries.

Ancient Ghana is not ethnically, geographically or in any other way related to the modern country of Ghana, about 600 kilometres to the south-east. Originally known as Wagadou, the empire adopted the name 'Ghana' from its Soninké founders – the word means 'king.'

We stopped beside a lake that was most likely Koumbi Maré, where young cowboys were watering their cattle. Three of them were very keen to show off their accomplished horsemanship by making a spirited run through at full gallop. From the settlement's beginning around the third century AD until its decline in 1250, the land would have been greener and much more productive. The shallow lake, now about half a kilometre across, would once have been much larger and an important source of food and water.

As we rested under an acacia tree at the southern periphery of the mounds, Seyid spoke to locals from the nearby village, trying to find out more about the ancient royal capital. He was particularly excited

A cowboy at Koumbi Saleh

to explore the site as he had learned about Koumbi Saleh in his history books. In the couple of days since he knew we were going there, he had been connecting with academics in Nouakchott to learn more about it. By the time I was ready to look around, he had determined the urban layout and, accompanied by two locals, was able to guide me through a tour to see where the royal palace, courtyard, gold chamber, mosque and military quarters were believed to exist.

There are a few theories as to how the earliest of the most significant empires in West Africa evolved; the most plausible is that the highly developed Dhar-Tichitt culture from around Tichitt, Oualata and Nema migrated south because of pressure from advancing desert nomads and the increasing aridity. The introduction of the camel in trans-Saharan trade boosted the volume of goods that could be transported and the new powerful civilisation evolved with a rich and stable economy that would dominate West Africa for about 500 years.

We headed to the highest mound from which we could survey the site. Only a couple of walls have been excavated of this, the royal palace (according to Seyid). It was difficult to imagine, from this pile of stones how this place must have appeared during its glory days when the divine king ruled all the land between the Senegal and Niger rivers, the Sahara Desert and Niani in the north-east of present-day Guinea. Oualata would have merely been a satellite trading post on the desert boundary of the Ghanaian Empire, its fortunes fluctuating with the flow of camel trains. Most of the detail of what is known about Koumbi Saleh comes from archaeological excavations and the Arab writers who travelled there or interviewed merchants returning from the West African capital. In 1067, the most articulate and prolific scholar and geographer Al-Bakri fuelled future fertile imaginations with his description of the court of Tenkamenin, the emperor of the time:

> The King adorns himself like a woman wearing necklaces round his neck and bracelets on his forearms and he puts on a high cap decorated with gold and wrapped in a turban of fine cotton. When he gives an audience to his people he sits in a pavilion around which stand his horses covered in gold-embroidered material; behind the King stand ten pages holding shields and gold-mounted swords and on his right hand are the sons of the vassal kings of his country, splendidly clad and with gold plaited into their hair. The governor of the city is seated on the ground in front of the King, and all around him are his ministers in the same position. The gate of the chamber is guarded by dogs of an excellent breed, who never leave the King's seat. They wear collars of gold and silver studded with a number of balls of the same metal.*

The palace is said to have contained glass windows and outside the divine leader kept a menagerie of elephants and giraffes. From his palace, the king was surrounded by his protectors – his army and his priests. Inevitably, traders brought Islam with them, but the king retained his traditional beliefs. To accommodate the two religions, and to avoid Islam permeating the animist philosophy of his subjects, the capital was actually two cities ten kilometres apart. The regal town, El Ghaba, and the Muslim town (the name of which has not been recorded) were connected by a single road. Between these two towns were continuous habitations so that they might be merged into one. The main buildings and walls were made of stone while other houses were most likely made of wood and other perishable materials.

The treasury, partially excavated in 1949

We were walking through the ruins of the El Ghaba section that functioned as the royal and spiritual capital of the empire. What remains of the walled city covers an area of about one square kilometre. Around the king's town were domed dwellings and sacred groves and thickets where the sorcerers in

---

* A quote from *Corpus of Early Arabic Sources for West African History*

charge of the religious cult lived. The Muslim section was for the traders and contained twelve mosques with scholars, scribes and jurists; it was most likely to be the primary hub for West African and trans-Saharan trade. The king drew on the book-keeping and literary expertise of Muslim scholars to help run the administration of the territory.

Seyid led me down the mound to the treasury, partially excavated by Raymond Mauny and Paul Thomassey, French archaeologists, in 1949. It was in these vaults that the wealth of the empire was stored in gold. The gold trade was largely responsible for the development of Ghana into a powerful, centralised kingdom. The peoples of West Africa had independently developed their own gold-mining techniques and began trading with merchants from other regions of Africa and later Europe as well. Gold was traded for equal amounts of salt that came down from the Sahara. But it was the collection of taxes that allowed the citizens to live in such opulence. There were two distinct types of taxes that were paid to the royal treasury: import and export tax and production tax. The import and export tax was paid by traders for the right to bring commodities in or out of Koumbi Saleh. Al-Bakri noted that merchants had to pay a one gold dinar tax on imports of salt, and two on exports of salt. The second tax, the production tax, was applied to the production of gold. The king claimed as his own all nuggets of gold, and allowed other people to have only gold dust.

A little further along, just off the Grand Avenue, we investigated what was the front of the mosque. This was one of the most intact remains: the stones of the *mihrab*, from where the Imam delivered prayers, had been reassembled with cement grouting. Initially the mosque was built to accommodate visiting foreign dignitaries but gradually, as Islam's importance increased to overpower traditional beliefs, so did its scale. The Ghanaian empire was conquered by the Almoravids, a Moroccan Berber dynasty which stretched from southern Spain to ancient Ghana at its peak. The kingdom recovered somewhat after the initial conquest in about AD 1075, but the damage was done. The once-well-organised, controlled peripheral states fragmented as they were gradually

A fallen kingdom. Fragments of the ancient history of Koumbi Saleh lay concealed beneath the rubble waiting to be unearthed

overwhelmed by the tide of the new creed. Associated with the emergence of some of these new states were the Fulani people, who served to spread the word of Islam. At the same time drought was beginning to have a long-term effect on the land and its ability to sustain cattle and cultivation. Koumbi Saleh's importance as the centre of trade diminished as gold was discovered elsewhere and the balance of power shifted to the realms of the Niger River. Unable to collect taxes from the vassal states, the economy atrophied and the empire fractured and crumbled over the next 150 years. Ghana was incorporated into the emergent Empire of Mali but retained function as a sort of kingdom within the domain.

We moved on to where the central square would have been. The enormous mosque would have once encroached over part of the extensive plaza. Seyid joked that if Oualata had 'Times Square' then the centre of Koumbi Saleh should be 'Red Square' in comparison. From his palace above, the king could overlook and maybe address his army paraded before him. At the height of his powers, he could recruit from all corners of his empire to field forces including 200,000 soldiers, 40,000 archers and a cavalry, if required. Along with being able to process gold, the ability to smelt iron to make weapons and tools played an equally important role in the expansion of the empire and maintaining control over it.

'Red Square' would also have been the high church for the people's traditional religion: a place for cult practices and sacrifices. The decline of Ghana's wealth was also explained mythically through the story of Bida, the black snake. This snake demanded an annual sacrifice in return for guaranteeing prosperity in the kingdom. Every year a virgin was offered up until, one year, the fiancé of the intended victim rescued her. Cheated of his sacrifice, Bida took his revenge on the region. A terrible drought took hold of Ghana and gold mining fell into decline.

At the southern end of the square, directly in front of the divine ruler's palace, stood the remains of some sort of statue or obelisk of worship. Fittingly, the monument was being eroded by the ravages of time, gradually being returned to dust by the very forces of nature which the king and his subjects once worshipped.

Our mini-circuit ended there, along with a journey back in time. There were small plaques located around the site indicating that Koumbi Saleh had been added to UNESCO's 'Tentative List' for World Heritage classification as a place of great archaeological importance. The main issue now is to preserve what is there and ensure that the local people understand its significance. The flat stones make great building blocks and in a region where such materials are scarce, it is understandable that some have been used to construct their modern dwellings nearby. Even more pressing is the need to protect the site from modern-day trophy hunters so that archaeologists can learn more about the capital of West Africa's first major kingdom.

Since we had left Kayes and the Senegal River, our 700-kilometre diversion had allowed us to explore some of the roots of modern West Africa. Kingdoms rise and kingdoms fall – Ghana, Mali and Songhai were all consecutive dominant empires – but what is clear is that, prior to colonialism, West Africa harboured highly organised, economically successful societies with a level of sophistication and intellectual development comparable to Europe in equivalent times. This history is rarely taught.

Seyid – 'Which way to the border?'

❋

The village-to-village slog resumed. Advancing towards the border was a real test of resolve. It would have been easier to dig deep if we knew exactly where we were heading or how far we had to push, and we were fast exhausting our ability to repair tyres. We'd resorted to cutting an old tube into pieces to fix the punctures but soon we would run out of glue. In the heat of the following day, only about 20 kilometres from the border, it was Dan's turn to lose patience and seriously doubt our route. The futility of the situation was taking its toll and Dan had had enough. John and I had to reassure him that he had done most of the hard work and convinced him that we could not be all that far from Nara across the

Mali border. I was starting to feel stronger, although I had lost a lot of weight. Full fitness was certainly not there yet.

By the end of the third day we crossed back into Mali. There was no demarcation so John celebrated by driving his vehicle round and round in a tight circle when the GPS indicated we were there. Although there was no sign of a border post, the villages changed dramatically in architecture and culture from one side to the other. The last village in Mauritania was typical of what we'd seen, with square mud houses, whereas across the imaginary line the next Mali village was totally different, with round grass and thatched houses and distinct village design. The women wore beautifully coloured clothes with jewellery and beads through their hair, as we had seen before. The track improved in quality a little, although it wasn't devoid of long sandy sections, especially where we passed by fields in fallow or cultivated with millet and sorghum. As we neared Nara, villages became a more regular occurance.

Nara had been the focus of our efforts for the last four days from Timbedra. As the sun sank behind us, Dan and I paused for one last break. We could see the communications mast on the horizon and estimated it to be about 10 kilometres away. The sight set us off, fantasising about the icy-cold beer and shower we were going to enjoy when we soon reached our Shangri-la. It didn't quite work out like that. Just as the team left us to go on ahead into town to find accommodation, an enormous thorn embedded into my tyre. With nightfall fast approaching I elected to leave the spike in situ so that it plugged the hole, and I kept pumping up the tyre every 800 metres or so. This all took up more time and so the last few kilometres were done in the dark. We could just see headlights, of motorbikes mainly, weaving through the woodland on the spaghetti maze of tracks. Wondering why we hadn't arrived, John came looking for us. Finally we could hear the distinctive, reassuring diesel engine-purr of the Land Rover in the distance and headed cross-country towards the sound, flashing our inadequate torch lights. My tyre was completely down again, and without a path to follow, Dan simply ditched his bike and sprinted towards the vehicle, finally shouting out to catch John's attention.

Reunited, we walked into town and, like the Pied Piper, gradually accrued a trail of followers. The hotel was hardly the paradise we had imagined but the headlights illuminated the word Novotel painted across the fence. Obviously this was not part of the international hotel chain and the standard of the amenities certainly confirmed that. Rather than a warm shower, I ended up washing the standard way

Dan asks for directions through the Canal du Sahel region just outside Sokolo

with a bucket of cold water. As there were no rooms available, we were given the meeting room – a noisy room beside the bar – to roll out our sleeping mats on the dirty concrete floor. The bar did serve that cold drink and I relaxed, simply pleased that we had arrived in Nara together and in one piece.

This was also the end of Seyid's time with us. The following day, John and Dan had to drive about 100 kilometres back to the Mauritanian border on the main road towards Nema to get the customs clearance and carnet stamped for the vehicle. Seyid returned with them over the Mauritanian border and then caught a lift to cover the 1400 kilometres back to Nouakchott.

While the others were away, Paddy and I wandered through Nara's well-supplied markets, stocking up on provisions for the next few days to Ségou. Of the many unusual items Paddy spotted for sale, it was the Obama perfume which took the prize. President Obama was proving to be an incredibly popular figure in this part of the world. Throughout the journey so far we had seen t-shirts showing his portrait, sometimes on a background of US stars and stripes, or displaying the words of his campaign slogan, 'Yes we can.' There were billboards, portraits, cafes and bars all renamed in honour of the American leader.

With all the necessary passport stamps and customs papers in order, we pushed on with the Niger River and Ségou in our sights. Thankfully the route improved immensely between Nara and Sokolo. The gravel road had actually been built and it was almost as good as cycling on tarmac except for the last 30 kilometres into Sokolo which were horrifically corrugated.

Reaching Sokolo, a busy market town, signified quite a change in the journey. On the town's western perimeter a huge livestock market was underway, pastoralists gathering from the surrounding dry lands to sell or trade their animals. The dusty streets led to the centre of town, an atmospheric labyrinth of rickety stalls offering a huge variety of products and services.

After a decent pause and a couple more *cafés au lait* to kickstart the afternoon, Dan and I set off in a south-easterly direction and entered into a very different environment. Sokolo sits on the outer limits of the Canal du Sahel region, often referred to as Mali's breadbasket. In the 1930s, the French used forced labour to build the huge Office du Niger project. Their chief interest was to 'develop' Mali as a source of cheap cash crops for export. Covering an area of about 50,000 hectares, the present-day project is on a scale not seen anywhere on our journey to that point. Between Sokolo to Niono, an administrative centre for the project, we wove through a patchwork of rice, cotton and wheat fields and vegetable plots. The canals are fed from the waters of the Inner Niger Delta, where the mighty Niger River disperses into a flat, marshy wetland. Along the main canal we passed people travelling by foot, bicycle or cart, carrying wares from their local markets. There was a buzz about each of these small communities. The roads that run alongside the canals are of well-maintained gravel and water pumps produce clean water. Finding a secluded campsite was difficult, but at last light, somewhat fittingly, about 10 kilometres north of Niono we camped near a crumbling old colonial building used as a warehouse to store flour.

From there we knocked off the 134 kilometres into Ségou, capital of the ancient Bambara Kingdom, on a beautiful tarmac strip in very good time. We were eager for a good break after a tough eight-day stint.

Total distance: 2301 kilometres

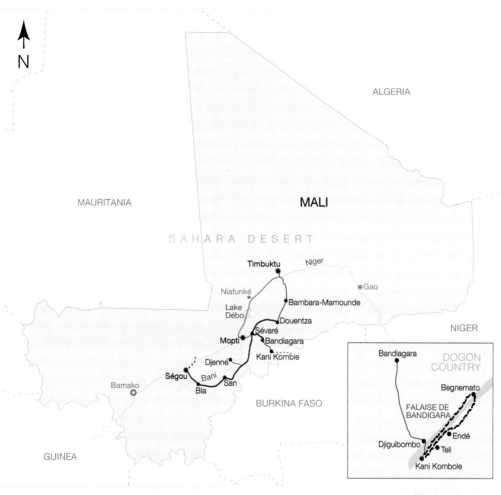

ALGERIA

MAURITANIA

MALI

S A H A R A   D E S E R T

Timbuktu

Niger

Niafunké

Gao

Bambara-Mamounde

Lake
Débo

Douentza

Sévaré

NIGER

Mopti

Bandiagara

Kani Kombole

Djenné

Bamako

Ségou

Bani

San

Bla

BURKINA FASO

GUINEA

Bandiagara

DOGON
COUNTRY

Begnemato

FALAISE DE
BANDIGARA

Endé

Djiguibombo

Teli

Kani Kombole

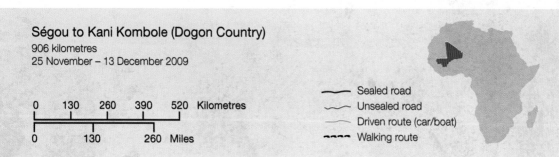

Ségou to Kani Kombole (Dogon Country)
906 kilometres
25 November – 13 December 2009

| 0 | 130 | 260 | 390 | 520 | Kilometres |

| 0 | 130 | 260 | Miles |

———— Sealed road
∿∿∿∿ Unsealed road
———— Driven route (car/boat)
- - - - Walking route

3
MALI'S LIFELINE

Ségou to Kani Kombole (Mali)

Stern of the pinnace to which our pirogue was attached. The River Niger carves a life-sustaining path through the semi-desert near Niafunké

Agriculture, fishing, livestock; that's my work in Malian society. Everyone has the right to have at least one job and there is plenty of work to be done. Our future prosperity depends on work. So let's work!

These words were translated from the sleeve notes of Ali Farka Touré's 2006 posthumous album, *Savané*. Outside the hotel where we stayed in Ségou, hawkers would hover to sell us whatever they could – artwork, t-shirts, bottled water. A number offered CDs of local music – virtually all Ségou or Mali blues, and at the top of their pile would be a catalogue of Ali Farka Touré's works. In the end I could not resist and bought another of his masterpieces, *The Source*, to add to my collection.

Around the time I was developing and organising the expedition, I had acquired a taste for Ali Farka Touré's music. He used a mix of traditional instruments, such as a single-stringed violin, the *njarka*, and the *ngoni*, a Malian lute with more standard instruments like the guitar. The ambience of his music fired my imagination as to what it might be like travelling through his home territory, the realms of the

River Niger between Ségou and Timbuktu. Ali Farka Touré is internationally known as the 'King of the Saharan Blues,' a genre from which all blues music has its origins – via the US slave trade. For Ali, every performance had to say something. Towards the end of his life he became weary of touring and the expectations of international audiences and decided to devote himself to the agricultural development of his hometown, Niafunké, on the Niger's remote Sahelian banks, where he served as mayor for two years. Despite receiving his country's highest accolades for his musicianship, he considered himself a farmer first and foremost and cared most about his roots.

The waters of the River Niger, the essence of Ali Farka Touré's heartland, spring from the Fouta Djallon in Guinea, the same highlands as the Senegal and Gambia rivers originate in. West Africa's largest and the continent's third-largest river carves a 4200-kilometre path from the tropics through the savannah and the Sahel and kisses the Sahara Desert at Timbuktu before arching south through Niger, forming a border with Benin and finally through Nigeria to the coast. The largest portion of the river, though, is in Mali, including what some cultures refer to as the Camel's Hump. Just as the hump of a camel provides sustenance for the animal in times of hardship, the Camel's Hump of the Niger River is a vital source of life for the twenty or so cultures living in its dry hinterland. And just as the camel itself is a mode of transport bringing trade and culture to desert regions, the Niger's Camel's Hump does the same.

The unusual crescent shape of the river baffled European and North African geographers for some two millennia. They could not understand why the waters flowed north from its source – 240 kilometres from the Atlantic Ocean – to the desert before bending east at Timbuktu. Early explorers such as Ibn Battuta, who passed through Oualata on the way to the region, had the Niger drawn in as the Western Nile. The first Europeans who explored the African west coast thought it was connected to the Senegal River. It wasn't until the early nineteenth century that Mungo Park solved the riddle of the river's course (outside of local knowledge). Even when Park became the first European to set eyes on the river at Ségou during his first expedition to the region in 1796, he believed that the Niger might be joined to the Congo River. On his return journey in 1805, the Scotsman managed to navigate the Camel's Hump and down to the Boussa rapids in Nigeria before drowning after an ambush.

After his first expedition, Park reported on the hospitable nature of the people of the Bambara Kingdom and was astonished at the opulence and extent of cultivation he found everywhere. Ségou, the Bambara capital, had a population of around 30,000 at the time and the countryside around was beautiful, intersected on all sides by rivulets. A positive legacy of Park's explorations was that he was one of the first Europeans to 'humanise' Africans at a time when the overwhelming perception of them was of savage, primitive creatures. Writings of his first expedition influenced thinking that would eventually lead to the abolition of the European slave trade. Almost 500 years earlier, during the height of the Mali Empire, Ibn Battuta wrote that he found the territory safe to travel through without fear of robbery or violence and that the Mande people of the same region were of a kind and gentle nature. They were, he recorded, 'seldom unjust, and have a greater abhorrence of injustice than any other people.' On his arrival at the River Niger, somewhere in the Ségou vicinity, he received a lesson in common decency, Bambara style.

I saw a crocodile in this part of the Nile (Niger), close to the bank; it looked just like a small boat. One day I went down to the river to satisfy a need, and lo, one of the blacks came and stood between me and the river. I was amazed at such lack of manners and decency on his part, and spoke of it to someone or other. (That person) answered; 'His purpose in doing that was solely to protect you from the crocodile, by placing himself between you and it.'

Our theme for this phase of the journey was to explore the environs of a section of the Camel's Hump from Ségou to Timbuktu in order to look at some of the cultures, history and issues of the region.

❊

In colonial times, Ségou experienced strong growth because it was chosen as the hub of logistics and management for the Office du Niger and the Inland Delta developments. Ségou was a good place to have a pit stop as it is a centre for many international development organisations and is therefore well-connected. I spent two days visiting the nearby Millennium Village Project at Tiby while John and Dan drove to Bamako, Mali's capital, to collect supplies and vehicle parts. After being disheartened by the calamity of development attempts in Oualata, I hoped Tiby's story would provide some kind of positive karma.

We had passed through one of the most prosperous-looking agricultural regions on the way in to Ségou (due to the irrigation systems on the river's western bank) yet on the opposite side benefits from irrigation were limited. Tiby is a cluster of eleven villages situated 65 kilometres north of Ségou. Local community leaders and elected committee members identified the site as most vulnerable due to a compounding set of circumstances. The region experiences low and increasingly unreliable rainfall and the naturally poor soils have been degraded due to a breakdown of traditional farming systems. Child mortality rates were high, chiefly due to malaria which is endemic in the region. Literacy was incredibly low, with only one-third of the population being able to read and write in some pockets. Before the program began, only 20 per cent of the residents had access to safe drinking water.

As with Potou in Senegal, a mix of international, national and local stakeholders fund the programs and retain control of the overall direction. Most impressive, however, is that the whole project is being implemented and run by local Malian people – leaders, scientists, professionals. My time visiting the project was coordinated by Dr Bocary Kaya, team leader and science coordinator. I could not have had a better-qualified person to show me around. Dr Kaya studied for his master's degree in Bedford in the UK and earned his PhD in the US. He could have had a successful life with his family living and working in the US or UK, yet was motivated to make more of a difference in his homeland, on the banks of the River Niger where his expertise and experience are so much in demand. He is an inspiring example of someone who is defying the brain drain.

On the first day, Dr Kaya invited me to sit in on the annual planning meeting. This was where the direction of the project was presented to the community leaders and employees to be discussed and then implemented. As we drove to the villages, Bocary explained that the program, as in most Millennium Villages, had been going for three years. In that time, the Tiby Millennium Village Project team had been able to stabilise many of the basic problems. Now he and his associates are able to focus more of their energy into developing the region as a whole, even beyond the selected villages, using advancements in science and business to make changes sustainable. At one point, as we crossed a bridge over a small waterway, Bocary slowed down to acknowledge some young fishermen. He pointed out that the nets they were using were too fine: they were catching tiny hatchlings as they were about to enter the big river. The nets were illegal because they were harvesting the young before they matured into a decent meal. This was just one more behavioural change, born out of a culture which was often short on food, that they had to get right.

Dr Bocary Kaya (left) with the mayors of two of the main villages that make up the Tiby Millennium Village cluster

The meeting took place in Dioro, a town of approximately 20,000 people, set beside the river banks 60 kilometres north of Ségou. There we were welcomed by the mayors of the two largest communities, the doctor and other leading professionals. The development strategy for the next year was presented by different specialists, led and facilitated by Dr Kaya. Infrastructure was first. Details were outlined for the improvement of roads, irrigation banks, transport, street lighting and, importantly, communications. In the following year there would be improvements in mobile phone reception and internet connections, communications being key to sustainable development. Agriculture is dominated by sporadic low rainfall and climatic conditions, something I could relate to as they are not too dissimilar to what is experienced in many parts of Australia. The river is the lifeline here for just about everything: food production (irrigation, fishing), transport, forestry. I listened to detailed plans for use of fertilisers (urea, di-ammonia phosphate) for staple crops such as millet, sorghum and rice. An artificial insemination program was being introduced to improve the standard of the herds for milk and meat production. Also to be introduced were new, specifically designed milking machines, which can process 1000 litres a day as well as pasteurise, pack the milk into one-litre bags, and control the temperature for storage.

Bocary explained that the project had made great strides in improving basic education and health. Within the first three years, average literacy levels had almost doubled to over 80 per cent. Malaria had been a serious issue but now people have free access to medication. Morbidity rates for HIV/AIDS (2 per cent in Mali), tuberculosis and childbirth had also been reduced. An education program aims at changing the cultural

Bocary Kaya outlines the plan for the coming year

practice of FGM (female genital mutilation), a major threat to maternal health, which is still widely practised in many African countries. Much more is being done to improve reproductive health care, such as baby kits to assist home births, and provide medical treatment for fistulas. The final presentation concerned governance and the empowerment of local women.

Listening in on the development planning meeting, it was clear to me that the initiatives covering the basic needs of the communities were gaining momentum. On the second day I was shown a small-scale example of a sustainable business project. This time I travelled out to another of the villages with Paddy and Severin Oman, an MBA graduate working for the Millennium Promise organisation. His project involved delivering onion seeds to the 243 women working the six-hectare village garden. A number of different organisations have had a go at aiding development of the large market garden over the past thirty years but all have broken down, rather like in Oualata. Millennium Promise had received a specific grant to make the garden viable in the long term and to produce a model which could be replicated in at least eight other village gardens in the area.

The chief oversees onion seed distribution for women from his village

Being an outsider, Severin could not simply move in, deliver the business plan and expect the women to show up to collect their seeds. This would not work. Much of his effort had been spent fostering relations and gaining trust and acceptance from the village chiefs. The process took time and was much more convoluted than he could have imagined. Severin's local staff had to assess the plot sizes owned by each of the women so that they received the right amount of seed. An auditing system was developed to record everything transparently and fairly within the community protocols.

woman receives her quota of onion seeds – her insurance against the hungry season

Having worked on the project for eight months, Severin was excited that this was the day that he finally got to distribute the seeds. Why onions, you might ask? They are easy to grow and the project requires a simple business model. An equally important part of the project is the provision of special well-aerated warehouses to significantly extend the storage life of the onions. This way the growers can take advantage of market fluctuations and choose to sell their produce when the prices are higher. Dr Kaya added that this can double or even triple the women's income. During the course of the year, when stocks are low, villagers are often forced to sell off some of their staple crops to make ends meet. By about August they would normally run very short on food and go hungry. By growing the onions and making more of a profit, they will not be forced to sell their staple produce and therefore avoid hunger. The initial investment involved fixing the fence and irrigation system and providing the right variety of seeds.

It is important to note that the seeds are not a handout. Once the crop is produced, the women are expected to pay back the costs using some of the profit. Education is given as to how to maintain the economic viability: keep the books, apply for a micro-loan, banking, trade – even how to 'fix the pump.' In fact, while all these initiatives are subsidised, farmers and villagers are all expected to at least pay for a percentage of what they receive (everything from the milking machines to the artificial insemination program). All the ingredients are there to ensure that they will not experience another 'Oualata situation.' When the Millennium Village Project finishes in 2015, the once-vulnerable communities should be resilient and well placed to continue to develop on their own.

Off to plant their onion seeds

Before setting off from Ségou we decided to have a team meeting to assess how we were going after five weeks on the road. Overall, we had done well. To prevent us from falling behind schedule we had altered the route slightly without compromising the purposes of the journey. There were minor hiccups with communications and illnesses but nothing that we couldn't overcome.

The biggest concern by far was Paddy's attitude. Being green to this level of expedition, we'd all accepted that there would be a few errors early on but we had presumed he would learn from these. John, Dan and I in our own ways had tried to guide him through. The trouble was, the situation was not improving. During downtime in Oualata we'd finally had a chance to view some of Paddy's work, which up until that point he had closely guarded, not permitting anyone else to use the main camera. We were dismayed at the small quantity and overall quality of his output. Fortunately, Dan had proven his natural talent with a camera. He had been diligent at recording with his small video camera, which could compensate for what was missed. The first instalment of expedition footage had been sent back to Australia and I was desperately waiting for a professional opinion.

During the meeting, Paddy asked whether he could just work five days a week. This was the last straw. The request rendered the three of us momentarily speechless – the expedition could not work like that. His heart obviously was not in it. Dan offered to take over on Paddy's rest days, saying that cycling every kilometre was not specifically important to him and he would be happy to relieve Paddy. We could not continue with someone who was not enthused by what he was seeing, who did not have the right work ethic, who was not learning from mistakes, particularly with regard to security issues, and was not producing the quality or quantity of footage required. John, Dan and I unanimously agreed that I should start looking for a replacement. This was difficult to manage while on the road, heading for Timbuktu.

We set off early towards the ancient town of Djenné, our next port of call along the realms of the mighty river, passing through the regional centres of Bla and San. For the first time on the expedition I felt like we were starting to find a good rhythm and cover the distances to which I am usually accustomed.

Even with a constant north-easterly wind we were clocking up 130-140 kilometres consistently. It had taken the team as a whole some time to reach this point. Extended lunch breaks had really been eating into the daily distances, and from Nara to Ségou, this had been bugging me. Initially we took longer breaks to avoid the heat of the day but now it was cooler (still up to mid-30s), we could make better use of the day. If we continued as we had been, it would have meant losing one day in four or five, and over ten months that would make a big difference. I always had to be mindful of the big picture. At the same time, I valued the fact that Dan and John were easy-going. They were becoming soulmates and I felt the three of us had developed into a strong team.

✻

The main asphalt road we were following to Djenné skirts the Niger River floodplain. The terrain was so flat that perhaps the highest landmarks were the giant termite mounds! Waiting for the ferry to transport us across the Bani River, the Niger's principal tributary, it was obvious we were heading for the country's premier tourist attraction. Sellers crowded their captive audience in the hope of flogging trinkets, jewellery, carvings, masks, clothing – whatever they had. They wanted to trade everything – the bicycles, my sunglasses, even the shirt off my back. I understood all the reasons why they wanted everything we had but they were never going to understand that we were travelling for the best part of a year and only carried what we needed to get through. We were not made of money and could not simply replace our gear.

Djenné, built on the floodplain between the Niger and Bani rivers at the southern end of the Inner Niger Delta, is Mali's oldest town. 'Modern' Djenné is a walled city, settled approximately one thousand years ago, but archaeological excavations indicate that the Iron Age civilisation at Djenné-jéno, a couple of kilometres from town, was first settled around 200 BC.

Often referred to as Timbuktu's sister city, Djenné's *raison d'être* was its location at the head of the Saharan trade route. Merchants would travel from the tropics of Guinea to trade gold for salt (and many other items) with those arriving from Timbuktu and beyond. Arabs brought their religion with them and Islam infused into the melting pot of Djenné's culture. The city became prosperous through trading with all corners of the vast Kingdom of Mali while avoiding being captured by its armed forces. (The military reportedly tried ninety-nine times to conquer the city walls.)

A dusty, winding thoroughfare led us past an unusual array of double-storey adobe residences to the main attraction – the Grande Mosque, the world's largest mud building. Our reason for making good time to Djenné was to arrive in readiness for the famous Monday market, where traders still travel from as far away as Bamako, Ségou and Mopti. We were all up early the following day in readiness to capture the scenes as they evolved with the morning light in front of the Grande Mosque. However, we had not realised that the national holiday on Saturday extended into Monday and the bustling market never eventuated. All was not lost as our guide, Amadou, was able to show us around his town and the mosque and enlighten us about their colourful history.

The first mosque was built in 1240 by the sultan Koi Kunboro, who converted to Islam and turned his palace into a place of worship. In the mid-nineteenth century it was let go – all adobe buildings need constant maintenance. The Grande, or Kunboro Mosque as it is often called, was rebuilt in 1906 in the same architectural style as the first building.

Djenné mosque: one minaret had collapsed after seasonal rains

The Grande Mosque, which sits on an enormous raised plinth of dried mud bricks, is constantly being renovated. During the recent floods, one of the three minarets of the front façade collapsed and preparations were under way for its repair. Before the Wet season, the whole community gathers to repair the walls, adding a layer of fine mud render where required. Amadou told us that the spring festival to preserve the premier jewel in their crown has a real carnival atmosphere. Year after year of adding to the thickness of the walls eventually means they become too thick, absorb too much weight after the rains and collapse in places. Some of the walls are therefore being reduced in size to keep the balance. Mud for the render is mixed with rice husks to make a smooth surface, while mud for the core of the walls, usually about 30-40 centimetres thick, is combined with straw. The palm-wood beams are built into the walls to act as scaffolding to make the annual renovations easier. Positioned atop of each spire, like the decorations of a giant cake, ostrich eggs symbolise fertility and purity.

Even though we had offers to enter the building (for a decent price), we respected the wishes of the Imam (head of the mosque) and local community, and elected to stay outside. Some tourists allegedly abused the privilege a few years ago so now entry is officially reserved for all local men and women who have visited

Entrance to the Djenné library – an example of the Moroccan-influenced architecture present throughout the town

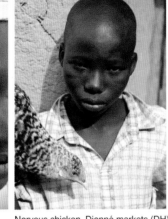

A Fulani girl on market day (DH)   Nervous chicken, Djenné markets (DH)

Mecca. Women can only enter the mosque via a special entrance around the back of the building and are not permitted to even see men once inside.

Like Oualata and Timbuktu, Djenné has a strong tradition of education with twenty-two Qur'anic schools, many madrasas and now government schools. A library houses ancient manuscripts of similar vintage to those of its sister towns.

Despite the national hol-iday, some vendors still showed up – mostly the poorest – to sell their produce. The market these days is based around agricultural trade rather than gold. Some Fulani women we spoke to had carried firewood for many miles to sell. In the main market I noted salt, spices, soap, onions, dried fish and a pungent kind of fish stock, dried meat, groundnuts, chillies and live chickens – still a wide variety of produce for sale. There were the usual omelettes and dough ball fry-ups, music and clothing stalls. Mothers worked with babies strapped to their backs and there were children and goats everywhere.

Superficially, the beautiful mud buildings of Djenné, with influences from Morocco, Egypt and Ethiopia, could resemble a theme park. In reality, though, the architectural beauty is very fragile, and it is what goes on in and around the town that give Djenné its character and identity: its markets and its educational and religious traditions. The trading post that fed off the gold and opulence of the Mali Empire no longer contains such wealth. These days the town's economy relies on agriculture and tourism. All around are threats to its existence. When people are unable to feed themselves, as happened in droughts in the 1970s and 1980s and during more recent challenges to livelihoods, the buildings are let go. Artisans drift to the cities and the walls 'melt' with the first rains.

Fortunately the masons, whose family lines stretch back half a millennium, did not leave and the community did revive after the droughts, albeit with some outside assistance. The masons still mix clay dug from the surrounding plains with water from the Bani River. Then, drawing on knowledge passed from father to son, they create an architecture that attracts visitors from all over the world.

These local Mande people have a fundamental concept called *nyama* which infers that there is a source of power or energy behind every task or movement. *Nyama* is present in all the rocks, trees, people and

Backyard kitchen. It is what goes on within its walls that keeps Djenné alive (DH)

animals that inhabit the Earth. In Western cultures the nearest parallel is that of the soul, but *nyama* is a more all-encompassing belief of occult power – a kind of divine current that is tapped by adepts. In

Restoring a village granary

Mande culture, words can have a high level of *nyama*. The life-force an animal once possessed can be retained in the leather, and inorganic materials such as minerals release *nyama* when they are melted. By combining clay with water to make mud for the buildings, *nyama* is released by the masons who contribute to the soul and life-force of Djenné.

Djenné's future survival depends on its ability to hold on to the essentials of the past. It must continue to adapt to changing circumstances while guarding what lasts. For example, farmers in the Djenné region who are struggling to make ends meet during the increasingly erratic seasons could adjust by adopting successful initiatives pioneered in the Tiby Millennium Village to build resilience, even prosper. The city could do much to improve sanitation and infrastructure. However, it is within Djenné's collective power, or *nyama*, that it endures.

❊

Back on the road, a positive *nyama* between foot and pedal and backside and (leather) saddle needed to be created to get me through. Leaving Sévaré, the next main village north, my powers were further boosted by the special breakfast served at Mac's Refuge accommodation. My metabolism had suitably cranked up to process the vast amounts of food needed for the challenge ahead. To start the day on the road I would normally put away four or five ladles of porridge. Rather than eating from a standard plastic plate like my teammates, I ate out of a large mixing bowl which we affectionately dubbed the 'dog bowl.' At Mac's I felt obliged to make the most of the variety of food offered. After consuming two huge buckwheat pancakes (made from millet flour) soaked in honey, numerous pieces of French toast, a large bowl of homemade muesli, two helpings of fruit salad, juice and coffee, moving at all was a challenge.

I cycled the 400 kilometres from Sévaré to Timbuktu alone as it was Dan's turn to be head cameraman – a role he seemed to relish. I quite enjoyed cycling on my own but for the first day and

A typical grain store of the region – built off the ground to prevent moisture from seeping into the grains

The landscape as I approached Douentza

a half, from Sévaré to Douentza, I was never by myself for long. Beside the road an almost continuous procession of nomadic herders moved their stock, usually goats, sheep or cattle. The Fulani men would be dressed traditionally, some wearing conical straw hats, others turbans. Here, donkeys are real beasts of burden, often dwarfed by their loads. Firewood, grains, salt, goats, people – they hauled just about anything. On my journey through Africa so far I had witnessed donkeys receiving some of the cruellest treatment. I decided that anyone who returns to this world in another life as a Malian or Mauritanian mule must have done something pretty horrific to deserve such punishment.

From about 50 kilometres before Douentza, the landscape transformed gradually into open savannah and the distant range of weathering buttes which form the northern end of the Falaise de Bandiagara made increasingly imposing and spectacular views. It was one of those inspiring mornings when I simply had to keep stopping to photograph what I was seeing. Fanning north-east from Douentza, a dramatic tabletop mountain range with sheer cliff faces rising over 600 metres above the plains would be considered by rock climbers as paradise.

To ensure our safety through this region, John had reconnected with Cheikh Ag Baye, the head of a Tuareg organisation from Kidal (in Mali's north-east), with whom he had worked on a previous expedition. The desert and its margins across Mauritania, Mali and Niger are all classified as red zones – areas of extreme danger – on Western government websites (such as Australia, UK, US and France). Recent kidnappings and executions in Gao, 400 kilometres to the east, and in Mauritania had led the French government to embargo the region and pull out all nationals. Before the journey I had been negotiating with Cheikh and his people to accompany us through the region if required. But after checking out the situation, Cheikh's advice to John was that travelling along the road between Douentza and Timbuktu would be safe enough without their help.

As I turned off the bitumen and on to the gravel my mind was prepared for a battle of a different kind – with the road which our Sahara Desert 4WD guide book described as an horrific sand trap on which motorbikes struggled. Locals in Douentza told us that the first section was good but that there would be sand after Bambara-Maounde, the village at the halfway point, so we stocked up in Douentza with extra supplies in case the 200 kilometres took three or four days. The mountain range not only served as a picture-postcard backdrop, it also shielded me from a strong north-easterly crosswind. As I headed the escarpments and entered the nondescript Sahel scrubland, the wind picked up; gusting into my face, it knocked me down to 13 kilometres an hour at times. The road had been recently made and, true to the locals' information, was excellent for the first 40 kilometres. By the end of the day, however, it had deteriorated into a rough washboard surface. Assuming that this would be the standard for the next 140 kilometres, I tried to just go steady to conserve energy.

The better road to Timbuktu (JD)

John was careful to find a well-concealed campsite, perhaps a kilometre off the road. We were aware that this was still a potentially dodgy region and that traffickers frequent the road at night. They are known to use routes such as this to smuggle people, arms and drugs. For example, as European ports tighten their security, the South American drug trafficking organisation, FARC (Revolutionary Armed Forces of Columbia), has employed AQIM (Al-Qaida in the Islamic Maghreb) to smuggle cocaine through the empty spaces of the Sahel and Sahara to Algeria and on to Europe for a lucrative slice of the profits. The best line of defence for us was to ensure they didn't know we were there. At night we turned off all lights as soon as we heard a vehicle hurtling along the road.

Most of the road was corrugated. Cycling along it took full concentration as I constantly scoured the path in front of my wheel, searching for the smoothest looking option. I removed all but one rear pannier which made for a rougher ride but reduced the risk of broken equipment. Travelling over these surfaces, the wear and tear on everything, body and bike, is immense. My whole body, but particularly my legs, works much harder to take weight off the seat, absorb the shocks and maintain balance over the bumpy and often soft surfaces. The team set up for a lunch break about 100 metres off the road and about 30 kilometres north of Bambara-Maounde but I was in such complete concentration rattling over the corrugations that I didn't see or hear the others shouting at me to stop. I cycled straight past and John had to drive a couple of kilometres down the road to catch me.

That evening we stayed beside a farmer's encampment for protection, again well out of sight of the road. Life for the farmer and his family was simple but obviously harsh: they lived in semi-permanent tents and mostly tended to their animals. Their sandy, infertile soil supported little more than scrubby thorn trees and doublegee-infested grasses; growing anything of nutritional value here would have been a challenge. The farmer insisted on providing us with an open-sided tent for shelter, swept the vicinity and collected wood to make a fire. Before leaving the next morning, in return for his hospitality we donated some food – basics they probably didn't have much of, such as sugar, potatoes, onions, rice and some tinned food. We were going to make it easily to Timbuktu, now only 60 kilometres away, where we could restock. The gifts were much appreciated.

On the final push to Timbuktu I did have a tussle with the sand but, unlike in Mauritania, I had changed over to my wider 'Expedition' tyres which I had brought for the job. This made a noticeable difference and I was able to power through most of the sandy patches, even if doing so did sap the last of my energy.

I was amazed at the width of the Niger River here at the apex of the Camel's Hump. We took the barge across what I estimated to

Reaching the Niger River crossing to Koulikoro

be about two kilometres of water. From there it was a simple 18-kilometre ride along a eucalypt-lined paved road to the Sahara's fabled 'city of gold.' The route from Douentza had been in better condition than we expected and I was pleased to have conquered it in two days.

❋

I remember when, growing up, people often used the expression 'from here to Timbuktu' to refer to a place that was an inaccessible or an unimaginable distance away. This had its origin in the fact that, until 1828 when Frenchman René Caillié travelled disguised as an Arab, no European made it out of Timbuktu alive. A number, including Mungo Park, were killed trying. Nowadays people can fly, drive, take a boat, walk, ride a camel there...but not too many cycle to the ancient, mystical city of approximately 50,000 inhabitants. As I arrived at the Bouctou Hotel where we had chosen to stay, I was suddenly besieged by a flock of national press, including a well-known Malian media personality with his cameraman. This took me by complete surprise. The embargoes sanctioned by the French government in response to recent kidnappings had rocked the local economy, which relies heavily on tourism. The scene was orchestrated, possibly by government security officials, in an attempt to demonstrate to the public on national and African television that Timbuktu was *so* safe that 'even a woman on a bicycle can arrive in one piece, only experiencing friendly, helpful people.' Of course, it was completely true.

We being among only a handful of foreign tourists, like bees to a honey pot, guides, sellers and anyone seeking our business swarmed to compete for our attention. It was difficult to get any peace. Eventually I settled on hiring a guide, Idrissa, who quietened things down somewhat. When Idrissa learned where I was from he said that for the people of Timbuktu, the idea of Australia evoked similar notions as a mystical, faraway land, unreachable to them. Ali Farka Touré expressed a similar sentiment to Idrissa when he said, 'For some people, when you say "Timbuktu" it is like the end of the world, but that is not true. I am from Timbuktu, and I can tell you that we are right at the heart of the world.'

That afternoon the Timbuktu commune laid on an event which Idrissa explained was 'an impromptu celebration for peace', an attempt to promote tourism and raise the spirits of the town. A large crowd milled expectantly in the sandy expanse behind our hotel, Timbuktu's version of the village green. A band added to the ambience by filling the dusty haze with Saharan rhythms. (Ali Farka Touré's music would have suited the mood perfectly here.) Traditionally-clad Tuareg horsemen showed off their fine riding skills racing by at full gallop while boy jockeys mounted their camels and gathered at the start line. For some reason the camel race never eventuated, but the pomp and colourful processions succeeded in entertaining the masses.

A meeting place for many cultures

A celebration for peace

Legend has it that Timbuktu started as a Tuareg camp in the eleventh century. In the Dry season, the inhabitants grazed their animals on *burgu* grasses (wild millet) around the Niger and in the Rainy season they roamed the desert. Realising that if they camped too close to the river they became sick from mosquitoes and stagnant water, they chose a site a few miles from the banks. When they moved their herds north they left their heavy belongings with a woman named Bouctou. In Tamasheq (Tuareg), *bouctou* means 'large navel' and *tim* is the word for well. Timbuktu, or Tombouctou as it is called in French, therefore refers to the well belonging to Bouctou, lady with the large navel.

Because of its location at the point where the big river meets the desert, Timbuktu evolved as a meeting place for many cultures – a crossroad 'where camel met canoe.' African merchants from Djenné traded with Tuareg and Arab traders from the north. Djenné's architects designed Timbuktu's first constructions using the same *banco*, or pounded clay, to which they were accustomed; the Muslim influences came later. Timbuktu's development gained momentum during the Mali Empire and it was Mansa Musa, the tenth emperor of Mali, who effectively put Timbuktu and his kingdom on the world stage. During his pilgrimage in 1324 to Mecca, accompanied by an entourage including 60,000 men and 12,000 slaves, Musa was so generous with gifts to the cities he passed through, such as Cairo and Medina, that he flooded the market with gold. As a result, the Egyptian currency crashed in value and did not recover for a decade. From that point, the names of Mali and Timbuktu became legendary and were featured on Islamic and European fourteenth-century world maps, whereas previously little had been known beyond the western Sudan.

Returning from his *hajj,* Musa brought architects from Cairo and Morocco to design the famous Djinguereber Mosque (which was the first attraction Idrissa showed us on his tour). Timbuktu soon became a centre of trade, culture and Islam. Merchants travelled not only from Nigeria, Egypt and other African kingdoms but also from the Mediterranean cities of Venice, Granada and Genoa. Musa founded universities in Timbuktu as well as in Djenné and Ségou. Islam was spread through the markets and university, making the city a new centre of Islamic scholarship.

Over the following centuries Timbuktu's reputation grew as a Mecca for academia, and Saharan trade routes became more important as 'ink roads' for its economy. Our fourteenth-century roaming friend Battuta reported on the piety, tolerance, wisdom and justice of the city's inhabitants. By AD 1500, Timbuktu's population of 100,000, twice the size of London at that time, included 25,000 scholars. Arabic professors who took study sabbaticals to Timbuktu were no match for the black academics of Sankoré University, the Oxford or Cambridge of the time, and were sent away to complete bridging courses to bring them up to speed. At a time when Europe was emerging from the Middle Ages, African historians were chronicling the rise and fall of Saharan and Sudanese kings, replete with details of great battles and invasions. Astronomers charted the movement of the stars, physicians provided instructions on nutrition and the therapeutic properties of desert plants, and ethicists debated such issues as polygamy and the smoking of tobacco.

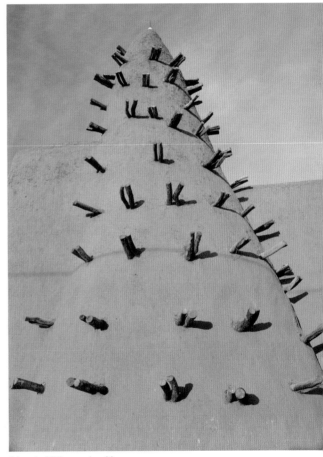

A turret of Djinguereber Mosque

The Songhai Empire, centred 400 kilometres to the east on the River Niger in Gao, succeeded Mali as the next superpower of West Africa. Intellectual and trading status was maintained until the Moroccans invaded and ransacked the city, which started its downward spiral in the late 1500s. The army plundered the wealth, burned the libraries, killed or incarcerated the scholars and pilfered many of the manuscripts. Intellectuals resisted and scholarly activities were driven underground; hundreds of their manuscripts found their way to Fes and Marrakesh in Morocco. Much of the economy dried up as gold was discovered in other parts of the world and European traders, starting with the Portuguese, used ocean routes to connect with Africa rather than crossing the Sahara. During the French colonisation of Mali between 1893 and 1960, many more books and manuscripts ended up in French museums and universities. Only after independence did families again trust that their most prized possessions would not be taken away. West Africa's historical records slowly began to trickle out from rusting trunks, musty storerooms, dry wells, caves in the desert or from holes dug under the arid sands – wherever they were stashed to protect them from conquerors and colonisers. There are estimated to be up to 700,000 manuscripts held in and around Timbuktu, mostly still kept within the families. The sixty private or public libraries in the city hold about 10 per cent of the manuscripts.

Idrissa arranged for a visit to the Imam as-Sayaouti Library, named after the father of the present Imam of the Djinguereber Mosque. On display was a small collection of manuscripts representative of the 11,000 it contains. Boubacar, a curator and our guide, indicated that the cabinet against the wall, which was crammed full, contained some of the 3000 recent contributions from the community. Over the coming year, the staff's 'to do' list included conserving, digitising, translating and cataloguing each script, although some would have been beyond rescuing. Boubacar explained that people's private collections were so precious they would sleep, and even choose to die, beside their books. Convincing owners to part with their prized family heirlooms for the purpose of preserving and documenting their content was a challenge and often costly. In villages it might mean building a new mosque or much-needed amenities, or trading a flock of goats in exchange for manuscripts.

For presentation purposes, the displays were kept out of direct sunlight in a climate-controlled environment. The room was dimly lit by diffused natural light that beamed across the glass cabinets, accentuating the filigree shadows cast by decorations above the front door. On show were books of varying condition but all were priceless. Boubacar didn't know the exact age of the oldest volume: it was not new when it was first found in the eleventh century, and then in the fifteenth century the Moroccans stole it and buried it six metres underground. It was rediscovered centuries later and returned to Timbuktu. The curators cannot touch its termite-damaged pages for fear of them atomising into a puff of dust. We also saw an eleventh-century medical text-book about the heart and stomach and a thirteenth-century script bound with goat leather and written in Fulbe (Fulani) – this was unusual because most

The oldest book in the Imam as-Sayaouti Library

documents were written in Arabic. We heard from Boubacar about how sixteenth-century Islamic scholars advocated exp-anding the rights of women, explored methods of conflict resolution and debated how best to incorporate non-Muslims into an Islamic society. A 500-year-old book of Qur'anic law, illustrated with the most skilled, delicate calligraphy, outlined the rights of women, explaining that all Islamic women have the right to spend time to make themselves more beautiful. Detailed astrological diagrams depicted the advanced knowledge of the night sky used to navigate by the stars across the sandy sea.

I could not help but compare and contrast Timbuktu's fortunes with Oualata's. As the various kingdoms superseded one another over the centuries, the towns' scholars sought each other's sanctuary. If Timbuktu is the 'navel' (Bouctou) of the West African intellectual universe then Oualata is merely a satellite in its galaxy. I started to wonder whether there could be some sort of partnership formed with Oualata to share knowledge of conservation and cataloguing of their treasures. Boubacar said that the doors are open but Oualata would need to come to Timbuktu.

He explained that conservation of the scripts is passed down through the generations but that further expertise had been required. The need to locate and preserve the manuscripts was raised four years after independence but Mali being one of the poorest countries in the world, the government has to prioritise its basic tasks of keeping the nation fed, watered, healthy and secure. Without the collaborative support of UNESCO, South Africa, the US and Spain in particular, the written record of Africa's ancient history would gradually be lost.

Stepping outside was like being transported back through the time warp. In the full brightness of day, the sun's white light bleached the colours of the courtyard. The glare was too much: my pupils recoiled, my eyes watered. Squinting to the point where my lashes joined over the slits in my eyes to filter the blinding rays, I fumbled around for my futuristic cycling sunglasses. Once I'd slipped them on I was back in the present. Completing the contrast from ancient to modern, my mobile phone rang – the Western world calling – someone from London. I made use of the small internet café across the courtyard. With such mod cons, communicating with the outside world from Timbuktu is a little easier these days.

The streets of Timbuktu are certainly not paved with gold as the legend has it. The mud buildings stand as weathering embattlements struggling to resist the encroaching sands, and today they are barely distinguishable from it. We drove the impoverished back lanes to the dune-covered outskirts which serve as the terminus for the camel trains that still bring salt to and from Oualata or Araouane. But we were out of luck: just a handful of camels and goats grazed the sporadic clumps of spiny greenery and the odd nomad went about his business. As we waited out the serene late afternoon in case something appeared on the horizon, Dan and John pulled out their football for a kick around with a couple of lads who had followed us from town. Eventually, the inevitable happened and the ball was spiked by a thorn. The boys pleaded to keep it and, to their delight, got their way. The fact that it was flat wouldn't have stopped them having hours of fun.

The landscape around Timbuktu

I wandered off to photograph the dunes in the now-beautiful low light and became fascinated watching a Sisyphus beetle (a type of scarab or dung beetle) scurrying up a sand slope. As the gradient became too steep, as if surfing a wave the beetle would slide back down with the mini-avalanche it caused, and then restart the climb all over again, and again, and again... Eventually it succeeded. These little bugs have extraordinary mechanisms for conserving moisture – from the dung they roll into balls to transport, to sucking in dew from the desert night air. To escape the heat of the day, they burrow underground. When there is no skerrick of damp, they first create and then drink their own sweat. From this little observation, it is easy to see why they have cockroach-like abilities to survive.

Sisyphus beetle

While Africa's recent troubled history cannot be rewritten, the records of its glorious past may be a key to the future. By unearthing ancient manuscripts, conserving and analysing the writings, many Malians are rediscovering their heritage. Most people have heard of Timbuktu but don't have a clue where it is, let alone know that it was central to one of the most advanced cultures of its time (around AD 1500). Often people, Africans and non-Africans, make the mistake of assuming Africa has no written history, that its heritage was only passed on by spoken word, art and dance. When South African president, Thabo Mbeki, visited Timbuktu in 2001 he was so moved by Mali's efforts to conserve the manuscripts with inadequate funds and resources that he pledged to help 'preserve Africa's heritage and intellectual property' and the South Africa-Mali Timbuktu project was born. Its aim was to conserve manuscripts and train conservators, construct a state-of-the-art library and archives building (the Ahmed Baba Institute of Higher Learning and Islamic Research was completed in 2010, six months after we left Timbuktu) and create public awareness about the need to safeguard the books. For the first time, a collection of manuscripts left Mali's landlocked borders to be exhibited in South Africa, to share a 'common patrimony.' The wider African community is taking up the baton via NEPAD (The New Partnership for Africa's Development). The manuscripts are being used as a cultural motivator and are Timbuktu's next potential 'goldmine.' They help to clarify identity – and it is essential to be clear about identity before anyone can be clear about everything else.

The Sisyphus beetle should be Timbuktu's mascot; like the manuscripts, it seemingly appears from its burrows in the desert sand, serving as a symbol of rebirth and an ultimate survivor with a hell of an attitude to work.

✽

From Timbuktu, the plan was to return to Sevaré and then rejoin the line, heading for Burkina Faso via the Dogon Country, Mali's third World Heritage Site on our agenda. Rather than backtracking on the bike, Paddy and I were to take a pirogue down the river to Mopti just a few kilometres from our Sevaré base and John and Dan were to drive back the way we came.

The day after we arrived in Timbuktu, Paddy felt ill and suspected it could be malaria. Although John in particular was well-versed in assessing the signs of malaria and he doubted that Paddy had it, we could not afford to take any chances and combed the pharmacies for the right medication. It was soon evident that it was just another bout of diarrhoea – still not pleasant, but at least we knew it was not serious in the long term. Because of Paddy's condition, Idrissa arranged for us to travel on a traditional pirogue to be attached to the side of a public pinnace. We were effectively quarantined from the other patrons but, being towed by the larger motorised vessel, we could still make the journey within two days. We set off from Koulikoro, the same river port where we had arrived two days earlier.

The great artery varied between one and two kilometres in width for most of the way. When we veered close to the river's edge I surveyed the shallows for hippopotami which graze on

A crew member of the pinnace maintains the diesel engine

the amphibious grasses, surmising that much of the river must have been shallow to support such broad zones of reeds. It is generally accepted that the Niger is two ancient rivers which joined together. The upper Niger travels from the source past Timbuktu to the most prominent bend near Gao and once fed into a now-extinct lake. Dating back to when the Sahara was green, the lower river originated in hills near that lake and flowed to the Gulf of Guinea. When the Sahara dried up 1000-4000 years ago, the rivers hooked up to become the Niger.

Small settlements were nestled along the banks every few kilometres. With no significant roads connecting them, the Niger really was their lifeblood, providing water, fish and an avenue for transport. We floated past cameo scenes of life beside the river: washing, cooking, fishing, playing. The occasional

Djenné's architecture influences the whole region along the River Niger and its environs

Life goes on beside the river

small-scale irrigation pump fed water back to vegetable gardens and staple crops. Life on the banks of the Niger, however, was once much more urban than it is today. According to new archaeological revelations, the River Niger between Djenné-jéno and a site near to where Timbuktu now stands was once an almost continuous Mesopotamia-like conurbation. In fact, it has been said that if someone wanted to send a message a long distance up or downstream, they would just have to shout and it would be passed along. Over the last twenty-five years, the forces of erosion have blown away the sand dunes to uncover the remains of a city at Tumbouze, about 12 kilometres south-east of Timbuktu, which is estimated to be have been about twice its size. While much more remains to be unearthed to reveal how these people lived and what happened to their civilisations, it is known that they existed peacefully between about 500 BC and AD1000 (the same vintage as the Dhar Tichitt civilisation in Mauritania) and cultivated grains and used iron and other metals which were traded from far away.

Our strange-looking ensemble continued past Niafunké in the dark, occasionally docking to pick up and drop off passengers. The large pinnace was carrying all sorts of ballast such as bags of grain, people's belongings and even a goat. Locals travelled self-sufficiently, cooking their own food using equipment they brought along. One fellow I spoke to was a businessman who used the boat as a normal means of travel from Niafunké to Mopti.

About 100 kilometres from Mopti, the waters sprawled into a huge reedy expanse, Lake Débo, the largest lake of the Inner Niger Delta. Mud houses belonging to the Bozo people were built on low-lying islands; from my line of view at water level, they appeared to be floating amongst the reeds. Bozo are the indigenous people of the region who for centuries have been living off the riches of the river delta they call the Macina. Fulani nomads travel from as far away as Mauritania and Burkina Faso to graze their cattle on the

A traditional form of sailboat navigating through the reeds of the Inner Niger Delta

nutritious grasses in the fertile delta. At the head of the lake, our pilots skilfully navigated a network of narrow channels through the reeds. It was incredible to think that we were meandering through a series of braided waterways and marshy lakes which cover an area the size of Belgium in the Rainy season.

Boubacar, the pilot of our pirogue at sunrise

All was calm as the sun sank behind the sea of reeds. Bird life was abundant, fishermen using poles propelled their canoes through the grasses. Our boat caused the only significant disturbances: the grumbling bluesy tones of its diesel engine and the ripples left in its wake. On a far grander scale, waves of disruption throughout the Macina are being caused by the manipulation of the river's gentle flow by way of dams and irrigation schemes and the drying climate. The wetlands are a Ramsar site, recognised internationally for their wealth in bird life and the need to conserve their threatened habitats.*

Travelling down the Niger had been an invigorating experience until the final morning. Then it was my turn to be ill again. Our lovely crew, Boubacar and Ousman, who had been cooking all our food had made the same sauce last for three days, combining it with fish they caught from the river or goat they bought from a riverside village. Paddy had been off all but plain rice during the journey but I had been eating normally, and this had taken its toll. My body's response was violent and total. Arriving back in Sévaré, John and Dan needed another day to repair the Land Rover power steering which meant I had twenty-four hours to starve myself to try to kill the stomach bug before setting off. Given that we were staying again at Mac's Refuge, which served some of the best food going around, this was particularly disappointing. I had to be content with the water and papaya seeds I was given to settle things down. Dan rejoined me on the bike and we pushed off the next afternoon, reconnecting with the line of the journey, heading for the Dogon Country. I felt fragile but managed all the same. Although I was over the worst of my gastro quickly it affected my health for the next week, all the way to Ouagadougou.

❋

---

* The Ramsar Convention, convened in Ramsar, Iran, in 1971, is an intergovernmental treaty that embodies the commitment of its members to maintain the ecological character of their Wetlands of International Importance.

The land of the Dogon people is set amongst the Falaise de Bandiagara. These cliffs run roughly parallel to the River Niger through the Sahel for about 150 kilometres between Douentza, which we passed through on the way to Timbuktu, and Gani Do in the south. The Dogon live on the plateau, cliffs and Plaine du Séno hundreds of metres below. The three-hour afternoon ride from Sévaré to Bandiagara, done in the one hit, gave clues that we were on our way to see something spectacular: we climbed gentle gradients through a backdrop which could well have been a set for an old Western movie – rocky escarpments, mesas, weathering rock formations. As the sun sank it was like drawing the final curtain on the 'Wild West' landscape. From there the last 20 kilometres to the delightfully named Djiguibombo (pronounced Jiggiboombo) was done in the dark. At first Dan and I cycled by the dim glow of the moon until the Land Rover caught us and illuminated our path, the low angle of the headlights behind distorting our shadows, elongating our figures so that we appeared like ogres on wheels. The high beam magnified the appearance of stones and corrugations and the regular dips became gaping black holes. These we negotiated in blind hope. In one dip we apparently cycled straight past a snake, thankfully only revealed by John's headlights after we had gone through. In Dogon mythology it was the serpent Lébé that led the tribe to settle in the Bandiagara region so perhaps crossing the snake's path was a kind of spiritual welcome. The headlights served as blinkers so that we could just see the path in front. We could only imagine what our surroundings looked like until the light of the new day.

The view from the creaky, louvred window of my guesthouse bedroom the following morning confirmed we had arrived at some kind of fairytale world. I looked down from the second storey over a constellation of flat-roofed mud and stone houses topped with piles of drying millet and other grains, among which were dotted thatched tipi-like roofs of grain stores. From Djiguibombo at the top of the escarpment we descended for nine kilometres on an exhilarating ride down to Kani Kombole on the plains. There we left our bikes and vehicle for a two-day diversion on foot with our Dogon guide, Moumimi, Momo to us.

The precise origin of the Dogon is not known. They migrated to the Falaise de Bandiagara area around 500 years ago after fleeing Muslim invaders and/or drought. The Dogon and Bozo people arrived in the region at roughly the same time. Being fishermen, the Bozo chose to inhabit the banks of the River

The granaries of old Teli overlooking new Teli below

The Falaise de Bandiagara at Teli

Niger while the Dogon, as cultivators, chose the plains and cliffs. Excavations have revealed that prior to the Dogon's arrival the region was home to two separate cultures; the Toloy lived there between 300 and 200 BC, and the Tellem were around between the eleventh and fifteenth centuries AD.

The beautiful little Kani Kombole mosque is another example of Djenné's architectural influence. Momo explained that Islam and Christianity (latecomers in the scheme of Dogon history) co-exist with more traditional Dogon animism. Adherents respect each other's religion but they do not tend to intermarry. The Dogon's tolerance and isolation are keys to their cultural longevity. Living in the difficult-to-access cliffs has allowed their mythology to remain in a fairly pure state, even with the interventions of Muslim and Christian missionaries. One of the last groups of people to come under French rule in the 1940s, the Dogons, who maintained their own beliefs and religious practices, were thought to have been one of the best examples of 'primitive savagery' known in the world at that time.

Tellem houses above the granaries

From Kani Kombole it was a simple four-kilometre trek along the donkey track at the base of the craggy cliffs to Teli. In the distance we could see a series of boxes and dwellings set into the rock face and on reaching them we climbed up to explore. The boxes were an extensive series of elevated granary stores. As most grains are now warehoused in the newer village at ground level these stores are only used to hold millet, sorghum and beans after a very good year.

Above the granaries were tiny houses which once belonged to the Tellem. Momo explained that the Tellem, whom he referred to as Pygmies, lived off the fruits of the forest below. Living high up would have given them a great vantage point to defend themselves and stay safe from large predators. The Dogon believed that the Tellem could fly and had magic powers to reach them but, more plausibly, in the wetter climate of a few hundred years ago, the Tellem probably used overhanging vines to climb to their houses. When the Dogon arrived in the region they cut down the forest for firewood, cultivated fields and raised animals, gradually destroying the Tellem's habitat so that they were pushed out and had to retreat east. From the Tellem's crow's nest view over the plains, the landscape is now typically dry and bare and studded by regular, compact villages. The mosaic of cultivated fields is carved by a network of cart tracks which connect the villages.

Before we descended, Momo showed us the home of the Hogon, the spiritual leader. Normally, the Hogon would live alone but there was no one at home: the last Hogon of Teli had

The Teli Hogon residence showing Lébé the serpent and a crocodile totem, a symbol for water

died about ten years earlier and although a new high priest had been chosen by the village elders he was not yet ready to assume the mantle. Being brought up to speed with such a complex religion can take a long time – Ogotemmêli, a sort of Dogon professor who first disclosed the intricate details of the complex belief system, had taken more than twenty years to master it. Dogon mythology is of oral tradition but it can be deciphered because of the consistent and elaborate use of symbolism. The people's famous artwork, particularly their sculptures, preserves the knowledge.

Dogon beliefs are centred on three distinct cults: Binou, Lébé and Awa. The totemic cult of Binou deals with immortal ancestors. Spirits often make themselves known to their descendants in the form of an animal that interceded on behalf of the clan during its founding, becoming the clan's totem, for example, at the Teli Hogan's residence were totems of crocodiles. The Lébé cult is concerned with agricultural cycles and land fertility. The Hogon is chief priest of this cult, responsible for guarding the purity of the soil. In this Earth-centred religion, human spiritualism is directly linked to biological make-up which is in turn connected to the Earth itself. The Awa or mask cult is the faction of the dead. Awa dance ceremonies lead souls of the deceased to their final resting place in the family altars. The ritual masks worn during these ceremonies contain iconographic messages that are the codes of their religious philosophies.

By the end of the day we reached Momo's home town, Endé, which had a population of about 3000 people. A simple 'Hello, how are you?' is not sufficient in Dogon culture. Their typical greeting sounded almost melodic. The older person usually asks the younger a series of six to eight questions, such as: 'How are you?' 'How is your family?' 'How is your wife, house, village, animals, crops, sick uncle...?' The answer is always 'sewa' or 'fine', even if things are not good. On the way into Endé a steady flow of 'sewas' were exchanged.

Momo took us to meet his family and share in some millet cream, a blend of pounded millet and baobab juice. Sap from the plentiful baobab fruit is poisonous if not specially prepared. I was, of course, going easy, given my delicate condition but had to at least try it. The drink tasted like sour, tangy porridge:

A Dogon village in the intensively cultivated Plaine du Séno

an acquired taste but quite palatable. Momo told us that as a kid he virtually lived off millet cream – he loved it. The Dogon are generally very poor and often consume millet for breakfast, lunch and dinner, varying porridge and millet cream with the odd millet beer. They rarely eat meat such as chicken or goat, whose limited supplies are generally reserved for tourists like us.

From Endé we continued along the base of the *falaise* amongst overworked cultivated fields dotted with skeletal baobabs. African folklore, like in the Australian Aboriginal Dreamtime, has it that an angry god turned the baobab upside down and made its fruit taste vile. On day two we put in a decent distance, walking along the base of the escarpment and then climbing a natural thalweg gorge to Begnemato on the plateau. Compared to the kind of day I'd usually put in on the bike, walking 20-odd kilometres was a doddle on the cardiovascular side but my feet and knees, especially on the downhill, weren't used to it. In contrast to the harsh environment of the plains below, the high, terraced slope was lush and green. A permanently flowing stream provided a life-giving artery to the mature trees draped with overhanging vines and ficus. Ravines such as this, which score the escarpment face at regular intervals, are important ecological sanctuaries in a landscape where most indigenous flora and fauna has been lost to desertification and human pressures. As we passed by, we saw many locals tending to their vegetable plots. They enhance the humus-rich soil by spreading bird droppings collected from ledges in the escarpment.

Views from the head of the chasm over the Plaine du Séno about 500 metres below were spectacular. The village of Begnemato, set in a natural sandstone amphitheatre, is separated into distinct animist, Christian and Muslim sections. Momo led Paddy and myself to the village hunter's house in the animist quarter. Inside, the mud walls of the compound were decorated with his many trophies and fetishes, mostly monkeys' remains. The small pet monkey that flitted about the premises was probably an orphan. The womenfolk sat out the heat of the day preparing bissap flowers (a type of hibiscus) to make into the fragrant bissap syrup, served as a refreshing cordial drink throughout the Sahel region. The hunter

explained that there isn't much game around these days and that he only takes an animal for meat every couple of weeks. This is the extended family's main source of protein. Leaning up against the granary wall were the hunter's tools of trade – five shotguns crafted by the local blacksmith. Compared with the semi-automatic AK-47s which are commonplace around much of Africa, these weapons were Homo erectus. The hunter offered to give us a demonstration of how he would normally use his gun. After reassuring us that this was just a silent dummy run, he secretly loaded a small amount of gunpowder and fired, the blast reverberating over the walls of the compound, over the town and resonating off the natural rocky auditorium. We jumped out of our skins and the pet monkey, which probably had good reason to be more than a little nervous, dived for protection behind the women. They all thought it was a great joke. Gotcha! We were obviously the dummies but laughed along after the initial deafening shock.

A fly whisk fetish, hunter's residence, Begnemato

Our path on the return journey to Kani Kombole was a kind of scaled-up version of snakes and ladders. We picked our way over the rocks, across fertile fields and along the crest of the escarpment to Indelou, the most pristine animist village on our tour. In this multi-dimensional board game the snakes are metaphysical. Unlike all the other villages, Indelou has no mosque. In the centre of the village was the blacksmith's foundry. Blacksmiths have a powerful position among the Dogon (as in many West African cultures) because of their skills in transforming material from the Earth and their ability to control fire. They are believed to produce great life force (*nyama*) and to possess special powers, and they usually assist the Hogon with agrarian ceremonies. These days they have lost their ancient smelting skills and, like the blacksmith we watched in action with hand bellows, make tools and weapons by melting down scrap metals. Through the Hogon and blacksmith, Lébé the Earth God (represented as a serpent) had obviously been looking after the villagers' needs.

We climbed on to some boulders to gain a vantage point over a checkerboard of flat roofs piled with produce – millet, chillies, beans, sorghum – intermingled with the usual thatched grain stores. Energetic children seemed to materialise from every house and street corner, competing for our attention. The ladders in this game were in the form of traditional Dogon steps, hewn by cutting right-angled wedges out of tree trunks to make rungs. We negotiated a number of these along with roughly cobbled stone stairs as we made our way down to the plains by descending a narrow ravine.

Rooftops in Indelou, used for drying grains and other food as well as sleeping in the summer

Having visited a trifecta of Mali's World Heritage Sites which are all within relatively close proximity – Djenné, Timbuktu and the Dogon Country – I had been interested to note how they managed tourism. Since 1996, in these main tourist destinations – Ségou, Mopti, Timbuktu and the Dogon Country – poverty rates have decreased, whereas in the country's non-tourist regions, they have increased. The

Dogon area accounts for about one-third of tourism in Mali. There, poverty has been reduced by almost 20 per cent so far – but at what cost? Tourism is seen as both the Dogon's cultural saviour and destroyer. On the plus side, nearly all walkers travel in small groups with a Dogon guide; this ensures people keep to the paths and remain respectful of Dogon property and religion. And compared with most other places we had been, there appeared to be less litter (although this aspect is far from perfect). Incorporated in the guide's fee was an allowance for a tourist tax which Momo distributed to the villages we visited. On the minus side, many souvenirs are extracted legally and illegally from the region every year.

The Dogon people originally chose to settle in the Bandiagara cliffs to safeguard their religion and culture. While over the centuries they have adopted Islam and Christianity to varying degrees, it is now tourists who bring their ways of the world to infiltrate the plateau, cliffs and plains. Many of Momo's generation leave for Mopti, Sevaré and beyond, some returning as guides. Living away, they distance themselves from their families and from cultural traditions which, like the mud buildings, need to be maintained during the annual cycles. The Dogon of today are in a more precarious position due to outside influences than were their forebears, who dangled from baobab ropes in order to scale the escarpment. Responsible tourism, which is happening in part, seems the only way forward – to preserve their culture while reducing poverty with all its associated issues.

Responsible tourism is in the hands of the traveller as much as the locals. 'Leave no trace' not only refers to litter and human waste or leaving things where they belong. Momo mentioned that the well-intended but random giving of gifts to children was a problem. It usually resulted in jealousy amongst those who missed out and encouraged kids to beg when they are meant to be at school.

The following day we farewelled Momo and set off towards Bankass, Koro and the Burkina Faso border. After about 40 kilometres, Dan could cycle no longer as his knee had become sore on the ride into Djiguibombo. He had kept pretty quiet about this, hoping that the two days off the bike would allow him to work through it. After leaving Kani Kombole he soldiered on for quite some time, basically cycling with one leg but the pain eventually became too much. Disappointed, he reluctantly rode in the vehicle and hoped that a few days rest would be enough to recover. I cycled on alone – 162 kilometres that day on a gravel road, across the border and all the way to Ouahigouya, then 189 kilometres the following day to reach Ouagadougou, the capital of Burkina Faso.

Total distance: 3207 kilometres

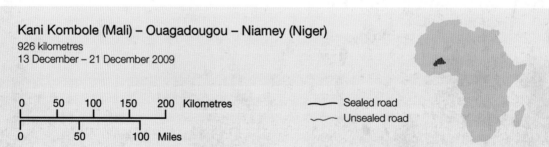

Kani Kombole (Mali) – Ouagadougou – Niamey (Niger)
926 kilometres
13 December – 21 December 2009

| 0 | 50 | 100 | 150 | 200 | Kilometres |

| 0 | 50 | 100 | Miles |

———— Sealed road
~~~~~ Unsealed road

4
A COUNTRY ON THE MOVE

Kani Kombole (Mali) - BURKINA FASO - Niamey (Niger)

Starting the day on a brand-new road between Kaya and Bani

You educate a man; you educate a man. You educate a woman; you educate a generation.

Brigham Young

If it weren't for having to have our passports stamped out at the Mali border-post and in at the Burkina Faso post a few kilometres later, we would not have recognised that we had entered a new country. Between the flags, the Sahelian backdrop was uniformly nondescript. The flat scrubland had been flushed by the most destructive floods on record that had swept through four months previously, displacing 150,000 people and taking the topsoil with it. In a landscape where some of the greatest deviations were the gullies carved by raging torrents, there was little for the grazing animals to eat. But if my passing encounters with locals were anything to go by, the people seemed to take the recent devastation in their stride. First impressions of the Burkinabé people were of gentle friendliness and, over the coming days, I learned of a deep-rooted pride. A laid-back lot, even they refer to themselves as 'tranquil.'

As I cycled through small villages or passed a donkey cart, local Burkinabé would respond with the most enthusiastic double-handed waves (rather than the usual single-handed wave) which were very difficult to reciprocate from over the handlebars on rough, unpaved road. The kids in particular expressed unprecedented enthusiasm. As I pedalled alone through the regular villages, small groups would rush to the roadside, form a line, clap and wave me through as if I was competing in the Tour de France – not quite what I had expected pushing along in a backwater of a country of which many people in other countries would never have heard.

This reaction may have been learned from the Tour du Faso, an international ten-day cycle race which has been held every October since 1987. Professional competitors travel from Europe to pitch themselves against Africa's best. While participants would not have raced over unsealed roads such as this (north-west of Ouahigouya) the event receives much publicity nationally and thousands of Burkinabé of all ages, particularly children, line the streets to watch the action. The carnival atmosphere is also the perfect stage to pass on important messages about wellbeing, education and survival. 'Hand wash with soap,' 'Use insecticide-treated mosquito nets to prevent malaria,' 'How to avoid mother-to-child transmission of HIV,' 'The importance of breast feeding,' 'Problems associated with child labour' were all communications from UNICEF, which recognised the public relations value of sponsoring the 2010 event. These basic messages are often life-saving in this statistically third-least-developed country in the world. Compounding these problems, according to the UN Development Program, Burkina Faso suffers from the highest levels of illiteracy of any nation. In the Sanmatenga region in north-eastern Burkina Faso, there was a focus on girls' rights to access education in the Sahel region. This was where we were heading via a regrouping pit stop in the capital, Ouagadougou.

In the Sanmatenga region, where there is a focus on girls' access to education, a young audience pays full attention to the messages (JD)

So how did civilisations of the West African region, some so advanced for their time, diminish to the present-day situation? In Burkina Faso, just over one-quarter of its citizens can read and write. In truth, I was more interested in how Burkina Faso is moving forward than concentrating on the alarming figures, but to understand where they are going it is first necessary to look at where they have come from – briefly. Burkina Faso's historically contentious leadership along with its susceptibility to natural disasters has a lot to do with it.

Burkina Faso is the crossroads for many cultures, people and languages. About half of the current population of 16 million are Mossi. Now predominantly farmers, the Mossi claim descent from warriors who migrated from neighbouring Ghana and established an empire that lasted more than 600 years. During colonial and post-colonial times, the Burkinabé people have been dealt an adverse hand. In 1896, the French overpowered the Mossi Kingdom of Ouagadougou and moved in; they struggled however to gain control of other groups of their fledgling protectorate. Between then and independence in 1960, the borders of Upper or Haute Volta, as it was called by the French, were shuffled back and forth five times, damaging the social fabric. Upper Volta was used as a kind of colonial landfill, made up of bits of other colonies the French failed to effectively exploit or which were in the too-hard basket to administer. Ethnic groups were further fragmented when the French army forced the removal of tens of thousands of people to work on plantations in their adjacent Ivory Coast colony. Since independence, the country's house of parliament has been more like a house of cards made up of too many jokers and wildcards, and without sturdy foundations. Every time a power-hungry, wealth-sapping leader was deposed by the standard military coup d'état – some bloody, some bloodless – the 'house of cards' would collapse and the Burkinabé people would have to absorb and endure the disruptive consequences all over again. In card-playing terms, the resilient Burkinabé have no choice but to adapt to a game of patience.

One leader who bucked the trend was Thomas Sankara. He still achieved power via a bloody coup in 1982 but his radical left-wing policies and his alignment with Cuba's Fidel Castro earned him the title of Africa's Che Guevara. Determined to stamp out government excess, Sankara initiated a blitz on corruption. He cut government salaries by 25 per cent, dismissed most of his cabinet and sent them to work in the fields, and even got around in a modest Renault 5-series car. To sever ties with the colonial past, he renamed the country. Upper Volta became Burkina Faso which translates as 'Country of Honourable (or Upright) People.' Community self-reliance was promoted and the economy benefited from financial transparency and minimal debt financing.

Thom Sank, as he is still popularly known, made notable reforms in health and education. In one 15-day marathon, two-thirds of Burkina Faso's children were vaccinated against measles, meningitis and yellow fever. More than 350 communities built their own schools and primary enrolment increased. During the five years that he was in power, people developed genuine pride in their country. But while stirring the pot so radically may have made Sankara a hero to the average Burkinabé he was despised by those who were worse off: politicians, trade unions, the urban elite and the West (USA and France). In 1987, Thom Sank was betrayed by his once-loyal soldiers and friends and was assassinated. Blaise Compaoré, his former ally, became president and he immediately set about 'rectifying' Sankara's revolution. A new constitution paved the way for elections in 1991, which Compaoré won easily, although they were boycotted by opposition parties. Compaoré has clung to power ever since, amending the constitution once his official terms were up, and suppressing and eliminating political opposition and journalists who have stood in his way.

The upside of Compaoré's reign, which has at present spanned nearly a quarter of a century, is that Burkina Faso has benefited from long-term stability. Making friends with Western nations and institutions such as the World Bank has led to an environment more conducive to foreign investment and development assistance. Even though there is obvious poverty, construction of new roads and buildings seemed to be going on just about everywhere. All along the 190 kilometres of paved highway from Ouahigouya to Ouagadougou were signs indicating the presence of international and local NGOs. In Ouagadougou we were guests of one of our sponsors, Gryphon Minerals, which itself was attracted by the stable economic conditions and the prospect of mining gold tenements in the Banfora region in the south-west of the country. I first came across Burkina Faso's minister for mines at a Sydney resources conference which I had attended just before I left Australia. He was presenting there to encourage Australian business partnerships.

One of the most important parts of Burkina's development strategy is its qualification for debt relief. Like many of the countries on my route, Burkina Faso had a history of racking up unserviceable debts. This began with poor management and bad investments during the 1970s and 1980s. Then, rising oil prices and slumping commodity prices conspired to cause debts to start spiralling out of control. Loans that were meant to generate exports and other long-term benefits were exacerbated by poor governance, unfair trade rules, droughts, floods and civil unrest. Borrowings amounting to hundreds of millions of dollars were being taken out just to pay the interest on existing debts, stifling any efforts to reduce poverty. Burkina Faso was one of the first sub-Saharan countries to prepare its Poverty Reduction Strategy Paper which qualifies it for debt relief, meaning, in short, that it has drafted effective plans to combat poverty using monies saved from not having to pay interest on national loans. Compaoré's government satisfactorily demonstrated to the World Bank and the International Monetary Fund that it has a strong donor coordination strategy and an environment conducive to foreign investors. Since 2002, Burkina has focused debt relief savings on fighting AIDS, improving education and providing safe drinking water. For example, money freed up from debt service payments has been used to build 746 schools and put over 110,000 students in school within three years from 2006. The spread of HIV/AIDS (6.5 per cent) has been controlled and over a million more people have access to clean drinking water.

Critics say that forgiving debt is merely a Band-Aid if the funds are not also used to effectively change basic flaws in institutions such as judicial systems and governments, as well as stem corruption and improve trade liberalisation. There is evidence that some countries, including Burkina Faso, are at risk of slumping back into a cycle of incurring unsustainable debts if these are not better addressed. Debt relief is just one piece in the puzzle that does help free funds to reduce poverty. Across the continent, the cancellation of Cold War debts has so far helped 52 million more African children go to school – an investment that can only fortify many societies in the future.

✻

Compared to other African cities, Ouagadougou seemed a little more friendly and orderly – well, there was organised chaos at least. I reached the city's outer limits after a nine-hour day of pedalling. This was my second consecutive day of such magnitude and my legs were beyond tired, continuing to turn the pedals robotically as if detached from the rest of my body. My stomach was still fizzing from the last gastro attack, but over the final 15 kilometres I had to find a little extra and stay alert. I soon sharpened up as the odd donkey cart and cyclist I normally shared the roadside with gradually merged with peak-hour traffic. There was certainly no chance of responding to any double-handed waves here either. If one were to assess the range of vehicles on the move, then the main thoroughfare into the city could have constituted an ark for road users. Every type of vehicle was represented, in a range of working states and burdened with all sorts of loads; four wheels, two wheels, four legs, two legs, horse-powered, mule-powered, human-powered... It was hardly a system of two by two but there was a type of hierarchical slowest-to-fastest natural selection, particularly in the outside lane. I hovered between the motorised and non-motorised traffic. Burkinabé cyclists, true to their natural disposition, tend to amble along upright and in no hurry, so I found my niche between them and the scooters mostly, trying to keep a constant pace while darting in and out with the flow. Atmospheric conditions at peak hour on the 'ark' were definitely not conducive to the long-term survival of any 'species' and while I found the experience of cycling in this African city surprisingly exhilarating, I was glad I did not have to do it every day.

In Ouaga, as the capital city is referred to locally, I broke the news to Paddy that he would be going home for Christmas, and we arranged for his departure. Obviously missing home, he appeared to welcome the suggestion. He was to courier camera equipment which had been damaged, and have it repaired and returned to us at the next opportunity. I wanted him to review his work with professionals at the production company before I confirmed that we no longer needed him on the team.

Other than that, there was the usual mountain of work to do: writing, arranging visa extensions, sorting out Paddy's replacements, giving a radio interview, organising the connections for accommodation and security ahead. John always had work to do to maintain the Land Rover and Dan worked as a loose man in defence, filling in the gaps where needed. There was never enough time to cover everything and, subsequently, I began the next leg tired from lack of sleep. John and Dan dropped me back on the ring road to recommence the journey, rejoining the line, direction Kaya, while they spent the day waiting to collect our visas.

❋

My main focus in Burkina Faso was to look at the state of women's and girls' education by visiting one of Plan International's projects based in Kaya in the Sanmatenga region, approximately 100 kilometres to the north-east of the capital. Traditionally in Burkina Faso, as with most of the Sahelian countries, boys are given priority for education – girls are expected to work, marry at an extremely young age and produce a large family. In 2009, only 30 per cent of adults over fifteen years were able to read and write and of that number, there was one literate woman for every three men. As I found out, sustainable improvements are being made, particularly with regard to cultural changes. It doesn't matter how good the institutions that are put in place are if the local people do not embrace the changes.

Our visit was hosted by Plan Burkina's Ms Francoise Kaboré and the program operations manager, Mr Oumarou Koala (and, yes, we got the obligatory joke about the relevance of the director's name to a certain Australian marsupial out of the way during the introductions). Once in Kaya, the regional capital, the three of us and a cameraman drove out to a small village where I was to be shown a new BRIGHT school. (John and Dan were still stuck in Ouagadougou.) BRIGHT stands for Burkinabé Response to Improve Girls' Chances to Succeed. The project was initially set up in 2006 by a US organisation called the Millennium Challenge Corporation. Plan International is a major stakeholder. Since then, 132 BRIGHT schools have been built, educating over 17,000 new primary students, more than half of whom are girls.

We arrived at the school to find many of the villagers waiting under a shady tree to greet us. Mr Koala first sought permission from the community for us to take photos. We introduced ourselves to the audience, Francoise translating for me. After the courtesies and formalities were over and we were accepted, the elders selected a representative cross-section of the community for us to meet. Elders, teachers, women with their babies and community members of all ages filled the largest of three classrooms and Francoise, Oumarou and I sat out the front. What followed was a two-way forum where we asked each other questions. In response to our queries the community members articulated their thoughts about education, how it affects their lives and their greatest hopes and needs. I found the heart-to-heart interactions deeply emotive. These people had taken time out to share their experiences and educate me about the subject I most closely identified with. I had learned much of the theory but now I was hearing how it was put into practice straight from those most deeply affected. I felt a strong sense of duty to absorb all the information to pass on to others.

Here is a summary of the questions I asked.

How has the village changed in the three years since the school was built? What was it like before?

'The school brings the community together; it gives hope for the future. Now our children have opportunities which we never had.'

One of the more outspoken men explained that he had never had the chance of education – he could not read or write (although he was an exceptional spokesperson). He said that now girls are no longer expected to marry and have children when they are very young; they are encouraged to go to school for formal and non-formal classes. In this particular school, more girls than boys attend and the girls' results were marginally better overall.

Wise village elders explain how they now encourage girls to go to school (FK)

This is a big cultural change. In the past, the main motivation for communities to provide their children – usually boys – with a primary education was to progress to secondary school and, after graduation, obtain a salary-paying job. This income would be contributed back to the subsistence-based community in times of drought, flood or other economic crises. Before, the general perception was that educating girls was not worth it. As girls are expected to spend more time than boys carrying water, collecting firewood and performing other menial tasks, the community therefore believed that they were less likely to achieve success from education. Giving birth at a very young age meant girls were unlikely to finish their education. They would never progress to secondary school and move on to find an outside job. And although school fees were very low, paying them was still a significant expense for Burkinabé farmers. It was also felt that educated girls were more likely to refuse an arranged marriage. This would be shameful for the father who would incur a financial loss as a result.

How has the project encouraged more girls to attend school?

Initially, partners of the BRIGHT Project educated the community leaders who in turn spoke individually to each family to explain the importance of attending school. Community consensus is required before anything goes ahead here. As an incentive school lunches were provided for those who attend; these people are very poor and this ensures the students get at least one good meal every day.

(To the three teachers) *What can be done to improve the quality of their work? What do they need?*

The young head teacher read out the class sizes. The average was fifty-five students per class. Currently there are three classrooms and teachers are expected to tutor two year groups at a time. Their dream would be to have a classroom for each of the six primary year levels. Another request was really simple – 'We need electricity so the school can have light.' Teachers are restricted to daylight hours to prepare lessons. If there were lights, the school could then be the focus for community events after dark and students could also do their homework. A normal school day would entail starting at 7:30 a.m., working through to lunch at around 11:30 a.m, then a break before resuming at 3:00 p.m. for the two-hour afternoon session.

What are the main types of non-formal education?

There is a special program for young mothers to improve literacy as well as give them practical lessons in subjects such as agriculture, nutrition and mothercraft. Having better-educated young mothers ensures that children receive the support and encouragement they need to attend school every day.

The benefits of educating women reverberate right through the society as women are the cornerstones of every community. But while Burkina Faso's women do most of the physical work they have little say in decision-making. Improving their level of education gives them a greater voice. Educating women is also a priority because, as it is well-documented, educated women tend to have smaller families and their children are generally healthier.

(To the women) *What changes and improvements would you like to see in the village over the next five years?*

Water was the main issue. The village only had one well and there was just enough water for drinking (but not growing things). A man who had walked from a neighbouring village said that often young girls missed the first three hours of class because they had to queue to collect water, then carry it some distance back to their land. Here, as in much of the Sahel, only millet can be grown as a staple crop; it thrives in poor soils and in dry conditions and has a short four-month growing cycle.

Another woman contributed that the other outstanding need is for a health centre. At present the women have to walk many kilometres to get medical help. She said that education is good for preventing health problems, including delaying having children until the mothers are older (and their frames ready for pregnancy and birth), but they need a health centre as well.

Overall, there was an air of positivity among the people we met. Community members seemed genuinely inspired by their improving

Access to clean drinking water is still a problem in many of the smaller villages (JD)

circumstances. But this was just a start and there was a long way to go on many levels.

With visas in hand, John and Dan joined us the following day for part two. Francoise and Oumarou took us to another, larger village to be guests at a special non-formal educational gathering. Facilitated by Plan Burkina and promoted by local radio, the event was presented by a group of senior students from the secondary school. Hundreds of kids of all ages, their teachers and a few others gathered around where the young leaders were to perform. This was designed to be a fun way to convey important information and was a great example of child-centred development.

The main theme of the day was stopping violence in schools. The twelve senior students individually delivered their lines, nervously at first, starting with (roughly), 'Education is a basic human

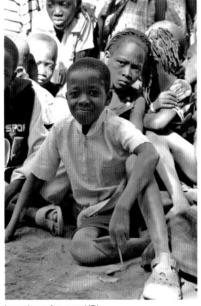

Learning a fun way (JD)

right; everyone has the right to receive an education.' Another continued, 'If students are afraid to go to school because of violence, then this affects their learning, their health and their community...' After the main messages were performed (and this was really well done), the students invited their teachers to individually join them to dance a little. Later, Francoise, myself and Oumarou were in turn invited up for a brief solo bop. Possessing about as much rhythm as these kids probably have in their little toes, I started to dread the situation as soon as I realised it was unavoidable. When the moment arose I knew I had to bury my inhibitions and go with the flow: it was more important for the kids to see me taking part than it was for me to be worried about embarrassing myself for a couple of minutes. I got stuck in. There was definitely a level of appreciation for my cameo but I was not sure whether they were laughing with or at me! Finally, Mr Koala took to the floor and then he wrapped up the morning's proceedings.

After the event was over, I met the English teacher, Karime Zongo, and encouraged him to become involved in the Breaking the Cycle education program. He was exasperated because he would have liked to do so but it was too difficult and too expensive for him to gain access to the internet. Karime explained how challenging it was to work at the secondary school: there was effectively only one decent classroom and he had to teach classes of 130 children at a time! Not surprisingly, he said he was burnt out. We lunched with the teachers before farewelling Francoise and Oumarou, two very inspiring people. It was time to move on.

The projects seen in the Sanmatenga region are a microcosm of the national picture. The government, whether through creating a favourable climate for effective development assistance and investment, or through its poverty-reduction strategies using debt relief, was fostering a trend which was washing over the country. This trend carried within it broader positive implications for combating extreme poverty. But, according to the United Nations, if the needs of women and girls were not fully attended to, six out of eight of the Millennium Development Goals will not be achieved. Many, however, consider the elephant in the same room of fighting acute poverty to be increasing population pressure.

As in most developing countries, Burkinabé families are traditionally very large because they require many children to do all the time-consuming jobs – a kind of unpaid workforce. Given there is no medical insurance or social security, children are needed to fill in the gaps when a family member is sick and to care for their parents in old age. In recent times, however, the average family size in Burkina Faso has reduced from 7.2 to 6.1 children. As education levels, particularly of girls, keep increasing and general living conditions improve (health, food security, infrastructure, economics, etc.), population growth will continue to decrease naturally. What has happened elsewhere in the world is starting to occur in Burkina Faso. The longer it takes to realise these conditions, the larger the scale of the problem and the more difficult these trends will be to reverse. This makes tending to the cultural barriers that form an impervious screen for women's rights to education and empowerment one of the major issues. The good news is that the screen appears to be developing holes.

Educating tomorrow's leaders, girls and boys

✣

In Kaya we stayed in a standard Burkinabé hotel rather than the usual hotel accommodation assigned to NGOs and other foreigners – that was beyond our budget. But the Burkina 'standard' quickly reminded us of why we preferred to camp where possible. The Land Rover may have been secure but that was the hotel's most redeeming feature. As I tried to close the door of my room, the door knob fell off. On closer inspection, the shower vestibule had been used as a lavatory and mosquito nets in all our rooms were full of holes. The shower itself proved to be just a folly and so I managed a brief wash with the bucket of water provided. Staying in a place such as this may have been cheap but it was bad value – we were at risk of contracting any one of a number of serious diseases. Luckily we got away with a clean bill of health this time.

The road to Dori, in Burkina's far north-east, was newly constructed, with only short sections through some of the regular villages left to seal. I continued alone, pushing into a steady headwind, as had become the norm. Dan's knee was still painful and so he manned the camera. It was obvious as we headed north again that the people, land and climate were changing. The region around Kaya and further north, near to Dori, offered inspiring variations in an otherwise level landscape. An ancient rocky knoll just after the Islamic centre of Bani, too rugged for cultivation, made a people-free, pristine campsite – much appreciated after the Kaya hotel experience. We were back into a region of mosques and kaftans, whereas around Ouagadougou there were more churches and Western clothes.

If judged only by the roads shown on our maps, the 90-kilometre route from Dori to Tera (Niger) should have been straightforward. As we were quickly learning on this expedition, we should have assumed nothing. Leaving John and Dan to replenish and filter our water supply from the town well, I set out on the good gravel road towards Sebba. The directions, verified by a number of locals, were that I should turn left at a sign about four kilometres along. But this did not materialise and I cycled back and forth searching for the elusive indication to Sitenga and the Niger border. Exasperated, I returned to Dori, reunited with the boys and quizzed several more locals, all of whom sent us back down the same road. We remained baffled until a motorcyclist eventually set us on the right path. The sign was four kilometres from town, but no wonder we missed it; this was no road sign, just a rusting advertising 'plaque', as they called it, partially concealed by some scrub. I had assumed that the road to the border would be a made

The road to Sitenga and the Burkina-Niger border

gravel road, like the Sebba road we were on, but it was an inconspicuous bush track marked with a small piece of orange tape! I'd done an extra 15 kilometres for nothing.

From there our path was more like a braid of tracks weaving through the sparse acacia woodland. Where the trees petered out into desolate open expanses the tracks amalgamated to just one or two sets of wheel ruts. For much of the day I battled into the teeth of a headwind so strong that a local cyclist travelling from the opposite direction sailed by without even pedalling – he nonchalantly sat up tall and let the wind catch his loose attire. The two-handed wave was downright showing off! And a little disheartening. The track was sandy at times, especially where I passed by cultivated fields of maize or through creek beds. Like back on the Mauritania-Mali border, there were no road signs anywhere and villages were not named … it was a case of cycling from one to another asking for directions to Sitenga on the frontier. As these folks rarely see white people, if I did stop to ask for directions, the whole village would materialise and crowd around, intrigued.

Times were about to change dramatically for these people though: a brand-new road was being pushed through on both sides of the border. On the Burkina Faso side, it was still being surveyed but on the Niger side, the pristine paved route started from within one kilometre of the national boundary, 40 kilometres from Tera. When I was organising the expedition, Niger had the dubious honour of being

My friendly 'upright' co-cyclists enjoy the brand-new road on the way to work

classified as the poorest country in the world – or thereabouts – so I had hardly expected to be cycling along such an amenable surface. They may as well have rolled out the red carpet. Being so new, there was virtually no traffic on the road; not many people here would own a vehicle in any case. The route would most likely remain little used until the connection was completed through Burkina Faso. Then the floodgates would open for international trade.

For much of the first 20 kilometres, I shared the road with two cyclists, enjoying their now-much- easier commute to work. Both had radios strapped to their handlebars so that when I cycled between them I got Nigerien radio in stereo. Radio is the most important form of media in Niger because few can afford television sets, even if they did have electricity, and high levels of illiteracy hamper the effectiveness of print media. People still waved enthusiastically but there were more bemused looks. Although it was early many of the women were already pounding away, pulverising millet or beans into flour. A constant, deep, partially-muffled 'thud, thud, thud...' resonated like a baseline beat, keeping time for the rhythm of their daily lives – from dawn to dusk, sometimes later. In the semi-nomadic dwellings between the villages it looked to be a particularly tough grind. Kids were up and about too, carrying buckets of water, tending to livestock, doing the chores. I wondered how many would be going to school that day. Dominating the symphony in my ears were the crackling sounds of our three pairs of tyres gliding over the loose blue metal stones, in harmony with the static-filled radio broadcast. I was a part of a new procession signifying that change was on its way. No wonder I was getting some perplexed glances.

The daily grind, dawn to dusk. A typical scene taken while I was on the move

Much of the road was still under construction, forbidden for vehicles to use. About halfway to Tera, all users were channelled on to sandy and corrugated side tracks. I forlornly followed, but thankfully a road worker directed me back up on to the new surfaces. As I neared Tera, it was like peeling back each layer of construction until eventually I rode along a half-metre-wide strip of compacted earth beside a wet tar pour that resembled sticky treacle. That was the start of another 160-kilometre into-the-wind slog to get within reach of Niamey, Niger's capital. By dusk, I made it to the Niger River crossing at Farie. John arrived there a little before me and was able to put the Land Rover on the barge, which only crosses when it is fully laden. Dan waited behind for me. Eventually we took a pirogue across the river at last light.

Waiting for us in Farie was Alichina Mamadou, Ali to us, our main contact and fixer organised by another sponsor, NGM Resources. There was little in Farie, certainly no place to stay, so Ali led us down to Niamey where he had comfortable digs arranged. This was to be our base for a few days over Christmas. The following morning we drove back to Farie and I cycled the final 60 kilometres, accompanied by John and Dan who did stints of about 20 kilometres each.

Nearly there. Appreciating the new roads in Niger, built using European Union funding (DH)

❊

That afternoon, Ali arranged for us to walk with West Africa's last herd of wild giraffes. There are nine giraffe subspecies in Africa, each distinguished by its range of colour and the pattern of its coat. Now only found in Niger, the endangered Peralta Giraffe has large orange-brown spots on its body that fade to white on its legs. These graceful animals used to roam the Sahel from Senegal to Chad. During the course of the last century, the destruction of their habitat through desertification and deforestation as well as threats from poaching, farmers protecting their land, disease and road accidents had led the population to shrink from about three thousand to fifty by 1996. Their remaining habitat is a small pocket of land in Niger's south-west, where they coexist with humans. These are the only giraffes in the world that roam in entirely unprotected territory… all others live in national parks, sanctuaries or zoos.

At Kouré, about 70 kilometres south of Niamey, we collected our compulsory local guide to track the wild giraffes. As the wardens monitor their movements daily our guide knew where to start searching, but since the giraffes are constantly on the move, it is never guaranteed that they will be found. Soon we diverted off the main road and were bouncing violently over rough sandy tracks. After about half an hour the guide spotted a group of five, two males and three teenagers foraging in the treetops. Once close enough, we followed on foot. Apart from a few monkeys and vultures, the giraffes were the first wildlife we'd seen. What a thrill it was to keep pace with our galumphing subjects as they loped along, barely breaking their enormous stride as they nibbled a few select leaves. How could the vile-tasting spiky acacia provide the main sustenance for this beautiful creature? With their demeanour of such innocence and grace, it is hard to imagine how they could agitate anyone.

The Peralta giraffes have to compete for resources with some of the world's poorest people, and the zone they inhabit is the most populous in Niger. The Zarma people are sedentary farmers who grow maize, beans, millet and sorghum. The Fulani, who roam through the region, mostly herd cattle. While locals admire the majestic creatures from a distance, when a giraffe spies a field of beans as dinner (and anything must be better than acacia spines), they are considered a threat to the farmers' livelihood. On our ride from Farie to Niamey, I bought a bucket of ripe, juicy mangoes from a roadside vendor. They didn't stay in my panniers for long as we unashamedly gorged them as a rare, irresistible treat. In 'giraffe-land' a tree full of ripe mangoes is like a tree laden with lollipops – at giraffe-eye level. They cannot resist, much to the dismay of the Zarma.

The Peralta consume between 35 and 75 kilograms of leaves a day, which provides all their nutrients and moisture. Unfortunately for them, many locals subsidise their incomes by cutting firewood to sell. The side of the main road into Niamey had constant supplies of firewood for sale – a major cause of deforestation in the region, even though steps have been taken to reduce the problem. As a result, the giraffes have a diminishing food supply, which causes them to wander further afield, into unfriendly territory.

In the giraffe zone, locals are now mostly well educated as to why they should tolerate the endangered species, and the benefits from ecotourism over-ride crop losses in general. Roaming into neighbouring Nigeria, where such education does not occur, the elegant, eyelash-batting beauties are sometimes seen as one tonne of prime bushmeat.

Since 1996, the Niger government and some international conservation groups have conducted a campaign to save the endangered species. The initiatives focus on improving the circumstances of those who live in the area; creating a greater value through ecotourism, providing micro-loans to encourage alternative incomes, and teaching how to better manage their drought-prone environment. Poaching is outlawed and more severe penalties have been applied than before. Our guide explained that 200 Peralta giraffes had just been counted wandering through the region. Man and beast appear to be coming to the party, intermingling successfully and generally moving in a positive direction.

A family of Peralta giraffes continually grazing on the move

Total distance: 4133 kilometres

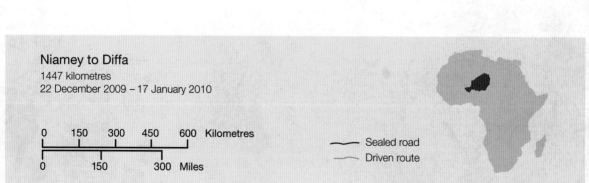

Niamey to Diffa
1447 kilometres
22 December 2009 – 17 January 2010

Kilometres: 0 150 300 450 600

Miles: 0 150 300

—— Sealed road
—— Driven route

5
PUSHING BACK THE DESERT

Niamey to Diffa (Niger)

A struggle (DH)

The old song 'I Want a Hippopotamus for Christmas' seems a bit extravagant in one of the world's poorest countries. But on Christmas Day we were taken to at least observe the hippopotami at the Niger River. Niger being a predominantly Muslim country, Christmas isn't really big there – just a few token tinsel displays around town, mostly to make the expats feel at home. After speaking to all my main family members, I hadn't any major expectations. But Christmas in Niamey turned out to be unforgettable thanks to Ali – or 'Super-Ali', as I had started to call him. There didn't seem to be a problem Ali couldn't fix, or a person in Niger he didn't know. On Christmas afternoon we were driven for just under an hour north of the city to see the wild hippos which are resident in and around the river.

From walking with the Peralta giraffes south of Niamey to watching the hippopotami just to the north – there could not be more contrast between these two evolutionary anomalies. The statuesque giraffe is like the Elle McPherson of the African animal kingdom. Sporting nature's beautiful camouflage designs, giraffes' deportment is the epitome of balance and poise: they parade their Sahelian catwalk with a graceful swaying gait, fluttering their long Mae West eyelashes and teasing each others' affections with a little necking (intertwining of necks). The hippo, on the other hand, is more the Sumo wrestler with its squat frame and stumpy legs. Its fierce smile bears a dental formation that hardly exudes a ring of confidence. Hippos hang out in gangs of up to thirty, collectively known as a 'bloat'. While the giraffe defends itself by deft but deadly backwards kicks (they can kill a lion with a single kick), hippos are incredibly aggressive. On land, their 'Michelin Man' physiques are capable of charging at 30 kilometres an hour in short bursts and they are responsible for killing more people than any other animal in Africa.

With this in mind, our mode of transport seemed inadequate and flimsy, and a fair degree of trust

was assumed as our guides pointed the bows of our shallow-bottomed dugouts into the fast-flowing current. The river was narrower and deeper than when we last encountered it in Mali, and had certainly gathered power. Our guides paddled vigorously upstream, avoiding the strongest current by shadowing the bank. From a distance, the 'river horses' appeared like floating logs. Once we had spotted them, we continued past for a way before our boatmen turned the pirogues towards the centre of the river and drifted back, skilfully manoeuvring closer to three enormous beasts. But not too close.

Keeping a distance from the most dangerous animals in Africa, but where is the other hippo?

Although hippos' nearest evolutionary relatives are actually cetaceans (whales and dolphins) and not pigs or horses as first postulated, they do not swim fast. They don't exactly swim either, rather hold their breath and sink to the bottom to graze on water grasses, bounding along the riverbed until they are ready to resurface for another breath, often several minutes later. I tried not to dwell on the notion that an angry three-tonne hippo could suddenly surface nearby and capsize our fragile craft. Better to focus on the massive animals basking maybe 20 metres away. It appeared as though there was a happy hippo family before us – a bull, cow and calf – but all three never surfaced at the one time. They hovered, facing upstream with often only eyes and nostrils above the waterline, the rest of their bulk remaining submerged to keep cool and prevent sunburn. Eventually we drifted out of sight and returned to the safety of the shore. Afterwards, chicken and chips seemed a reasonable substitute for Christmas turkey.

✻

The causes of Niger's poverty concerns are similar to those of Burkina Faso's (and other Sahelian nations). Four-fifths of the country is desert and much of the remaining fifth is fighting to push back the ravages of desertification. Most of the 16 million inhabitants live in the narrow Sahelian strip that lines the River Niger in the west and borders with Nigeria in the south. About 60 per cent of this burgeoning population exist on less than one US dollar a day. Catastrophic natural crises such as drought and locust plagues used to occur on average once a decade but in recent times the incidence of moderate to severe extended dry spells has increased. It is a combination of poor governance, unsustainable population growth, drought and desertification that undercuts Niger's economy. Living conditions are harsh for most of the people who rely on agriculture to survive. My plan was to follow this populous belt from Niamey, through Maradi, Zinder and on to Diffa near Lake Chad to take a closer look.

Niger's history, like Burkina Faso's, has an all-too-familiar pattern. The French were unable to pacify the assortment of ethnic groups within the boundaries they imposed until 1922, when the Tuareg from the north finally succumbed. Since independence, Nigeriens have lived under five constitutions and three periods of military rule. Over the years, there have been many serious skirmishes with disgruntled Tuareg and other minority groups, in particular over lack of government representation, unfair economic circumstances and environmental disregard. The country is known to contain at least 10 per cent of the world's uranium in deposits centred in and around the Air Mountains in the far north; it also has substantial deposits of gold, oil, coal, iron and other minerals. Exploiting natural mineral wealth is seen by the government as one of the ways to improve the economy but others question the competency of the governance. Ali and his business-minded friend Cissé (who aspires to be a politician) were exasperated by the government's recent resource negotiations with the Chinese. They said that the government was so desperate to improve infrastructure, such as building a new bridge over the Niger River in south Niamey, that it signed off on an unfair long-term binding deal, virtually 'giving away its natural wealth.' The Chinese are shrewd negotiators but my friends blamed their own government's incompetence.

Moving forward, there are some brighter lights. Debt relief is making a difference here too. But there is another movement afoot, driven by village leaders and ordinary farmers, that is gradually infiltrating through the rural communities, instilling resilience and shoring up the fly-away sands. When researching the expedition I learned of this incredible agro-forestry initiative called Farmer Managed Natural Regeneration (FMNR) which has been transforming many regions here for thirty years. Niger seems such an unlikely setting for what has now been acknowledged as one of the world's top nineteen most significant agricultural innovations – ever. I very much wanted to learn more about this exciting success story. In Niamey I looked up (with Ali's help) Professor Boubacar Yamba, who has been an instrumental figure in educating the mostly illiterate rural population about the process and virtues of FMNR while also developing and streamlining the procedure. Professor Yamba explained that in the region where we were heading, between Galmi, Maradi and Zinder, more than five million hectares of poor, marginal farmland – an area the size of Costa Rica and which amounts to half of Niger's cultivated land – had

been restored. Here, the desertification process is being reversed, soils enriched and livelihoods are being transformed. As I traversed Senegal, Mauritania, Mali and Burkina Faso, I was struck by the dreadful state most of the Sahelian land is in – due to population pressure, over-grazing and poor land management practices. FMNR is also being introduced in these countries, as well as other African nations and beyond. In fact, FMNR is fast becoming a global movement, but Niger seems to be the epicentre.

With Ali, Cissé and Professor Yamba at the Université Abdou Moumouni de Niamey (JD)

✳

From Niamey we were joined by documentary film-maker, Stuart Kershaw, for two weeks. A hardened adventurer and athlete, Stuart immediately melded seamlessly with the expedition, his expertise, professionalism and enthusiasm really spurring the three of us on. Stuart's contribution was far more than just being the cameraman – he directed us with great energy and instilled confidence in what we were doing on the filming side of things. To make the most of Stuart's time with us, I planned a schedule crammed with a variety of content, from visiting a FMNR project near Maradi to diverting into the Sahara 'proper' at Termit.

The road from Niamey to Dosso was flanked by a single power-line which runs all the way in to Nigeria. Nigeria supplies Niamey and in fact most of Niger with electricity, so if relations fail, Nigeria can literally turn off Niger's power at the flick of a switch. And during our time in Niger, the internal political situation was on tenterhooks. On 22 December, the day we arrived in Niamey, President Mamadou Tandja's second, and what should have been his final term was up. He had been in power for 10 years but, not wishing to step down, had tried to implement a reform so he could stay in office. The opposition objected and the resultant impasse was condemned by the international community and the UN, US and European Union withdrew all non-humanitarian aid to put pressure on the president. Such political instability really hurts the country, especially when nearly half the national budget is derived from foreign aid donors. Cissé thought that the reasons Burkina Faso was a little more developed than Niger were because it has benefited from two decades of relative political stability and because of the lasting effects of Thomas Sankara's previous regime – a legacy of greater unity and social organisation.

Perhaps the most remarkable feature between Niamey, Dogondoutchi and Birnin-Konni was the quality of the road surface. Signs advertised that the road was funded by international donors, chiefly the European Union. It was one of the best standards we had come across on the journey to date and belies the economic condition of the country. This road receives special attention because it is part of the 'Uranium Highway': from Arlit in far north Niger (the town central to France's uranium mining interests), liquefied uranium is transported overland through Agadez, Tahoua, Niamey and on to the ports in Benin. The beautifully smooth road transported me across the landscape as easily as would a sterile conveyor belt. Maybe it was fitting that I felt somewhat removed as I passed through regular small villages with square earthen houses and thatched granaries. Niger may not be able to supply itself with power but it does provide 80 per cent of the uranium needs of France – a country which is totally reliant on nuclear energy. In 1996, the Niger government received less than one-tenth of the total value of uranium exported by the principal French company, AREVA. And it appeared as though very little of even that sum was reaching the citizens of Niger. The road that serves to siphon a big chunk of Niger's natural resources is a symbol of the disconnection of wealth between the Nigerien people and their government and foreign partners. Pushing along the Uranium Highway, a reality jolt soon reminded me of where I was – the begging reached a new level of desperation. Rather than politely asking for 'un petit cadeau, s'il vous plaît' ('a small gift, please'), here many villagers plainly demanded 'argent' (money).

Dense woodlands had given me some shelter from the wind for much of the first 300 kilometres but after Dogondoutchi I faced wide open expanses and seriously strong headwinds. Daniel decided he was ready to give cycling another go and we left Dogondoutchi together. Initially I was the one in trouble from debilitating muscle spasms, a condition which recurred several times during this journey and has plagued my cycle touring career. The spasms typically occur after I have been pushing hard and then have total physical rest for a few days. When I resume cycling, waste products collect in major working muscles such as my quadriceps, gluteus and lower back and the resulting pain is so intense that all I can do is try to push through it. I can only cycle short distances until I have to stop to stretch and massage the area, then repeat the process. Usually after an hour or two, the problem dissipates, but the resulting soreness can last for days. After about 25 kilometres, I had mostly worked through my issues but by then Dan was in difficulty. His knee was agony and he was forced to stop. We were all very worried about Dan's knee. Over lunch we discussed his options and decided to consult some contacts we had in Maradi as to where to seek appropriate medical advice.

Grain stores near Galmi

In major towns like Birnin-Konni and smaller villages I noticed Nigeria's influence. Much trade creeps over the border, at times just a few kilometres away. Fuel is significantly cheaper in Nigeria, one of the world's leading oil producers, and much is sold on Niger's black market, vendors setting up their stalls in random locations along the roadside. John preferred not to buy from the black market because there was no guarantee of fuel quality – much of the diesel was dirty. In Niger, a litre of diesel cost about AUD$1.30, in Burkina Faso $1.80 and Nigeria about $0.80.

Niamey to Maradi was a long 700-kilometre, five-day slog into the Harmattan. These seasonal trade winds which had been constantly repelling my journey to date intensified over December and January. Prevailing from the north-east, they whip off the Sahara, filling the air with sand and dust. At worst I was knocked down to 13 kilometres an hour on the flat and was forced to put in many consecutive dawn-to-dusk days just to make the distances planned. In these conditions the sunrises and sunsets produced an eerie kind of filtered light. The sun never touched the horizon: in the morning it seemed to gradually materialise through the dust-filled atmosphere which blankets the land and then in the late afternoon it slowly diffused back into the haze. The extended twilight produced a soft, delicate light – the colour of the pale sands it reflected – which washed over the powdery pastel landscapes.

Dust sweeps across the road and into my face, making breathing difficult: a typical day into the Harmattan

❋

We arrived in Maradi, Niger's third largest city and commercial capital, on New Year's Day. There I had arranged to meet and stay with Sally and Peter Cunningham, who had been living and working in the region for SIM (Serving in Mission) for ten years. Specialising in Farmer Managed National Regeneration (FMNR) and associated agro-forestry initiatives, they arranged for us to visit a village which has fully embraced FMNR practices. We spent a captivating afternoon with the Cunninghams, Jaho, a Nigerien radio personality and FMNR activist, and our interpreter in the village of Djido, 25 kilometres south-east of Maradi. This was all about communities taking control of their own destinies.

We first gathered in the shady central meeting place. Once the elders and village leaders finished their Friday prayers we received their official welcome. Jaho, being a familiar personality to the audience, did most of the talking. Larger than life both in the way he animated his confident delivery and in his physical presence, Jaho is a colossus of a man. After the introductions were over and we were accepted, the hospitality continued with a special lunch which the women had prepared from produce they had grown themselves on their now-more-productive land – beans, millet and chicken (including head and feet). Being served chicken was a great honour in a culture that traditionally experienced poor food security. Normally a chicken would only be slaughtered for a special occasion and I appreciated that this kind of welcome did not happen every day. Stakeholders in the FMNR initiative – Serving In Mission, World Vision, Care International – have been fostering a relationship over a number of years, developing trust and friendships. I learned that the villagers' quality of life has improved dramatically in that time and from what I could see the people of Djido seemed happy and extremely motivated.

So what is Farmer Managed National Regeneration, or FMNR? The trigger for this farmer-led transformation of the landscape stemmed from an ecological and humanitarian crisis in the 1970s that threatened the lives of millions and undermined the ability of Niger to sustain itself. Prior to colonial intervention, land use in southern Niger was characterised by sparse rural populations cultivating small fields amidst surrounding bush. Families were smaller, yields were sufficient and there was plenty of timber from natural sources: people co-existed in balance with the environment. Land clearing and tree felling became more common in the 1930s due to the French colonial government, which drained the country of its land resources by pushing farmers to grow export crops and providing them with disincentives to care for the land. A new law was passed transferring tree ownership to the government and Nigeriens had to purchase permits if they wanted to make use of the trees.

At the same time the French improved the healthcare system, the outcome of which was longer life expectancy and lower infant mortality. However the increased population and lower productivity of the land strained resources and left people vulnerable to famine and natural disasters. Post-colonial governments in the 1960s and 1970s continued to implement the tree ownership law, but following the four-year famine from 1969-73, positive steps by NGOs (such as Serving In Mission, World Vision and Care International) and the Maradi Integrated Development Project eventually led to a change in the law and ownership of trees was returned to the farmers. This long-drawn-out process was only officially realised in 2004. Once educated about the law, people took responsibility for their own trees. This was part one of the big change.

Our little party, along with a selection of the community who were to showcase the FMNR procedure, relocated to a field near the village. Peter Cunningham explained that the trees that have been clear-felled are cut off at the stumps, leaving the roots intact and ready to re-sprout. These root systems are often referred to as 'underground forests'. The bush which sprouts from the roots has many stems. Jaho gave the first rather theatrical demonstration of the FMNR process, which simply involves pruning away the lesser branches, leaving the four or five most robust ones. The stems are also cleaned of side shoots and runner roots are cut, which encourages the nutrients to be channelled into developing four or five strong trunks, and so the trees are trained to grow taller. If an owner needs to cut a trunk for firewood or use as building material, for example, he or she can extract one or more of the stems and still have two or three trunks to use later. In times of hardship the owner may take the whole tree, knowing it will re-sprout. But with whatever is taken, not even a leaf is wasted. The whole procedure is extremely low-cost, practical and adaptable, especially when compared to previous plantation-type initiatives trialled in Niger.

Where FMNR is fully established, villagers typically grow about 200 trees per hectare. Facilitating the trees to regenerate improves soil fertility as the trees provide wind-breaks to counter soil erosion; the fallen leaves are used as mulch and most of the trees

Applying the FMNR pruning technique to a mature acacia tree. Tending to acacia trees is a priority because the roots fix nitrogen in the soil, improving fertility naturally, and the pods make high-protein fodder

are acacias which fix nitrogen naturally in the soil. As a result, crop yields increase. Introducing FMNR has, in some places, allowed farmers to reclaim land totally lost to the desert but mostly it has substantially increased productivity of farmed soils. Pods and leaves provide fodder in the Dry season and diversity is restored as local species of plants and animals return. In addition, trees provide shelter for the animals.

Demonstration complete, Jaho invited the men and then the women to give testimonies as to how FMNR has changed their lives. Enthusiasm bubbled into uncontained smiles as each person spoke.

Jaho asks the men to share with us how they have benefited from FMNR (JD)

Afterwards, they could barely wait to show us the techniques they had now incorporated into their traditional culture. Prior to the introduction of FMNR and associated re-greening initiatives, the farmers could normally provide enough food for only eight months of the year. Then, typically, the younger men would have to leave the village to find work to keep their families for the remaining four month *soudure* or 'hungry period': now they can stay and contribute to the village economy and community life. Women no longer have to spend hours collecting firewood every day (they used to average 2.5 hours a day) and can use the time productively to farm trees and grow food, which has improved their social status. When the land was subjected to wind erosion, farmers had to regularly reseed their millet and sorghum fields several times to produce one crop. With added protection from trees they need only sow once, saving time and money, and surpluses are sold off. In fact, trees are now referred to as 'banks': instead of putting money into a savings bank, when villagers need funds they can simply draw on their wood surplus, selling firewood to supplement income. One study* found that protecting forty trees per hectare, leaving five stems per tree, would typically bring farmers an extra US$140 a year after four years – increasing

Unmanaged land near Maradi

their average income by almost half. With added productivity, farmers are developing export markets, mostly with Nigeria, reversing the general trend.

On the bumpy return journey to Maradi, we stopped off to inspect land which had not been managed. The open, windswept expanses were devoid of all but a few skeletal trees and stumps, the barren soils a stark reminder of how all of this land used to look and of how households were forced to burn dung for fuel rather than use it as compost to improve the soil fertility. When the concept of FMNR was introduced in the early 1980s, farmers were challenged to abandon lifelong practices. Lighting the flame of FMNR initially resulted in a slow, smouldering 'dung burn' rather than a fast-moving 'bush fire.'

Adopting FMNR all depends on the leaders of each community. Only twelve farmers out of thousands approached were brave enough to 'risk' the new methods. They were mocked by other farmers and some of their young trees deliberately damaged, chopped down or stolen for fuel wood. Despite the peer pressure they boldly persevered, but the program needed another boost. During droughts in 1984 and 1988, in ninety-five villages around Maradi FMNR was incorporated in a Food for Work program whereby, in return for food, farmers were required to regenerate native vegetation on their land. Mostly farmers were reluctant, motivated by the desire for food aid rather than the virtues of the initiative. After the program ended and despite the obvious benefits, two-thirds of the half-million regenerated trees were lost. However the 30,000 farmers who did choose to continue the movement provided a critical mass, which allowed the roots of FMNR to take hold. An important component of the initiative is that it is the farmers and their communities who decide how to implement the changes: they determine how many trees to regenerate per hectare, how many stems to prune, how much wood they need to sell and how they spend the benefits. There are few 'rules', and the adopted FMNR principles emphasise choice

---

* Rinaudo, 2005

'The one who cares for trees will not be hungry.' The Hausa motto for the FMNR Project on Peter's vehicle

and experimentation. The greatest gains against poverty and desertification have been shown to occur when communities work on their own behalf to achieve their own objectives.

Now FMNR is spreading like wildfire from farmer to farmer, community to community, as their leaders become enlightened. Pockets of bare ground are becoming isolated islands around Maradi, thanks to the persistent hard work of the instigators of FMNR, especially Tony Rinaudo, an Australian missionary who developed the re-greening program, academics such as Professor Yamba, activists such as Jaho, the continued cooperative work by the many stakeholders, the government and community leaders. In some regions, the transition between the FMNR instigators and leaders to local communities is complete. After an earlier coup d'état in 1996, when most aid was suspended, woodland regeneration continued to spread without the assistance of outsiders. A decade later, densely populated parts around Zinder, where we were heading, had almost universally adopted FMNR practices over a million hectares without major donor intervention. As the climate, already marginal, becomes subject to more extremes, FMNR has even greater importance for the future. In the famine of 2004-05, FMNR villages fared much better than those denuded of vegetation. The BBC reported that around fifteen children a week died in the bare regions around Maradi, whereas 80 kilometres away in the Aguié district, where farmers could harvest trees for food, fodder and firewood to sell in exchange for grain, not only did they not rely on any food aid, they avoided a single death. A drought may bring hard times, but it is extreme poverty that causes famine.

Back at Sally and Peter Cunningham's place – a welcome little Australian sanctuary in the middle of Niger – we were treated to some magnificent home cooking. During the evening Peter mentioned that he considered Niger's biggest challenge now was to stem population growth. The national figures cite each woman as having 7.8 children, the highest rate in the world. Ruth Perkins, another Serving In Mission (SIM) worker who joined us and who has lived in Niger for twenty years, added that in this region, the average is closer to ten children. Polygamy is

With some FMNR experts (JD)

widely practised here, as in most of West Africa: the number of wives a man has is a symbol of wealth and status. Peter knows a man who has thirty-eight children! A population explosion has already occurred in the five years since the 2005 famine and associated crises, so in a few years from now there will be a whole new generation with little to do and the pressure on the land will mount once again. Given the rate of population growth in the region, FMNR alone will not enable Niger to stay ahead of the food and livelihood needs of its people. When people are hungry and half the children suffer from malnutrition, it is difficult to prioritise anything above the emergency needs for food, medicines and clean water. By increasing the sustainable threshold of the land, FMNR serves to buy the rural population some time.

A girl in Djido displays some home-grown produce

On the whole, Niger is on the up. Although I had been deeply affected by some of the situations I had witnessed, I had nothing to compare them to and conditions are not uniform. Niger is gradually clawing its way off the bottom of the Human Development Index. Having earned full debt relief means it has developed an effective poverty reduction plan focusing on improving health, primary education, rural infrastructure, agricultural production, environmental protection and judicial reform. Despite the recent political hiccups, the economy is benefiting from better coordinated foreign aid and investment. For example, 122 new mining exploration leases were granted to international organisations and even AREVA doubled its royalties in 2007. Better than before. More of that revenue is being channelled in the right direction. For example, a joint program between the Niger government and USAID is concentrating on girls' education, combating corruption and enhancing business creation strategies. But although things are moving, will enough be done to moderate the population growth? Educating 16 million people in time is a hopeful challenge, but not as difficult as educating 25 million people in 2020.

✳

Because we only had Stuart with us for a limited time, we needed to adapt the program to make the most of his considerable skills. From Maradi we diverted for a week's tour by vehicle into the desert to gain first-hand experience of the pure sands of the Sahara, the beauty of the Termit region and an insight into the culture of the semi-nomadic Toubou, the indigenous people of the east Termit region and adjacent Tin Toumma Erg. We were to return to Maradi to resume the continuous line.

From Maradi we drove to Zinder, Niger's first capital city (in 1927). There we met up with Limane Feldou and Mamane (cook), our guides from the Tuareg organisation, Tidène. Limane and Mamane had driven non-stop from their home town of Agadez, almost 500 kilometres north of Zinder. Unfortunately for me, just as we arrived in Zinder, gastro attack number three of the journey manifested itself. This one was intense and I was violently ill for about twelve hours with a high fever. I seemed to recover fairly well over the next few days but it wasn't a good start to my week of recuperation off the bike. Stuart had had a similar experience two days before and defiantly soldiered on, filming the FMNR project while barely finding the energy to stand.

We followed the main road to Gouré then turned towards Tasker, 160 kilometres to the north, along a dirt track that had once been made but had not been maintained. The spectacular landscape north of Gouré featured the crumbling escarpments of the Koutous Hills amidst wide open expanses. This tabletop range forms the southern boundary of the Termit region and defines the extent of the Hausa people's territory (dominant in southern Niger and the northern half of Nigeria). The Hausa are cultivators and the Koutous Hills are at the limit of where land can support the growing of crops. Continuing north, Hausa villages of *banco* dwellings became increasingly sparse as semi-nomadic encampments of pastoralists became more common.

Men carrying water to their livestock, Kellé village well

After camping at the base of a stunning mesa north of Kellé and midway to Tasker, we stopped off at one of the best examples of a working well that I had seen. The well is the focal point for all-comers in the area; both villagers and nomads rely on the water, whose level, judging by the length of the ropes being used to haul the containers up, was about 70 metres down. The well had five wooden pulleys operating at once. As the large canvas buckets were drawn, the unoiled pulley wheels collaborated as an improvised, screeching quintet, the raising and lowering of the buckets creating a rhythmical background to the morning's activities, a kind of 'Days of Our Lives' on the edge of the Sahara. For the men, women, children, lone horsemen, cameleers and cattle herders, the well was the hub of their working and social lives. The 'music' reflected that this was no soap opera though, more 'A Day in the Harsh Working Life of ...' The high-pitched tones tested my ear drums' tympanic limit and sent chills down my spine in the warmth of the morning sun. In contrast, the mules and bullocks hauling the water bags appeared to be either deafened by the sounds or hypnotised by the drudgery of their task. About 20 metres away from the well were positioned clusters of small, round troughs for people to water their grazing animals. Men strained to lug the heavy buckets across from the well to fill the troughs. Water to be transported was stored ingeniously in containers made from old tyre tubes tied at the ends which were loaded on to donkeys, bullocks, camels or horses and taken away for later use.

Tasker is basically a military town and Limane led us straight to the gendarmerie to check-in. There he presented the special travel permits he

Old tyre tubes make ingenious vessels to transport water

had pre-arranged – essential to be allowed passage through the protected Termit region. It was the last opportunity to top up with fuel which John and Limane carefully filtered as there was no telling where the diesel was sourced. As we travelled away from Tasker, the land became noticeably barer as most of the tufty brush grass had either been eaten down or cut for use by the villagers. Amazingly, in these parts we still passed women carrying firewood, yet there were few trees to be seen, and after Tasker, no permanent settlements. They must have walked for long distances every day. Vegetation gradually phased out over the next 120 kilometres to Termit. The late afternoon light accentuated a green tinge of grass, still hanging on after the October rains. The same system that caused Burkina Faso's floods had also damaged Agadez and swept through the desert corridor. For most of the way, the sandy track was just a pair of wheel ruts with a few alternatives which ran parallel between two sand ridges.

The jet-black volcanic peaks of the Termit range appeared almost sinister as they loomed through the morning haze. They didn't look impressive at first – more like a heap of mining rubble. As we ventured closer and around the south-eastern perimeter, a distinctive palate of colours was revealed. Honeycomb-coloured sand spilled over the layers of charcoal grey and white gypsum rocks. Bonsai-sized acacias clung from precarious positions in the rock face, growing out of fissures in the massif. Termit qualifies for UNESCO World Heritage listing for three reasons. Firstly, it is an ecological island right at the point where the Sahara and Sahel meet. Secondly, it is a sanctuary for some critically endangered species, the best known being the Saharan cheetah and the desert addax, a type of antelope sometimes called the white or screwhorn antelope. Thirdly, it is known to be of immense archaeological importance, containing a wealth of ancient artefacts and rock petroglyphs. We had to check in once more, this time at the Termit-Kaoboul military checkpoint, before setting off.

Limane led us around the southern edge of the massif to meet some Toubou nomads. The Toubou originate from the Tibesti region in northern Chad but some minority groups have dispersed into eastern Niger, Libya, Sudan and north-eastern Nigeria. Often portrayed as 'born-guerrillas,' the Toubou are historically a warrior people renowned for their capacity to fight and for their endurance. Having lived in this region for at least 2500 years, their way of life is supremely adapted to surviving in the desert for extended periods. Toubou people claim indifference to exhaustion, hunger and thirst. One story maintains that it takes three days for a Toubou to eat a date: one for the skin, one for the flesh and the last for the pith! Tales abound of their legendary toughness and ability to cross deserts on a piece of mutton and a *guerba* (goatskin) of water.

We collected a couple of nomads who rode in Limane's vehicle to guide us to what was probably the main encampment. Being semi-nomadic, the Toubou have little material wealth. After warm greetings outside, our group was invited into the men's tent for tea, and we joined a gathering of about a dozen

Tea with the Toubou men

sitting on woven mats around the tea-making ensemble –
a pot simmering gently over a small wire basket of coals.
Communicating for us meant embracing a whole range of
gestures and plenty of smiles. Limane managed the negotiations as he could converse freely and he relayed in simple
French for us to struggle with. The Tuareg and the Toubou
traditionally share a cultural camaraderie. The tea ceremony
involved an exchange of convivial pleasantries between us and
the men, but amongst the Toubou it appeared to be more like
a good old-fashioned chinwag. It was hard to imagine these
people as the oasis-raiding warriors they were once famed to
be.

Women have more responsibilities in Toubou
culture, which helps to ensure their survival in
the extreme environment

As a woman, I was privy to the best of both worlds.
Soon I was invited into the women's tent, a place where men
are not usually permitted to enter. (Stuart was allowed to do
so after a while to film.) Women have a more equal standing in
Toubou society than in other Saharan cultures. Although the
husband or father is the head of the household, he rarely makes decisions without consulting his wife,
and when he is absent, she often takes complete charge of moving family tents, changing pastures or

A beauty queen of the desert

trading cattle. Women are also regarded as the
better navigators. They travel without maps,
guided by the sun, stars and memories of
dune sequences. If they get it wrong, they die.

The sturdy traditional women's tent,
made from woven matting and constructed
as an enclosed tunnel 10-15 metres long,
is built to withstand the harshest Saharan
conditions. Inside it was divided into several
cosy vestibules. The kitchen area was near
the front entrance to make the most of the
ventilation. At first I communicated with a
woman making lunch, stirring a huge cast iron
pot. The digital camera was once again the ice-
breaker and pretty soon they all wanted me to
take their portraits.

From there I was ushered into a second
room where the older generations sat by an
open fire making – surprise, surprise – tea. I
may not have been able to speak Toubou, but
the wrinkles on their weathered faces told
tales of their lifelong battle with the desert.

A Toubou grandmother and great grandmother in the women's tent. The older women seemed to be suffering from cataracts and eye conditions

The lines accentuated facial expressions as we attempted to make ourselves understood – a cross-cultural version of charades. After accepting a couple of shots of tea, I was offered sweet camels' milk. High in essential nutrients and a boost to the immune system, camels' milk is the local elixir for health and wellbeing. Still nursing a dodgy stomach and having learnt the hard way about mixing water and raw milk, I hesitated at taking the drink but felt I couldn't refuse their hospitality. I decided I had no hope of making them understand my reservations and so I downed it. Then another tea was offered. Sensing a pending disaster, one of the wise old grandmothers snatched the glass from my hand. She pointed to her stomach, then gestured an explosion by splaying her fingers in front of her wide-eyed face and making an appropriate sound. She was definitely looking after me. She taught me that tea followed by camels' milk was fine, but not tea–camels' milk–tea. I stored this in my memory for next time.

Pure Sahara

We set off, skirting the eastern perimeter of the Termit Range. Tufts of grass made our cross-country excursion rather bumpy but gradually they became less until finally, by late afternoon, we hit pure sand. Our views to the north and east across the Tin Toumma Desert, especially of the ergs and ridges, are what most people imagine the Sahara to be like. In fact, only one-third of the Sahara is sand – and we were enjoying the desert at its purest. We saw plenty of gazelles, initially in pairs or groups of four, and before the day was out we watched a herd of about fifty bound into the sea of sand, apparently disappearing into infinity. These were most likely to be Dorcas gazelles. The other type of gazelle found around Termit, the Dama gazelle, along with the addax antelope, the Saharan cheetah and Barbary sheep, are on the critical list. While we scoured the landscapes for signs of these animals, our cause remained optimistic. Termit and the surrounding Tin Toumma Desert are home to the last viable population of desert addax, prized by poachers for their horns. There are about two hundred left in the vicinity. Saharan cheetahs can survive without a permanent water source by gaining enough moisture from the blood of their quarry. The elusive big cats are perfectly adapted to the heat and their light-coloured spots make effective camouflage. Any cheetahs would have most likely detected us from high on their rocky thrones, their radar ears twitching in the calmer-than-usual Harmattan breezes. There are only about ten of them left in the Termit region but rare sightings have been reported elsewhere along the Sahelo-Saharan limits.

Sadly, the gazelles, along with the other endangered species, are accustomed to being chased. Uncontrolled poaching and hunting expeditions from countries such as Libya, Saudi Arabia and the Emirates are pushing the animals of Termit's Sahelian ark to extinction. These foreign 'VIPs' obtain special hunting concessions to take only the most abundant game but largely ignore them. Locals have reported seeing refrigerated lorries transporting large numbers of gazelle carcasses and helicopters flushing out animals at night, to be captured alive and removed in crates. The informants have disclosed that this was largely the work of Seif Al Islam, a son of

First drink. A camel with her newborn calf, no more than an hour or two old, in the Gosso Lolom Bo region of Termit Range

Libya's Colonel Gaddafi, who even built a permanent hunting lodge about 50 kilometres west of the mountains, north of Tasker.

The northern end of the 130-kilometre range, the Gosso Lolom Bo region, consists of bare volcanic peaks which rise up to 700 metres like rocky islands emerging out of the sand. True to Tuareg tradition, Limane navigated without a GPS. He knew where he was by reading the formation of the dunes and the position of the sun. Given that he hails from the Tidène region just north of Agadez, the Termit environs

Ancient volcanic landscape, Gosso Lolom Bo region

must be less familiar, but for the Tuareg the desert is their home. Driving through the sand was a whole different skill set but John in his Land Rover and Limane in his Land Cruiser revelled in the challenge.

I had a go at cycling in the pure desert. Mostly it was at Stuart's instruction to create some special scenes for the video but I also wanted to get a taste of what this was like and how it compared with some of my previous Australian experiences. In the valleys between the ergs, where undisturbed sand was surprisingly hard-packed, I was able to cycle along quite well. At the other extreme, ascending the steep side of a dune was a futile exercise. In the steepest, softest sections, where I sank into the sand almost up to my knees, the only way to ascend was to lift the bike to head height and then ram it into the sand above,

Stuart and I at work (DH)

horizontally to the slope. I used the bike as an anchor to then lift myself up, one step at a time.

The Gosso Lolom Bo harboured more surprises. On the third day we lunched beneath some rare shade in a broad valley. Fallout from the eroding peaks, which defined the valley, formed a gibber plain that was partially blanketed with sand. A mirage appeared to melt the landscape so that the colours of the ochre sands, basalt and gypsum bled together with the bluest of skies. Closer inspection revealed that the ground was covered by more than just stones and sand. Scattered amongst the volcanic rubble was a treasure trove of ancient artefacts: within about half an hour, the team had amassed an impressive cache of grinding stones, cutting tools and spear heads. Limane discovered a beautifully fashioned stone axe.

The implements we found were made of stone and iron. According to a UNESCO study in 2002, prehistoric inhabitants at Termit were the first iron-smelting people in West Africa and among the first in the world – around 3500-5000 years ago. The findings concur that these early Iron Age blacksmiths developed their smelting techniques independently rather than importing the knowledge from the Middle East, as was first hypothesised. The ability to smelt iron transformed the lives of Termit's early

An ancient grinding stone (SK)

residents. Here and across many African cultures, past and present, blacksmiths were and still are revered to the extent that they are assigned divine status – believed to release the strongest *nyama*. This being a protected area, we replaced our trophies, leaving them where they belong.

It was a long drive back to Zinder where we farewelled Limane and Mamane – perfect guides, hosts, gentlemen. Limane's organisation, Tidène, is more than a desert-specialist adventure travel company: it has also set up its own NGO to build wells, improve education and health and preserve culture in the Tidène Valley, about 80 kilometres north of Agadez. In partnership with the French organisation Les Puits du Désert, Tidène is making a difference. Among its activities,

it plans to build about one hundred more wells similar to the one we saw in the Koutous Hills. The holes, up to 70 metres deep, must usually be bored through solid rock. Limane explained that it takes about six months to build a well and that importing the materials is an expensive business. Each well costs €10,000 ($AUD15,000), with funds generated through private donations and from the profits from the adventure travel business.

John and our guide Limane Feldou of the Tuareg organisation, Tidène

Zinder also spelled the end of Stuart's time with us. 'Super-Ali' and Cissé drove 1000 kilometres from Niamey to collect him as internal flights could not be relied on to fit in with his tight schedule. By Stuart's account, the return trip was about as fast as a speeding bullet.

A struggle (DH)

*

John, Dan and I drove back to Maradi and I resumed the cycle journey the next day. Dan had earlier seen a physiotherapist in the Serving In Mission compound at Maradi, whose verdict was that he needed a month of rest. He adapted his role to remain an integral part of the support team, becoming the official cameraman for the next couple of weeks after which Zdenek Kratky, our new cameraman, would join us. Dan also took on the role of cook, inspired by Mamane's ability to produce great food out of very limited stores. This was another skill he was quite good at.

Miraculously, in the desert the Harmattan had eased and we enjoyed several clear sunny days. But setting off from Maradi, it returned with a vengeance, like a persistent stalker sensing my every move. I managed to pick up a cold during the freezing Saharan nights. Believing it to be insignificant, I ignored it and pushed hard the first day back on the road – I wanted to catch up some time on the good paved surface. Pushing into the dust and wind sent my system over the edge. My body struggled internally to combat the resultant chest infection and externally to resist the force of the Harmattan.

These conspiring circumstances were most testing on my mind. I had done almost three months and just over 5000 kilometres but, if all went to plan, I still had at least seven months and 17,000 kilometres to go. I'd had three gastros and two chest infections in that time. Dwelling on these overwhelming thoughts did not help as I crawled along at 12 kilometres an hour at times. Retaining the most aerodynamic position – doubled over with my back flat and head down – for extended periods of time was wearing. During the worst of the sand blasting, in a crude attempt to filter the grit, I covered my nose and mouth with my neck scarf. But I couldn't keep the scarf in position for long because I could not breathe: my whole air tract was gummed up and the dust exacerbated the situation. Back in Maradi, Sally had mentioned that locals call December and January the 'nose-picking season' because the Harmattan causes endless respiratory infections. I could see why.

This stage may have been mental torment but there was never any intention of giving up. I reminded myself of all the effort that had gone into reaching this far, of all the people who had invested time and money into the venture and the many children and adults who were following the journey, learning more about Africa. That was motivation enough for me. I was still looking forward to seeing how this story would unravel and could not wait to find out what lay ahead. I may have felt low, but in reality there was nothing stopping me from turning the pedals. I just needed to accept this particular set of circumstances – my health, the weather and the road – and work with them, adapt and endure. I dropped down a gear or two and kept spinning at a reduced speed, at a reduced intensity. It was essential to focus on answering the question 'How do we get there?' rather than 'What will stop us?'

Pushing along with my head down, watching my own legs go round as I rolled over the monotonous stream of broken white lines, could lead to being consumed by negative thoughts. I developed different techniques to coax myself along. One was to enforce photo stops. Even if there was nothing particularly noteworthy, I'd pull up every so often to capture a record, which would also force me to search for the beauty in my surroundings. In this landscape, which for those who travel at faster speeds appears to be nothing but dull scrub, I learned to look for the finer details. I would also break up the time by keeping a handful of sweets or a packet of biscuits in my handlebar bag and every five kilometres I would allow myself another treat. Other times I would try to balance on the white lines on the road as if they were a tight-rope. That was difficult in the blustery conditions but it kept me entertained. Sometimes I would imagine how elated I would feel when I reached the finish, or I would trap favourite songs in my head. Although using earphones would have helped it is extremely dangerous to do so: I needed to remain alert to my surroundings, especially to traffic approaching from behind.

Searching for the beauty. A typical riding shot of the desertification between Gouré and Maine-Soroa

The battle in my mind reached a crescendo on the morning into Gouré. Three hours for 45 kilometres – I barely noticed that the land had morphed into rolling hills during my personal emotional rollercoaster. At the top of town I spotted John and Dan waiting for me and veered off the road – straight into a sand trap. It was a gentle, slow-motion tumble, but although the only thing dented was my pride, it felt like a slap in the face. A couple of rogue tears escaped. These served to fog my sunglasses, which remained firmly affixed to mask my emotions, otherwise the floodgates could have burst. The boys were suitably empathetic and had even sourced a packet of morale-boosting bonbons.

Seemingly out of nowhere, an older woman sidled in between me and John. She talked non-stop in a language we could not recognise, possibly Hausa. We nodded and smiled, with plenty of approving 'uh-ha's, although we didn't have a clue what she was on about. Our limited response did not seem to perturb her and she pulled official papers out of her bag to show us she was of good standing. Despite departmental stamps from different regions with signatures beside them we could not work out what they were for. The woman continued to babble on as I reapplied sunscreen to protect myself from the midday sun. She thought that if this beauty cream was good enough for me, she'd like some of it too, so John squirted a liberal, manly dollop onto her forearm. She tried to rub it in but there was far too much for one use. Not wishing to waste any of it, she found a small container in her bag and scraped the cream off to be used later. Then she turned her maternal attention to me, who must have looked a mess. She noted that I hadn't properly worked in all my sunscreen, and proceeded to do the job for me. Before I knew it she was rubbing cream on to my nose, and then started to run her finger around the edge of each of my nostrils, picking away any impurities. I couldn't quite believe she was actually doing this and didn't know how to react. Her actions were gentle, caring and completely natural, her face a picture of concentration. She was just being a mother to me – cleaning me up, preening my feathers. After all, this was supposed to be the nose-picking season. Soon, I couldn't keep a straight face and before long I was almost crying with laughter. I resumed the struggle with my spirits uplifted. John joined me for the next short session, as he had started to do regularly. His company really helped my mental battle.

Oasis at Guidimouni, the 'garden town'

A daily pattern evolved where I 'did my time' against the strongest winds in the mornings, usually managing about 60 kilometres. Exhausted, I would rest out the afternoon heat for about three hours. Usually after 4.00 p.m. the wind eased so I could cycle on until dark. I still managed to do between 100 and 120 kilometres a day, just to keep the odometer ticking along. Overall we kept the schedule on track.

Between Maradi and Zinder, it was easy to pick out which land had been managed by FMNR and which pockets had not. Between Zinder and Gouré, FMNR fields gradually phased out, although there were impressive developments at the oasis town of Guidimouni, which we labelled the 'garden town.' After Gouré, the level of desertification increased significantly and we passed sections of pure dunes, created by overgrazing, deforestation and shifting sands. The United Nations Development Programme (UNDP) and some other organisations have been carrying out effective dune stabilisation work in the region: 20x15-metre sections of brushwood formed a patchwork of barriers over some of the dunes, halting further wind erosion. FMNR should be a priority here. The people seemed even friendlier – if that was possible. Rather than demands for *argent*, I was greeted with big two-handed waves, words of encouragement and smiles the whole way to Maine-Soroa. Occasionally I stopped to shake peoples' hands, but I couldn't afford to stop on every occasion or I would still be riding!

Pushing through the pink sands of the encroaching desert on the way to Maine-Soroa (DH)

In Maine-Soroa we stayed with Phil and Carol Short, Australian missionaries introduced to us by Sally and Peter Cunningham in Maradi. Phil, Carol and family have been working in Maine-Soroa on and off since 1974 and have seen plenty of changes in that time. The new tarmac strip now goes past Maine, all the way to Diffa, making travel to Zinder, Maradi and Niamey, 1400 kilometres away, much easier. The Shorts arrived during the terrible four-year drought, and have seen a few more over the years. Now, Phil says, the people are better equipped to deal with the dry years than they were but there is still much to do to improve food security. The new year, 2010, was shaping up to be another lean one. The nomads' transhumance (seasonal movement of people and their livestock) had begun. Already they had been forced to drive their herds over greater distances than usual to find suitable pastures – either further south into Nigeria, where it is not so safe for them to travel, or north towards Bilma.

Phil and Carol's son, Warwick, was looking into the use of native trees as food sources and as a means of generating income. He said that over the last few decades, due to the compounding circumstances of chronic poverty and a string of crises, local knowledge of the uses for native flora had been lost. One tree Warwick had been studying was the *Boscia senegalensis*, also known as *anza, dilo* and various other names throughout the

Lone cavalry atop of Diffa's 'triumphant arch' at the town boundary

Sahel, which can be used as a food, timber, fodder, medicine, fuel, poison or alcohol. Warwick is working to reintroduce this knowledge as a way of building resistance to famine. On the way in to Diffa, I passed large fields of the evergreen shrub laden with fruit, which had just set after flowering.

Back in Maradi, Peter Cunningham translated the motto on the Farmer Managed Natural Regeneration logo, written in Hausa, as 'The one who cares for trees will not be hungry.' For the majority of Nigeriens who live a tenuous existence in the desert margins, fighting to push back the ravages of desertification, this motto seemed perfectly apt.

Total distance: 5580 kilometres

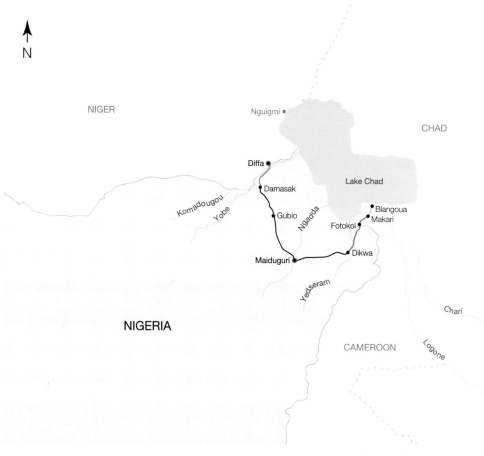

N

NIGER

Nguigmi •

CHAD

Diffa •

Lake Chad

Damasak •

Gubio •

Komadougou

Yobe

Ngadda

Blangoua
•
Makari

Fotokol •

Maiduguri •

Dikwa

Yedseram

Chari

NIGERIA

CAMEROON

Logone

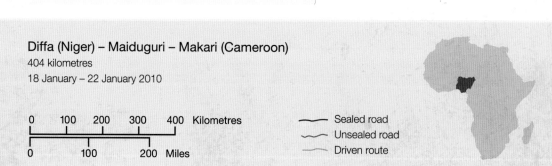

Diffa (Niger) – Maiduguri – Makari (Cameroon)
404 kilometres
18 January – 22 January 2010

| 0 | 100 | 200 | 300 | 400 | Kilometres |

| 0 | 100 | | 200 | Miles |

——— Sealed road
～～～ Unsealed road
——— Driven route

6

AROUND LAKE CHAD – THE SAHEL'S VANISHING JEWEL

Diffa (Niger) - NIGERIA - Lake Chad (Cameroon)

The unmaintained highway between Dikwa and Ngala. It was quicker to cycle across the adjacent floodplain

Reaching Lake Chad was always meant to be both a focal point and a turning point of the expedition. The once-huge lake, which is draining much faster than the natural rate, is almost at the geographical centre of Africa and in the heart of the Sahel – the borders of Niger, Nigeria, Chad and Cameroon meet here. It is the last remnant of a string of lakes which once ran all the way from the Air Mountains to the north-east near Agadez and which gradually dried up over the last 11,000 years.

There were two options to travel around the lake to reach Cameroon. My original plan had been to cycle through Chad to the capital, N'Djamena, and then on to Cameroon but this would have included about 600 kilometres of straight sand. The region was lawless and bandits could have attacked us at any point, especially as we would have been slow-moving targets. Cycling through the Borno region in the far north-east of Nigeria certainly wasn't recommended, according to the government warning list, but according to trustworthy local advice, this was the better option. Super-Ali sorted out our Nigerian security contacts and John consulted with them both before we left Diffa, for our own peace of mind.

Our instructions were that we should be fine, but to call them if we had any concerns.

Diffa was the end of the line for us in Niger. From there we crossed the Komadugu-Yobe River which, when it rains, flows into Lake Chad. The river demarcates the border with Nigeria. The border crossing was a minor one and guards on both sides were very friendly. Nigerians speak English, so conversing with them was much easier for us, even with their distinctive accents. The guards told us that the first 35 kilometres to Damasak along the sandy tracks that run parallel to the river would be impossible on a bike so I prepared my mind for a struggle. But although it was rough and sandy riding, there was enough hard-packed ground for me to get by. Turning south, I finally got to enjoy a decent tailwind; this was only the third day during the whole journey where I had the wind at my back. I was able to generate enough momentum to get through the soft sections and made good time to Damasak and the tarmac.

Damasak seemed to be populated by swarms of children, whom I thought should have been at school when we arrived mid-morning. With 152 million people, half of West Africa's population, Nigeria is the most populous African country. It has by far the largest economy in West Africa, mostly due to the exploitation of its massive oil reserves. Almost anything made in West Africa is made in Nigeria and exported to neighbouring countries and beyond. A former British colony, Nigeria's biggest trade partners are Britain and the US.

❋

Nigeria's far north-east is a hub where the three contriving extremes at the root of the Sahel's main problems – extreme poverty, extremes in climate and extreme ideologies – intersect. The prime source of instability, particularly in the Borno region, is the Islamic militant group Boko Haram. Loosely translated from Hausa, Boko Haram means 'Western education is forbidden.' Its fundamentalist followers are said to be influenced by the Qu'ranic phrase, 'Anyone not governed by what Allah has revealed is among the transgressors.' The group's enemies are anyone, Christian, Muslim or otherwise, who takes part in any political or social activity associated with Western society; this includes the Nigerian government. Any person who votes, wears Western-style clothing or receives a secular (government) education is at risk of being killed or punished by Boko Haram.

The organisation was formed in 2002 in Maiduguri (Borno's capital) by a charismatic Muslim cleric named Mohammed Yusuf. He set up a religious complex, including a school and a mosque, the school attracting poor, vulnerable Muslims from across Nigeria and neighbouring countries. The group's political goal is to create an Islamic state and the school became a recruiting ground for young *jihadis* to fight the government. In 2009, six months before we arrived at the border, Maiduguri erupted after a series of attacks on government and police buildings. Shoot-outs in the streets killed hundreds of people and thousands more fled the city. Yusuf was captured, executed by police and his body paraded on TV – a sure way of embedding hatred in the bellies of remaining Boko Haram members.

North-eastern Nigeria is the nation's poorest region. Illiteracy is widespread and as a result, it has become a breeding ground for groups with similarly fanatical religious ideals. Many analysts believe the threat of Boko Haram will only disappear if the Nigerian government manages to reduce the region's acute poverty and build an education system that gains the support of local Muslims. Knowledge can dissolve ignorance and misunderstanding and, subsequently, erode the power of Boko Haram, al-Qaida in the Maghreb (AQIM), al-Shabab and other extremist groups.

This volatile situation was the reason why I had originally planned to give north-eastern Nigeria a wide berth. There were also reports that corruption was rife amongst the police and that there was banditry. In order to minimise the likelihood of a robbery or worse, our strategy was to pass through to Cameroon as quickly as possible: the longer we stayed in this region the more chance there was of something going wrong. We consequently travelled closely together, especially through the police and customs posts stationed at the entrance and exit of each village. In between towns, John kept a much tighter rein on me: the vehicle was never more than 10 kilometres or half an hour away, whereas normally I might spend many hours alone. Heading south towards Maiduguri, although we were still in the Sahel the land was more prosperous, with better tree cover and pastures for grazing. This is where farmers from Niger drive their cattle when there is not enough to eat on their land.

Leaving Maiduguri's city limits

On the outskirts of Maiduguri I was struck by the number of different signs advertising evangelistic and fundamentalist Christian religions, each faith competing for new followers. Searching for accommodation, we came across a Christian hotel which did not permit two people of the same sex to share a room, such was the level of its homophobia! (We didn't stay there.) As we'd heard there might still be a curfew in the city we made sure we were safe and sound in a hotel by dark. Everything seemed calm though.

Maiduguri, a city of just over one million people, was quite different from any of the other West African cities we'd stayed in. All around were Western influences which would have riled the members of Boko Haram. Maiduguri had more business and manufacturing activity, an abundance of fast food places, and the streets were abuzz with motorbikes. The markets were excellent, supplying the largest range of produce we had seen. On closer inspection, however, many of the operations were failing – infrastructure, supplies, services. The streets were filthy, the internet cafe operated at a slow drip, similarly the power and water worked sporadically in our hotel and, of the numerous service stations in this petroleum-rich state, John struggled to find even one that had fuel to sell.

From Maiduguri we turned the corner and headed north-east towards Lake Chad and the most northerly border crossing into Cameroon at Ngala. This meant pushing directly back into the headwind. On the half-day ride to Dikwa I noticed that not only were there all the usual police and customs checks but groups of armed men in vehicles marked with 'Flush II' were regularly stationed along the roadside. Generally they stopped us but were friendly, emphasising that they were there to protect us. It was explained that if we had tried to use the road two or three years before, we would have almost certainly been robbed or attacked. 'Operation Flush' is a government crackdown to 'flush out' banditry and extreme groups such as Boko Haram. Apparently the original Operation Flush didn't work but Flush II was a success. With no tree cover to screen our campsite from the busy road, we made friends with the customs officials near Dikwa. Camped just behind their station, we were guaranteed 24-hour surveillance by the guards.

✻

A few kilometres out of Maiduguri we entered a deadpan flat landscape. The waters of 'Mega Chad,' once an inland sea, would have extended over these fields. The area immediately to Maiduguri's north-east is

Jere Bowl, originally a swampland fed by the Ngadda River. The Ngadda, Yedseram and Komadugu-Yobe are Nigeria's three principal rivers which used to supply about 10 per cent of Lake Chad's water. The flow of each river has been manipulated by dams and irrigation schemes, many poorly engineered and managed, so now it is much reduced. For example, the Ngadda's flow was halted in 1988 with the construction of the Alau Dam, with the intention of supplying Maiduguri with water and irrigating the Jere Bowl. The dam has never been very effective

Pushing hard over the ancient bed of sand and clay that was Mega Chad. This was my preferred route, a faster option to the original dilapidated highway (DH)

because it was built over what was once Mega Chad's sandy beach. Now much of the reservoir's volume is lost to seepage. As usual, it is the local farmers who shoulder the burden of the consequences: their thriving rice, wheat, fishing and pastoral businesses were badly affected. As they can no longer count on the seasonal inundation of floodwaters they now have to make do with the unreliable rainfall to grow lesser crops on the treeless, wind-blasted plains.

The main international route is now a thoroughfare only used by locals

I had mistakenly assumed that the A3 between Maiduguri and Ngala would at least be bitumen all the way, as the map depicted it as a major highway and because it was a thoroughfare for the many large trucks delivering goods between Nigeria, Cameroon and Chad. Up to Dikwa the road had been quite acceptable but on the eastern side of town it deteriorated to hopeless, gaping potholes gradually merging until the tarmac had worn away completely. All that was left of the road, built up above the flatlands to avoid the seasonal flooding, was the ridge where it had once been and the concrete kerbs that outlined the tarmac strip. Mostly it was impossible to cycle or drive on it. Ironically, on a surface designed to encourage the flow of international trade, the only people who used the highway were local pastoralists and impoverished farmers. At one stage we watched a herd of about one hundred cattle with enormous horns pass along the raised avenue. The lead cowboy serenaded the beasts as he walked by playing a traditional two-stringed lute called a *kontigi*. Given the size of their horns, it made good sense to attempt to keep the cattle docile.

A cowboy serenades his herd, leading them up the embankment of the old main road

Mostly we followed unmade tracks on either side of the road, dust from the traffic and wind so thick at times I struggled to see. We paused for lunch beneath some rare shade. Adjacent to us a network of dry irrigation canals extended across the desolate plain. Two girls from the nearby village, out collecting dung to burn for fuel, came to see what we were up to. With no trees left to use for firewood and no oil available, they were obviously hungry so we gave them some of our food. They sat under a tree and demolished every last morsel.

One of the girls out collecting dung. She is standing over a dry irrigation channel beside the alternative highway

We had been unable to obtain our Cameroon visas in the usual way (in any of the preceding countries we had travelled through) but fortunately, after a long-winded process over preceding weeks, Nerice, our Cameroon contact, had managed to secure them. She emailed them to a fellow travel agent, David, from Maroua in northern Cameroon. David then enlisted a guide, Martin, to travel to the border, a 400-kilometre journey, with a photocopy of the documents. I had been coordinating all this in Maine-Soroa and Maiduguri, and then by satellite phone as we neared the border. Miraculously, just as officials were stamping us out of Nigeria, Martin arrived in Ngala. A consular administrator had somehow omitted John's passport number from his visa, which added to the tension. Martin more than proved his worth negotiating our way into Cameroon with photocopies of visas with incomplete details. We had no trouble at all, even though Cameroon officials are notorious for being difficult. We crossed the north-east corner of Nigeria in three-and-a-half days without any incidents.

✤

The road on the Cameroon side was a bumpy dry-weather thoroughfare. Every so often there would be a rain barrier gate to prevent traffic from passing and destroying the road when it was wet. The theory was good but, judging by the state of the surface – which was sculpted into a continuum of choppy waves through heavy vehicles using it before the mud was dry enough – these barriers were largely ignored. By evening I had cycled to Makari village at the Lake Chad turn-off. We then drove the 50 kilometres on a minor road up to Blangoua, the only way to see the lake from Cameroon. With Chad being just across the Chari River to the east and Nigeria only a few kilometres to the west, this is a very sensitive region, especially as there is an on-going border dispute with Nigeria. Having Martin with us was very important in these parts – he knew the processes and how to deal with tricky officials. There were forms to fill out, papers to sign and fees to pay. It all took time, but patience was rewarded in the end.

It was essential to visit Lake Chad to learn about the state of the Sahel's beating heart. We set off on a powered boat up the Chari River, the eastern bank of which was actually Chad.

Bororo man

Bororo woman

Firstly we were taken to an island in the river to meet a group of Bororo people. The Bororo are nomadic cattle herders, related to the Fulani, whose lives revolve around ensuring their cattle have enough to eat. These people had migrated from Niger to the fertile shores of Lake Chad to escape the dry seasons. The lake's environment was a real departure from the parched windswept plains we had been travelling through. Its waters transform the landscape. The leafy riverbanks supported a series of vegetable gardens whose produce was grown for local consumption and export.

The boat ride to the lake took a couple of hours, passing small villages, fishermen, checking in at a police outpost. Dense vegetation gradually merged with the reedy wetlands and eventually the river flowed into the lake. The jewel of the Sahel was not spectacular, more a murky aquamarine than a sparkling sapphire, the vast expanse of open water melding seamlessly with the horizon. Still, I was pleased to simply be there – our target for more than three months. Lake Chad may have looked immense from our perspective but in fact is a shadow of the inland sea it once was. NASA satellite images show that the surface area has shrivelled 90 per cent since the 1960s, for reasons including climate change, population pressure and poor water resource management, and a lack of rain has meant less flow. At the same time, more people than previously are drawn to the lake to eke out a living, like the Bororo.

In response to the 1970s droughts, the Cameroon government built the Maga Dam on the Logone River, the Chari's principal tributary. The plan was to improve food security in Cameroon's far north with new irrigation schemes but in reality it served to cut off much of the water supply to the lake. As the Chari/Logone

Export harvest, Lake Chad

Made it to the lake with Martin, Dan and a local guide

rivers contribute 90 per cent of Lake Chad's water, this displeases Cameroon's neighbours. The Lake Chad Basin currently supports almost 30 million people in the four countries whose borders intersect within it. The Sahel's heart is in critical health and stabilising its condition requires a concerted effort and cooperation from all sides.

Total distance: 5984 kilometres

Lake Chad to Yaoundé

2218 kilometres
23 January – 18 February 2010

| 0 | 100 | 200 | 300 | 400 | Kilometres |

| 0 | 100 | | 200 | Miles |

Sealed road
Unsealed road
Driven route

7
AFRICA IN MINIATURE

Lake Chad to Yaoundé (Cameroon)

In Librou, a Koma village in the foothills of
the Atlantika mountains, the chief's wife still
wears a traditional girdle of leaves known
as an *arama*

Tourist brochures promote Cameroon as 'Africa in miniature' because it contains the full complement
of climatic zones, from the near-desert Sahel around Lake Chad to savannah, mountains, coastal and
dense tropical rainforest. Due to its geographical location at the hub of the continent, where the desert
graduates into the tropics, Cameroon's environs have always been a meeting point of cultures – for
10,000 years at least.

The original inhabitants lived in the south. These people belonged to ethno-linguistic groups
whose members were generally short in stature and who were collectively known as 'Pygmies.' In the
extreme north around Lake Chad, the most significant early culture was that of the Sao people who
migrated from either the Nile Valley or the Bilma region (in northern Niger). Cameroon's modern-day
borders envelop a diverse cultural package where 286 different recorded languages are spoken.

Even Cameroon's colonial history is a hotchpotch. The Portuguese first ventured to its coastline
in the fifteenth century, sailing up the Wouri River which they named the Rio dos Camarões, meaning
'River of Prawns', and it is from this that the country's name is derived. The coast was frequented over the

next two centuries by Dutch, Portuguese and British slave traders. As a result of 'the Scramble for Africa', the protectorate of Kamerun was allotted to Germany and then after the First World War the country was further segmented into French and British colonial administrations. In order to reflect such diversity our plan was to explore a convoluted path through Cameroon from the shores of Lake Chad, along its mountainous spine to Mount Cameroon on the coast, then head east through the largest city, Douala, to the capital, Yaoundé. We would finally venture out to Bertoua in the south-east to meet the Baka, some of the first inhabitants of the rainforests.

When organising the journey through Cameroon, I learned that there is a cultural divide between the north and south of the country. The general perception of the southerners is that the regions north of N'Gaoundéré are a more hazardous place to travel, with problems consistent with the adjacent Sahel nations of Chad, Niger and Nigeria. This view was consolidated on my first day pedalling south to the town of Waza, when I encountered two United Nations peacekeeping convoys. The first, a trail of possibly a hundred shiny new vehicles, was being deployed to oversee unrest in Chad. A smaller band was heading to mediate a border dispute with Nigeria. Martin, an experienced guide, was like our insurance policy. He knew the lie of the land and where the sensitive areas were; he negotiated with officials and minimised the possibility of encounters with bandits. Luckily, he was also a fountain of local knowledge, allowing us to make the most of our time in the Extreme North and North regions.

I resumed from Makari village, continuing the struggle from where we left off on rugged 'dry-weather' clay and sand surfaces. To save time, the boys drove ahead, diverting into Kousséri, the major market town on the Chari River and the border with Chad, to collect Zdenek Kratky, our new camera operator. This was Zdenek's first experience of Africa and, fresh from the depths of a freezing European winter, he must have wondered what planet he'd arrived on. Against the billiard table-flat backdrop of the Waza-Logone floodplain, this tall beanpole of a man cut an alien, ghostly-white figure. This was our first meeting too. Back in Mali, when it was evident that we needed to change camera operators I turned to successful documentary film-maker Claudio von Planta, whom we had met in London. Claudio provided valuable advice and the eventual solution. He found both Stuart and Zdenek, the latter about to return

to his native Czech Republic after living in London, trusting us enough to commit at least three months to the expedition, maybe longer. From the outset it was evident that Zdenek was a consummate professional with a creative passion for taking both moving and still images. When filming, he would shadow his subject, like a cat stalking its prey, aiming to document the action without affecting it and waiting patiently for exactly the right moment. His quiet enthusiasm meant he slotted into the team causing barely a ripple.

Horse antelopes, Waza National Park

North Cameroon is little spoilt by tourism, which for us meant we could enjoy the many sights I had lined up without too many hassles. In Waza National Park where we spent dawn and dusk the next day, we rarely encountered anyone else. Against a backdrop of two distinctive granite hills and open savannah and bush we spotted giraffes, horse antelopes, an ostrich, deer, warthogs, jackals and many birds.

Sixty kilometres south of Waza, at Mora, the plains ended abruptly as the parched, craggy Mandara Mountains gradually filled my viewfinder. Since the start of the journey we had been travelling along the relatively level Sahel and so the first sign of real mountains had a spectacular impact. I set off alone from Mora, leaving the team in the market town trying to send emails – a process which usually took hours thanks to an impossibly slow and intermittent internet service. Since eastern Niger, we'd encountered all sorts of problems connecting with the outside world, this area seemingly a black hole as far as communications went. In the evenings I would draft messages in advance, so that if an opportunity arose, John or Dan could at least send these off without me wasting valuable cycling time.

The dirt road through the Mandara Mountains over the next couple of days was to become a personal favourite. From Mora, the track, which was sandy at times, wove along the base of the stark granite range, passing through a string of lively villages. Occasionally I watched Fulani herdsmen driving their stock through the bush and across my path, oblivious to the fact there was even a road there. Cycling off the main tarmac strip, I felt a more intimate connection with my surroundings and, now that I was heading south, the wind was at my back.

The flat road came to an abrupt end at the picturesque town of Koza (a further 60 kilometres from Mora) nestled in at the base of the mountains. Its square and cylindrical mud houses and granaries with conical thatched roofs reminded me very much of those in the Dogon country – without the tourists. From Koza the only way was up, the next seven kilometres ascending into the mountains like a stairway – steep inclines and switchbacks were engineered into the exquisitely terraced landscape. This was the first real test requiring considerable climbing mettle and legs of steel. Normally when doing such severe climbs I prefer to keep my head down and concentrate on the rhythm and effort rather than look up at the task above but here this would have been sacrilege. Although I often had to focus on the path just ahead of my front wheel to pick my way through the stones and crevasses, I gazed out when I could afford to. The views over the plains below and the ancient terraces that sculpt the slopes beyond were inspirational. At my slow pace, the roadside was like a rolling movie set: people working their gardens, women carrying calabash gourdes or heavy containers of water on their heads, kids returning from school. My presence tended to put most conversations on pause and elicit plenty of bemused, if not friendly, acknowledgements.

Stone terracing and intensive land use: a scene from my 'rolling movie set' climbing out of Koza

The people of the northern Mandara Mountains are collectively known as Northern Montagnards. There are over 70 different ethnic groups living in this small locality of northern Cameroon and north-eastern Nigeria. The Montagnards originally settled there because the mountains offered better sanctuary from Islamic slavers from the desert and because the region receives higher rainfall than the Sahelian plains below. Land use has to be intensive to support the densely populated slopes. The terraces and stonework that have been continually maintained and extended for at least 400 years have not only a functional purpose but also spiritual significance. The traditionally animistic people of the region work to a thirteen-month lunar calendar – each month starts with the new moon. As this does not exactly fit with the 365-day solar year, they modify their calendar according to the changing seasons, particularly to ensure harmony with the coming of the first rains. If the rains are early, then the thirteenth month can be cancelled, and if they are late, the first month may be repeated. We were travelling through in the eleventh month, *Te Yawal*, when the women were predominantly threshing grains and the men mainly building or repairing houses, cutting wood or making mats.

At Mokolo we camped beside the hotel but still patronised their facilities. This was convenient for Martin so he could watch the football (soccer). His country may be characterised by a patchwork of time-honoured traditions and cultures but everyone passionately embraces football – it is truly a religion here. Football, especially following the success of the Cameroon Lions in the 1991 World Cup, has an important cross-cultural unifying effect. The African Cup was in its final stages when we joined Martin and his countrymen in the packed bar – they love their beer just as much as football – and I could feel the waves of tension and anxiety. Much to Martin's dismay, Cameroon lost in extra time to the eventual victors, Egypt.

Ancient volcanic plugs at Roumsiki. A view across to Nigeria, here about three kilometres away

Winding our way south through the homeland of the Kapsiki people to Roumsiki (also known as Rhumsiki), we were treated to the geological landscape for which the area is most famous. The skyline is dominated by the remnants of an ancient volcano field, the cathedral-like lava plugs protruding spectacularly above all else. Roumsiki, Martin explained, was named so after a man called *Siki* led his people to safety from the invading Arabs. To survive they hid in caves in the mountains, or *roum*.

The road runs very close to the Nigerian border at times and, according to Martin, much smuggling goes on. Motorbikes loaded to the hilt with cheap fuel from Nigeria would often pass. Martin insisted that we divert away from this road for the final 100 kilometres to Garoua because of the potential dangers some of these smugglers posed. We turned east for 60 kilometres to Guider, then back on tarmac again we diverted to explore the little-known Gorges de Kola, impressive chasms carved out of an ancient lava flow. The brand-new highway took us through Garoua, capital of Cameroon's North Region.

The land between Garoua on the Bénué River and N'Gaoundéré in the Adamawa Plateau or Central Highlands was undulating but not so spectacular, and generally used to grow the standard millet, maize, sorghum, groundnuts and beans. For a significant stretch of the way, the highway formed the western boundary for the Bénoué National Park, a UNESCO-designated Biosphere Reserve. As with the giraffe zone in Niger, this is a critical reserve where there is a focus on integrating conservation, development and scientific research to sustainably manage the ecosystem. The western fringe was characterised by tall savannah grasses and native woodland ... we had definitely left the Sahel behind. The next time we would reach these latitudes would be in Ethiopia and Somalia at the finish of the expedition. Here, as with other reserves we passed through in central Cameroon, the locals burn the grass regularly to keep down ground fuel and encourage fresh growth for the animals to graze. This prevents wildfires causing excessive damage to people and wildlife. Along the Bénué River and nearing the Central Highlands, the land was more productive – market stalls, laden with vegetables and cotton, were strung out along the roadside. It was the first time I had seen raw balls of cotton for sale – sold like popcorn in small containers.

✳

At the village of Gouna, about halfway between Garoua and N'Gaoundéré, we turned off for the Atlantika Mountains, 100 kilometres to the west. Martin was primarily taking us to meet the Koma people. The Koma, or 'lost people' in Kanuri language, are now a small ethnic minority who, like the Montagnards, originally fled into the mountains to escape from slavery and to protect their animist religion from Islam imposed by the peoples of the north. They remained 'in hiding' during the times of the early European slavers and colonial tax collectors, preserving their simple way of life. The women, Martin explained, still wear only a girdle of leaves, renewed daily and known as an *arama*, to cover their private parts. The men, however, now rarely wear their traditional attire – loins of leather or local cotton known as a *bentin*. Many Koma are gradually integrating with the outside world and its influences while others continue to cling to their culture living on the mountain slopes.

Zdenek hitching a ride with the Pastor of Poli

The road was incredibly rough. At Poli, after 36 kilometres and two hours of driving, we stopped to visit the Baptist pastor, a friend of Martin's. Here we dropped off luggage which we didn't need for the next two days of walking, to reduce the load for the Land Rover. Continuing west, we bisected the Faro National Park, occasionally catching a glimpse of a few baboons and warthogs. Finally, at last light, as we crossed the mighty Faro River, the Atlantika Mountains materialised as a spectacular but imposing wall, silhouetted by the sun's pink and violet afterglow. Wangai was the end of the line. Here we were welcomed by the village chief and crowded by many eager potential porters. While we could have skimped on using porters, we realised that this is an important source of income for them. We employed three along with a guide and set off early the next morning, one of the porters carrying an 18-kilogram bag of salt on his head. The Koma tend to still use a barter system rather than money, so Martin organised for us to take the salt, along with soap and matches as gifts, to present to the chief of the village where we were to stay that night.

We were led along a well-trodden path up the valley floor to Bimlerou Bas, a lowland village. The Koma who live here have a lifestyle that reflects their heritage – that being the Sahelian plains to the north from where they fled. They rely mostly on traditional cultivation and the raising of animals. As with the people of the Mandara Mountains, this was the time of year for harvesting and milling grains for the women, while the men were busy basket weaving, making repairs to their mud buildings and trading goods. People here traded produce regularly at the markets outside Wangai and had better access to schools, healthcare – and Christian missionaries.

The range itself, which rises to almost 2000 metres, straddles the Cameroon-Nigerian border. The Koma tuck themselves away in isolated communities on both sides of the frontier – the borderline to them is inconsequential. The higher into the mountains they live, the more isolated their existence and the less affected they are by the outside world. Our path steepened until we reached the protected enclave at the head of the valley and the community of Librou. The chief was ill when we arrived at around midday, so we were welcomed by other elders and the chief's wife. When Martin last visited seven years before, most Koma still did not wear clothes but now, with a stronger connection to the outside world via the missionaries and trekkers, nearly all were doing so. Only the chief's wife was attired traditionally when we turned up.

In Librou, and more so further up into the mountains, the Koma exist self-sufficiently. They grow and hunt all their food and possess a vast knowledge of how to use the natural vegetation for medicines. As the Koma are virtually cut-off from the outside world, this knowhow is essential for survival – they don't have access to healthcare and children don't go to school.

Sampling tiny wild figs, Bikeba (ZK)

Leaving the bulk of our gear in Librou in the foothills, we climbed the steep slopes to a tiny, more isolated community called Bikeba. Here few women wore modern clothes. When we arrived a man and a woman were up in a tree collecting wild figs. I tried the pea-sized fruit, which tasted like a normal dried fig but had a more intense flavour and had candied naturally, making it extra sweet. These Koma seem to live a very peaceful and uncomplicated lifestyle with sweeping 'penthouse suite' views over the valley.

When we returned down the slope to Librou, the women and girls were traditionally dressed in their *aramas* and preparing to perform some dances for us. A number were smoking pipes which I understood contained a native grass with mildly hallucinogenic qualities. Martin said that it was a great pleasure for the people to perform for outsiders. For us it was an honour and a privilege. Their enjoyment was certainly genuine, their excitement palpable: no pre-performance nerves here. The men kicked off the twilight performance, playing their handcrafted drums and flutes as the women stirred up the dust and encircled them, ululating. All of the women joined in, from the oldest grandmother to children and babies strapped to their mothers' backs. Young boys danced enthusiastically off to the side. By the end, the groups had all collaborated in a mass celebration of their culture. After the dancing Martin thanked them and we presented the gifts: salt, matches and soap. That night we erected our tents on the terraced land, washed in the nearby stream and slept in a very different 'fairytale world.'

Some of the older women smoked pipes containing mildly hallucinogenic native grasses in preparation for the performance

All ages were involved in the celebration

But this is a world not as idyllic as our short adventure revealed. Population and development statistics for the Koma are difficult to collate because births and deaths are not recorded. Without birth registration, they have no basic human rights in Cameroon society – no right to education or healthcare, and no justice. They are simply not in the system. Life expectancy is around forty-five years. A high child mortality rate (one source puts it at 70 per cent, but this I cannot confirm) is exacerbated by malnutrition, malaria and other diseases.

The Koma originally chose to live in the hills to escape slavery and protect their animistic beliefs but now they are at a crossroads. As the outside world comes to them – and this seems unavoidable in one way or another – they have to strike a balance between preserving their proud heritage

Koma women have their two front incisors extracted by their husbands – a traditional belief to help ensure fertility

and integrating with the foreign influences. For example, many Librou inhabitants have now converted to Christianity. To opt out completely would almost certainly mean cultural extinction; they will have

to evolve to adapt. As we set off back towards Wangai, some children passed us in a hurry to reach the village to go to church. We in turn greeted them with 'tika tika' – the only Koma words I learned, meaning 'hello'. I wondered what would be left of the culture in a few more years.

On the return journey from Wangai, Martin suggested we stay at the Catholic Mission at Fignolé, about halfway back to Gouna and the main road. Just before the mission we stopped in a small village named Godé as there was an interesting-looking market in progress and we needed some supplies. Some of the locals became upset at Zdenek's filming and Martin

John and Martin on the return trek from the Atlantika Mountains

had to intervene to smooth things over with the chief. I followed to introduce myself, apologise and present him with an expedition badge. A little courtesy goes a long way. The chief signed his name as Sa Majesté (His Majesty) Haman Bangari, the Lamido of Godé. As the Lamido, he is the traditional ruler, in charge of fifty villages around the Godé district. He proceeded to show me photographs of himself in full regalia. Formalities over, the Lamido began to open up, explaining that he and his people were feeling very emotional as two of his nephews had drowned the previous day while drawing water from the river.

He then proceeded to pour out all the problems of the community – water, health, education. The children wouldn't have drowned fetching water if the village water pump hadn't broken six months previously, he said. Now everyone had to find water, often dirty, sometimes several kilometres out of town, and carry it to their homes. 'Why can't you fix the pump?' (Heard that one before?) The Lamido said the government would not give the people any money to do so and that they are too poor to raise the funds needed. A teacher by profession, the Lamido is a well-educated man and he genuinely loves his people but like the academics of Oualata and others whom I had already met during the journey, he

could not see how to fix a simple hand pump. He needs help to learn how the people could repair the pump; as the saying goes, 'Teach a man to fish...'

Other issues facing his community, he told me, are that there is only one headmaster for fifty schools, making the Lamido's task impossible, and that there is no hospital or even a health centre for 20,000 people. On top of all this, there is little infrastructure, and no telephone or internet services in the area. We discussed how the local community might create extra income but he couldn't envisage how they could trade their way out of the poverty they are trapped in.

Raising spirits. Lamido of Godé (photo: Z Kratky)

Martin explained that in regions such as this, near the national borders, people tend to be struggling much more than in central-southern Cameroon. Improving infrastructure is also important but it seems that the 11 million Euros spent by the European Union on building the Faro River Bridge could have been put to better use by looking after the people of the region. Not for the first time during the journey I felt helpless, and could only promise the Lamido that I would try to publicise the plight of his people. At the conclusion of our chance encounter he at least seemed in better spirits.

The Fignolé Catholic Mission was just five kilometres further on, set in an idyllic location at the base of the mountains beside Fignolé village. The missionaries there help to educate and provide support for the locals. We were greeted by Sister Agnes (originally from Canada) and Sister Laure (from the Republic of Congo), and later we briefly met a Polish missionary who was busy building wells in the region. When asked about the pump at Godé, his opinion was that the

Sister Laure de Fignolé, originally from the Republic of Congo

problem was so simple that the people should be able to source the small amount of money required to fix the pump. He didn't show much sympathy for the Lamido of Godé.

We revisited the pastor in Poli to collect our belongings and then it was back to Gouna. Here we farewelled Martin. He was such a terrific guide and friend that he continued to give us advice by phone from his home in Maroua over the coming weeks. I did a quick 60 kilometres that afternoon and then another full day of cycling, including an 800-metre climb on to the Adamawa Plateau to reach N'Gaoundéré.

✳

The Adamawa Plateau stretches the breadth of the country from the Nigerian to the Central African Republic borders, forming a geographical divide between north and south. With an average elevation of 1100 metres, the ancient volcanic ranges are the source of almost all Cameroon's major river systems: the Logone that feeds Lake Chad, the Bénue and Faro that drain into the Niger River (in Nigeria) and the Mbam, Djerem and Lom, all tributaries of the Sanaga River that enters the Bight of Bonny on Cameroon's coast. But the Adamawa Plateau provides more than just a geographical division. It is the country's most thinly populated region and is the least impacted by human development. It is also a land forgotten by the national government and so has little infrastructure: poorly maintained roads, inadequate amenities (except in a handful of principal towns), too few schools and health centres. Literacy runs at 20 per cent when, nationally, over three-quarters of Cameroon's 20 million citizens can read and write. This is partly due to the same cultural factors we'd seen across the Sahel. The population is comprised largely of Fulani or Bororo, nomads who rarely send their children to school and generally marry off their daughters by early puberty. The incidence of HIV/AIDS runs at 17 per cent when the national average is 5.6 per cent.

In N'Gaoundéré I got no sense at all of these problems. We stayed at the aptly named 'Nice Hotel,' which was clean, had motivated staff, decent food and was good value all-round – rare among our experiences of African town hotels to this point. In fact, from my perspective, N'Gaoundéré was refreshingly well-organised: the streets were swept and generally rubbish-free, the stores were well-stocked, cafes and bars were busy – even the internet was reasonable (all relative though).

It is also the transport hub linking the north and south. To the north, a well-maintained bitumen highway extends as far as N'Djamena in Chad, while Yaoundé and the southern ports are connected to N'Gaoundéré by the Trans-Cameroon Railway. As the railway is the principal method of travel south of N'Gaoundéré, the roads are neglected and unpaved and most travellers either take the train or domestic flights. For us there were two road options. The route to the south-east through Bertoua is a little shorter but it is also the main truck route connecting to the Central African Republic and, by all reports, in appalling condition. We chose the westerly route through Tibati and Banyo – still frequented by heavy lorries transporting goods to and from the port at Douala, the west country and Nigeria. The attraction was a visit to the English-speaking North-West region and Mount Cameroon on the coast.

Initially I had difficulties even finding the main road. As usual there were no signs to direct me to the route to Tibati. Eventually, after missing the turn-off and asking several truck drivers and moto-taxis, I found the unremarkable gravel road. The name Adamawa Plateau suggests that the uplands are a level table-top but I soon discovered they were anything but even. Here, altitude ranges between 900 and 1600 metres.

The first section was well-made and it was easy to avoid the worst of the washboard surface. But from about 100 kilometres out of N'Gaoundéré the road condensed into a series of steep ascents and descents, camouflaged by the dense temperate rainforest. Tiny settlements were tucked away off the road, their earthen houses characterised by high-pitched thatched roofs designed to repel the frequent downpours. The more vertical the terrain, however, the more hazardous the track surface. Gully erosion,

potholes, embedded granite boulders and loose stones were masked by a thick blanket of bulldust, sometimes 30-40 centimetres deep. Bulldust is dust as fine as talcum powder caused by constant heavy traffic on dirt roads. On these mountain tracks it is the curse of drivers and motorcyclists – and this cyclist – on all steep slopes.

At the 48-kilometre mark on day two out of N'Gaoundéré, I was at the start of a particularly sharp descent when my front wheel struck a large rock concealed beneath the dust. Unable to brake effectively, I came flying off, diving head first at speed. I lay there for a few moments

Dr John cleaning out the main wound (photo: Z Kratky)

The dust could be knee-deep in patches, concealing stones, potholes and gutters

assessing the damage – no broken bones, the bike was okay. My helmet saved my head and my gloves protected my hands but I had badly grazed my elbow in particular. I pulled to the side to wait for the team. Five minutes later a motorcyclist came careering down the slope, crashing in the exact same spot. I raced over and helped him up. He too was badly grazed and suffering from shock but his motorbike had sustained more serious damage. When the Land Rover arrived about fifteen minutes later Doctor John, ably assisted by Nurse Dan, did a great job cleaning my wounds, trimming away loose, lacerated skin and patching me up. The key concern was to prevent infection. The fall dashed my confidence and over the next few days on these appalling roads I approached each descent feeling so brittle I could have been made of glass. The accident was a reminder that one mistake, one break in concentration, and it could be all over. I had to ride to survive. It was a wake-up call, heightening my focus on the task at hand.

Road conditions deteriorated on the 115-kilometre track from Tibati to Banyo; there were even steeper inclines, worse bulldust and heavier truck traffic. Hidden beneath the dust was a surface riddled with giant potholes (approximately three metres wide by a metre or so deep), rocks and corrugations. To see how some of the massive trucks, usually dangerously overloaded, negotiated these conditions was astounding – sometimes their wheels were entirely airborne. Drivers were on the whole very courteous; some would actually stop and wait for me to slip by, and I would pause for others to pass at times.

Dust particles lingered in the still atmosphere of the dense forest making it impossible to see or to breathe without pulling my scarf over my mouth and nose. The fine powder made a mess of everything, especially my bike: the drive train was often submerged in dust as I pedalled. In these conditions I could not use oil for the working parts because it would immediately cake everything. I carried a special 'dry lube' for this type of situation but the dust was so bad it would 'wash away' within half an hour and would have to be reapplied. Most of the time I simply kept grinding away as if there were sandpapers coating the working parts. Poor bike. I came off a few more times, once landing directly on the

Waiting for the team on the outskirts of Banyo. The Adamawa region has Cameroon's highest incidence of AIDS at 17 per cent and signs like these, educating about AIDS prevention were commonplace in major towns and villages

injured elbow, but there was no more major damage. It was a war of attrition that I felt I had deservedly won by the time my bike grated and groaned into Banyo.

From Banyo the road was still gravel but of better quality, the many steep sections sealed to prevent dust and erosion problems. At the village of Mayo Darle I stopped at the primary school to watch the kids marching off to their morning exercise classes. Each class passed in formation, singing marching songs. The older students sang in French but I noticed that the nursery children, who were being strictly drilled outside their classroom, were chanting in English, 'Happy, happy new day, happy, happy new day...'

I spoke to the head teacher, Evita Sumna, who was in charge of the 760 students. She explained that due to pressure on school facilities, classes were divided into morning and afternoon shifts. The drills installed discipline, she said, necessary for teachers to control their large classes – usually of about fifty students. There were major difficulties in enticing teachers to work away from the cities, and so Evita's staff were overworked and underpaid. Teachers earn about $US20 per day, which is little incentive in these parts.

A short pause at Sabongari, last break for the day before arriving in Ngu (photo: Z Kratky)

✻

Soon after Mayo Darle we descended from the plateau into the sultry cauldron of the lowlands. At Nyamboya we turned off the busy gravel Trans-Atlantic Highway and across the plains towards the high mountains of the North-West Region. I worked my way through some beautiful stratified rainforest literally crawling with life. There was so much diversity here. Coffee plants flourished beneath the protection of the canopy, and raw coffee beans were laid out on mats to dry in front of many village houses. Tropical fruits such as mangoes, papayas, avocadoes and bananas grew in abundance.

When locals from Sabongari, Ngu and near the foot of the massif learned that I was to cycle from Ngu at 700 metres, up over 2060 metres to Ndu, many were lost for words and simply shook their heads in disbelief. This was my first proper high mountain pass and by the time the Great Wall was in front of me, I understood their reservations – at the first hairpin corner a sign warned of a 20 per cent gradient. I frequently struggled to turn the pedals over the next eight kilometres up to the village of Sop, and at times had to pull so hard on the handlebars that I had a job keeping the front wheel on the ground. Occasionally vehicles laboured past leaving sooty exhaust clouds lingering in their wake, and motorcyclists rolled downhill with their engines switched off to conserve fuel. My body had already taken a battering since N'Gaoundéré and was screaming out for a rest as I zigzagged back and forth across the steepest part of the road in an attempt to reduce the severity of the climb. I may have only been progressing at walking pace at times but the key to avoiding mental defeat was simply not to stop. By Sop, the plains were merely an undefinable misty green haze below. From there, the acute gradients eased as the path wound in steps and stairs through regular small communities. The volcanic soils appeared very fertile and the steep, terraced slopes produced all sorts of fruit and vegetables – available for sale at the roadside. At 2000 metres we arrived at a very different land. A patchwork of tea and eucalypt plantations appeared to thrive in a milder climate.

In one long ascent, we'd not only graduated from coffee to tea but also from French to English. By the time I reached the top, I switched from saying 'Bonjour' and 'Ça va?' to 'Hello' and 'Good morning.' People greeted me with a cheery 'Good morning' even if it was five o'clock in the afternoon! Officially Cameroon is a bilingual country. The North-West and South-West regions are Anglophone while the remaining eight regions are Francophone, in keeping with old colonial influences.

Other greetings that I initially did not pick up on but heard often were 'How na?' or 'Ha yu dey?' ('How are you'?). The unofficial language of Cameroon is *Kamtok*, a kind of Pidgin English, or in these parts, more a Pidgin 'Franglais'. *Kamtok* translates as either 'come talk' or 'Cameroon-talk'. Sometimes referred to as Cameroonian Creole, it is believed to have evolved from as far back as the fifteenth century when the Portuguese arrived. The language began as a means of the locals communicating with the various visiting Europeans and across their own native cultures. The semi-phonetic, English-based language also has influences borrowed from other European and West African languages. By the time the Germans arrived, *Kamtok* had become the lingua franca. Many strands have subsequently developed. For example, almost a century ago a Catholic version,

Asking for directions in Sonkalong near the base of the climb, where the language was starting to change from French to English (photo: Z Kratky)

Grafi Kamtok, a liturgical form of *Kamtok,* was devised by European missionaries to spread the Word. Today *Kamtok* is spoken by more than half the population and has an important place in enhancing communication between the dialects and across borders. The nomadic Bororo have their own version, understood wherever they graze and trade their livestock in Cameroon and Nigeria. Children learn *Kamtok* from their mothers at the same time as they are exposed to their own native tongue, usually before they learn French or English. *Kamtok* is used on university campuses, in political campaigns and in the spoken media as a way of communicating to the masses.

During the journey I had been amazed at the occurrence of eucalypt trees, native to my own country, but which have been introduced to all corners and climates across Africa, from Timbuktu to Lake Chad, Rwanda to Ethiopia. Here, and across the grassland region in the middle belt of Cameroon, German missionaries in the early 1900s had made extensive plantings of eucalypts. In the 1960s, plantations were boosted to compensate for the fall in coffee prices and with the aim of solving the problem of wood for fuel shortages. Prior to this introduction, fuel wood had become scarce and households were deficient in their only source of cooking fuel. The problem with the fast-growing eucalypts is that they are capable of draining water and nutrients from the soil in very large quantities and therefore tend to choke out any other crops or trees planted near them. They are now vermin here, and what was once considered a useful cash crop for both fuel wood and timber is regarded as the main reason why one-quarter of all standpipe taps in the area no longer supply water during the dry season. As a result, women have to walk many extra miles to collect water and to find productive land that they can farm. With the cooperation of traditional leaders, landowners and the government, projects are underway to fell many of the eucalypt plantations and replace them with native trees that in most instances are of more use to locals.

It was easy to see why the Brits were attracted to the North-West Region with its amenable climate and grow-anything soil. The centre of Ndu was unmistakably British colonial with rusting architecture, little tampered with since the Brits left fifty years ago. The broad, dusty main street was lined with tea-houses and trading cooperatives. Dispersed amongst these ramshackle relics of a bygone era, modern hotels and bars, restaurants and a service station stood out like white elephants. There was definitely some new money around.

Nearing Ndu the road is flanked by tea and eucalypt plantations
(photo: Z Kratky)

Judging by the street signs advertising various religions, God was all around too. The importance of religion in Cameroon, and in fact the whole of Africa, is nothing new, but now it is on the up. People in large numbers are converting to Christianity and Islam and there is a big revival in traditional practices. There are many conflicting figures, but roughly speaking, the continent has equal numbers of Muslims and Christians (about 400 million of each). In many instances, both these dominant religions have been overlapped and fused with traditional beliefs. It is estimated that Christianity is growing by 2.5 per cent annually, attributed mostly to the increasing popularity of evangelism. Muslim populations are expanding due to many influences, particularly with large investments coming from Saudi Arabia and as a result of the work of missionaries from the Indian subcontinent. Many Africans associate themselves with religious networks for purposes beyond strict religious practice – for social, political and economic reasons. Where people have experienced a traumatic past, have lost faith in their current political institutions and / or face an uncertain future, religion offers structure and security and instils a sense of belonging. The effects of religion in Africa are profound – for good and for bad – and cannot be ignored.

For most of the journey to this point we had travelled through Muslim-dominant countries, but arriving in the North-West Region of Cameroon it was Christianity that held sway. Baptists, Presbyterians, Catholics, evangelists and various offshoots of these creeds compete to recruit believers. In Ndu we stayed in the Baptist Mission on recommendation from Martin (our guide in northern Cameroon). Like all the missions we stayed in, it offered cheap, clean, secure accommodation – cheaper, though, if you were the 'right' religion. Here the tariffs were: 2000CFA ($US4) for Baptists, 3000CFA ($US6) for Christians and 4000CFA ($US8) for non-believers and Muslims!

At the start of the expedition, people would comment that clean-shaven Daniel could be the double of Chris Martin (from the band Coldplay), but walking through Ndu's market sporting his scraggly beard and hair, he was likened to Jesus. And then when Dan explained that he was a carpenter, I could see peoples' eyes just about popping out of their heads!

Cycling from Ndu through Kumbo to Bamenda, the capital of the North-West Region, there were two standout features – the lung-busting, bone-rattling terrain and the dominance of evangelical forms of Christianity. The landscape constantly oscillated between 1100 and 2200 metres in altitude and the bulldust was so bad on the descents that at times I had to walk the bike down to avoid further accidents. A lack of infrastructure is really holding back the region, whereas with decent paved roads they would be struggling to hold back the tourists. As usual, when the conditions test my physical boundaries, I focused on the beauty of my surroundings to remain positive. Here that part was simple: there were spectacular scenes for 360 degrees most of the time.

Tucking into some Ndu-style fries. 'Jesus' has the bananas (photo: Z Kratky)

Finding a secluded campsite in the populous productive high plains (50 kilometres before Bamenda) proved a challenge. Eventually we settled for a hilltop just above a small village near Ndop. As darkness encroached, so did the wending sounds of an evangelistic church service below, replete with brass band to awaken the spirits – ensuring that I remained awake too! The music meandered into the night, floating past us on the way to Heaven. By 3.00 a.m., it sounded like the euphoric all-night 'love in' with the Lord had reached its climax but when I awoke again to the clash of cymbals and resonating bass drums just before dawn, the celebration was still holding out. I wondered how the congregation could front up for a productive day's work as their modern economic doctrine demands. I was sure struggling.

❋

Just as suddenly as we had entered the English-speaking North-West Region, after another massive climb out of Bamenda we were abruptly back to French in Bafoussam. This time we'd gone from lunching at the Beverley Hills Cafe in Bamenda to indulging in a 'hungry cyclist' calorie bonanza at La Pâtisserie on the outskirts of Bafoussam. Finally, after ten days of relentless steep hills and appalling roads, it was down, down, down on the busy paved N5, out of the highlands through Bafang and Loum to virtually sea level, 100 per cent humidity and a constant 32 degrees Celsius.

We spent an incredibly clammy night camping beside a pineapple field near the forestry town of Loum, well secluded from the road. The farm workers were a little surprised to find us the following morning when they arrived for work – but they were very friendly and our presence didn't seem to interrupt their tight schedule. The pineapples were being cut and packed for export to France. They were to be transported within a few hours of being picked and would potentially be on French supermarket shelves the next day! The manager loaded us up with as many ripe pineapples as we could deal with; they were too ripe for export but perfect for eating immediately. When the team caught up to me later that morning carrying the pineapples, I gorged myself. The flesh was so juicy it was impossible to eat without making a mess – not that it concerned me too much. I was already drenched from cycling in extreme humidity so a sticky bath of pineapple juice only made a refreshing difference.

Pineapple farm, south of Bafoussam

By reaching the coastal lowlands of the Littoral Region we'd completed a full cross-section of the country. The wet tropical climate is characterised by higher rainfall than just about anywhere else in the world – almost four metres of rain is received each year. The intimate villages and slow-paced lifestyle of the regions to the north suddenly seemed another world away from the highly developed coastal plains. In the shadow of Mount Cameroon, the black volcanic soil supported a seemingly endless array of large-scale agriculture. Plantations of tea, rubber, bananas, papayas, paw paw, coconut and palm trees are big business here – often internationally owned. I took the existence of a garden centre as a sign of prosperity. So far on this journey I noticed most people only gardened in order to produce food but here they could also afford the time to grow plants to beautify their surroundings.

We had been doing so well through Cameroon that we had caught up time. Diverting from near Douala to Buea – the original German, then British, colonial capital – to climb Mount Cameroon was Dan's suggestion and an extra to the original plan. I thought this would be a great team-building exercise, a non-technical climb that we could all do together. For me, who had just done eleven days on the trot, it was never going to be a rest, more an active recovery session. The local Bakweri people call the highest peak of this live volcano, standing at 4090 metres, 'Mongo-mo-Lobo' or 'Mountain of Thunder', and the entire massif 'Mongo-mo-Ndemi' or 'Mountain of Greatness'. It is thought that Phoenician explorers witnessed the volcano erupt when they sailed by in about 450 BC.

Accompanying us up the mountain were our guide Peter, three porters and Charlie, a young New Zealander who had been travelling independently and whom we invited to join us. We chose to take the Guinness Route, the most direct and steepest path up the mountain. Being so close to the Equator (six degrees north), the mountain is of great scientific significance. The slopes are home to many endemic species and the distinctive climatic conditions make it a biodiversity hotspot. Our route bisected the three significant ecosystems – the tropical rainforest, savannah and alpine zones.

The climb started from virtually straight out of the back door of the mission where we stayed at about 1000 metres elevation. The first stage involved ascending through dense rainforest to Hut 1 (at 1900 metres). Grand ficus trees with ribboned buttress roots and draping epiphytic vines cocooned the well-worn track, the canopy filtering out direct sunlight and sealing in the moisture. The microclimate was so muggy that I was able to wring out my clothes during the first short break. Here Peter used his machete to demonstrate how he dug out cocoyams, one of the locals' staple root vegetables. About half an hour's climb from Hut 1 the forest ended abruptly and we entered the savannah zone. Exposed now to the elements, the wind chill was momentarily refreshing but then the cold set in and we wrapped ourselves in layers of protective clothing. Rising above the mist, we made an extremely steep ascent past the lone 'Magic Tree', the division point between two enchanted worlds. The tuft grasses made stable stepping stones amongst the loose volcanic rubble.

We reached Hut 2 (2860 metres), our overnight campsite early, so there was time to relax and explore the area. A scattered stand of weathered trees stood barely defiant of the forces of nature, mosses and lichens bearding the gnarled, tormented skeletons. Tolkien would have surely created wise old characters out of these trees. By dusk I had almost lost myself in this mythical world above the clouds, half-expecting a goblin to surface from one of the many caves – extinct lava vents. Too much rarefied air? Maybe not. For once I had some downtime where I was not struggling with shoddy internet connections or stressing under the constant pressures of the expedition. These were cherished glimpses of clarity which gave me perspective through the fog swirling in my mind. The night was freezing but the air was so clear I could see the lights of Buea almost 2000 metres below.

Climbing through the alpine zone over the final 1300 metres to the summit completed the epic trilogy of climatic zones. Any trees and shrubs – that by this stage

Dan taking a break beside the Magic Tree, ascending through the tropical clouds on Mt Cameroon

only lingered in protected pockets – gradually became more stunted until they petered out altogether. Here the highest bald peaks were carpeted by hardy grasses and delicate alpine flowers. Peter pointed out some hotspots of a more literal sense. The 'Mountain of Thunder' last blew its top in the year 2000 and steam still trailed from live vents: mortal whimpers from that eruption. Reaching the summit, we were rewarded with vast views of the mountain high above the clouds, the rainforest, the towns and the ocean. We were sitting on top of the highest point in West Africa.

The most difficult part of the Mount Cameroon excursion for me was descending. Climbing uses similar muscles to cycling so I could cope well with that but the descent put an agonising strain on my injured knee. I hobbled down very slowly and cautiously, using only my good leg and a green stick to balance. I had real concern that I had incurred more permanent damage to the joint which, by the time I reached Buea, had swollen indefinably.

John and I had noted that Dan had become somewhat disillusioned and stale as the expedition unfolded. Some of this was probably born out of being cooped up in the vehicle when he needed more energy release. His temperament was more suited to the timeless freedom of a backpacker, and the demands of our tight schedule frustrated him. I would have liked more flexibility myself, but this expedition could not work that way. I offered him a week off to chill out on the beaches of Limbe and he accepted. John, Zdenek and I returned to the junction near Douala where I had stopped cycling to resume the ride through that city and on to Yaoundé.

Back on the bike, I initially struggled to push my swollen knee through full revolutions. Trekking steep mountains was definitely out for the remainder of the journey. Gradually the joint wore back into its cycling grooves and the regular motion reduced the swelling before the severe undulations kicked in on the way up to Yaoundé. Negotiating Douala's chaotic backstreets was a little hairy and I had to keep my wits about me. Once out of the industrial port zone and over the Wouri River Bridge it was straight on to the main thoroughfare and out. The highway connecting Cameroon's economic and administrative capitals was hellishly busy and had some of the best surfaces of anywhere I'd encountered. Unaccustomed to such roads, drivers travel at breakneck speeds, often with unsafe loads. I passed a sickening accident where a logging truck had failed to take a bend, had careered into the embankment, and a log had smashed through the cabin. There were no survivors. Cameroon's road toll is horrific and I saw plenty more evidence of carnage.

Finding a place to camp when the roadside was either flanked by villages or rainforest required all of John's experience. He eventually found a palm plantation off a side track. Much of the forest in this region has been or is being cleared to make way for palm trees for producing palm oil. We spoke to a worker who explained that a French businessman owned this land, while the Chinese were buying up big tracts of forest nearby to turn into palm plantations. Beneath the canopy was a steamy, sterile environment of long rows of palm trees. Nothing else grew below the treetops. The ground was littered with prunings and the rotting corpses of what were once majestic trees of the original rainforest. It seems a big sacrifice of diverse rainforest to create a monoculture that produces relatively small amounts of oil per hectare. The worker added that his employer provided unskilled work for the locals but little else benefited the economy.

Humid campsite beneath a palm oil plantation. The decomposing logs are the only remnants of the tropical rainforest before it was levelled

By the time we arrived in Yaoundé at the headquarters of Sundance Resources (which kindly supported our stay), I was looking rather bedraggled – exhausted, filthy and very sore from fifteen consecutive days of either mountains or extreme humidity. We'd been on the road for almost four months and despite the various hiccups remained on track. We were spoiled by being able to base ourselves at Sundance's headquarters thanks to Robin Longley (senior geologist), Jeff Duff and a dedicated local team, especially Guillaume and Promise.

✻

I had to time our arrival in Yaoundé with the arranged visit to Bertoua in the East Region to learn about Plan Cameroon's Baka Rights and Dignity Project. At the head office in Yaoundé I received an overview of the organisation's projects from the national director, Amadou Bocoum before John, Zdenek and I set off for Bertoua, a 350-kilometre drive to the east.

The Baka people belong to the ethno-linguistic group of the Pygmies. Roughly 75,000 Baka live in isolated communities spread throughout the rainforest in south-eastern Cameroon. Almost half of Cameroon's forests have been allocated to logging operations, and as a consequence the government requires that the Baka make the transition from their traditional nomadic way of life to settle in small villages in the forest periphery. This poses many challenges, such as access to Cameroonian nationality, social services and landownership. The Baka Rights and Dignity Project (BRD) supports the Baka to improve their bargaining skills and empowers them to claim their rights – including rights to education and healthcare, the rights of women and children (in these matriarchal communities), knowledge about legal procedures and the right to be registered at birth. For example, without birth certificates for identification, children's nationality is not recognised. With no official registration they are not entitled to receive healthcare or sit matriculation exams. The program also aims at strengthening the Baka's self-esteem by focusing on problems of integration with the rest of society. Serious issues faced by Baka youths include suicide, malnutrition, sexual exploitation, child labour, trafficking, unemployment and drug abuse. Other marginalised ethnic groups in the region, such as the Mbororo and Bantu, are included in Plan's work. Fortunately we had an opportunity to learn about these groups too.

A birth certificate officially recognises this boy's nationality and ensures he qualifies for his basic rights

Thomas Ngala, Plan's Monitoring and Evaluation Coordinator for the project, led us deep into the forest of the Doume District about 50 kilometres south-west of Bertoua. Initially the aim was to make brief visits to two villages to obtain a snapshot of the communities, their issues and how they live.

The first Baka village, Nkolbikon, a community of about 250 people, was at the end of the rough, narrow and overgrown track. These people came out of the forest in 1982 and it was evident that they were really struggling to adapt to a sedentary lifestyle. Although Plan had built some permanent buildings, a school and infrastructure, in general everything appeared quite run-down. The village chief was not a dynamic personality and kept his distance, although other community leaders were more forthcoming in communicating with us.

We gathered under a tree to have a discussion with some village elders, surrounded by a swarm of inquisitive children. Tom translated the dialogue that revolved around what it was like to live in the village and what their most pressing needs were. One elder explained that they were in need of better roads so they could more easily transport and trade their produce and reach help in an emergency. He thought two other important priorities were to build a health centre and ... to have the water pump repaired. Not another fixing the pump issue! John, a little exasperated (as I was too), asked whether we could see the pump, which had been broken for two years. It was difficult to understand why they couldn't repair such a simple problem. Tom explained that Plan had twice shown them what they should do about it but no paperwork had been submitted and no action taken by the community. Plan's work here is to train them in management and leadership skills so that the Baka can implement their own initiatives – a sustainable theory, but evidently there was still much work to do. According to Tom, the Baka's self-esteem was so low that they didn't yet have the will to implement the changes they had suggested to me. I found this very saddening, and set off for the second village feeling pretty frustrated. I wanted to know and understand more.

The second Baka village, Mayos, which Tom explained was a showcase example, was larger and much more developed. Settlement began in 1970; there was more space, more food grown, a cultural centre and the pump worked. Apparently the pump had broken down in the past, but the people had learned how to fix it and took the initiative themselves. They had much stronger leadership and organisation than the Nkolbikon community. Tom said that Plan was arranging for a delegation from

The chief of Nkolbikon with his people

the first village to visit the second village to learn from them and hopefully be empowered by what had been achieved. John bought a hand of bananas as a token of support and we set off for Bertoua where we based ourselves for two days.

In Bertoua we met with Denis Tchounkeu, the Regional and Baka Rights and Dignity Project (BRD) Coordinator, to learn more about what the project is doing. He explained that the picture is complex as different communities are faced with their own specific problems that require individual solutions. Much of Plan's work with educating the Baka about their rights and legal procedures goes unseen, but without making this work a priority, all the improvements in infrastructure and other more visible actions would be a waste of time and resources. These people have had to start from scratch; for example, business acumen and money know-how is not in their make-up. The Baka also need to learn how to communicate, trade and negotiate with other cultures, work within the law and make democratic decisions. In addition, they need to develop farming skills and be taught about land ownership. Denis

Debao, the head teacher, Samuel and I displaying donated text books (photo: Z Kratky)

said that the most advanced villages are adopting a 'council approach' to better manage community needs.

The following day we returned to Mayos, the more advanced Baka village, for a closer look at its culture and issues. This time Samuel Londo, Plan's Capacity Building Coordinator, took us around. At the school we were greeted by the three teachers. It was a Monday but there were no students in class. Debao, the head teacher, explained that all the children were out in the forest gathering food. Food security, she said, was the biggest obstacle here: if pupils are hungry they cannot concentrate and learn. While some food is produced in the village, it seemed very much to be a hand-to-mouth, day-to-day existence. When I suggested that the students grow a garden at school to help alleviate the food shortage, Debao pointed to an overgrown patch of weeds and grass beside the classroom. She'd already tried that. Her students had planted cassava and other vegetables but before they were ripe, an inebriated member of the community came and pulled everything up, destroying the garden.

Samuel added that although the Baka may not be natural cultivators, the food crisis stems from deeper, long-term social issues. Many of the adults are employed by the more business-like Bantu people who pay inadequate salaries, and this, coupled with a lack of business and management skills, means the Baka cannot get ahead financially. Low self-esteem has led to alcohol and drug problems being pervasive throughout the community. It seemed that even Mayos, the showcase village, still had a long way to go to adapt to their new circumstances and integrate with Cameroon society.

Bark scrapings from a solea tree are boiled and taken to settle the stomach

As the Baka specialise in knowledge of the forest I asked if they could take us into the bush to search for some of the plants they use for traditional medicines. Their 'medicine woman' was summoned and she led us on a short excursion into the undergrowth. One of the several remedies she picked was a large, fleshy fruit the size of a small cantaloupe. Noel Olinda, the village leader, explained that he could prepare the seeds of this plant, the motoko-toko to treat diabetes or malaria. At his insistence I tasted the seed and immediately spat it out. It was shockingly bitter – a little like quinine in tonic water but about 1000 times stronger – and the taste remained with me for the rest of the day. All four Baka in the group thought my reaction was a great joke. Noel said that he had successfully treated many people from abroad. He was open to sharing his knowhow but in the past experts had wanted to extract his knowledge without rewarding him. Noel was aware that he had something of value and was adamant he was not going to be taken advantage of.

The Baka Rights and Dignity Project is helping give the Baka people the tools to successfully manage their forced transition to a sedentary lifestyle while preserving culture and rebuilding self-esteem, and has the potential to assist in preserving their forest environment. Learning how to better exploit their intricate knowledge could be significant in helping save the Baka and their very own treasure trove, the forest.

❊

While in Bertoua, Denis arranged for us to visit an Mbororo market at Bazama. The same village was also home to a few thousand refugees who have fled from the rebels in the Central African Republic (CAR). Although the three-year Central African Republic Bush War officially ended in 2007, unrest continues in the bush communities in the

According to Noel Olinga, motoko-toko seeds can be prepared to treat diabetes or malaria form of human rights abuses and outbreaks of fighting. Valentine Alobwede, Plan's Early Childcare Development Coordinator, accompanied us as we drove east along the Batouri Road to the town of approximately 5000 people. On the way we passed scores of logging trucks, many overloaded, all transporting massive logs from the rainforests of the Central African Republic. The Lebanese and Chinese-owned companies allegedly have few restrictions on what they extract, and it appeared as though these prime natural resources were literally haemorrhaging out of the forest. We were told that loggers concentrate on hauling out the tallest trees, leaving the understoreys for local people to exploit for their own use.

The Mbororo are another branch of the Fulani culture – the same ethnic group we had been encountering since Senegal. As with their Sahelian cousins, they are tall and thin in stature with striking features. The women are usually beautifully dressed, signalling their wealth and status by what they wear. Although the Mbororo are marginalised as a group in southern Cameroon, their being nomadic does not necessarily mean they are poor. They congregate to trade at bazaars like the one in Bazama, which was in full swing when we arrived. Even a travelling medicine man was there, keeping his audience, mostly children, spellbound by his demonstrations of magic powers and remedies.

A travelling medicine man touts his trade to a young, impressionable audience at the Bazama market

Valentine found Hannatou Modibo, the early childhood teacher, with whom he regularly works. Hannatou not only teaches the children aged two to four years old but is also responsible for their vaccinations, healthcare, nutrition and general development. Demand for care for this age group along with teaching primary students is overwhelming due to the influx of refugees from across the Central African Republic border and a new classroom had recently been opened behind the primary school.

Communicating with the refugees is an important part of Hannatou's work. She led Valentine, Zdenek and myself to one of the refugee dwellings to have a chat with the women. This was a rare opportunity to gain insight into the situation in the Central African Republic. The exchange was also my most confronting, harrowing experience of the journey to this point. A mat was laid out for us to sit on, and Hannatou interpreted from Fulbe to French and Valentine then translated to English. A matriarchal grandmother figure told us her story – sadly one that can be replicated many thousands of times over in these parts.

She lived with her husband and about eight children in the forests of the south-west of the Central African Republic. They were wealthy cattle herders. About three years ago they were visited by rebels – disgruntled failed opposition to the Central African Republic government. The rebels kidnapped three of the couple's children, threatening to kill them if they did not pay a ransom of ten million CFA ($US25,000). The husband was able to pay and the children were returned. The rebels came back, kidnapped the same children and demanded the same ransom, again threatening to kill them. This time the couple was forced to sell all that they had to pay the rebels. The bandits returned a third time and once more took the children. This time the parents could not pay so the rebels killed the husband and three children.

The woman fled with the rest of her family and gave birth to a child while on the run. She said that she did not know where she was going, she just ran in fear and did not sleep for months. As she recalled the horrors, her already wrinkled, weathered face creased up and her eyes transformed into deep wells of unfathomable grief. There was no need for the translators here. No words could describe the connection she made or the effect she had on me. I tried to be strong for her but a few tears worked their way to the surface.

Mbororo refugee woman from the Central African Republic tells her story while Hannatou translates (photo: Z Kratky)

Valentine and Hannatou had heard it all before, so while they also felt for the woman, they were somewhat hardened to such stories. Anyone working in these situations has to be for their own sanity. For Zdenek and myself, the level of inhumanity was incomprehensible. The woman spoke on behalf of the group; they all had similar stories to tell. She said that they are grateful to have a safe, secure place to live and do not wish to return to the Central African Republic. In Cameroon they have a fresh start and an opportunity for their children to grow up without fear. They are being educated and have access to healthcare facilities, clean water and sanitation thanks to the combined efforts of a number of agencies. Here Plan works with UNHCR, the Red Cross and a couple of other French organisations.

Back in Yaoundé we completed a ten-day pit stop. It was a time to catch up on writing, respond to a myriad of emails, answer students' questions, connect with sponsors, send off footage and damaged equipment, organise visas and confirm timings for project visits down the track. Even at this stage, I was keeping my contacts in the government of the Puntland State of Somalia informed of our progress and estimated time of arrival into Somalia. Obtaining Angolan visas was looming as the most problematical administrative hurdle. Guillaume from Sundance Resources at least sorted visas for the next three countries – Gabon, the Republic of Congo and the Democratic Republic of Congo.

Total distance: 8202 kilometres

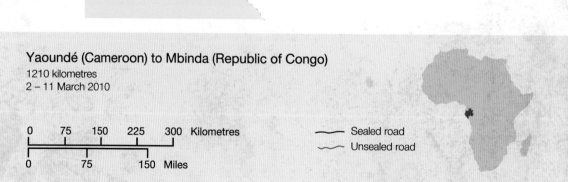

Yaoundé (Cameroon) to Mbinda (Republic of Congo)
1210 kilometres
2 – 11 March 2010

Sealed road
Unsealed road

8
ACROSS THE EQUATOR

Yaoundé - GABON - Mbinda

The team endures steamy conditions at the Equator
(photo: Z Kratky)

The ten days spent off the bike in Yaoundé and Bertoua had been important to recharge the batteries and make a smooth transition within the team. John returned to Scotland to honour his farming commitments and Simon Vernon came out to take over the driver's seat for the next two months. Although we had all been getting on pretty well the change in team composition would keep us fresh.

Team dynamics altered significantly as a result of Simon's arrival. Although he was a very experienced touring driver for paying groups, apart from the drive down to Dakar with John he had no experience in Africa or of this type of expedition. Dan's role was important in assisting Simon to adjust to the conditions and the rhythm of the expedition. He'd learned a lot from John and helped maintain continuity. Zdenek had been with us for a month and had settled in well in his own quietly creative way.

Setting off on 2 March, we were heading into the tropics during the early stages of the Rainy season. In crossing the Equator twice, no matter how I scheduled the journey, it was always going to be impossible to avoid all four Wet seasons completely. I was fully expecting a torrid time with the Wet at some stage. There were other question marks over security and gaining permission to travel through some of the regions ahead. I was relying on advice and assistance from my contacts in the Republic of Congo to get us through the rebel-controlled Pool Region just west of Brazzaville. The Congolese capital was also our last chance to secure the appropriate Angolan visas. From Brazzaville we had to cross the mighty Congo River into the Democratic Republic of Congo where we would have to negotiate our way through Kinshasa and the Bas-Congo Region, notorious for banditry and lawlessness. With all these factors playing on my mind, my goal was to minimise potential problems by pushing through as fast as possible.

Pretty fatigued and dehydrated when I arrived in Yaoundé, by the time we left I felt refreshed and much stronger. All the same, it took a while to regain my cycling legs after such a long stint off the bike. This phase was to require an intense, sustained effort, so I needed to be up for it. We returned to the exact spot where I stopped cycling, just outside of Yaoundé, and set off.

It took only two days to reach the Cameroon-Gabon border village, nearly 300 kilometres from Yaoundé. In pushing through the South Region, the expedition had travelled through all ten regions of Cameroon. On the whole the going was pretty straightforward, which allowed the new team combination to become settled. The region – at least along the main highway – looked more developed than most other parts of Cameroon that I had seen. There were bigger houses with more satellite dishes. Since colonial times, this has been a land of plantations – cocoa, coffee, forestry, rubber, palm oil – and now the economy has been bolstered by tourism and the resource industry to some extent.

Once through the many checkpoints and across the Ntem River, we were into country number eight without a hitch. Gabon's brand-new highways were in pristine condition, slicing through the verdant, steamy rainforest, occasional villages and a continuous procession of long, steep rolling hills. The path was a taxing yet smooth rollercoaster ride. In these conditions I was able to descend at a fair speed but the enjoyment was short-lived and subsequently it felt as though I was always climbing.

Contributing to the testing circumstances were the side-effects of taking the anti-malarial drug Doxycycline for the first time. Travelling across the Sahel and savannahs, the team had elected not to take anti-malarial medication as it is not advisable to be on it for extended periods. Now, heading into the tropics, we conceded that we had all better give the malarial prevention medicine we'd bought for the expedition a try. After three days the strong antibiotic had started to build up in my system. Even though I was well-acclimatised to the sun and heat and applied sunscreen twice a day, due to increased sensitivities from the Doxycycline, I suffered from sunburn and developed heat rashes and severe chafing for the first time on the journey. The anti-malarial drug also played havoc with my digestive system and generally put my finely tuned body under more stress. I hoped things would settle down in time. The others did not suffer such intense reactions. Zdenek was advised to use a different drug, Lariam, which is associated with neuropsychiatric side-effects, including depression, hallucinations, headaches and anxiety if taken for extended periods of time. Not a great choice.

❊

Gabon's flag is a simple design of three horizontal bands of colour. The green symbolises the lush forests that encompass 80 per cent of the country; the yellow band stands for its abundant natural resources and the line of the Equator that divides the country in two; and the bottom blue stripe represents the sea of its 1000-kilometre coastline. Gabon's coat of arms signifies a similar theme except the shield is guarded by two black panthers standing on their hind legs on either side representing the 'president's vigilance and courage to protect the nation.' Delving deeper, this coat, the coat of arms, is a facade of many more colours and hues.

In the fifty years since its independence, Gabon has only had three presidents. Léon M'ba became the first leader until his death in 1967. His vice-president, Omar Bongo Ondimba, assumed the reins and held on for forty-two years until he died suddenly in 2009. After flawed multiparty elections, Omar's son Ali Bongo Ondimba came to power. While the French colonists had officially abdicated from running the country by 1960, they served to prop up their exploitative interests in Gabon's considerable natural resources long after M'ba and then Bongo came to power. An extreme culture of corruption and blatant exploitation has been upheld by the Bongo dynasty: the Bongos have treated Gabon as their own private property, allegedly siphoning off hundreds of millions of dollars to fund a life of outrageous luxury. The open cheque book is chiefly fuelled by Gabon's oil industry, the third largest in sub-Saharan Africa, along with other primary exports such as logging, manganese and uranium. Despite such corruption, Gabon has remained relatively peaceful and stable. The Bongo leadership has maintained strong foreign support and created an environment conducive to attracting big investors. Mr Ali Bongo promotes that his country will be an emerging 'black panther' economy by 2025.

A forestry operation near to our second campsite in Gabon

On paper, Gabon's population of about 1.5 million has one of the highest per capita annual incomes on the continent (almost $US15,000). These figures are skewed because there is a drastically lopsided distribution of wealth. It is estimated that 20 per cent of the population receive 90 per cent of the country's income while about one-third live in abject poverty.

It is abuses of power such as these in Gabon that stymie development relief efforts. There is no other reason why Gabon's small population should suffer. There are, of course, many other well-documented incidences of corruption throughout the continent, often buffered by Western interests. It is estimated that as a result of corruption sub-Saharan Africa loses $US148 billion each year, which amounts to approximately one-quarter of the region's GDP. Cases such as Gabon's are disheartening and off-putting for those who wish to give yet fear that their generosity is money down the drainpipe. There are a number of African leaders and non-government organisations setting the pace for tackling corruption in their countries. Some of them are making significant strides in introducing strong anti-corruption legislation and punitive measures that will ultimately discourage the graft culture that has plagued African governance for decades.

Foreign investors can play a significant role by disclosing all transactions so that they are traceable. One global civil society organisation that is leading the fight against corruption is Transparency International. As an organisation it has formed a powerful worldwide coalition that raises awareness in order to diminish apathy and tolerance of corruption, and devises and implements practical actions to address it. For example, in 2009 the French government froze $US900 million of the Bongo family's assets in response to a lawsuit filed by Transparency International on behalf of a Gabonese citizen, who accused the family of corruption, embezzlement and fraud. Other leaders are also being challenged for their irregular high expenditure. While corruption may never be stamped out completely such organisations and strong leaders carry the candle of hope.

✤

Initial impressions as I cycled through the Gabonese countryside were congruent with a wealthier set of circumstances. Some houses were quite grand and there was a lot of construction underway. The standard of cars was high – I rarely saw the usual African bombs cobbled together with improvised bush mechanics. Population density was sparse compared with southern Cameroon where there were always people around. I made several more unsubstantiated observations that I attributed to a higher standard of living. These included that roadsides were generally rubbish-free and that gardens appeared well-maintained. People were cutting grass with lawnmowers rather than by hand with machetes or scythes. And then there was the unavoidable matter of dogs! For the whole of West Africa, the dogs had been just one breed and poorly treated: battered, abused and submissive and certainly not revered as man's best friend. Arriving in Gabon, I was regularly lined up and ambushed by dogs of all shapes and sizes. From groomed yapping ankle-biters to German Shepherd types with deep-throated barks that sounded like they were capable of tearing off a whole leg, they elicited an immediate response of wanting to take my feet out of the toe clips and lift them over the handlebars. At least I'd had my rabies injections. From past experience I knew it best to ignore their bravado and not look at them directly in the eye as they deem this as a threat, which turn encourages attacks. Once I was out of their owners' territory they would always give up the chase. The better-off Gabonese obviously treat their dogs as pets which I took as another sign of greater prosperity, although you certainly won't find this detail in any of the economic indicators.

I noticed little agriculture. Gabon relies on importing just about everything, including fresh produce from Cameroon's southern plantations and goods from France. There were regular pockets of slash-and-burn land use – some recently razed, others where forest was regenerating. Land cleared of tropical rainforest by the age-old slash-and-burn technique is traditionally only good for one or two crops and soils in the jungle are generally very poor because most of the nutrients are contained in the dense biomass above the ground. Burning the vegetation releases some of these nutrients but after a couple of uses the land is rendered infertile and is left to regenerate. Slash-and-burn agriculture works in harmony with the environment when the population density is sparse, as in parts of Gabon. Once the delicate balance is destroyed by unsustainable numbers of people, the pressure on the land becomes too much.

About 40 kilometres north of the Equator, we were lunching in a small roadside shack when we heard a gunshot, a silent pause, then a thud as a dead monkey dropped from a tree onto a corrugated iron roof. The small gathering of villagers cheered with excitement – they would have a good feed on the table that night. In Gabon and surrounding countries of the Congo Basin – southern Cameroon, Equatorial Guinea, Republic of Congo, Democratic Republic of Congo and the Central African Republic – there is a heavy reliance on food from the forest, including bushmeat. Bushmeat means basically any wild animal with a heartbeat, including monkeys, gorillas, chimpanzees, elephants, antelopes, lizards, snakes, wild pigs and porcupines. We regularly saw evidence of the practice – a hunter proudly emerging from the forest with his bounty of 'Porky Pig' (porcupine), lizards and snakes for sale on the roadside, trailer loads of wild boar and gazelles, monkeys and dogs draped over the back carrier of a motorbike and a display of chimpanzee skulls in a Baka village cultural centre. A Baka leader explained how they would not hesitate in taking a gorilla for food. With conditions generally ill-suited for raising domestic animals, cultures of the rainforests have always hunted bushmeat as an important source of protein. Consuming bushmeat is so much a part of everyday life that it can be served up anywhere throughout the region, from state banquets to small backstreet restaurants.

When this controversial practice is combined with loss of habitat, development of road infrastructure by the logging and mining industries and increasing populations, extinction of some species is a serious prospect. The most well-known and emotive issues are with our closest relatives such as chimpanzees, gorillas and bonobos. According to one estimate, 800 gorillas are poached in the south-eastern corner of Cameroon every year. Bushmeat trading is banned in Cameroon, as is hunting in the six-month off-season, or with locally-made guns and cable-snares at any time yet dozens of tonnes of meat arrive at Yaoundé's four bushmeat markets each month. Protected species account for only about 5 per cent of the total but are highly prized, with elephant and gorilla fetching twice the price of pork or beef. For the poor, living off less than two dollars a day, the bush-meat trade is an important source of revenue: a gorilla can fetch about $US60 and chimps $US30 at Yaoundé's markets.

Bushmeat means any kind of wild meat including this enormous lizard

Primates are susceptible to many of the same diseases as humans. Monkeys and apes in particular may have a role in the spread of new and virulent diseases to humans, including the HIV and Ebola viruses. Hunting, butchering and consuming primate meat places people at risk of contracting zoonotic diseases – diseases that cross over into humans. It seems ironic that HIV/AIDS, one of the key diseases keeping people trapped in a cycle of poverty, is related to the simian immunodeficiency virus (SIV), one theory being that it originally transferred across to humans through the primate bushmeat trade in the Congo Basin. The solution lies in the general concept of 'look after the people and then they will look after the forest.' Steps that need to be taken to save endangered species from extinction include developing means of improving people's economic situation, providing protein alternatives, better engaging leaders and decision makers, properly enforcing the laws, protecting larger tracts of forest, and increasing public awareness, research and monitoring. In most cases some actions are being taken but it is generally reported that they are too little, although not too late.

✳

While reaching the Equator was an important landmark in the context of the physical and mental journey in Gabon it is not a particularly pleasant place. We stopped for the obligatory team photo. Conditions were predictably steamy and uncomfortable, exacerbating my heat rashes and chafed, raw skin. Sitting on the bike had become a real trial and I could do little about it except focus on something else. The heat had even caused the asphalt to become malleable enough to be moulded, like plasticine, into waves under the weight of traffic. The Equator marked the end of the sealed road for us. At Alémbe, a few kilometres into the Southern Hemisphere, we turned east off the main road, over the rickety Okano River bridge and into the country's wilder depths, direction Franceville.

Just over the bridge some local foresters stopped to warn us about travelling through the Lopé National Park, a day's ride away on our route, because of the likelihood of elephants, buffaloes and panthers. This did nothing to instil confidence as I struggled, mostly alone, along a tortuously steep road made of large, loose gravel stones and flanked by the impenetrable bush. This was proper equatorial rainforest. As I ascended into the mist, the first thunderstorm produced such heavy rain and poor visibility that if an elephant or a buffalo had crossed my path, I would have probably ridden straight into it. Out of the clouds, the storm eased. I tried not to dwell too much on what might wander onto the claustrophobic dirt road but I got the feeling that there were many more pairs of eyes watching me than the other way round.

Although a black panther would have seen me as meals on wheels most animals of the Gabonese jungle are shy and elusive. The bongo is one such creature,

Okano River bridge

preferring to trail through the forest along tracks where elephants have grazed. Elephants push through the forest like nature's bulldozers, leaving a path that is more easily navigable in their wake. Bongos like to wrap their prehensile tongues around shoots sprouting after vegetation has been snapped off by the plentiful elephants. The bongo, the largest antelope of the rainforest and sought-after for its beautiful chestnut coat with fine white stripes and its spiralled horns, is dwindling in numbers due to all the usual reasons – loss of habitat, the bushmeat trade and poaching.. Maybe Gabon's coat of arms should replace one of the panthers with a bongo. The great antelope could symbolise the country's natural beauty, wealth and the plight of the average citizen, while the panther still represents the Bongo leadership.

The road loosely tracked the course of the magnificent Ogooué River, Gabon's greatest waterway. The river valley has served as the principal migratory route for the diffusion of people and languages into Central and Southern Africa. Archaeological evidence in the Ogooué valley demonstrates 400,000 years of almost continuous history. From the Palaeolithic through to the Neolithic and Iron Age and on to the present day, Bantu and Babongo (Pygmy) migrations from West Africa along this cultural superhighway have shaped the ethnic landscape of sub-Saharan Africa. As we travelled through the realms of the river valley, the dense rainforest gave way to tropical savannah, a relic of the last Ice Age, that has made the

The tropical rainforest and savannah landscape in the realms of the Ogooué River (photo: Z Kratky)

passage more suitable for agriculture and the gradual migration.

We crossed to the south side of the fast-flowing Ogooué and into the Lopé National Park towards the end of a slow, gruelling, eight-hour day. The road also runs beside the Transgabonaise Railway line skirting the park perimeter. Spooked by the warnings of the foresters the previous afternoon, we decided that the vehicle should travel close to my tail. We had no trouble and, in fact, didn't even see an animal!

In 2002, then-president Omar Bongo created thirteen national parks and set aside 11 per cent of the country as nature reserves in an attempt to encourage ecotourism as an alternative to the logging industry.

Ogooué River near Lopé National Park – a corridor that provided a principal migration route for the diffusion of people to central and southern Africa

Lopé National Park, already recognised since 1946 as Gabon's first protected area, was included. Gabon became a focal point for international efforts to conserve some of the world's largest intact tropical rainforests for carbon capture and endangered species protection. Five years later, the park was inducted as a UNESCO World Heritage Site because of the importance of its ecosystem and relict cultural landscape. Having endured six days of camping, we decided to treat ourselves by staying at the Lopé Hotel. Nestled in the park in a bend in the river, complete with mown lawns and an airport nearby, the lodge is definitely geared to entice international ecotourism. Spending the night there was really beyond our means but after some negotiation we were allowed to all cram into one chalet.

Continuing east along the park boundary, we encountered one of the most unpleasant annoyances of the journey – sweat bees. Our first experience of them was back in the temperate rainforest just south of N'Gaoundéré on the Adamawa Plateau in Cameroon. If we stopped anywhere in the forest we would have about ten minutes grace before the insects detected our scent, whereupon they would swarm in their countless thousands. Sweat bees are like tiny black flies, about two or three millimetres long. Attracted to perspiration, they don't bite, they just crawl and wriggle in your ears, up your nose, in your hair, in

the corners of your eyes and down your shirt. I reckoned I must have drowned a fair few with my work rate in such high humidity. As far as the annoyance factor goes, Australian bush flies are tame in comparison with these blighters. None of us had experienced anything like it.

Sweat bees disappear at night, but as we set up camp after Lopé, and again at first light the following morning, they toyed with our sanity. We were totally incapacitated by the marauders. It was like a horror movie – attack of the killer sweat bees – and in this instance, normal bees too. Desperately we fumbled around, trying to prevent being stung while packing up camp. In the end, everything was flung into the vehicle in a frenzy. As I escaped down the forestry track and back to the main road attempting to shake off my assailants, perversely I started to see the lighter side of the situation. Out of nowhere my mind was filled with the theme music from the farcical 'Benny Hill Show' – in fast forward. Maybe I was going mad but the silliness did bring a smile to my face. A few kilometres later we were able to take sanctuary in a sweat-bee-free village and set up for breakfast – porridge as usual.

Lastoursville was the biggest town we'd seen for a while. I arrived absolutely soaked to the bone and covered in mud from head to foot after pushing through another day of steady rain. At least the rain was warm and kept the sweat bees at bay. Lastoursville had a very different ambience from the towns we'd passed along Gabon's main highway. Originally named Mandji, it had started out as a slave depot on the Ogooué River (pre-1883). Palm oil became the main industry of the region and Lastoursville grew as a colonial administrative centre due to its position on the river and later the railway. Its karst landscape

Rain clouds hover over the forest surrounding Lastoursville beside the Ogooué River. This was at the start of a long climb out of the Ogooué valley

contains a labyrinth of limestone caves that give the subterranean architecture the texture of Swiss cheese. The grottos, now on the tentative list as a potential World Heritage Site, harbour further archaeological evidence relevant to the Babongo culture and the prehistoric migration to the interior of the continent.

✳

Despite the hardships, it looked as though we were going to reach our next port of call in Mayoko, just across the Congolese border, a day ahead of schedule. In Lastoursville we made the most of the facilities, phoning and emailing ahead, restocking and refuelling, finishing up with breakfast in the Barack Obama Cafe. Out of the town, the road rose steeply away from the Ogooué valley and then continued to bisect the folds and valleys all the way to Moanda. The piste was particularly sticky under my tyres, making for heavy going. The clay surface had barely dried enough to ride on; had it rained at all, the road would have transformed into a quagmire, rendering our efforts futile. Nearer to Moanda, the Chinese were hard at work, preparing the road to be sealed, and after one exhilarating descent to the Leyou River I was pleased to hit a solid section of tarmac. I guessed it wouldn't be long until the whole road was paved. The Chinese presence was evidence that we had entered a mineral-rich zone. The Chinese here, as in many other parts of Africa, are building infrastructure as part-exchange for natural resources.

Moanda is the epicentre for Gabon's mineral boom. In the first years of political independence, manganese and uranium began to be extracted from the environs, which are estimated to contain one-fifth of the world's known manganese reserves. In 1953 a French-American corporation was established – Compagnie Miniéré de l'Ogooué (COMILOG) – to mine the manganese. The main problem was that tucked away in the far south-east corner of Gabon, surrounded by hundreds of kilometres of dense forest, the area had no roads or trainlines to convey the mineral to Gabon's ports. During colonial times, the Haut-Ogooué Region was administered by Brazzaville rather than Libreville, Gabon's capital. In order to transport the manganese ore from the region, COMILOG built an aerial ropeway conveyor system, the longest of its kind in the world, from Moanda across 76 kilometres of difficult terrain to Mbinda on the Congolese side. From there the ore was transported via a purpose-built railway line (completed in 1962) a further 250 kilometres to connect with the existing Congo-Ocean Railway and finally down to Pointe-Noire, on the coast. From Moanda, we were to follow a similar route, although we planned to branch east to Brazzaville, rather than west to Pointe-Noire.

Starting from our secluded campsite about halfway between Mounana, a uranium mining town, and Moanda, I set off early with the intention of reaching Mayoko, approximately 140 kilometres away. It promised to be a monster day because I knew there would be difficult conditions and a border crossing ahead if all went to plan. Moanda is a bustling outpost built on four small plateaus. Before the discovery of manganese, it had been an isolated backwater but with the mines, the cableway and an influx of refugees fleeing the Congolese civil war, the town has undergone waves of expansion. As usual, the signposts were either absent or confusing. I veered off the Franceville road, passing scores of students walking to school and businesses being set up for the day, and down through the town. Confirming directions from the police, a taxi driver and another knowledgeable-looking person, I worked my way through the streets. On the urban outskirts, the Moanda-Mbinda road made a part-causeway through the dank Miosso Swamp. Finally, I rode between Mount Moanda and Mount Boundinga, the two prominent sandstone mounds that are said to be spiritual guardians of Moanda, and out.

Over a distance of about 20 kilometres, the road surface gradually reduced to potholes, then broken islands of old tarmac and finally gravel and clay. As I continued deeper into the forest, the inclines became progressively more severe – the steep sections were sometimes completely eroded into washaways and gullies. Occasionally I glimpsed the decrepit pylons of the now-defunct COMILOG cableway, rusting and overgrown with vines. The conveyor system, engineered to be telegraph-line straight, bridged the vertical terrain whereas the road I followed cut a convoluted path. The cableway closed in 1986 after the Transgabonaise Railway was completed from Moanda to Libreville. During the twenty-seven years prior, one-tonne cars had carried manganese ore around the clock. Now lifeless, they stand like sculptural installations, slowly being incorporated into the stratified forest. The pylons make great scaffolds for birds to affix their nests and the drooping wires that connect each tower make

The COMILOG cableway was built in 1957 to transport Gabon's manganese to Mbinda in the Republic of Congo, from where it was railed to Pointe-Noire. It was closed in 1986

effective perches. I imagined the whole system would be a first-class adventure playground for monkeys!

Having given up on taking my anti-malarial medicine back at the Lopé National Park, I had more vigour, but now after ten days on the trot in oppressive conditions, fatigue was starting to kick in. The morning mist was soon burned away by the overhead sun whose white-hot light seemed to pierce straight through me. I was barely casting a shadow and shelter was scarce as I moved along the road, unsure when I would reach the next village as my maps were useless in this remote area. I realised I hadn't seen the boys since I set off almost four hours earlier and started to worry. Had I taken the right road? What if something had happened to the team? I was running low on water and had been rationing my sips for some time. I also hadn't seen a car for an hour, maybe longer, and began to wonder if I should turn back. When finally I reached a village I hailed the first passing car and asked the occupants whether they had seen a red 4x4 Land Rover. To my relief they had, and soon after the team caught up with

Struggling after the rains at Bakoumba (photo: Z Kratky)

me. There was always a checklist of maintenance required to keep the Land Rover running reliably, and sometimes that, along with other chores, took longer than expected. Simon had been equally worried that I'd taken the wrong road. The poor surface had been slow-going for the vehicle too.

Bakoumba was the headquarters for the COMILOG cableway. There had obviously been a lot of investment in its facilities but now most of its infrastructure was crumbling along with the whole system. Here we had our passports stamped out of Gabon and Simon had customs to deal with. Conscious that I still had a lot of work to do, I set off just after a brief but violent cloudburst. The rains changed everything, transforming the piste to thick, sticky clay – perfect for moulding ceramic pots but not to cycle over! It caked my tyres and drive train so that I could not turn the wheels: I was constantly forced to stop to clear the bike workings. If I gathered enough speed, the clay and small gravel stones would flick off with the centrifugal force – it was as if I was riding on a pair of

mud-flinging Catherine wheels! On the uphill slopes, though, there was no chance of cycling. I tried the side of the road but that was worse. At times there was no alternative other than to carry the bike.

Conditions improved slightly and it looked as though we would at least make Mbinda, 25 kilometres from Mayoko, at last light. But as we traversed the range just before the border, another thunderstorm erupted. I could only push on a few metres before I had to stop to scrape out the mud. I managed just 500 metres in half an hour by this means. It all seemed futile. With the light failing we decided to stop and return to Lekoko, a tiny hamlet we had passed two kilometres before. The villagers

The Lekoko community provided a refuge from the wet, just three kilometres from the border

treated us like family, providing me with a bucket of water to wash and the team with shelter for the night. At least we were warm and dry.

The following morning we reached the border post which was just four kilometres from Lekoko, but the gate was locked and no one seemed to be around. No one really used this crossing anymore, probably since the cableway was closed. Eventually, we spoke to a woman and her husband was able to process our passports. He phoned through to Mbinda and someone rode out on a motorbike with the key to unlock the gate to let the vehicle through. I was able to slip around the side of the barrier and got a head start. It was only seven kilometres to Mbinda but the track was as slippery as a skating rink. The road to Mayoko improved as it started to dry out. Here we soon picked up the decaying Mbinda branch of the Congo-Ocean Railway line that we were to shadow as far as Makabana.

Nearing the Gabon-Congo border (photo: Z Kratky)

Total distance: 9412 kilometres

REPUBLIC OF CONGO

CENTRAL AFRICAN REPUBLIC

CAMEROON

GABON

DEMOCRATIC REPUBLIC
OF CONGO

Atlantic
Ocean

Pointe-Noire

CABINDA
(ANGOLA)

Mbinda
Mayoko
Tsinguidi

Makabana

Dolisie
Nkayi
Madingou
Loutété
Mindouli
Kinkala
Brazzaville
Kinshasa

Oubangui

Congo

Congo

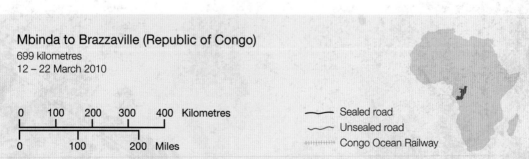

Mbinda to Brazzaville (Republic of Congo)
699 kilometres
12 – 22 March 2010

| 0 | 100 | 200 | 300 | 400 | Kilometres |

| 0 | 100 | 200 | Miles |

—— Sealed road
~~~ Unsealed road
++++++ Congo Ocean Railway

9

THE TEN-THOUSANDTH KILOMETRE

Mbinda to Brazzaville (Republic of Congo)

Pushing hard along the main road (RN1) between Dolisie
and Nkayi

The Republic of Congo (ROC), sometimes called Congo-Brazzaville, should not be confused with the Democratic Republic of Congo (DRC), formerly the Belgium Congo and then Zaire. The two Congos are entirely different countries. The Republic of Congo, a sparsely populated nation of four million people, the size of Germany, lies to the north and west of the Congo and Oubangui rivers (the Oubangui is a major tributary of the Congo River). The much larger Democratic Republic of Congo, home to more than 70 million people, is situated to the rivers' south and east. The countries have different histories and cultures. The land that is now the Republic of Congo was claimed by the French during the times of 'the Scramble for Africa'. Then explorer Pierre Savorgnan de Brazza competed with King Leopold of Belgium's International Congo Association for control of the river basin. De Brazza signed a treaty with the Bateke leaders and the north bank was secured as the French protectorate they called Middle Congo. In 1908, in order to more efficiently control the regions and to harness the exploitation of people and resources, Brazzaville was made the capital for the newly created French Equatorial Africa – Middle Congo, Gabon, Chad and Oubangui-Chari (present-day Central African Republic).

The initial reason for choosing our unusual and more interesting route through Gabon and into the Republic of Congo (rather than down the main highway) was to link up with another expedition supporter, DMC Mining Limited, which was exploring for iron ore reserves in the region. Here was more than just a pit stop; it was an opportunity to experience a part of Africa few get to see. Thanks to DMC's government connections, we were in a privileged position to gain greater insight into the country from the highest level down. On our recovery day I asked the DMC staff if they could show us something of the region that was gradually recovering from the brutalities of the 1997-99 civil war. They did a pretty good job. In one day we were introduced to the issues facing some of the indigenous people, met an ageing political figure, and were taken to appreciate some of the Mayoko District's natural beauty.

The deserted border post between Gabon and the Republic of Congo

Our tour began in Mayoko village where we collected the mayor's representative and the chief of police along with an armed security unit. Simon drove the Land Rover, following a DMC pick-up through the forest. I thought they were being a little over-protective, a theme that continued throughout our time in the country, but we were under their protection and had to respect that they were not going to leave anything to chance. I felt honoured by their efforts to showcase their region and to keep us secure. We developed a relationship of mutual respect and trust.

First stop was an emotive visit to Lessoukou, the last village of Babongo people in the Mayoko region. I thought this would be a good follow-up opportunity to compare their situation with that of

The youngest seller at the Mayoko market. UNICEF calculate that 54 per cent of children here live below the poverty line (less than $US1.25 a day)

On the road between Mbinda and Mayoko. According to a UNICEF study, more than half of the children in the country are either not attending school or are lagging at least two classes behind   (photo: Z Kratky)

the Baka, their ethnic cousins whom we met in Cameroon. I was shocked to learn that there were just thirty-seven people left in the village – that is all there is remaining of these, the first inhabitants, who have their own language and customs. Indigenous people only make up about 2 per cent of the Congolese population, and over time they have been largely overwhelmed, marginalised and displaced by the various tribes of the more dominant Bantu people, such as the Bakongo, Sangha and Bateke. I tried to find out why the Babongo people are disappearing as a group, and deduced that the main reasons were that some have integrated and moved away, and others suffered from the impact of the civil war, were marginalised by other ethnic groups, or were unable to adapt to the change of lifestyle. As with the Baka, this has resulted in loss of self-esteem and in alcohol issues. The Babongo have lost land and livelihoods due to deforestation, broader scale agriculture and other land uses.

The villagers knew we were coming and had prepared two letters, neatly hand written in French, that read as a desperate plea for help. The one from the chief of the village had the official Lessoukou stamp.

By the tone of his voice, Debi Rodrigue, our interpreter, obviously found it difficult to translate their words. They made grim listening. The leaders wrote that they can't get any help, and that they feel forgotten by the government. This part of the country is still reeling from the effects of the civil war and, with poor infrastructure, the environment is not yet conducive for international NGOs to set up. The Babongo do grow and produce food and handicrafts to sell, but they have no facilities.

Debi interprets the letter from the chief of the Babongo people (DH)

Lessoukou's Babongo community show concern for their future (DH)

We moved over to the school that they had built themselves. The village has three teachers but can only afford to pay one. The total learning materials amount to chalk and a blackboard, the students using their wooden desks as slates. There are no health facilities for when people are sick – malaria is the main killer – so health problems usually have to be treated with traditional medicines. The chief explained that sometimes the villagers receive gifts from outsiders and that these are appreciated but the people cannot build a future from these random acts of kindness alone. Instead of gifts they need help which brings about long-term changes. The village's focus is on improving primary education, health and building capacity to sustain them economically. Debi translated the last line of the chief's letter: 'We are the last people here, so please help.' As before in similar situations, I felt totally helpless. All I could do at that point was to promise that I would tell the world about their plight through my blog.

Indigenous discrimination has been ingrained in Bantu culture. In the extreme, many indigenous people are bound to a lifetime of servitude under their Bantu masters. Changing these customary ties is taking time. There is hope though: in 2011 the Congolese government moved to protect the indigenous minority, passing a law making it illegal to refer to the indigenous population as Pygmies – a term that is considered derogatory and synonymous with the idea that they are second-class citizens. The law details all forms of discrimination in an effort to promote equality in all basic rights – education, health, employment, etc. Many indigenous women had avoided going to hospitals to give birth because they were afraid of how they would be treated. Now the right to access health services without discrimination is written in law.

Our entourage moved on. Next was a courtesy call to the brother of the ex-president of the Republic of Congo, Mr Lissouba. At eighty-six years of age, he might have been a little frail but he was still the chief of his village, Tsinguidi, and was treated with respect by all those around him. There are two dominant characters to remember when it comes to Congolese politics, Denis Sassou Nguesso and Pascal Lissouba. Sassou Nguesso rose to power in 1979 after the all-too-familiar cycles of power struggles, military coups and assassinations that had plagued the Congo's political scene since independence. During that time, the country had been aligned with the Soviet Union, China, North Korea and Cuba to become the People's Republic of Congo. Sassou Nguesso continued with the Marxist-Leninist ideology but with the collapse of the Soviet Union in 1990 Congolese officials gradually moderated their political and economic views. By 1992 the Congo had transferred to a multi-party democracy and Professor Pascal Lissouba defeated Sassou Nguesso in the country's first democratic election. Political struggles and unrest festered away until they exploded into a brutal civil war in 1997. Pro-Sassou Nguesso forces, aided by Angolan troops, captured Brazzaville, forcing Lissouba to flee. The fighting devastated Brazzaville and the most populous

regions that concentrate along the railway lines, including where we were in Niari, Lissouba's home region. Pascal Lissouba remains in exile in France, although he was pardoned in 2009. Sassou Nguesso remains in power after the 2002 and 2009 elections were boycotted by the opposition. Being brought up to speed with this turbulent history, it was strange to be sitting with the elderly brother of the ex-president in his home and studying the photos of that bygone era hanging on the dimly lit walls. Mr Lissouba was hopeful that his brother would soon return home to Tsinguidi from France.

Policewoman at the Louesse River rapids

The finale for the day was a trek through the jungle to see a spectacular cataract on the Louesse River. Our party traipsed for about an hour through thick vegetation, the village leader with machete in hand to trim the overgrown path. Most of the forest appeared to be secondary regeneration after it had been clear-felled in earlier times. A policewoman with us took time to collect some bush tucker along the way. We tried the two types of fruit which were both varieties of what they called *ntounde*. The flesh tasted like a cross between a lemon and passionfruit and was probably packed with anti-oxidants such as vitamin C. I made the mistake of crunching on the seeds, which were horribly bitter. Another villager picked a type of wild plum which was so chalky that it was definitely an acquired taste!

That night Simon noticed his chest was covered in spots. He was also experiencing cold sweats and felt feverish. Mohammed Munkailah (Munks to us), DMC Mining's country manager, arranged for Simon to visit the company doctor. His condition was assessed to be an allergic reaction to an insect bite but later when one of the DMC staff checked for malaria with a self-testing kit, the result was inconclusive. We knew that if in any doubt about malaria that we should assume the worst and treat it accordingly. Simon was immediately put on a dose of Coartem (the artemisinin-derivative drug that stops malaria). The following morning he seemed much better but we decided to stay another day with DMC Mining Limited to make sure he was all right.

✻

The monsoonal storm that set in the evening before we restarted had me worried. The road ahead was more of the same and would have been equally as shocking in the Wet. Fortunately, by morning it had dried just enough so that I could slalom around the last of the puddles as I set off from Mayoko. DMC Mining had ensured our security for the journey to Brazzaville. As I headed out through the village, the team diverted to the gendarmerie to collect Richard, our armed escort. Over the next 300 kilometres, all the way to Dolisie, Richard sat in the front seat in military uniform with an AK-47 slung over his shoulder.

Richard, our security guard, watches on as Daniel changes my chain

After about 20 kilometres my bike chain suddenly wore out. Constant grinding of sand and mud had already destroyed my chain wheel and gear cassette back at the Gabonese border and now the chain would no longer catch the teeth of the cogs. I'd hoped to get through the tropics before the drive train died but it was not to be. Dan set to and changed the chain very efficiently.

After passing through Tsinguidi village the road merged with a logging route. Massive trucks belonging to a Malaysian timber company frequently hurtled along the road, compacting the clay into a smooth, fast surface. Richard had warned me of the dangers that these trucks posed but my experience was that the Malay drivers were aware and courteous. There was give and take from both parties, although

Being passed by an empty Malaysian-owned logging truck just after Tsinguidi (photo: Z Kratky)

157

in deference to their Goliath-like bulk, there was a little more give from my side.

As per Richard's security protocol, we checked in with the Commissariat at each of the main towns down the line – Mossendjo, Tsimba, Makabana and Dolisie. Since we travelled through the region, DMC Mining Limited was bought out by another company, African Iron, which in 2012 sold its stake to Exxaro Resources, a South African mining company. Exxaro Resources intends to export iron ore via the existing Mbinda narrow gauge railway line by 2014. From what I could see, the line obviously needed some major restoration work in order to safely carry laden iron ore cars.

As I rode along a rickety wooden bridge near Makabana that served as the only river crossing for

After the thunderstorm (photo: Z Kratky)

both rail and road, I considered how the region I had just pedalled through might change in the coming years. The government has earmarked the Niari Region for development and I noticed construction work underway in most major towns along the railway track. I hoped that a good portion of the wealth generated by the iron ore mine would be invested right the way down the line, to stimulate a flailing local economy and improve living conditions for all citizens.

After Makabana we turned away from the Mbinda railway line and towards the main road. The land opened out and the hills thankfully had gentler gradients. The main road – officially it qualifies as a highway on the maps – that connects the Congo to Gabon was a little better maintained but heavily corrugated and much busier. I began this short stanza being regularly enshrouded with clouds of dust from logging trucks in particular, then halfway along a thunderstorm converted the dust to mud and made a mess of me. I'd allowed three days for the Mayoko to Dolisie section to account for the worst monsoonal conditions, however by cycling for more than eight gruelling hours a day on mostly dry roads, I managed to reach Dolisie a day early.

✳

In Dolisie, the Congo's third biggest town, we were joined by Inspector Évariste, who travelled in plain clothes and with a concealed gun. Although Dolisie is within a few kilometres of the border with Angola's troubled oil-rich state of Cabinda, we weren't expecting any issues around there. The security stakes were to become progressively higher as we neared Brazzaville, just less than 400 kilometres away. Évariste travelled with three mobile phones in his pockets, each with a different SIM card, and as the regions ahead were serviced by different Telcos he had to keep juggling his phones depending on the telecommunication zone. The inspector checked in with his colleagues more and more frequently as the team drove east.

Flippers and snorkel would have been handy, starting from where we left off the previous evening, 25 kilometres north of Dolisie. But this was definitely no seaside holiday. The route was often fully submerged and the monsoonal rains constant. If we'd had these conditions out of Mayoko, we would have been stranded but here at least the roads had been made with gravel at some stage. It was fun and games all day.

Initially I tried to avoid the puddles, even opting for portage through the bush when the roadsides resembled a quagmire. My feet sunk up to my mid-calf at times and the suction from the mud would have pulled off my shoes had they not been firmly locked on to my feet with an ingenious clasp system. Évariste was quick to warn me not to venture off the track no matter how badly it was inundated because he said there was a greater risk of being bitten – I assumed by the charades he meant by a snake. My disc brake pads eroded quickly in these conditions. I'd had to rely on them heavily to maintain control descending steep and very rugged slopes. Dan made more emergency repairs.

Due to the conditions and more so for security reasons, rather than camping free we needed to reach a town where we were safe. I therefore had to slip and slide my way to reach Nkayi, capital of the Bouenza Region, no matter how long it took. In the fading light I fell, sliding from a high point between the tyre tracks (up to two feet deep). I landed heavily on the same elbow I had damaged back in Cameroon and grazed the scar off. I'd had such a rough day – being rattled to pieces and soaked to the bone, covered in mud and suffering from severe chafing – that by this stage I was past feeling any pain. My injury was not so serious this time and Simon simply washed it before I was back to work. Soon I was following my own elongated shadow, made by the wavering beam of the Land Rover's headlights. It was difficult to decipher the depth of the puddles or

Pushing along the RN1 main road joining the Congo's two main cities (photo: Z Kratky)

the state of the surface as any dip just appeared as a black hole. It was times like these, pushing along in the pitch dark through the Congo with an armed policeman in the vehicle behind, that it all seemed one absurd dream. I was not afraid though, in fact I felt remarkably fine: we were all in one piece and I was on a bit of a high from a day's worth of endorphins. My mind was as numb as my body and full concentration was required to stay upright. Finally reaching the paved streets and bright lights of Nkayi was a little surreal. It had taken eight-and-a-half hours to cover just 113 kilometres!

The dream became even more random when we were directed to a Chinese-owned hotel. The flimsy, stark white walls were made of a single layer of plasterboard and the floors sported sheet plastic as coverings. The flickering white-blue fluorescent lights were in keeping with the minimalist decor. The whole building must have come as a flat-pack do-it-yourself kit, but it was perfectly functional and cheap – and spotless until I arrived. The first problem I had was to remove my shoes. They were stuck fast to my feet as mud had jammed the clips of the high-tech release system. Eventually, after several minutes of hosing down I was able to wriggle my feet free. Although I had enough decorum to do that outside, my pristine white bathroom was awash with mud by the time I finished cleaning up. I hadn't expected to later be dining on fried rice, omelettes and what I hoped was sweet and sour chicken in the middle of the Congo.

Nkayi was originally called Jacob, named so in 1887 after a French engineer who led the first mission to select a route for the Congo-Ocean Railway. Around the time the French assumed control of their new colonies, they identified the need for a railway line to bypass the impenetrable rapids of the lower Congo River to connect Brazzaville to the ocean. From Brazzaville river boats were able to navigate along the Congo, Oubangui and other major tributaries that once formed the principal arteries to access outposts in French Equatorial Africa. The railway was constructed in the 1920s and 1930s using forced labour recruited from its Central African colonies. The Congo-Ocean Railway quickly became the country's economic lifeline, not only to export raw materials but also because the Congo became a net importer. As in Gabon, only about 3 per cent of Congolese land is used for agriculture. As a result of the civil war and the guerrilla tactics adopted by militia in the ensuing years, use of the rail link was suspended for six years. This crippled the economy, causing food shortages and serious inflation in the cities and towns that relied on passing trains for trade, such as Dolisie and Nkayi.

In 2007, a joint mission by UNICEF, the Congolese and Japanese governments and some US organisations distributed insecticide-impregnated mosquito nets along the course of the railway. (The line was in a decrepit but useable state, although most of the trains remained broken.) This was part of a project to equip every woman and child under five with nets, an initiative aimed at saving approximately 15,000 lives a year. Malaria is responsible for almost one-third of the Congo's deaths under five years – more than 20,000 young children are lost there annually. The UN estimates that malaria costs African economies $US12 billion a year (2 per cent of Africa's growth rate) and kills more children than AIDS. Having secured assistance from major organisations such as the Global Fund (fighting malaria, AIDS and tuberculosis), the Congo is mobilising against its biggest killers. It seems ironic that the Congo-Ocean Railway that was built at a cost of at least 17,000 lives, many lost to malaria, has recently been used to 'roll back' malaria (as the campaign slogan says).

Apart from being a major stop on the railway line, Nkayi developed because of its location in the fertile Niari River valley. Large swathes of land were converted to sugar-cane plantations, which I guessed might account for a significant portion of the Congo's agriculture. For much of the way to Loutété we passed through sugar-cane country mixed with savannah. Where there was agriculture there was more development. Near towns such as Madingou and Mouyondzi I appreciated sections of old bitumen. Évariste explained that a French company had been commissioned to seal the Route Nationale No. 1 (RN1) all the way between Pointe-Noire and Brazzaville but only ever completed isolated strips around major towns. The Chinese now have the contract but only a small section had been done out of the two main cities when we passed through.

I hadn't imagined the Congo to be so beautiful. Most of our way was carpeted with tall savannah grasses rather than the dense jungle I envisaged, and we were treated to some extensive views pushing over the high hills – 200-400 metres up, then down again, up, down. Although the road was dry I could only average 15 kilometres an hour. When vehicles traverse these roads in the Wet, the surface is carved up and fist-sized globules of mud are flung out from their tyres. Although barely noticeable from within a 4WD, for a cyclist the dried mud creates a hellish surface. The lumps and pustules resembled the random degenerating cobblestones of a medieval street – guaranteed to rattle out any loose fillings and numb the hands.

I was on a roll as I rode through Loutété, possibly the Clapham Junction of the Congolese railway line. I had covered 85 kilometres and was psyched up for doing another 40 kilometres before dark. Just as I was through the town, the team caught up with me. Évariste insisted that I stop because I was about to enter a dangerous section of road still controlled by the Ninja rebels. Due to communication difficulties

I did not at first understand what he meant, and was annoyed because I had been busting my gut to cover maximal distance so we could reach Brazzaville a day earlier. Eventually I comprehended that we could not go beyond this point without permission from both the gendarmerie and the army.

During our time in the Republic of Congo, we were looked after by all three departments of their security forces – the police, the gendarmerie and the army. The police control security in the cities and larger towns. The gendarmerie is a paramilitary unit that maintains internal order, especially in rural areas. The army's primary role is with external security though their work overlaps with the gendarmerie. There was a high degree of coordination between the armed forces and Évariste conducted proceedings, ensuring all parties were informed of our situation. After cleaning ourselves up we visited the chief in the army barracks on a hilltop on the outskirts of Loutété.

There was a real air of negativity amongst the team. Virtually since starting out from Yaoundé I had sensed in particular an evolving disconnect between myself and Simon. Part of it I put down to him being cooped up in the vehicle in wet conditions. He wasn't pleased at having to drive eleven days in a row, although I don't know what else we could have done, travelling through the tropics in the Wet. In Mayoko, Simon said that he wasn't interested in visiting any of the projects I had organised to see because he had seen enough poverty in South America. Into our third week of travelling together, I was starting to wonder why he wanted to come in the first place if he wasn't interested in the purposes of the expedition and didn't like the tropics. When Dan had become negative earlier during the journey, John was very good at steadying the ship but since this particular combination of team-mates came together I could see Simon and Dan, who in normal circumstances were good company, starting to drag each other down. To their credit, both always did their jobs to a high level and were superficially polite, enabling the team to get through on time and budget, however I felt that I was constantly battling a negative undercurrent.

I took their perceived sufferance personally and found it a heavy burden in my own mind. I still believed firmly in the mission I had set. In such testing circumstances, the support I had from so many friends, sponsors and followers remained a powerful motivator. I was determined not to break the line of my journey and decided that the best plan was to focus on putting in a consistent effort, to keep grinding forwards hour after hour, day after day. I had to continue regardless of hearing comments about us not making it through, or that there may have been a better route according to a certain website for travellers. I had chosen this path for good reason but found I was constantly defending myself and the mission of the expedition. Positive thinking was the only way to approach this journey and so I only allowed myself to consider how we would get through rather than what would stop us. Zdenek never gave much away so it was difficult to know what he was thinking. He seemed happy to go along with my plan whereas the others did not share the same trust.

✳

Up at the military barracks, Évariste convened the meeting with the chief, who gave us his full support and formed a plan for our protection. To paint a context for why we had concerns about travelling through the Pool Region between Loutété and Kinkala, it is necessary to detail more of the complex political background. The Congo's shaky transition towards democracy in the early 1990s was fuelled by the struggle for control over the country's considerable oil resources. The conflict pitted Denis Sassou Nguesso, Pascal Lissouba and a third political leader, Bernard Kolélas, against one another. Each had

161

their own militia. Lissouba's stronghold was the south-west (we had just been there), where he exerted military and political power through his Cocoye or Zulu militia. Sassou Nguesso, whose stronghold was in the north, depended on his Cobra militia. Kolélas, whose power-base was centred in Brazzaville, relied on his Ninja militia. Regional divisions coincided with different ethnic loyalties that in turn added to the combustibility of the conflicts.

Kolélas's Ninjas, named after the Ninja warriors of feudal Japan, initially allied with Sassou Nguesso's Cobras to fight against Lissouba's Cocoye militia in 1993 after the election results came into question. During the civil war, Kolélas appointed himself initially as mediator but towards the end switched to side with Lissouba – as it turned out, the losing side. The Ninjas fled to the neighbouring Pool Region. In 2002, Sassou Nguesso was returned to power after his main rivals, Lissouba and Kolélas, were barred from the contest. The Ninja rebels, now fronted by the messianic Pastor Ntoumi, entered into a bitter conflict with government forces. Ntoumi's militiamen wore the colour purple, symbolising suffering, and sported dreadlocked hair. In March 2003, Ntoumi (aka Frederick Bintsamou) signed an agreement to cease hostilities in Pool. Despite the peace accords, many Ninja remained active, engaging in robberies of civilians and train hijackings. A handful of militia is still wanted for hostage taking, torture and extrajudicial executions. In June 2007, Ntoumi announced that the Ninjas were 'going into constructive opposition' and were determined 'to work for peace in Pool and across the country'. Ninja members led by Ntoumi burned about one hundred of their weapons in a ceremony in Kinkala. Although Ntoumi was offered a government post in September 2007 he remained in hiding until December 2009, when he went to Brazzaville to take up the position.

As of 2010, active Ninja remnants still existed in southern Pool but numbers were dwindling. In describing the current position of the Ninja, our Inspector Évariste said that 'we have cut off their head, but the fingers are still twitching!' The remaining rebels now have nothing to fight for and cause trouble because they know little else and have no other income apart from collecting 'tolls' from travellers to support their lifestyle. Villagers help hide them from the authorities.

The next morning there was a palpable air of anguish amongst the team; Simon was especially

Last of the old metalled road out of Loutété. The sabotaged power pylon was blown up during the civil war (photo: Z Kratky)

tense. We set off early, first checking in at the army barracks, before passing the railway junction and out of town. The tarmac slowly degenerated, phasing back to the rough road. The first thing we noticed was that the power pylons had all been destroyed – sabotaged so that they doubled over. The towers stood as wilted monuments to how war can cripple a country. After 15 kilometres we reached Kimbedi village where the army was stationed and Évariste negotiated the price for two soldiers to join us for the 73 kilometres to Mindouli. The Land Rover was suddenly overcrowded. Dan and Zdenek were squashed like sardines in the back between the soldiers, who sat with their AK-47s at the ready, protruding through the windows.

Basically I was required to do the distance non-stop – no time for rest breaks, water or food refills. We were forbidden to take photos, particularly of the military. The scenery again was stunning but there was no time to capture it; thankfully, Zdenek took a few sneaky snapshots through the windscreen. Although I had removed my bags from the bike to try and go faster I still ended up with the same average speed as there was less weight to keep me on the road. My speed was hampered by the extra effort that went in to absorbing the more violent shocks and I expended more energy keeping the wheels in contact with the ground.

Assuming we were Chinese, the kids in the villages here called out 'Chinois' rather than referring to us as 'le blanc' (white person) as villagers usually did. Instead of welcoming us with 'Bonjour' or 'Ça va?' they greeted us with 'Ni hao' or 'Ni hao ma' ('Hello' or 'How are you?' in Chinese). These children think that anyone who is not black African must be Chinese, such is their influence in this region. The Chinese have become the Congo's biggest investment partner and, according to some with whom I spoke, their 'best friends.' For example, on this route alone, Dolisie has a huge Chinese construction business, Nkayi has a Chinese hotel (where we stayed) and a hospital, Loutété has a Chinese cement works and the copper mines around Mindouli are Chinese-operated.

'Ni hao Chinois.' A beautiful sun-shiny day for some. Rough road out of Nkayi (photo: Z Kratky)

While I was busy cycling, Évariste was on the phone every fifteen minutes reporting our position to his colonel and the information that we were safe. It took roughly five hours to reach Mindouli which we managed without incident. There we were greeted by the military and gendarmerie before being taken to meet the army chief in control of the Pool region. I bolted down some lunch in preparation for the next section – a 63-kilometre ride to Kinkala that was reportedly in worse condition and more dangerous than the Loutété to Mindouli route we had just done. It was going to be a race to get there before dark. I probably would have just made it but there was no guarantee, especially if it rained or there was a breakdown. However the decision was made that we stay the night in Mindouli and prepare to be on the road first thing the next day. This was frustrating because we had to waste half a day but I fully appreciated the reason why.

We were asked to be ready by 7.00 a.m. – which we were – but as usual we had to wait for almost an hour for the security to arrive. African military timekeeping is only slightly better than normal African timing! When Évariste received the message that they were coming, I was instructed to set off ahead of them. About ten minutes later they caught up with me. I was expecting the same set up – two soldiers crammed into the Land Rover but this time we were to be escorted by a full military unit. When I counted seven soldiers, armed to the hilt, on the back of the utility I suddenly felt a little tense as the seriousness of their intent to protect us sunk in. It was very strange to be cycling sandwiched between a ute full of soldiers with Kalashnikovs and rocket launchers, primed, and the Land Rover. There had been a lot of recent activity in this section and the unmaintained road was laced with wobbly bridges and sections of bad mud and sand – all bottlenecks where vehicles would normally have to slow down, making them prone to an ambush. It had rained overnight although fortunately not too much, so the worst sites were navigable. But two trucks in separate instances had toppled over in the mud.

Being joined by a full entourage of soldiers on the outskirts of Mindouli (photo: Z Kratky)

Before the convoy caught up with me out of town I was passed by a Spanish motorcyclist and a blue 'roaring Corolla' with its exhaust pipe poking out of the back door window, Mad Max-style. The army immediately stopped to talk to the occupants of the Corolla. According to Évariste, they were a group of Ninjas that included a known assassin. Our security guards prevented them from travelling ahead so that they couldn't forewarn their colleagues of our impending arrival. Thirteen kilometres on, the motorcyclist slid over in the mire, causing a minor traffic jam. I simply picked up my bike and found a pathway dry enough along the embankment to avoid the muddy bog. In a bizarre moment of cooperation, Dan found himself working alongside the Ninja assassin and the Spaniard to manoeuvre the motorbike free. Once a soldier had scouted the path ahead, I was permitted to set off while the convoy sorted themselves out.

I had been watching my odometer closely as I was just about to click over the 10,000-kilometre mark. I managed to pull my little compact camera out of my bar bag while on the move in readiness to take a quick photo to record the big moment. Just as it occurred, a gunshot was fired from the bush on my left. I jumped as I heard the shot, blurring the image. At this stage I was standing without cover about forty metres behind the escort, feeling extremely vulnerable. The Land Rover was about 50 metres behind me (I think). The soldiers instantly swung into action; the commander and two soldiers remained to protect the vehicle while the others scattered into the bush to chase the assailants. A soldier fired two shots in return for the first. At this point the commander waved me forward. 'You're kidding' was my gut reaction but had to trust the professionals and crept up hesitantly, stopping behind a mound of sand. I thought at least the mound might obscure the Ninjas' direct line of view. The commander proceeded to wave us past them as the military made a final check of the area. Needless to say, my average speed for the second half of the journey to Kinkala increased! I will never forget the 10,000th kilometre of the Breaking the Cycle Expedition.

From about that point, the road surface turned sandy, so there was water, mud and sand traps to deal with for the remainder of the section. Several times the soldiers stopped to check out who was watching in the bush. We also passed through several Ninja checkpoints; had we been travelling alone, a 'toll' would have been demanded before we could continue. For travellers like us it was likely that we would have been allowed to pass through although it may have been expensive. After the initial shock of the gunshots, it dawned on me that the Ninjas weren't firing at us, they were attacking the government's forces. By travelling with the armed escort, we were cutting off their main source of income. Congolese who travel independently through the region are more at risk of physical attack because they may not be able to pay the fees. The government and its combined security forces were gradually winning though; relative to situations over the previous two decades, this was akin to rounding up the stragglers. While with us, Évariste received the news that the government forces had just

Securing an area not long after the shooting incident (photo: Z Kratky)

captured a wanted assassin – and his response bordered on the ecstatic. To say that we were relieved to reach Kinkala after 60-odd kilometres and four hours of non-stop drama is an understatement.

That was the first half of the day – now I just had to cycle 75 kilometres on smooth, Chinese-built tarmac into Brazzaville. The RN1 has been a casualty of poverty, a difficult terrain and climatic conditions and, in more recent times, civil unrest. As the Ninja banditry is brought under control, it is becoming possible to build and maintain the highway. In March 2010, when we went through, most people still either took the train or flew; few dared to drive! The situation makes transportation of commodities difficult but once the road is through, it will make a significant difference to the development of other infrastructure and businesses.

❊

The new tarmac ended abruptly as we entered the city limits. The outskirts of Brazzaville were a dusty, chaotic mess. As we crossed a small bridge we were surprised to be met by television cameras and traffic police ready to escort us through the city. Talk about a day of extremes! Usually, negotiating traffic in African cities is a hair-raising experience and we'd had enough of those for one day. I don't know how many traffic jams our entourage caused over the next seven kilometres but it was a treat to have a clear run and even be able to appreciate some of the sites. The tour evolved into a kind of triumphant procession

– some locals waved, some clapped, while others stared in wonder as a white woman, still covered with mud from head to foot, was paraded through their streets. My legs had felt heavy, my body spent, but over the final few kilometres, buoyed by the enthusiastic reception, I found a new lease of life, smiling, waving and acknowledging some of the onlookers.

Police escort through Brazzaville (photo: Z Kratky)

Greeting us at the hotel was Mr Henri Okemba, an ex-minister who was in charge of government liaison and public relations for DMC Mining Limited in the Congo. Henri had been overseeing our journey from Mayoko. During twenty years of government service, Henri Okemba has been Special Advisor to the President, Minister for Youth and Sports, Minister for Agriculture and Director General of Planning. At the media interview, he stressed that the government supported the expedition because it wanted to showcase it as an example of what women can do – to motivate Congolese women in particular. This was coupled with a message about the importance of education. My journey was treated as a positive public relations exercise all-round, my actions presented as a confidence builder, an unusual demonstration of international cooperation. I sensed this straightaway and avoided mentioning anything about the shooting incident that had occurred that morning. I felt very comfortable and proud that our story was being used for good.

The following afternoon Mr Okemba arranged for a special reception to be held by the Minister for Mines, Mr Pierre Oba. The press meeting was in the gazebo of the minister's home on the Congo River waterfront. After receiving an official welcome, the discussion, again filmed for the evening news of the country's only television station, promoted similar messages. Mr Oba, clearly a politician, did most of the talking, using the meeting as a platform to deliver messages about procuring international investors, especially with Australia. He praised my courage and the credible purpose of the expedition. I did my best to respond accordingly but, in all honesty, not knowing a great deal about many of the specifics and certainly being no politician, I felt a little out of my depth at times. After, it was canapés and champagne in the garden. I think I coped with that part quite well!

That evening the team was invited as Mr Oba's guests for dinner, along with Mr Okemba and some other officials. The minister explained that the Republic of Congo had that week been

A reception with Mr Oba, Minister for Mines, and the head of the Republic of Congo's only television station. Beside me is Arsène, my interpreter (photo: Z Kratky)

awarded significant debt relief. I later found out that this was to the tune of $US1.9 billion – no wonder they were all in a buoyant mood. Due to many factors, the climate for investors had, in the recent past, been poor. The Republic of Congo still does not score highly on the international 'Doing Business Rating' but times are changing: despite a turbulent route towards democracy, somehow it seems to be finding ways of smoothing over deep-rooted differences to move forward. The international thumbs-up allows the Congolese to implement their Poverty Reduction Strategy. Civil warfare has been replaced by a war on malaria, AIDS and other diseases. A country blighted by 50 per cent poverty, according to UNICEF, is now in a position to change that. Through maintaining peace, improving transparency and governance, amending equal opportunities laws and developing a climate more attractive to foreign investment and aid partners, I hope benefits will trickle all the way down the line to improve health and education.

The Congo is diversifying its economy to become less reliant on oil, historically by far its greatest source of income. In the past, its fortunes fluctuated with world oil prices, but now it is looking to its other mineral wealth, agriculture and various other trades to make its fast-growing economy more resilient. (In 2010, the Republic of Congo's GDP grew by 8 per cent and by 5 per cent in 2011.) Like their Gabonese neighbours, the Congolese too have aspirations of becoming one of the 'emerging panther' economies by 2025.

I felt empowered by the treatment we received from the Congolese government. With five months done and hopefully five months to go, its response and support really spurred me on. But we weren't going to get much further without its help once again. Obtaining visas for Angola had been the biggest bureaucratic obstacle threatening the challenge of cycling across Africa from west to east in a continuous line. No travellers' websites listed anyone as being successful in obtaining an Angolan visa to travel through the country from north to south; for some unexplained reason, going the other way was more acceptable. People can intermittently get five-day transit visas but this would have been inappropriate for us as I had to cycle nearly 2000 kilometres through the country.

Initially we came up against a brick wall. The invitations I had secured from an Angolan business were not sufficient. It seemed that the officer in charge – a woman with a scowling face (as I wrote in my diary) – had a mandate to make our experience as difficult as possible. She rejected anything that was irregular: any slight error in our handwriting and we had to start our complicated forms again. My passport photocopy was too big – go back to the city and have another one made. I had to write a 'letter of demand' but that was rejected until it was translated into perfect French. I got the feeling she enjoyed creating maximum inconvenience, and the trick for us was not to show any frustration because that would add another brick in the wall. But it was difficult not to. In the end, it was only due to an intervention made by the Minister for Mines, who spoke to the Angolan Ambassador on our behalf, that we received 30-day 'ordinary' visas. We had only lost four days. If we didn't have the visas it was likely we would have not been allowed into the Democratic Republic of Congo, our next country, because it required evidence of our onward journey. It could have been much worse.

Total distance: 10,111 kilometres

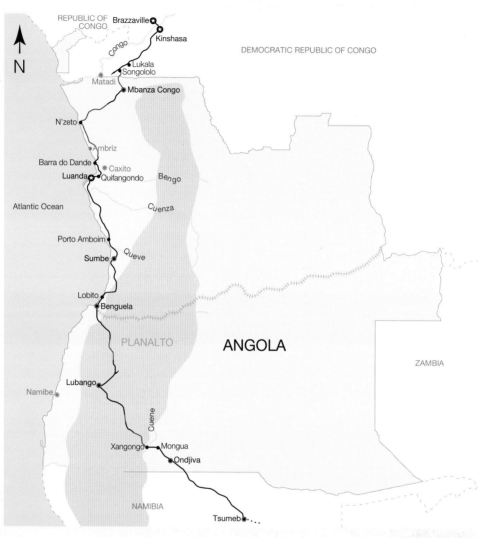

REPUBLIC OF CONGO

Brazzaville

Kinshasa

DEMOCRATIC REPUBLIC OF CONGO

Congo

Lukala
Songololo

Matadi

Mbanza Congo

N'zeto

Ambriz

Barra do Dande

Caxito

Luanda

Quifangondo

Bengo

Atlantic Ocean

Cuenza

Porto Amboim

Queve

Sumbe

Lobito

Benguela

PLANALTO

ANGOLA

ZAMBIA

Lubango

Namibe

Cuene

Xangongo

Mongua

Ondjiva

NAMIBIA

Tsumeb

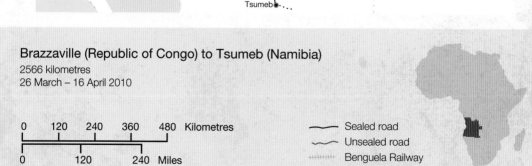

Brazzaville (Republic of Congo) to Tsumeb (Namibia)

2566 kilometres
26 March – 16 April 2010

| 0 | 120 | 240 | 360 | 480 | Kilometres |

| 0 | 120 | 240 | Miles |

——— Sealed road
⌒⌒⌒ Unsealed road
╪╪╪╪╪ Benguela Railway

10
FROM THE DEVELOPING
TO THE DEVELOPED

Brazzaville to Tsumeb
(Democratic Republic of Congo and Angola)

Turning towards the Angolan border from Songololo (photo: Z Kratky)

With visas for the next two countries securely affixed in our passports, we boarded the slow boat to Kinshasa. Our vehicle was the only one on this crossing – the rest of the deck gradually filled with an assortment of passengers and cargo. Chaos ensued as hundreds crammed on board. I felt most for the disabled who struggled to manoeuvre their cumbersome makeshift trolleys and homemade wheelchairs out of the intense midday heat. The sides of the boat were counterbalanced with piles of wares destined to be sold in the neighbouring Big City, Africa's third largest. We took sanctuary in the Land Rover for most of the ferry ride, slow-roasting in some coveted personal space while maintaining an eagle-eye on our equipment as looters nonchalantly tore open sacks of goods, took what they wanted and then sewed the bags up again!

The ferry route is at the western neck of Pool Malebo (formerly Stanley Pool), the lake-like widening of the Congo River that separates Brazzaville and Kinshasa, the two closest capital cities in the world. From this point, the river is navigable deep into the interior of the Democratic Republic of Congo and the Central African Republic. Downstream, the river descends hundreds of metres in a series of rapids known as the Livingstone Falls before entering the Atlantic Ocean.

The boat set off half an hour late, then returned to the Brazzaville side three times to collect more passengers and cargo, fuelling frustration amongst some of the mob, before finally making the short crossing. As it docked, agitated passengers swarmed like pack animals and surged forward, crushing each other in the rush to disembark. Port police were heavy-handed, wielding their batons, beating people back indiscriminately. Dan, Zdenek and I were required to leave on foot; we waited calmly to the side until the commotion had dissipated somewhat. Simon had to stay in the vehicle to drive it off.

Two of our friends who had helped host our stay in Brazzaville, Emmanuel and Arsène, travelled with us to ensure we made it through unscathed. Despite their presence, it took a further hour and a half for the authorities to process our passports. And then the first scam. Immigration officials insisted that it was necessary to disinfect the vehicle! We demanded they show us the paperwork that demonstrated this to be 'normal procedure' and eventually a document was produced. It may not have been exactly what we had asked to see but we felt we had no choice other than to pay the $US60 fee. Both the Land Rover and my bike were subsequently sprayed haphazardly – hardly a serious attempt to ensure we did not carry vermin matter into the country. In the end we were just glad to get out of there! Once through the port gates and into the frantic world of Kinshasa, I cycled close to the vehicle. Noel, a friend of Arsène's, led us back to his family-run hotel, about 15 kilometres from the port. At least we had a guide to see us through Kinshasa and a safe place to keep the vehicle for the night.

Despite an overwhelming number of travel warnings, I'd also learned that the Democratic Republic of Congo is not all bad. In the Republic of Congo we'd crossed paths with Olivier, a Belgian cyclist who had just pedalled solo from Burundi, through the centre of the country to Kinshasa and out. I thought this seemed very brave, especially considering his nationality and the levels of exploitation and suffering the country had endured under Belgium's colonial rule. Olivier only reported positive experiences. The roads may have been difficult, but he had loved his time there and could not speak highly enough of the local people. But to reach the Angolan border, we still had to negotiate Kinshasa's urban sprawl and the Bas Congo region, notorious for banditry, corruption and high prices.

Even though we set off early, the ring road soon resembled a car park. Riding through the fringes of most large cities is rarely a pleasant experience, but here there was an uneasy tension in the oily-tasting smog. Young men would repeatedly lean out from the open doors and windows of minibuses to try to touch me, making all sorts of sexual suggestions. The most unnerving moment came when, as I picked my way through the traffic, one fellow stroked my face. All I could do was totally ignore these advances and try to appear unflustered, keep my distance where possible and continue pedalling until I was out of there.

Away from the city, locals' responses were more normal but the following day near Kimpese I had an encounter with a traffic policeman who pulled me up just as I was leaving town. I felt that it could go horribly wrong as I could tell by his demeanour that he was a man who liked to exercise his position of authority. Initially, when he demanded my passport, I tried to casually divert the conversation with my poor French. I felt vulnerable, knowing that if he took it from me that he would have greater bargaining power. I tried to explain where I was from and what I was doing but in the end I had to hand over the passport. In the meantime, local men started to gather around as he deliberated over the many pages, visas and stamps, then moved away to his motorbike. By now ten men were encircling me. I endeavoured to appear calm and in control, aiming to acknowledge them in a respectful but confident manner. One of the men then demanded that I give them money. I explained that I wasn't carrying any cash. Then another asked straight out, 'Do you want sex?' (He spoke a little English.) I replied firmly and clearly, looking at him straight in the eye, 'No, that's not what I do'. That seemed to be enough. After a few more questions, my passport was returned and I was free to go.

As I set off, the endorphins flooded through my body so that my heart raced on the immediate downhill and I could hardly feel my legs as they laboured up the next incline. That was the most uneasy I had felt during the journey so far, maybe because I was also aware of one of the DRC's most alarming statistics – that a rape occurs every forty seconds somewhere in the country.

The boys also had an encounter with the corrupt police force. When Simon, Dan and Zdenek stopped to ask the police for directions, as they normally did in any other country, they were asked for money. Needless to say they didn't try that again.

It took just two days to cover almost 300 kilometres from Kinshasa to Songololo and the Angolan border. I did have the best tarmac strip in the country to savour. There was a fair amount of traffic moving between Kinshasa and the main port of Matadi; quite a contrast to the muddy, unmaintained road we had experienced between Pointe-Noire and Brazzaville. Other features were more similar to those we had encountered north of the border. The terrain consisted mostly of long, rolling hills carpeted by long savannah grasses. Where the countryside was flatter there was also more agriculture and heavy industry, especially around Lukala where a Chinese cement factory belched pollution into the sky and children greeted me with 'Ni hao.'

❋

Angola had been the most difficult country to research and plan for. Both before and during the journey I tried to make connections through the resource industry, via UNESCO and other organisations but my efforts were fruitless and I therefore lacked a specific project to focus on. Angola is associated in most Western minds with landmines and corruption, blood diamonds (diamonds traded to finance Angola's civil war) and poverty, the outcomes of a fourteen-year struggle for independence followed by a complex civil war lasting twenty-seven years. I wanted to learn about how the country was coping in the wake of two generations growing up knowing nothing but insecurity; for many, life had been a day-to-day, hand-to-mouth existence. Setting off towards M'banza Congo with our hard-won visas in hand, I felt relieved that I would not have to break the line of my journey and privileged that we had the opportunity to spend up to thirty days in the country. I was really looking forward to how the Angolan experience would unfurl but knew little of what to expect.

The immigration officer was pessimistic about my chances of cycling the 70 kilometres to M'banza Congo because he thought the road would be too difficult and muddy, however after my experiences in the Republic of Congo my concept as to what can be cycled had broadened. His predictions about the track quality were indeed accurate but it was only a half-day ride to reach the historic city of M'banza Congo. The first 25 kilometres were on the flat as the sticky clay road tracked along a broad valley, but then it veered up into the ranges. Although the steep climbs and steamy conditions were energy sapping my spirits were buoyed by vast open landscapes and welcoming villagers. Few travellers use this route and the locals responded to our passing with overwhelming enthusiasm. As I entered each village, I would usually be spotted first by children who would run towards and then alongside me waving and shouting.

The road to M'banza Congo (photo: Z Kratky)

I smiled and responded with 'Bom dia,' the only Portuguese phrase I knew, which usually set off a chain reaction down the street. I had to maintain a steady pace or I would have been mobbed by inquisitive friendliness. These small towns appeared to be poor and generally lacking in amenities, for example, there were no water pumps – residents' water supply relied on the collection of rainwater from their roofs.

As I neared M'banza Congo, or São Salvador do Congo as the Portuguese once called it, I was joined by a young teenage boy riding a bike with a frame far too big for him. Initially he tailed me, but then decided that the pace was too slow. He would race past me on the downhills, performing tricks such as standing on his seat and holding all sorts of poses with the flexibility and balance of a circus artiste. Show off. I felt a little boring and inept. He entertained me for a few kilometres along the muddy road and through the grassy woodlands. M'banza Congo's sprawling settlements, where I presumed he resided, gradually fused with the forest. Finally I laboured up onto an impressive flat-top plateau, known as Mongo a Kaila, where the muddy streets led us into a vibrant urban landscape; a contrasting mix of ancient and modern, poor and well-off.

I chose to divert to M'banza Congo, capital of Angola's Zaire Province, because of its historical significance. When the Portuguese first arrived in what is now northern Angola in 1482, M'banza Congo (population 50,000) was the long-established capital of the Kingdom of Kongo. The most significant empire of central-west Africa at this time, the Kingdom of Kongo extended from present-day Gabon to the Cuanza River, just south of Luanda. The Portuguese befriended Nzinga Nkuwu, the all-powerful king or 'Manikongo', who was intrigued by their sophisticated culture, religion and technology. Nzinga Nkuwu asked the Portuguese crown for missionaries and technical assistance in exchange for ivory and other goods. The Manikongo and ruling elite were quick to adopt Catholicism and learn new methods of stone masonry.

We headed along the main street, which represents a jumbled timeline of M'banza Congo's 500-year history. At the northern end sat a modern supermarket that would not have looked out of place in the West, replete with European imports and high price tags. Nearby, on the same side of the road, was the royal cemetery where at least ten Kongo kings were interred. Beside the cemetery is Kulumbimbi Cathedral, built in 1491 at a time when Portuguese and Congolese rulers were considered as equals. Pope John Paul II conducted mass at Kulumbimbi in 1992. A little further down, on the opposite side of the road, stand two tall, graceful 'sacred trees'; tradition says that court cases were heard here and the convicted hanged from them. The streetscape is now fairly organic, with more modern buildings filling in the gaps between the ancient and pre-1900 sites. The historic buildings are under consideration by UNESCO for World Heritage listing. We stayed in a contemporary hotel and I found an internet cafe a few doors down where I reconnected with the outside world.

✻

To understand how Angola spiralled into twenty-seven years of brutal civil war, it is necessary to briefly look at the history that led to the conflict. Initially the Portuguese had no interest in colonising the mosquito-ridden territories of the Kongo and neighbouring Ndongo kingdom to the south. It all started going wrong for the various Angolan tribes in the 1500s when the Portuguese needed slaves to work as domestic labourers in Europe and on their extensive plantations in Brazil and on the islands of São Tomé and Príncipe, in the Gulf of Guinea . The primary interests of the Portuguese over the next 300 years were in using Angola as a collection centre for one of the largest forced human migrations in history and as a strategic base on the route around the Cape of Good Hope. They gradually extended their presence in the region, mainly using the local populations to bolster their slave trade. Not surprisingly, slavery did nothing to endear the Portuguese to the Angolan people, and neither did the forced labour system and rigid dictatorship that replaced it in late 1800s. When the decolonisation process was occurring elsewhere in Africa in the 1950s, the Portuguese rejected independence and treated Angola like another overseas province. White immigration was encouraged and racial antagonisms intensified, fuelling the basis for the War of Independence that in turn set the scene for the civil war.

The situation was exacerbated in 1961 when the colonial authorities began to crush increasingly zealous uprisings from dissidents. The independence movement was driven by three principal groups that were aligned with the different tribal affiliations and international interests. The National Front for the Liberation of Angola (FNLA) was supported by northern Bakongo people, the Democratic Republic of Congo and anti-communist Western countries (the US provided arms through the DRC). Its major interest was to protect the people of the Kongo Region. The Popular Movement for the Liberation of Angola (MPLA) began with Marxist sensibilities and was supported by southern tribes, the USSR, Cuba and other Soviet allies. They had greatest influence over the northern coastal strip, including Luanda and the oil-rich state of Cabinda. The National Union for Total Independence of Angola (UNITA) originally had the support of the Ovimbundu people but later formed alliances with the Portuguese right wing, the US and South Africa. From the early 1960s, elements of these movements collaborated to fight a guerrilla war against the Portuguese.

A coup d'etat in Portugal in 1974 established a military government that promptly ended the war and agreed to hand over power to a coalition of the three political movements. The sudden colonial withdrawal in November 1975 became a mad scramble that involved one of the biggest airlifts in history. In one fell swoop the country was stripped of its qualified human resources and administrative structure, resulting in an uneven and weak infrastructure, low levels of health and education, two feuding sets of tribally-based elites and a large slice of unused government oil revenue up for grabs. The ideological differences between the three movements eventually led to the civil armed conflict, with FNLA and UNITA forces, encouraged by their respective international supporters, attempting to wrest control of Luanda from the communist-backed MPLA. Add to this Western communist paranoia and the political agendas of Cuba and apartheid South Africa, and the ingredients were ready to boil over into a vicious and protracted civil war.

Almost continuous conflicts devastated Angola until the leader of UNITA, Jonas Savimbi, was killed by government troops, peace was brokered and democracy prevailed in 2002. Nearly five million people were internally displaced during the war; now all but a few hundred thousand refugees have returned to their homes. But how can a country of approximately 19 million people recover when few can remember what peace was like? With the effects of conflict scarring and tainting the mindset, years of constant fear and uncertainty, an inbred culture of corruption, a lack of health and education facilities (especially in the rural regions), infrastructure obliterated – where do Angolans start? Landmines still litter

the countryside, killing and maiming the innocent. Although many regions have been cleared there is always a degree of risk, which seriously affects the rural population's ability to farm and grow food.

A street in M'banza Congo

*

After pausing to take a closer look at Kulumbimbi, I headed back along the unpaved streets and past the lively market stalls, down the hill and out through a neighbourhood of new houses, direction N'zeto, Ambrizete to the Portuguese, on the Atlantic coast. I was interested to see any evidence of the conflict and how people were recovering from it. Just as I was passing the Sonangol fuel station, I caught a glimpse of a fellow on the opposite side of the road, hobbling along using a single crutch to compensate for his missing leg. (Sonangol is the state-owned petroleum and natural gas company that has become the government's fundraising machine.) The Angola of 2010 just slapped me in the face.

Just out of town I was most appreciative of sections of brand-new asphalt road. The Chinese were building the road all the way to N'zeto. Of its 232 kilometres, 70 had been completed in different stages when we passed through. Rural Angolan friendliness may have rubbed off on the Chinese engineers as they too greeted me with smiles and waves and regularly stopped to ask whether I was okay. The Chinese presence seemed more prominent here than anywhere else in Africa. Now that the country is at peace, the national and international communities are scrambling to get their hands on the extensive bounty of resources – especially oil, diamonds and other minerals. China is currently the world's largest importer of Angolan oil and Angola is China's largest trading partner in Africa. What we were seeing was a part of a six billion US dollar (approximate) investment strategy to gain preferential access to Angola's raw materials. Added to that, China had provided Angola with unconditional loans by 2009 worth between 13.4 and 19.7 billion US dollars – loans that are given with no questions asked regarding transparency and accountability.* Chinese engineers, Chinese machinery and predominantly Chinese labour were replacing shockingly poor and old roads with new tar surfaces. These projects are a quick fix and perhaps a short-term answer to the infrastructure problem as the roads did not seem built to last. We noted in many instances that the quality of the Chinese work was seriously lacking, as though materials and labour costs were being skimped on. It was impossible, of course, for us to gauge whether this was the fault of the contractors or the poor negotiation skills of the government; for a cyclist passing through, however, these new surfaces were a treat.

---

*'Transparency and Accountability in Angola', *Human Rights Watch, 2010*

Houses in the small villages were almost exclusively made of home-fired bricks, baked in their local kilns. There were no gardens, just bare hard-packed dirt that turns into a skating rink the instant it rains. There didn't seem to be much food on offer, apart from the odd pile of pale-coloured oranges. Many homes and administrative buildings flew flags, mostly the national or MPLA flag or both. It is not surprising that these are very similar since the MPLA has been in power ever since independence in 1975; the only difference is that the Angolan banner has a cog wheel and machete added to the central yellow star – a kind of African version of the hammer and sickle. Occasionally the flags of other political parties flew too, especially in N'zeto where I also saw the FNLA colours, amongst others.

Angola's flag, one of many flying in N'zeto, is a modification of that belonging to the MPLA who were largely sponsored by the Soviet Union

Scenically, the road sliced through large, rolling hills, some very steep, topped by either long savannah grasses or dense pockets of jungle. As we were hugely concerned about the prospect of landmines, venturing away from the roadside, even for a nature break, presented a dilemma. We knew that the land near to the road should have been swept for mines but there was always an element of doubt that it had. Throughout Angola, this added a challenging new dimension to selecting suitable, out-of-the-way campsites. When setting up camp, Simon and Dan would look for small sections of jungle that had been cleared by the Chinese to dump their road-building materials on or for minor tracks. We could guarantee there would be no landmines where the ground had been recently used.

I saw comparatively little evidence of the conflicts, probably because Angolans would like to erase this chapter of their history and move on. About halfway between M'banza Congo and N'zeto,

Wreckage of a Russian helicopter on a hilltop half way between M'banza Congo and N'zeto

after a very steep climb, we did come across the wreckage of a Russian helicopter and this warranted inspection. Apart from that, we noticed signs pocked with bullet holes, the remnants of bridges and some buildings which had been blown up. N'zeto's quiet main street, which had obviously been the site of intense fighting, was a combination of dilapidated ruins and more recent developments where flags wavered sporadically in the fresh Atlantic gusts.

As we neared the coast, the savannah and rainforest changed to a drier, less fertile landscape. The grass cover became shorter and wispier and the forest contained many succulent species such as cacti and majestic baobabs. The cactus trees, *euphorbia conspicua,* were particularly eye-catching. Endemic to Angola, stands of specimens up to about 15 metres tall frequently graced the roadside, soaring above the sclerophyllous scrub. The cool Benguela Current that wells up along the coast causes the dry conditions. The coastline is reduced to desert in southern Angola. In Namibia it becomes the Skeleton Coast, an infamous foggy graveyard for ships since the times of the early whalers and Portuguese sailors.

The road south from N'zeto was far worse than I had anticipated. It had been paved once – probably well before the war – but it had not been maintained in any way. The first 50 kilometres south from N'zeto were characterised by deep sandy patches which made the going very heavy. The bulk of the road was unsealed with a rare island of asphalt or strip of old kerbing. Zdenek wanted to experience what cycling was like on this surface; after accompanying me for a 20-kilometre stint of constant dips, sand and

Euphorbia conspicua. Latex from this cactus tree, endemic to Angola, is taken as a purgative to treat constipation, and also to treat breast inflammation, epilepsy, coughs and tuberculosis

corrugations he'd had enough, commenting that he had to stop before he incurred brain damage! To add to the discomfort, I encountered tsetse flies for the first time. I didn't know what they were at first when they swarmed angrily around as I rode, biting straight through my sweaty clothing like horse flies. If I paused, the cloud of marauding insects would intensify. When I was finally able to apply repellent, it proved relatively ineffective. The problem dissipated after I stopped for the evening and the sun set.

FNLA flag painted on a rock near Musserra, a village just north of Ambriz and the FNLA headquarters

I was suffering from having had to endure all this and nearly 900 kilometres of cycling in a week. In retrospect, it was more than that. The whole physical and mental journey, the late nights, organisational stresses, team tensions and minor illnesses gnawed away at my physical being. I was much fitter than at the start of the expedition but the cumulative effect, day after day, week after week and month after month, was taking its toll. Into my sixth month and with about half the total distance covered, I was battling my own war of attrition. I felt exhausted and ultra-sensitive to the constant heat and humidity – my heat rash and chafing returned, my neck muscles ached severely from being in permanent spasm and my knees grumbled from all the jarring.

On the second last day into Luanda after just 22 kilometres I was feeling terrible. My heart had begun to race and I would break into a cold sweat just trying to turn the pedals. Then I became shaky and light-headed. The boys were a real help, meeting me every 10 or 15 kilometres so I could take a short break, rehydrate and cool off. Somehow I managed to gradually push through it so that by the end of the day we'd still covered 110 kilometres and no real damage was done to the schedule.

Ninety kilometres out of Luanda, we finally hit good tar road. I cycled through Barra do Dande, a bustling fishing village, and across the open grassy plains to connect with the main highway into Luanda from the north. The heat penetrated to my core and in my exhaustive state, my throat felt as though it was being constricted. I struggled to suck in enough oxygen. Conditions on the busy Caxito-Luanda road were hectic, to say the least. It wasn't quite wide enough for the constant barrage of heavy traffic. There was no hard shoulder and I fought to keep balance as I tried to avoid the crumbling edges or being forced off the road and into the gravel. Around Quifangondo and the Bengo River I passed through marshlands studded by small market gardens but nearing the city limits the road was flanked by heavy industry, predominantly Chinese developments. Road-signs were written in both Portuguese

Phoning ahead to organise accommodation in Luanda

and Chinese to accommodate the Chinese drivers who mostly piloted the huge juggernauts.

This was phase one of the white-knuckle ride into Luanda. Phase two began as the asphalt strip abruptly ended about 20 kilometres out of the city and the busy highway disintegrated into patches of potholes, dips and sand. The constant stream of heavy vehicles heading for the busy port was funnelled into hopeless bottlenecks which evolved into free for alls, drivers becoming impatient and travelling along the verge, down the wrong side of the road. Normally in congested traffic I could slip around the outside of the jam, but here the roadside was often loose sand and I had to be aware of vehicles approaching from head-on. Car horns and sirens – an ambulance, police – added to the chaos, the opacity of the dense dust clouds causing further confusion. Despite my physical state and my surroundings, my mind had to somehow remain translucent, focused and alert as a matter of survival.

Death Road – The start of phase two of the white-knuckle ride into Luanda (photo: Z Kratky)

I may have struggled along Luanda's main northern artery, but to the FNLA, the same road from Quifangondo into the city became known as *Nshila wa Lufu*, the Road of Death. This was the site of the first major battle of the Angolan Civil War in which the FNLA lost hundreds of fighters, retreated to its base in Ambriz and was soon completely overpowered by the MPLA in the north. The Battle of Death Road, as they called it, signalled the end of the importance of the FNLA in the Angolan Civil War. The MPLA and UNITA went on to slug it out for over a quarter of a century, supported by their international allies and further financed by their resources – chiefly oil and blood diamonds.

✳

Like so much of Angola's infrastructure, even the Road of Death was being mended: near the port, sections of the old road were being replaced by a six-lane freeway. The condition of the rest meant that all concentration was on the task at hand, and I was only able to catch fleeting glimpses of the suburbs beyond my tunnel vision. The periphery of Luanda is characterised by ramshackle slums called *musseques*, markets, and generally poor-standard housing. Those *musseques* that sprawl beyond the city limits are largely a result of the civil war, when refugees flooded in from other Angolan regions. Refugees still arrive from the Katanga Region in the Democratic Republic of Congo. Since the war, the city of more than five million people has experienced a population explosion and we were travelling through the heart of the process of rebuilding and extension to accommodate the masses, rich and poor. Mixed in with these poorer regions were new satellite developments, gated enclaves, rows of townhouses and Western-style supermarkets.

Arriving at the centre, we still had no guarantee of a place to stay. As a result of the conflicts, accommodation is limited, infrastructure is poor and 90 per cent of food is imported. Luanda is ranked as the world's second most expensive city after Tokyo and we could not afford even the cheapest hotel. Eventually we connected with Adrian Fick through our Nando's South Africa connection – the company he worked for, AngoAlissar, had provided the official invitations for us to qualify for entry visas into the country. Adrian very kindly put us up in his tiny one-bedroom flat; a secure accommodation in the same building that housed the Israeli Embassy.

Central Luanda was a different world altogether; it would not have looked out of place on the Iberian Peninsula. Here were reminders of past glories and of future potential: vast mansions from the colonial era overlooking Luanda Bay sat next to multi-storied apartments with louvred windows and terracotta tiled roofs. Amongst the mansions were dotted more recent commercial buildings. Gaunt but functional, these high rises were almost certainly designs out of the Soviet school of architecture. There seemed to be new buildings and renovations underway just about everywhere I looked: the town was undergoing an extreme makeover. Construction cranes that pimpled the city skyline worked around the clock. Battle scars inflicted by bullets and mortar shells from the time when the city was under siege were being airbrushed from people's consciousness.

A city undergoing massive renovation. A view of Luanda from our accommodation

Yet it felt as though the 'real Africa' had been locked out of the city centre. The streets were swept clean, the parks were manicured, and I noted there were no beggars, no one peddling their wares on the sidewalks. There were only new cars on the streets – the clattering, smoke-bellowing African bomb was nowhere to be seen. Few taxis were available to ferry people in and out of the *centro da cidade*.

This brave, new, peaceful world is one of extreme inequality – perhaps an inevitable blight of the recovery phase. In the north of the country there are few facilities; hospitals do not have enough medicines and people generally possess little. Yet in downtown Luanda we saw money virtually dripping from the chandeliers of its luxurious hotels (I was trying to find a working internet portal on a public holiday) and boutiques selling designer clothes. Improvements in infrastructure, especially in Luanda, are mostly a facade, showcasing to international visitors and investors the impression of a higher level of development than the national reality. Between 1997 and 2008, Angola's GDP grew tenfold, yet more than 60 per cent of the population live on less than two dollars a day.

Since Angola's conception as a nation, its institutions have been brought up on a diet of cruel and domineering powers, uncertainty, mistrust and poverty – all ingredients that stunt a nation's growth and cultivate deep-rooted corruption. Under international pressure, President José Eduardo dos Santos's government has made some commitments to reducing corruption but governance remains as haywire as the traffic we encountered on the way in, and transparency as opaque as the dusty haze stirred up by vehicles. The president is into his fourth decade of power and with recent amendments to the constitution, as long as he stays leader of the People's Movement for the Liberation of Angola (MPLA), he is likely to remain president until 2022. The government relies on revenue almost solely acquired from controlling the exploitation of natural resources rather than from taxation or a more diversified economy.

Angola is sub-Saharan Africa's second largest oil producer. Sonangol, the state-run group set up at the dawn of independence to manage Angola's vast reserves, had never been audited until 2003 – and those figures were not made public. Even after the government made a commitment to the International Monetary Fund in 2008 to gain a development loan (due to low oil prices and the economic downturn), it has never fully revealed the company's financial statements. According to a Human Rights Watch report in 2011, 32 billion dollars were either spent or transferred without being properly accounted for between 2007 and 2010.

Angola is undoubtedly moving forward but if members of the powerful elite weren't siphoning off billions for their own benefit, fewer of its citizens would be struggling. The trends of the Human Development Index rankings illustrate the issue: Angola's development status has barely improved even with the 1000 per cent increase in GDP. During the civil war, Angola was ranked 157 out of 175 countries on the index; in 2006 it was 161 out of 177 countries and in 2009, 143 out of 182 countries. Although China may be cited as a threat to good governance for providing unconditional loans and funding, it is not solely to blame for fuelling the Angolan government's resistance to reform. Most of the grave mismanagement occurred when Western companies and governments were the largest investment and trading partners of the country. Western companies are still the largest investors in Angola's oil and gas sector, the US being the second biggest consumer.

❈

Leaving Luanda early in the morning of Easter Sunday could not have been more of a contrast with the traffic conditions when we arrived. I set off from where I stopped cycling, fittingly from opposite the beautiful colonial Banco Nacional de Angola building on the Marginale – Luanda's palm-fringed waterfront boulevard. At the southern extremity of the tranquil Luanda Bay I rounded the old fort, Fortaleza de São Miguel. It was built in 1576 as the administrative centre of the first colony but later became a principal holding house for slaves destined for Brazil. By the nineteenth century Angola was the largest source of slaves for the Americas, and many of them would have farewelled their homeland from this point. I wound my way through the older part of town, pausing to take in a shanty fishing settlement

just offshore, and the rocket-shaped mausoleum of Agostinho Neto, Angola's first president. Traffic flowed pretty well along the brand-new roads which tracked the coastline south. At Luanda's southern extremity, the new suburb of Luanda Sul looked like any Western development, with its chains of luxury apartments and even a golf course.

Shanty fishing village, a part of the city coastline

Knowing that we would have mostly decent roads in southern Angola and Namibia, I decided to put in some long days and make up time. Hence I put my head down and tail up from Luanda to Tsumeb in northern Namibia. I managed 930 kilometres in seven days from Luanda to Lubango in the mountains, climbing 1770 metres, had a day off and then covered 773 kilometres in five days over the high plains to cross the Namibian border and on to reach Tsumeb.

The coastal strip south of Luanda is almost like a separate country from the north – in terms of its geographic, economic and cultural landscapes. The barren-looking limestone coastal plain that became more desert-like as I headed south supported mainly scrub, cactus trees, yuccas, aloe vera and other salt-resistant plants. Where the plateau falls away to the sea, the forces of erosion are continually sculpting the spectacular coastline.

Sunset over the desertous coastal strip

Yuccas thrive in the dry conditions

Every so often a river carved its way to the ocean, segmenting the coastal plain. For me, this meant a short steep descent followed by a climb; otherwise, apart from a section of badlands, it was easy going. Not only were the roads tip top, port towns such as Porto Amboim and Sumbe were virtual building sites. Judging by the logos on the construction signs, Sonangol is also fuelling these growth spurts – new condominiums, grand seaside homes. In between all this change there were still many small villages tucked back into the hillsides, with traditional houses made of mud bricks with high-pitched thatched roofs.

Larger rivers such as the Cuanza, just south of Luanda, and the Queve, between Porto Amboim and Sumbe, formed ribbons of green through the desert lands. Where the highway crossed them they had splayed out into marshy floodplains, teeming with birdlife – and mosquitoes. The war was devastating for Angola's wildlife, but these difficult-to-penetrate wetlands became safe-harbours for the threatened animals. Upstream from the swampy sanctuaries, the rivers were strategic points for many military offensives, with most of the bridges destroyed at various stages of the conflict.

A back street in Sumbe

On our second night out from Luanda, about 20 kilometres north of Sumbe, we became the subjects of a different type of vicious attack – from mosquitoes. Simon and Dan had found what appeared to be a perfect, secluded campsite: a disused track running parallel to the main road. The Queve River floodplain was several kilometres away and our campsite was on the high, dry coastal plain. Just as we were relaxing

The Cubal River cuts a spectacular gorge through the elevated coastal plain, 15km south of Sumbe

at dusk with a cup of tea prior to supper, we were suddenly ambushed by swarms of mosquitoes. Paranoid about contracting malaria or dengue fever, we all made a mad rush to cover up and avoid being bitten. After dark I tried to wash by removing one limb at a time from my waterproof clothing (best at keeping the insects out) but it wasn't a very effective manoeuvre for keeping them at bay. Entering the tent required a well-organised strategy so that the fly tent door was not unzipped for longer than absolutely necessary. All goods to go inside were lined up outside and then flung in through the smallest of openings, and finally I dived in and zipped up the fly. But I wasn't quick enough – a few buzzing insurgents snuck in all the same. After a mossie-killing spree, I spent much of the next few hours stalking the survivors and trying to ascertain which side of the fly tent the blighters were taunting me from. In these conditions, writing my diary as I did every evening was a challenge – the result was virtually illegible. Not a comfortable night!

One of the most frustrating factors as we were travelling through was that no one on the team could speak Portuguese. Although Simon could manage a little as he can speak Spanish and has travelled through Brazil, communicating with the locals was impossible unless they spoke English or basic French. Quite a few did speak a little English because the education level in Angola is generally better than in most of the countries I had travelled through to that point, especially in the more developed regions. The population is also exposed to English television programs with Portuguese subtitles.

Angola has the Cubans to thank for preventing its education system, along with its health system and infrastructure, from regressing to ground zero during the war years. When the Portuguese made their sudden mass exodus, 5000 Cuban educational, technical and medical staff were posted in Angola to help fill the gaps the colonists left behind. According to the Cubans, their overriding mission in Angola was humanitarian, not military. Between 1976 and 1991, 430,000 Cuban foreign aid volunteers served in Angola. For the volunteers, this 'internationalist service' represented the highest ideal of the Cuban Revolution. At the time of independence, over 90 per cent of the Angolan population were illiterate. By the 1980s, a constant level of 2000 volunteer teachers served in Angola, and at one point, two-thirds of all doctors in Angola were Cuban. Thousands of students were granted scholarships in Cuba to train and return as teachers, medics and technicians. Cuba's engagement laid the foundation for Angola's social services and provided a springboard to post-war recovery. According to the World Bank, in 2010 some 70 per cent of Angolans could read and write: 80 per cent of men, 60 per cent of women. I did notice a new school in just about every village.

South of Sumbe, the route turned into the foothills of the Planalto-Angolan Plateau. It was much harder work to cycle on, but the scenery was inspiring. Jagged sandstone peaks formed a stunning backdrop and the land became more wooded and fertile. For the first time since perhaps southern Cameroon there was significant land cultivation and farmers produced more of their own food. I passed

A line of cactus trees on the coastal plain with the Planalto, or Angolan Plateau, forming a wall to the east

villages with active markets selling locally grown fruit and vegetables.

Our path diverted back to the Atlantic coast again, for the last time on the journey, to the port cities of Lobito and Benguela. Assuming (correctly) that finding accommodation would be an arduous task, Simon and Dan drove on ahead to Benguela, leaving me to cover the last 70 kilometres on my own. Lobito's hilly outskirts, like a smaller version of Luanda, were a mix of new industry and housing developments. Navigating my way through the port city was a case of continually asking people for directions – until I met a local named Carlos who promptly made it his duty to protect me and escorted me through the town on his scooter. Carlos had lived in South Africa for many years and spoke good English and I learned much from our conversations as he led me most of the way to Benguela (20 kilometres from Lobito). He mentioned that, during the war, the city looked much greener whereas now it is a dustbowl – a virtual building site. Pointing out a Chinese camp – a temporary town site built of dongas (as we call them in Australia) – he told me that many of the unskilled labourers rebuilding Angola's infrastructure were Chinese prisoners, sent over to do their time. He also confirmed what we had heard about corruption levels and when I mentioned the president he did not want to talk about the man! Carlos' sentiments echoed what we had heard time and again in Angola – that the people were

aware of the extraordinary levels of corruption and the need for greater transparency. On the other hand, Carlos thought the country was now stable and would never revert to war again. It was his view that people had moved on and that now cities like Lobito and Benguela were places of exciting opportunity. That is why he had returned there to live.

As we travelled along the new freeway – still under construction – a fellow in a 'standard' African car passed several times, waving at me to stop. Normally, if I was on my own I would have ignored him but as Carlos was able to find out what he wanted, I obliged and pulled over. The driver was Tony, a journalist for a Lobito radio station. I agreed to an interview on the spot and luckily it was not in Portuguese! In it I focused on the positive aspects of my journey and project.

Being interviewed for Lobito radio by Tony, a local journalist

As Carlos and I worked our way south of the Lobito city centre, the maze of a road system crossed over the Benguela Railway in the peripheral suburb of Catumbela, not far from its western terminus at the port. Until recently, the stretch between Lobito and Benguela that we followed was the only functional part of the historic 1344-kilometre railway, which had been built almost a century ago by British businessman Robert Williams and his Benguela Railway Company to connect the Copperbelt region of south-east Belgium Congo (DRC) to the port of Lobito. The British employed forced labour to complete the twenty-seven-year project by 1929, the main objective of which was to extract the abundant resources from the Katangan and Zambian copper regions as economically as possible. By building the line, they cut almost 500 kilometres from the existing land route through Zimbabwe (then Rhodesia) and a further 5000 kilometres from the sea route back to Europe. A key leg of southern Africa's only trans-continental route, connecting Lobito on the Atlantic to Dar es Salaam (Tanzania) on the Indian Ocean, the railway was destroyed during the civil war, mostly by UNITA insurgents. Trains and repair crews were ambushed, stations bombed and bridges dynamited, and the right-of-way was mined. The lifeline through Angola's interior was crippled.

One main reason for the existence of the temporary Chinese town in Lobito was to house workers employed to rebuild the Benguela Railway. In 2006, the Chinese began a six-year project to help Angola restore the railway but before any construction work could start, the line had to be cleared of landmines.

The HALO Trust, a Scottish-based NGO, cleared more than 2000 mines and unexploded ordnance with some assistance from Angolan government agencies. Within two years of our passing along the first part of the Benguela Railway, the rebuilding would be completed and access to the interior reopened, further stimulating development and trade within the country.

Many categorise today's China as just another imperial power out to exploit the riches of Africa. Its motives, it seems, are similar to those of other countries – to take advantage of the natural resources – but the terms are quite different. The Chinese provide the Angolan government with cheap loans, enabling it to pay for the costs of construction. These loans are paid off using Angolan oil, sold abroad at the prevailing market rate. This is dissimilar from the former colonial powers, in this case the British, who drained hundreds of millions of tons of precious African copper down the Benguela railway line without paying anyone for it. So, yes, the Chinese are providing unconditional loans at a bargain rate, and these in turn do nothing to combat corruption, but their involvement is contributing to getting the country back on to its feet in a time of need.

Benguela and Lobito are quite different beasts. Lobito, a young economic boomtown, exists because the deep water port was selected to service the transcontinental Benguela Railway whereas Benguela is the traditional administrative centre of the province. Benguela's history parallels Luanda's as a prominent centre of the colonial slave trade. It is now a combination of beautiful colonial architecture in the city centre declining to slums that grew to house refugees. Dan and Simon found the cheapest hotel available in town but we didn't get much more than amenable staff for under $US200. The plumbing in our communal hotel room did not work and gaps between the windows and wall allowed mosquitoes into the room at night.

✻

Benguela to Lubango took three days. Although I gained nearly 1800 metres in altitude, the climb on to the Planalto was reasonably gradual, apart from one section, and I was able to enjoy the beautiful, ever-changing scenery. Along the way I was spoiled by kindness. A number of people stopped to give drinks and food.

About an hour before the end of the first day up from Benguela a South African truck driver pulled over and waved a bottle of iced water. His name was Tienie Kril and after an initial conversation and a drink with the three of us, we agreed to camp together that night. As is normal for someone who spends most of his life on the road Tienie was well-equipped, with a few more comforts than us. He had a fridge and freezer and he even rigged up a shower for me by connecting a shower head to a five-litre bucket and setting it up in the vestibule between the cabin and the first of the two trailers. That night he pulled some steaks from the freezer and cold drinks from the fridge and we had a good old South African *braai*. Tienie spoke of his fears for his family's safety in South Africa. He called his wife every night while on the road to check that each other was safe, and they were planning to move to Canada for a less stressful life. Being a truckie in Africa is so much more complex and dangerous than it is in Australia or Canada; with dodgy border crossings, corrupt officials, high duty prices and poor security to be negotiated. Tienie recounted how he was shot at in the DRC and said he now preferred to work along the South Africa–Angola route because it was safer and there were better business prospects, even though expenses were high. Angola

A side road made the perfect spot for Tienie to park his truck and for us to camp in the wetter climes of the Planalto

was, he felt, a country with a brighter future than others where he had worked. Similar to our experience, Tienie found it, on the whole, to be a safe, friendly country to travel through.

I continued along the new Chinese-made roads, whose quality was appalling. In some places the bitumen was so thin it was cracking like egg shells and becoming potholed within just three months of being laid. The sections that were still to be sealed were stark reminders of how fortunate we were to have new tar roads. Heavy traffic streamed onto side tracks in an attempt to avoid the original road that had decomposed into an untenable condition.

Enormous semi-trailers had to negotiate dips, water traps and steep hills, making even more of a mess and a testing time for all of us. As we gained altitude, we entered wetter climes: storm clouds bubbled up each afternoon and lightning flashed at random in the evening sky. Localised cloudbursts appeared to erupt somewhere almost continuously through the night.

Once on the high, more fertile Huila Plateau, the land was very different. This is productive, well-developed agricultural country. I could see Lubango from about 30 kilometres out. Angola's highest city is set on the Planalto at 1770 metres with a spectacular mountainous backdrop. A huge 'Christo-Rei' (statue of 'Christ the King') overlooking the escarpment 300 metres above Lubango is reminiscent of the monuments in Lisbon, the Corcovado guarding Rio de Janeiro and other Portuguese-founded cities. Even the marble statue had not escaped the conflict. It

The 'Christo-Rei' monument keeps watch over Lubango

had recently been renovated to conceal bullet marks on its face but it still had some missing fingers. Predominantly founded by Portuguese farmers from the island of Madeira, who travelled to the fertile plains to explore new opportunities, Lubango's boulevards and reasonably well-maintained streets had a distinct Mediterranean feel. The walls of some grand colonial buildings were adorned with cascades of bougainvillea. The alpine climate was such a relief after sweating it out, day and night, in the humid tropics. Lubango was a perfect place to have a day off and re-energise for the next stage, and we took advantage of its high-standard cafes and restaurants.

Herero woman. Herero people regularly cross the Angolan-Namibian border when migrating with their herds

❊

From Lubango I dropped some altitude gradually over the next couple of days, but stayed above 1100 metres. I really appreciated the open space after feeling a little claustrophobic in the equatorial regions. I could 'breathe again.' Relative to what I had been doing in recent times, the cycling was less challenging and I was able to clock consistently long distances, averaging 155 kilometres a day for the next five days to reach Tsumeb.

The southern provinces of Huila and Cunene are home to more cattle than people. I regularly passed groups of nomadic and semi-nomadic cattle herders who were grazing their stock on the rich native grasses along the roadside and on common lands. Much of the hinterland was fenced off as privately owned ranches. These nomad groups, either Herero or Ovambo, mostly live in northern Namibia, although a minority call the environs around the Cunene River home. Unlike the Fulani peoples we met in the Sahel region, or the Khoisan who are the original inhabitants of southern Africa, the Herero and Ovambo cattle herders, who had migrated from central Africa around 500 years ago, were generally very muscular and thick-set.

There was evidence of fierce past battles near the border. Running parallel with Angola's struggle for independence and civil war was Namibia's (then South West Africa) struggle for independence from South Africa. That war spilled into southern Angola when the MPLA offered the South West African People's Organisation, SWAPO, bases in Angola to launch attacks against the South African military in 1976. Xangongo was the site of the headquarters for the north-western front of SWAPO. The South African Defence Force, already fighting against the MPLA in Angola to keep a buffer zone to segregate black Africa and their system of apartheid, attacked Xangongo from the north. The South Africans proceeded to push SWAPO back towards their other base at Ondjiva and the border. South of Xangongo we crossed the old battlefields still

Landmines cordoned off at Mongua. The land has to be swept for mines before the road can be widened

littered with the wrecks of many derelict tanks and military units. At Mongua we came across a fenced-off area warning of landmines. A villager explained that the government has commissioned the main road to be widened but to do so means the entire 20-metre strip of land has to be swept for mines first. He told us that there were many mines still scattered through the bush. This was another example of the kind of handicap affecting Angola's post-war development, although it is a handicap they seem to be overcoming.

Crossing into Namibia was a painless process. The border post was efficient. Australians and British can just get a visa on the border – free – and Zdenek, who'd had complications obtaining his visa in Luanda, had no problems. The change in culture and level of development was immediate and profound. Travelling through Namibia, which has a population of just two million people, was much more similar to Australia than other African countries. They even drive on the left-hand side of the road there – and the main roads are excellent. The population speaks English, which meant we didn't have to struggle to communicate. Supermarkets are well-stocked, as in a normal Western store. There is plenty of choice of product and prices are much lower than in Angola. Services seem to be efficient and people are only too pleased to help … they seem to be more relaxed and there is less pressure.

We continued to Tsumeb, used the campgrounds as a base and drove back up the highway to Etosha National Park, taking three days off to explore by vehicle.

The next generation growing up free from civil war, its effects gradually diminishing

Total distance: 12,677 kilometres

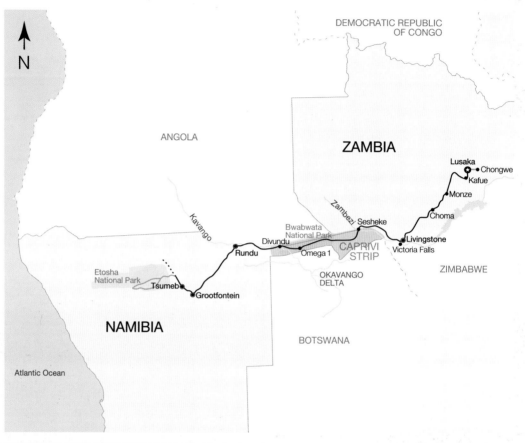

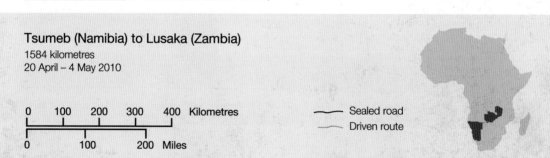

Tsumeb (Namibia) to Lusaka (Zambia)

1584 kilometres
20 April – 4 May 2010

| 0 | 100 | 200 | 300 | 400 | Kilometres |

| 0 | 100 | 200 | Miles |

— Sealed road
— Driven route

11
CONSERVING NATURAL WONDERS

Tsumeb to Lusaka (Namibia and western Zambia)

Etosha ostriches

Halali Camp Waterhole, Etosha National Park, Namibia. Halali's viewing platform is set into a small dolomite *koppie* (hill) safely above the floodlit waterhole. To watch the animals was a bit like going to the theatre while the performance was in progress. The audience creep in quietly in the dark, trying not to trip over the rocks or make a sound, not even whisper. The animals are the actors, stars of the show. The main difference is that they haven't done any rehearsals and rarely turn up on cue.

As we crept in, a greater kudu was munching the grass off to one side of the 'stage.' Gradually it grazed its way across the foreground, so totally focused on the larder of fresh shoots and flowers that it didn't flinch at the cascade of camera shutter-clicks. High-powered lenses framed its every move. The mature stag looked positively regal, crowned by its long horns that spiralled uniformly with two-and-a-half twists back from its head.

Kudu horns have long been prized for their shape and size, used as decorations, musical instruments, honey containers and symbolic ritual objects. In general, kudus are not aggressive animals but when males compete for dominance, they occasionally get their horns in a tangle: the large antelopes can become intertwined and, unable to break the double-helical deadlock, eventually die of thirst or starvation. Mother Nature distinguishes the kudu's taupe coat from other antelope by branding it with random fine white lines that run vertically across its torso, as if they had been sloppily dribbled from Her paintbrush. A brown-and-white striped beard forms decorative tassels down its dewlap. As it has done throughout its successful existence, the kudu's senses were attuned to what mattered – survival. This kudu stayed well away from the water's edge, constantly looking back to check for any predators.

On the far side of the waterhole, a small black rhinoceros emerged from the shadows of the *mopane* bush. It too moved cautiously – surprising, I thought, for an animal of such brawn (and small brain). Rhinos are agile and fast over short distances and defend themselves by goring their opponents. Their notorious unpredictability adds a dimension that has helped them survive for about 20 million years in Africa. Humans, latecomers in the rhino evolutionary time-scale, are their main predator. Unfortunately for rhinos, their horns are largely sought in Chinese medicine for their falsely claimed aphrodisiac and healing qualities. All five rhino species are threatened. In southern Africa in the late 1960s black rhinos numbered 70,000 but thirty years later this figure had dwindled to fewer than 2500. Rhinos are at their most vulnerable when they drink at waterholes, as they need to every day, so our rhino's caution was justifiable.

The odd couple kept us entertained for quite some time in the fading twilight. The kudu continued to chomp its way across the set until it eventually disappeared back into the bush. The rhino paddled about, causing the only ripples across the shallow pond. Despite its keen hearing and sense of smell, it too seemed oblivious to the snap-happy audience; it

The greater kudu and the black rhino, Halali Camp waterhole, Etosha National Park

must have known this was friendly fire. Exiting the water, it waddled across to a log that was just the right height for it to scratch its low undercarriage, and had a great time rocking back and forth over the log, arching its neck backwards and flapping its piglet tail in pure bliss.

❈

Up until Etosha National Park we had seen very few wild animals during our journey but our two-day visit to the 23,000-square-kilometre sanctuary changed all that. Not many wild animals are seen outside the parks these days, mainly due to loss of habitat, poaching and the bushmeat trade. Namibia is the only African nation with conservation firmly written in to its constitution. Since independence

Etosha means 'Great White Place'. The Etosha Pan covers 4731 kilometres square

in 1989 – perhaps an opportunity to create a more practical environmental agenda for the times – numbers of black rhinoceros and cheetahs have been increased significantly. The Etosha National Park, 80 kilometres north of Tsumeb, is Namibia's showpiece. The word 'etosha' means 'Great White Place', referring to the enormous saltpan and the limestone-based park grounds in and around which the animals live. The park was proclaimed over 100 years ago, which makes it one of the first designated conservation places in Africa.

We left the bikes and some unneeded gear at our campsite in Tsumeb and drove back to Etosha.

The park was easy to drive through, with good quality roads and plenty of side-tracks to access the many waterholes. Of course no one is allowed to get out of their vehicles (except in protected areas) and cycling is not permitted as there are plenty of man-eaters patrolling the land. At Sueda Waterhole on the edge of Etosha Pan we certainly needed no further persuasion to stay in the vehicle. There we spotted our first lions in the wild. For a moment I actually thought the male was a small elephant – it was huge! There was a lioness with him. They appeared delirious with contentment, having just consumed the morning kill. Almost as soon as we sighted them, they lay down in the shade of small shrubs and long tufts of grass. Later that afternoon, on the way back to the Namutoni entrance, we returned in the hope that they might still be there. And they were, but on closer inspection through the binoculars we counted a whole pride of lions. The male had a harem of seven females. The first two lions we had seen had not moved all day, except to follow the shade as the sun tracked across the sky. They were in deep relaxation mode – some lying on their backs, some with paws draped limply over another. Just as we were about to head off, Dan sighted two more lionesses, one asleep in a much closer location, another arriving from a different direction, moving with caution.

Over the two days in Etosha Park we also saw and identified elephants, black-backed jackals, a cape fox, a spotted hyena, a suricate, warthogs, black rhinos, giraffes, Burchell's zebras, steenboks, springboks, gemsboks, blue wildebeests, greater kudus, hartebeests, impalas, ground squirrels, honey badgers, ostriches, a martial eagle, kori bustards, southern yellow hornbills, lilac-breasted rollers, Swainson's spurfowl, starlings, owls and some other wildlife. Cheetahs and leopards were the main animals that remained elusive but which are known to inhabit Etosha – but there had to be some classic game left to see another time!

Giraffes gather around a waterhole

❊

I was determined to cover some decent distance, even catch up time on the way to Nunda River Lodge, near Divundu, West Caprivi. From Tsumeb I headed south east along the Otavi Triangle to Grootfontein, 60 kilometres away. Grootfontein has pride of place on the expedition as being the most southerly town we visited. From there, I headed north-east – finally in the right direction towards Somalia! Grootfontein had unusual beginnings. It was first settled in 1885 by an Afrikaans group from the north-west of South Africa known as the Dorsland Trekkers. They had tried to migrate to Lubango in Angola, but when the

Portuguese claimed the region as theirs, about forty families returned to call the fertile and mineral-rich environs around Grootfontein home.

I slipped through the tidy streets and back out into the vast bushveldt landscape. The road-sides were punctuated with regular picnic stops, conveniently located about every 10 kilometres or so. The organised infrastructure was such a contrast to the Africa I had seen prior to Namibia. Both sides of the Trans-Caprivi Highway were flanked by the fences of large, privately owned cattle-grazing farms, and the occasional Southern Cross windmill made me feel at home. On the first night back on the road we camped at a truck-stop at the border between the Grootfontein and Kavango regions. While physically the rolling veldt landscape of the Kavango region looked similar, the cultural landscape was quite different. The route appeared to be more heavily populated with the local Kavango people and, further on, groups of San, the first inhabitants. I passed through village after village with all sorts of handicrafts for sale by the side of the road and received an overwhelming number of welcoming 'hellos'. After Rundu, I pushed on due east, parallel with the Kavango River, and despite a nagging headwind, rose to my little personal challenge of reaching Divundu after three days and 532 kilometres.

We weren't only at the geographical low point in the expedition but also at rock bottom as far as team spirits went. Ever since the first phase out of Yaoundé I had sensed a growing air of negativity. Of course, no expedition, especially one of this magnitude in Africa, is going to run perfectly smoothly. Simon and Dan would pick holes and act cynically towards anything they didn't fully embrace. I felt that they were looking down on everything that I did. Initially I believed and hoped that such undertones would work themselves out, especially once we escaped the confines of the tropical Wet. But over the two months that this particular combination of personalities was in the vehicle, the negativity towards the expedition had festered into a serious division. Now, especially with such long hours on the road and with little else to stimulate the mind, boredom reduced activity to all but basic tasks.

Various minor issues that Dan had been prepared to tolerate at the start of the journey had become unscalable obstacles in his mind. He was now able to cycle but no longer wanted to get on the bike, saying I cycled too slowly for him. What he failed to appreciate was that his endurance cycling technique and workload had at least part-caused his injury in the first place. As he had never done the consecutive daily distances that I was covering here it would have been difficult for him to relate to the cumulative physical and mental effects the expedition had on me over the six months to this stage. For Simon's part, he drove and maintained the Land Rover faultlessly and diligently to the point where anything that challenged his neat equilibrium stressed him immensely, especially when I hadn't secured accommodation in the main cities days in advance. Despite this, to the team's credit, all essential duties were carried out like clockwork. Dan supported Simon, maintained the bikes, took pride in his cooking, kept the shopping to a minimal budget and turned his hand to whatever else was required. Zdenek kept very much to himself and so it was difficult to gauge how he felt.

I knew what was happening. I felt incredibly tense and uncomfortable in Simon's and Dan's presence, though I tried not to reveal it. The situation sapped the little energy I had left. For me it was a case of keeping the pedals turning, hour after hour for eight to ten hours a day. I realised this wasn't forever and I would only have to withstand another two weeks, until Lusaka. There we would have a change of team and John would return. It felt like nothing that I could do (without compromising the expedition) would be right in Dan's or Simon's eyes so it was better to work with the situation rather than against it. I had to respect that they had different views and that individually they were good people; it was the combination of circumstances that was threatening the expedition. I decided that, in order to keep the team together, the best plan was not to confront but rather remain on a steady course for Lusaka and endure.

✿

Long days on the Trans-Caprivi Highway (DH)

Nunda River Lodge near Divundu was flooded when we arrived. The Okavango River was the highest it has been for a century. We were now in the tail-end of the Rainy season and heavy falls up in the Angolan highlands catchment area had caused havoc downstream. The Okavango River passes through the western end of the Caprivi Strip and into Botswana, emptying into the sands of the Kalahari Desert, forming the renowned wetlands known as the Okavango Delta. To complete the basic geography lesson, the Caprivi Strip is the long narrow tongue of north-eastern Namibia, dividing Angola and Zambia in the north from Botswana in the south and Zimbabwe in the east. The German colonists wanted access to the Zambezi River so that they could connect with their empire in Tanganyika (mainland Tanzania) and the Indian Ocean. At the time the territory was administered by the British as part of Botswana. The Brits wanted German-controlled Zanzibar, and so the colonial powers traded the Caprivi Strip for Zanzibar during the big carve-up of Africa in Berlin in 1890. The Germans hadn't registered that Victoria Falls was downstream and their plan to use the mighty Zambezi to access the Indian Ocean was never going to be feasible.

Given my fascination with the quest for understanding more about where we, modern humans, come from, it was no accident that I had chosen this path. Recent genetic research has identified the origin of modern human migration to be near the coastal border of Namibia and Angola. We diverted to stay at Nunda River Lodge in order to meet Moira Alberts and the owners, Trevor and Eugenie Foster, who have a keen interest in their country's indigenous populations and the inequality of their circumstances. I had first learned about the plight of the San people when researching the expedition as UNESCO has identified their need for development assistance. The San have the oldest genetic lineages, suggesting they may be descendents of a population ancestral to all modern humans – they are genetically closest to the origin of humankind. This concept is based on the widely-accepted theory that the greatest level of genetic diversity is to be found in the oldest population – the group that has had the longest time to evolve.

I had planned to visit a program being run in Namibia's largest community at Tsumkwe but our course altered after I was connected to Moira and subsequently the opportunity to gain greater insight into one of the San cultures and some of their issues. There are twelve different groups of San (formerly Bushmen) living in southern Africa, the Kwe being one of these groups. I found it poignant that many of these groups of people, direct descendents of our most ancient ancestors, are now fighting to retain their culture and dignity.

Later the following afternoon, Dan, Zdenek, Trevor, Moira and I travelled to the edge of the park to meet with Friedrich Alpers and three Kwe people to learn about their concerns, particularly as a marginalised group. Friedrich worked for Integrated Rural Development and Nature Conservation

With Friedrich and Moira near Popa Falls (photo: Z Kratky)

(IRDNC), which is a Namibian NGO that supports and works with the 5000 people, mostly Kwe, who live inside the adjacent Bwabwata National Park (formerly the Caprivi Game Park). The three Kwe with whom we met, Tienie, Vasco and Jack, are representatives of the Kyaramacan Association who act for those living in the park.

The Okavango River was so high that the usually spectacular Popa Falls was barely distinguishable from the level of the raging torrent. Friedrich sat us down beside the water's edge beneath the shade of an enormous jackalberry tree, laden with the season's crop of edible fruit. Trevor explained that the local Thimbukushu name for the fruit was *nunda*. He decided to name his lodge after the fruit because it, and the jackalberry tree that bears it, is such an important resource for all who use the bush. Animals browse on the leaves and eat the fruit. Butterflies breed on the tree. The all-purpose hardwood timber is used to make dugout canoes and furniture while the leaves and bark are used in traditional medicine. And Moira added that in a few weeks, when the fruit was ripe, she would make a delicious *nunda* fruit pie to put on the lodge menu.

The Kwe, the original inhabitants of West Caprivi, have had a hard time in recent years. The region was declared a military zone by the South African Defence Force during Namibia's war of independence. (The South African government administrated Namibia until 1989.) South African troops, stationed in the strategic Caprivi Strip, also used the base as a springboard to fighting the war in south-east Angola. The Kwe were forced to take sides, and as the South African military were there, they chose to work for them, particularly as trackers because of their amazing bush skills. After independence, the Namibian government remembered this and the Kwe have been marginalised ever since.

Tienie, Jack and Vasco gave their side of the story. Tienie said they had been given basic handouts that were not only insufficient but had also created a feeling of expectation and dependency. Unemployment is very high among the Kwe and substance abuse is a debilitating problem. He told us that the children are discriminated against at school and sometimes sent away. Although there are two headmen in their village, Omega 1, stronger leadership is required to pull the communities together and to develop a more effective dialogue with the government.

Despite the obstacles, Friedrich's message was constructive and positive. He was enthusiastic about the Kwe's prospects. The IRDNC is working with the Kyaramacan Association on projects which aim to teach how to manage the park and resources sustainably so that the people receive greater benefits from the natural wealth and tourism. The park was decimated during the military occupation and from poaching; landmines were scattered through parts of the once-pristine bush, and the camp environment was tainted by diesel spillages and other toxic chemicals. But the Kwe are now starting to reverse the damage. In the 200-kilometre-long park, two areas have been sectioned off as core conservation areas; only animals exist here and they are protected. In the rest of the park, humans and animals co-exist. There are ten communities of Kwe in the Bwabwata National Park.

Hunting has always been essential to the Kwe way of life but the Namibian government embargoed the practice for several years and also stemmed poaching to allow populations of species to regenerate. In the future the Kwe will be licensed to manage hunting. They will only take animals in officially sanctioned groups rather than as individuals hunting at will, ensuring the animal populations are controlled and endangered species are not reduced. At the time of our visit, Friedrich was assisting the Kwe to document all the resources in the region using local knowledge gained from thousands of interviews and scientific observation. Under the age-old jackalberry tree, Friedrich, Jack, Tienie and Vasco unfurled their pride and joy – the fruits of their research, in fact – a piece of scrumptious *nunda* pie! An enormous detailed resources map was rolled out over the ground, the curly ends fixed down with a few stones. The map is the first visual representation of the collective knowledge of these masters of their environment. They took the map to government decision-makers to successfully argue their case for controlled hunting and land management in the park. Friedrich is guiding them so that they will have a stronger voice.

One of the most valuable veldt resources featured on the map is a tuber plant called Devil's Claw, used in the treatment of arthritis and prostate cancer and very much in demand in Europe. Friedrich has helped the growers gain an 'organic' tag that further increases the value of the product.

Tienie invited us to visit his village so I cycled a half-day to reach it. With a population of approximately 4600 people, Omega 1 is the largest of the Kwe villages. It was a base for the South African military during its occupation and many of the Kwe had been employed by the army. When the soldiers moved out, the villagers inherited the non-traditional houses and infrastructure. Once the headman gave us the all clear, Tienie acted as our host and guide. It was a Saturday afternoon and most activity was concentrated either on the soccer field or the drinking of a strong, home-made brew at the bar in the centre of the village. Sport, Tienie explained, was very important to the community's younger folk, many of whom are unemployed or rely on irregular casual farm labouring work. Playing football, netball and volleyball builds self-esteem, keeps participants fit and gives them something to do.

Some of the women of Omega 1 have retained their unique, traditional basket-weaving skills. Their distinct weaving techniques are used to transform a local variety of reeds, coloured using natural dyes, into fine baskets. The Kwe have aspirations of developing their tourist industry – the baskets are already objects of great desire – but it was evident in Omega 1 that they are not quite ready to receive tourists yet.

With Tienie and Vasco at Omega I (photo: Z Kratky)

Our little followers

We were led along the sandy streets, aligned, predictably, with military uniformity, to the blacksmith's house. He was out, but his wife, slightly over-awed by our towering presence, showed us in and demonstrated how her husband made tools. As in other African cultures, the blacksmith has a spiritually significant role – here making tools to till the soil to grow food. Looking inside the house it was evident that the flimsy walls encapsulate a culture in transition. The walls remain a symbol of the forces that were responsible for such a high degree of disempowerment, forming an impervious barrier for the flow of life forces (*nyama*) through the community. But these walls were not made to last. Cracks were forming and slits of light from the late afternoon sun beamed across the room.

The Kwe are trying to weave the threads of their ancient traditions, beliefs and skills into the Namibian nation's framework for development. They are learning to adapt and, according to Tienie, they are fast learners. As I found out from Tienie and Friedrich earlier, culturally appropriate foundations are being laid. For example, as a result of the prolonged military occupation and soul-destroying handout scheme, the younger generation was fast losing the Kwe's traditional bush skills. With a short life expectancy, the elders were dying out and with them the knowledge handed down since the dawn of humankind. Leaders from the Kyaramacan Association have initiated a priority program whereby the elders are transferring their time-honoured skills to the next generation.

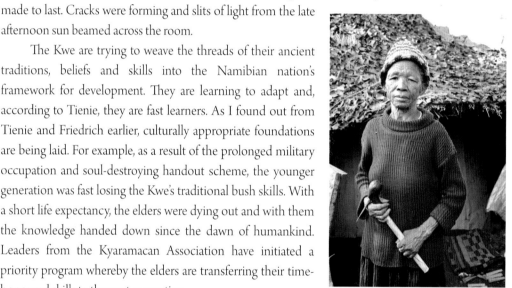

Blacksmith's wife

❊

I awoke to find my tent virtually floating in a small lake. The overnight rains continued for much of the next day. With the usual persistent headwind and late start out of Omega 1, what was going to be a standard 130-kilometre day turned into a beast – almost literally. Realising that it was going to be a race against time to reach Kongola, just outside the Bwabwata National Park border, the boys set off mid-afternoon to look for a campsite, likely to prove difficult as the boundary was a swampland. The plan was that Simon would return to lead me in. The shadows gradually elongated as I pushed on alone through the eastern core section of the park, and the last 15 kilometres were completed after sunset. As the backlight faded to twilight, my image melded with the grey asphalt strip. The wind died down and traffic no longer passed; the bush became eerily still and quiet. The loudest sounds seemed to be made by my bike – the seat squeaked with every pedal revolution, the drive train was in dire need of oil after the rain and as for the free hub when I coasted, I may as well have run a stick along a corrugated iron fence. A solitary warthog peered suspiciously at me through the veldt grass, like a sentinel of the bush. Spooked, I started to imagine the animals I couldn't see that might be eyeing me off as dinner. I knew there were lions... I upped the pace. No more freewheeling.

I was relieved when Simon arrived a few kilometres before the park gates; he had been held up helping pull someone out of a bog. Apparently the guard on the gate had told him there were many lions in this end of the park and that 'you should not leave your wife on her own...' From there Simon kept me on a short tether until I was out of the area. It was not a pleasant experience and, I must admit, for the first time on the expedition, I was genuinely scared.

At dusk two days later, descending from a highpoint of the gently undulating landscape, about 30 kilometres out from Livingstone, it was awe rather than fear that filled my thoughts. In the distance, to the south-east, against the fading tangerine afterglow, I could just make out the cloud from 'the smoke that thunders', or Mosi-oa-Tunya. To all but the local population, this was Victoria Falls – and judging by the height of the spray above the wooded landscape, the falls were going off. Earlier, where I'd crossed the Zambezi at Sesheke on the Zambian border, about 200 kilometres upstream, the river's flow rate had given the first inkling of what might be ahead: the waters appeared to be boiling with energy. The sheer force of the current, the waves and spiralling eddies that formed as the river swept around everything on its course – trees, islands, bridges – suggested that we were going to be treated to something spectacular. And here, with still about an hour and a half to go, I had only caught a fleeting glimpse of what was promised. The moment ignited my expectations for the next day. I used these positive images to coax myself onward as the night chill numbed my bare skin. My legs were past tired when I finally arrived in Livingstone by the light of the Land Rover – after a 204-kilometre, 10-hour day from Sesheke.

'... Scenes so lovely must have been gazed upon by angels in their flight.' These were the words of missionary explorer David Livingstone, believed to be the first European to set eyes on Mosi-oa-Tunya, which he renamed in honour of his queen. Gazing at Victoria Falls from every angle, I understood Livingstone's reaction. The world's largest curtain of falling water was in full flow, which according to mean measurements is around 500 million litres a second. The spray that I had seen from a distance spouted upwards before me like inverted rain, the mist rising higher than the falls are deep. When Arab slave traders, to whom Livingstone was ethically opposed, watched

The Zambezi River in flood at Sesheke, 200 kilometres upstream from Victoria Falls

the Zambezi's waters disappear over the mile-wide basalt lip and into the thundering cauldron they thought it was the end of the world. No wonder. Vapour clouds impede the view across the chasm and conceal the plunge pool, some 108 metres below. The atmosphere was so humid I could imagine the early trailblazers cutting it with their machetes as they would the dense greenery. Overhanging vines, mosses and lichens cling to moist fractures in the rocks and rainbows bridge the sodden sandstone walls of the main canyon. The humanitarian missionary explorer perceived the falls on Heavenly terms, whereas the cruel, seditious slave traders were afraid it was more like Hell. Spending the morning wandering around the site, taking images and being doused by the spray as it fell again as rain, I related to the joy of having my feet firmly grounded on this wondrous Earth.

Evidence suggests that humans have been drawn to the awesome power and beauty of the falls ever since Homo habilis chipped away there with his flint tools. Stone-Age cultures, the Iron-Age Khoisan and various Bantu tribes have all in turn displaced one another and left their calling cards. Of course, these days the emphasis is on preservation of the National Park so, rather than leaving their mark, travellers like us take away nothing but memories, photographs and the odd souvenir from the adjacent stalls within the compound. The Zambezi River and Victoria Falls which divide Zambia and Zimbabwe – Northern and Southern Rhodesia in British colonial times – are also the countries' major tourist drawcards. With the current political uncertainties in Zimbabwe, however, more tourists choose to visit the falls from the Zambian side.

Mosi-oa-Tunya, or 'The Smoke that Thunders'

✳

The journey from Livingstone to Lusaka was a fairly straightforward three-and-a-half-day ride up the main road. The Chinese had just about completed an upgrade as far as Monze (180 kilometres south of Lusaka), and the quality of their work was much higher in Zambia than in Angola. Here they were laying a much thicker layer of tar and taking care to protect the surface as the road was being built. At one point, I was given permission to cycle down the side of the new tarmac. It seemed dry enough for a start but then my tyres started sticking to the road. Treacly black tar and gravel stones flicked up, totally caking the tyre tread. Being the end of the Rainy season, the bush appeared fresh and alive with new growth and tall wispy veldt grasses. I really appreciated cycling through this countryside, which the team thought uninspiring from the vehicle. I took this as an illustration of the general difference between our mentalities at this stage.

Every school has its advertising sign, complete with school motto, beside the road. I had noticed these ever since arriving in Zambia. The mottos were always positive; many I found uplifting as I pushed into the breeze. One motto I read was: 'Education and hard work lead to survival and self-reliance'. Most were in a similar vein.

Zambia has a real cycling culture and many cyclists, especially boys and teenagers, would try to race me. Normally they ambled along and I would sail past them by just going my usual pace. Not to be outdone, they would respond with a burst of speed – not sustainable – and leave me in their wake. Once they had beaten me, the incentive was gone and their effort soon fizzled out. Their bikes were usually held together with whatever they could find. Often they had pedals missing, wheels were buckled and seats broken – and they regularly carried huge loads. On the final morning in to Lusaka, another young man sped ahead of me as I cycled through Kafue. As we hit the hill out of town, he struggled on his single-geared machine and I caught up with him. We rode together for about 20 kilometres and had an absorbing conversation. Other cyclists trailed us for short distances and then peeled off toward their destinations. The boy's name was Steve. He was fourteen years old and in Year 9 at school. He seemed a very bright kid and said he wanted to be a lawyer when he grew up. Steve's father had died of AIDS in 2006, leaving his mother, a farmer, to care for her ten children. She grew maize and sugar cane to sell to a local cooperative, but struggled to make ends meet. Steve said he was cycling to visit a friend just outside Lusaka. I thought he should have been in class and asked why he wasn't. He explained that he hadn't been able to go to school for the past month because his mother couldn't afford the school fees. Primary school, up to Year 7, is free in Zambia but to enter secondary school, fees must be paid and although they are low, for poor families this is a significant outlay. There are limited spaces for secondary students in any case, although the situation is improving: in 2000 only about 20 per cent of students progressed to Year 8, but now the figure is more like 40 per cent. When the Land Rover caught up with us, I gave Steve something to eat and water. We made a few small improvements to the bike, Dan repositioning a small piece of wood to stop the mudguards rubbing through the tyre.

Zambia is the most urbanised country in sub-Saharan Africa, with about two-thirds of the population living in its cities and larger towns. Despite many warnings that Zambian, and particularly Lusaka's, traffic is abominable, I didn't find it to be the case, certainly no worse than elsewhere in Africa. Entering the fast-flowing stream of cars in the capital city's outer suburbs, I was primed for a bunfight but as the Kafue Road merged with the Great North Road, traffic moved slowly through the central business district bottleneck. My experience from a bicycle saddle was that Lusaka was one of the most manageable African cities to cycle in, perhaps in line with Ouagadougou. For me, it was a major pit stop: I had projects to visit and team changes to coordinate, I needed to maintain connections, organise visas and shore up schedules for further down the track – in fact, all the way to Somalia. Trying to get the balance right was like conducting a finely-tuned orchestra in a complicated composition.

✻

First on the agenda was to meet Kristin Tweardy and Dave Neiswander from World Bicycle Relief, one of the expedition partners. WBR's mission is to provide access to independence and livelihood through 'The Power of Bicycles.' The organisation's bicycles are providing simple, sustainable transportation as an essential element in disaster assistance and poverty relief. In Zambia, these bikes fulfil basic needs by providing access to health care, education and economic development, and empowering individuals, their families and communities.

In response to the devastating Indian Ocean tsunami on Boxing Day 2004, WBR, founded by SRAM (which made the components for my bike), and Trek Bicycles provided Sri Lanka with 24,400 bicycles during a two-year program. In 2006, WBR turned its attention to Zambia and since then has established three different programs, with more projects being developed in other East African countries.

Project Zambia began with WBR partnering the organisation Reaching HIV/AIDS Affected People with Integrated Development and Support (RAPIDS) to provide 23,000 bicycles to HIV/AIDS caregivers. Once this program was completed, it commenced the Bicycles For Education and Empowerment Program (BEEP) which is now in full swing, providing 50,000 bikes to increase access to school for children in rural Zambia who need it most. Seventy per cent are going to girls. Now WBR is working with the micro-finance organisation, HARMOS, a partner of World Vision, encouraging the use of bicycles as a means of developing business opportunities.

The WBR bicycles are not donors' throw-aways; they are custom-built to withstand the challenging conditions in Africa and to meet the specific needs of the users. While many organisations believe they are helping to develop communities by donating 'normal Western' bicycles that have been perhaps gathering dust in the back shed, WBR perceives that although this may be helpful, it is a short-term fix. The majority of these bikes are not made for local conditions; finding replacement parts in Zambia is near-impossible and they can cause animosity in communities because people receive different standards of machine. Most bikes in Africa, such as the one Steve was using, are a poor copy of the old Raleighs made in the 1970s: nowadays they are usually made in China with nowhere near the quality and strength of the originals. The WBR bikes are basically work-horses – everything about them is built to last – the design modified after feedback from the end users and continually reviewed. They weigh 21 kilograms and the rack is made to carry 100 kilograms. The bicycle components used to be chiefly sourced from international companies such as TATA India, however more and more WBR is turning to South Africa. Bringing the business to the continent means fewer air miles and creates economic benefits for African people. The bikes arrive in Zambia as 'complete knockdowns' for assemblers to put together, and mechanics, located in villages where there are programs, are continually being trained to maintain them. At the time of my visit, nearly 500 mechanics had been tutored, provided with a toolkit and uniform and had received instruction in business principles and life skills.

Kristin arranged a special tour for Zdenek and myself so we could visit examples of each of these three projects in the Chongwe District, about 40 kilometres east of Lusaka. In Chongwe we collected Munangandu (Muna) who came along to help out and interpret. Firstly we travelled along a dirt track south of Chongwe to visit Chitentabunga Primary School that serves a zone of the same name. Here we met Evelyn and Fabby, who were in Year 8 and Year 9 respectively. They had received their new WBR bicycles as part of the BEEP Program, and Fabby lent me hers to go for a quick spin. It was so different from what I was used to. The back-pedal brakes and very upright cycling position made me feel like a beginner! The bikes are definitely coasters – with extremely comfortable seats.

I cycled about four kilometres with the two girls back to Evelyn's village to meet her family. Once I could get some momentum, the bike seemed to handle even the sandy patches with ease. On arrival, Evelyn was so proud that she had been chosen to show us how she used her new bicycle. Her mother has five children and is alone, her husband having died of AIDS a few years ago. She did everything: grew maize, sugar cane, pumpkins and onions, baked bread, sold her produce at the local market, brought up the family, and is a care worker. In fact, she qualified for a bicycle through the RAPIDS program a couple of years before.

The 50, 000 bicycles are being distributed in 500 schools to children who are especially at risk for extreme poverty and high local HIV/AIDS infection rates. Bicycles allow people to travel four times

With Fabby, Evelyn and their World Bicycle Relief bikes (ZK)

as far and carry five times the load compared to walking. Girls are a priority because they are usually required to work hard before school starts, and if they have to then walk 20 kilometres a day to and from school (as in some cases), they either miss class or are in trouble because they are late. As girls are more vulnerable than boys to harassment and sexual abuse during their long journey, reducing the travel time limits their exposure and encourages them to go to school. In Zambia, only 17 per cent of girls complete their secondary education. World Bicycle Relief has partnered with the Zambian Ministry of Education, community-based organisations and a number of NGOs to ensure the bikes are directed to those children who need them most. As long as the WBR bikes are used for the intended purpose, they may be used also as a means of transport by the family.

As we were leaving, Evelyn's mother tried to give me a sack of sweet potatoes she had grown – as if she didn't give enough already! I felt very humbled and insisted she keep them for her own use or to sell, telling her that I did not have anywhere to cook them. So she gave them to Joyce, the religious education teacher who also accompanied us. At least Joyce would make good use of them.

Muna and Irene, project coordinators, then took us to meet Jennifer, a healthcare worker who qualified to receive her bike during the RAPIDS initiative. Like Evelyn's mother, Jennifer already led a full life let alone volunteering to care for twenty-eight people on a regular basis. She received her training, which included a basic medical kit and counselling instruction, back in 2006. Carers like Jennifer are their community's first port of call if someone needs help. If more serious medical attention was required, she referred them to a hospital. The bicycle had increased her productivity immensely. Because of it, Jennifer was able to attend more patients more often than if she was on foot, and able to give more quality time

Jennifer didn't need her bicycle to care for her nearest patient, Emma, who lived next door. On meeting Emma and sitting with her on the woven mat she had laid out for us, I couldn't really tell what was wrong. She looked to be in reasonable health, strong and in good spirits. The only clue to her problems lay in the dark circles that emphasised her deep-set, sunken eyes. Muna explained in local Nyanja language what I was doing and that I had ridden my bicycle, *njinga*, all the way from Senegal. 'Uh,' Emma interrupted, causing Muna to pause, *'Njinga*...Senegal?' Her reaction of amazement was priceless. She held a wide-eyed stare for a second or two and then looked me up and down. 'Don't you get pains in your legs? Backside? Head?' I barely needed Muna's translation skills to communicate. Emma was so animated and we developed an instant bond. *'Njinga,'* she repeated, shaking her head.

I didn't want to spoil the moment or make her feel uncomfortable so I didn't like to directly ask why Emma needed a carer. Irene explained that Emma had nearly died of AIDS. Unable to eat because of the sores on her throat, she was at death's door when they took her to be diagnosed and receive treatment. Emma's tone instantly transformed to sombre when she recalled her pain and suffering as the disease advanced. She was a single mother with five children: who was going to care for them when she was gone? She had given up all hope of improvement but now, through taking the right anti-retroviral (ARV) medication, her life had been transformed. Her appetite had returned and she craved the best foods – T-bone steak, fresh vegetables, cakes – life was too short to be content with second best. Having stared death in the face, Emma was ecstatic about her new lease of life. She was productive once more, able to contribute to her family and community. She even had the strength to work in the fields. And in response to hearing about where I was heading after Zambia on my *njinga*, she joked that she would soon be fit enough to cycle with me. Emma would definitely be with me in spirit.

Jennifer (right) with Emma, one of her AIDS patients

The third initiative, which supports economic development through micro-finance loans for bicycles, seems to be the way World Bicycle Relief is heading – creating sustainable businesses. The WBR bikes cost around $US150 each, beyond the means for the average villager. When a person, or often a small group of people, decides they have a need for a bike, they make an appointment with the staff at HARMOS, a micro-lending bank. Typically they need to contribute one-third of the amount, and with a guarantee from the village headman can secure a $100 loan. The loans must be repaid within three to six months and about 90 per cent are honoured within the time-frame.

Joe (right) and his family. The micro-loan service has enabled Joe to make the most of his entrepreneurial vision

James Phiri from the micro-loans office took us to meet Joe, one of their success stories, to showcase just how effective the initiative can be. Joe seems unstoppable. He spreads the word with great enthusiasm, telling his story and educating others how to do what he has done. He explained that he used his first bike to carry charcoal to Lusaka to sell. This is all he did for six months: he put his head down and worked. With the money he saved he was able to buy a second bike, and within two years he had created six businesses. Joe showed us how he attached his custom-made goat cage to the carrier so he could transport his goats to market. He bought more land on which he and his family grow vegetables to eat and sell. He rents the properties he has acquired and on the day we visited he had just bought another sewing machine. He plans to employ six tailors to produce clothes.

Joe's incentives are to plan ahead – a concept rare in his culture – so that when he is too old to push the pedals, he has an income and his family a decent inheritance. Our group sat under a shady tree where Joe explained how with the loan giving him a leg-up, he has created so much. However, when he learned what I was doing, roles were reversed. He interviewed me, asking many very thoughtful and empathetic questions. We inspired each other.

Total distance: 14,266 kilometres

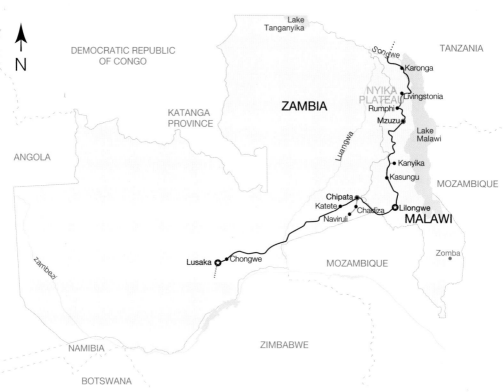

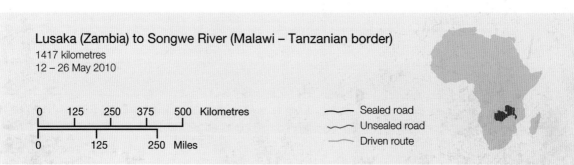

Lusaka (Zambia) to Songwe River (Malawi – Tanzanian border)
1417 kilometres
12 – 26 May 2010

| 0 | 125 | 250 | 375 | 500 | Kilometres |

| 0 | 125 | 250 | Miles |

—— Sealed road

〜〜 Unsealed road

—— Driven route

12
A NEW LEASE OF LIFE

Lusaka to Songwe River (eastern Zambia and Malawi)

A better diet has reduced some dependence on anti-retroviral drugs, helping to give a new lease of life to AIDS sufferers such as this man in Naviruli

Back on the bike, I felt revived after the long break and in high spirits. I noted in my diary that my enthusiasm for the Breaking the Cycle project had not waned at all. I could not wait to see how the next chapter of the journey would unfold. With just over three months to go to the finish, I was on the homeward run. I set off from Kristin's place (World Bicycle Relief), winding my way through Lusaka's suburban streets and back on to the Great East Road, direction Chipata, some 600 kilometres away.

During the Lusaka pit stop the team changed completely. After finishing seeding on the farm, John returned from Scotland to replace Simon. Dan had decided to move on. His knee was fine again but following his injury he never regained his motivation to cycle, and working as expedition support wasn't enough for him physically or mentally. By the time Dan left for the UK he was already planning his next adventure. Zdenek had to return to Europe for four weeks. In agreeing to join the expedition he had virtually dropped everything to catch us in northern Cameroon. He needed time to reorganise his life and arranged to rejoin the team in Kigali, Rwanda. All this meant it was just John and I who set out from Lusaka. We had a tight schedule to stick to through Zambia, Malawi and Tanzania to reach Kigali – almost 3000 kilometres in four weeks, including project visits. There was the added uncertainty of dubious road conditions through central Tanzania.

Lusaka's satellite industries quickly petered out and I was soon pedalling through open fertile-looking farmland. The busy highway was also a thoroughfare for cyclists transporting their wares to trade in the city and larger villages. Many had reinforced their bikes to carry loads of more than 100 kilograms of charcoal. I thought of Joe, the inspirational father and businessman I met in Chongwe a few days earlier, who had created opportunities by transporting charcoal, as these people were. Their work rate was intense, but even if their hands weren't free to wave, they always seemed to manage a cheerful 'good

Transporting charcoal to Lusaka

morning.' The landscape at times resembled a garden; tall meadow grasses were infused with sprays of bright yellow and, occasionally, delicate pink and white flowers. These gently undulating high plains near Lusaka (approximately 1100 metres above sea level) soon morphed into long, rolling hills out of Chongwe. Mostly I cycled through native *miombo* woodland intermingled with pockets of tall veldt grasses. Deeper into the countryside there was sparse arable land use beyond the subsistence farming around villages.

For most of day two out of Lusaka, the road tracked the northern perimeter of the Lower Zambezi National Park. I was enjoying the warm sunshine as I pushed along the more-or-less empty highway through pristine bushland, dwarfed by the towering grasses. The scene matched the idyllic picture I'd envisaged of the African bush prior to

leaving Australia. Moving at a steady pace, I was totally immersed in my thoughts when my mobile phone rang. I screeched to a halt and scrambled through my bar bag, managing to pick up just before it switched to message bank. It was my brother Tony ringing to wish me a happy birthday. He apologised for being a day late – the rest of my family had caught me on the day, before I left Lusaka. It was a surreal moment when two worlds intersected: I was standing on the gravel roadside in the wilds of Zambia, partially out of breath and with beads of perspiration trickling down my face,

Bush mechanics

chatting to my brother in Perth. He updated me on what his family was up to and mentioned how the children were growing up. The moment was an unexpected grounding. I was touched that my whole family had managed to contact me for my birthday. Travelling through Africa where the family unit is so integral to societies underlined to me how fortunate I am to have a solid family foundation – one from which I draw much inner strength. Of course, I missed them but here I was in my element. I was in a happy place.

Travelling became much simpler with just John and me. But although we shared all the normal cooking and cleaning duties, there was less flexibility. For example, when John did the shopping, there was no-one to watch over the vehicle, and when he travelled ahead to search for a hidden campsite, he would then have to wait beside the road for me to arrive rather than get on with setting up camp or making vehicle repairs as he usually did. All in all, though, we managed pretty well.

Around the Luangwa River, one of Zambia's principal streams, a more serious set of hills tested the legs. From there, as the main road closely tracked the Mozambique border, it was back to the high plains, studded with rugged granite outcrops and isolated mounds as I neared Chipata.

As we headed east, I noticed signs of an increase in the level of poverty. More people, especially women and children, would beg and hold out their hands as I rode by. I saw others washing their clothes in dirty puddles next to the road. Maybe a minute or two before I passed through Sinda, a small village just before Katete, a pig had been pulverised by a vehicle moving at high speed with the result that blood and guts were strewn all over the road. A group of locals had gathered with wheelbarrows and buckets at hand to salvage what they could of the unfortunate animal. Kids were rushing off with bloody pieces of the pig in their hands. To the average Westerner, the scene would seem pretty gruesome but here nothing was wasted.

❊

The nine countries of southern Africa contain about one-third of the world's HIV-positive population. As Zambia is ranked somewhere in the middle of this group, I wanted to take a closer look at how HIV/AIDS affects Zambian communities. In Chipata we met Benjamin Phiri, Plan Zambia's Health Coordinator for the Eastern Province and facilitator for their Chadiza Programme Unit. Benjamin led our day excursion, which began with an 80-kilometre drive over some rough roads to the town of Chadiza, tucked away in the south-east corner of Zambia, not far from the Mozambique and Malawi frontiers. Our path wound through small villages and fields of cotton, sunflowers and maize mostly. The countryside was adorned with craggy hills which developed into a more dramatic range towards the Mozambique border.

On the way we had time to discuss the HIV/AIDS situation in Zambia and learn a little about the project we were about to see. While we were focusing on a small part of the problem in Zambia, similar HIV issues are replicated across southern Africa. In Swaziland, Botswana and Lesotho, where up to one-quarter of the population is afflicted with HIV/AIDS, the very fabric of their societies is threatened by this disease. South Africa is dealing with an estimated six million sufferers, more than any other country (nearly one-fifth of the population aged between fifteen and forty-nine years is infected). Zambia sits in the next group, along with Zimbabwe, Namibia, Mozambique and Malawi, where between 14 and 11 per cent of the citizens have the virus. Around one million Zambians have HIV; Benjamin estimates that about 90,000 of these people would die from AIDS in 2010.

Benjamin had a gentle manner and was obviously a caring soul, but like most Zambians he drove at a speed way too fast for the road conditions. Midway through the journey he suddenly eased up to point out a couple of boys herding cattle along the side of the road. 'These boys are orphans, bound into unfair contracts of forced labour,' he said in a solemn tone. From the age of about ten, boys like them are taken in by 'foster families' and indentured for usually four years to herd cattle with no pay, no schooling and no protection. Sometimes they are given shelter and perhaps food, but no clothing to shield from the weather. Once their contract is up, they are 'rewarded' by being given an animal – perhaps a goat or a cow – that is usually in poor health and often dies within a few weeks. These boys reach their late teens illiterate, and having had no parental guidance or role models. A growing number of orphans are left in the wake of the AIDS epidemic. Of course not all are sentenced to forced labour – these were extreme cases – but at the time of our visit there were 993,000 orphans, 600,000 of whom were under the age of seventeen. About one- third of Zambian children have lost at least one parent due to AIDS.

Benjamin explained that in Zambia HIV is not just a disease of the underprivileged: all parts of the society are affected. Infection rates are extreme in some urban areas where the better educated and the wealthy live, though they may have better access to treatment. The most vulnerable group are women aged between fifteen and twenty-four; they are four times more likely to contract HIV than young men of the same age. Prevalence is highest among mothers aged twenty-five to thirty-five (approximately19 per cent) and among pregnant women (16.7 per cent), resulting in a high frequency of mother-to-child-transmission (MTCT) of HIV. A number of factors resulting from gender inequality contribute to this higher prevalence among women. Women are taught never to refuse their husbands sex or to insist their partner use a condom. About 15 per cent of Zambian women report forced sex but since many will not disclose this information, the figure is likely to be much higher. Young women usually become sexually active earlier than men with a partner who is on average five years older and who may have already had multiple sexual partners. There is much stigma and much misinformation about HIV/AIDS and possible 'cures', and as Benjamin gave us examples, he became so consumed by emotion that he started driving even faster, to the point where John politely asked him to slow down. One common myth is the claim that sex with a virgin can cure AIDS! Unfortunately this has led to children contracting HIV after sexual abuse – a crime rarely reported.

In Chadiza we paid a courtesy visit to the Chief District Commissioner and met the member of parliament for the Eastern Province who was in town to open a new school and hospital. Formalities over, we all piled back into the vehicle, along with Judith, a local reporter whom I employed to take

some video footage, and drove a further hour to reach the Naviruli community, still in the Chadiza district. We were a little late but the group of about 25 HIV-positive people still waited patiently. The Chadiza project was funded by Australian Aid (AusAID) via Plan International Australia to reduce community vulnerability to HIV and AIDS from 2005 to 2009. In a nutshell, the program involved setting up and running support groups to educate about the affliction, and encourage early diagnosis, acceptance and management.

The group was a lively bunch and we must have sat out in the drizzly rain with

An open discussion with the HIV-positive community at Naviruli

Remembering the pain and fear

them for almost two hours. I quickly realised that it would take much more than wet weather to dampen their spirits. All the same, communicating with the aid of an interpreter, it was quite difficult to get the conversation going. I introduced myself and asked some general questions – a little cautiously at first as I did not want to push them into discussing anything they might be sensitive about. I needn't have worried – within this support group they were accustomed to speaking about their situation. In many communities, being 'labelled' with HIV/AIDS, or even having a family member with the condition, may still lead to a loss of dignity, dishonour and humiliation. The resulting discrimination was, and in some cases still is, a major deterrent preventing diagnosis and treatment. The formation of support groups such as this in Naviruli is the cornerstone to the success of the program – a program that can be replicated throughout rural Zambia and further afield.

I asked whether individuals would like to share their stories – of how they knew they had HIV/AIDS, what led them to take the test, how they dealt with related ailments and how they make a livelihood. It was then that people really opened up. Most were members of woman-headed and grandparent-headed families – families where the traditional breadwinners had been lost to AIDS. It seemed as though it was therapeutic for them to describe their experiences. Sometimes I could see it was painful for them to relive what they had been through but they all seemed to finish with the positives.

The men and women tended to congregate in separate groups but contributed to the discussion equally. They reported a variety of signs of HIV such as chronic malaria, diarrhoea, pains in the legs, skin blemishes and irritations, or general body weakness. Overcoming the fears of stigma and prejudice here had proved to be the main barrier to being tested. As is the case throughout Zambia, there was a severe shortage of healthcare professionals. Plan trained up local psycho-social counsellors to work with existing doctors, nurses and lab technicians to instil confidence and encourage people to take the test. In general, the men were more reluctant than the women to be tested and to seek remedies. One fellow explained that when the headman of the village agreed to be tested, and was positive, it led many others, especially men, to take the test and face the outcome.

Pained expressions turned to unrestrained smiles as each member described how the anti-retroviral (ARV) therapy had transformed their lives. Most of the group were receiving ARVs. Like Emma, the AIDS sufferer we met from the World Bicycle Relief-supported project, these people could lead a productive life again. They were empowered.

A key aspect of the success of the project was that the group had been supported to maintain vegetable gardens growing cassava, sweet potatoes, pumpkins, tomatoes, rape, aubergines, capsicums, cucumbers, beans, sugar cane and bananas. On average they made around 100,000 Zambian kwacha per month (approximately $US20) from these gardening activities which they use mostly to meet their children's school requisites, pay for milling maize, and buy household items like sugar, salt, or soap.

Community 'banks' were set up and the group was educated about how to save any profits made from selling the excess produce.

After our discussion, some of the group members piled into the back of the pickup and we drove several kilometres to see a few of their vegetable plots. The member's garden we focused on was impressively lush. He had built gravity-fed irrigation channels to water his plants, used banana leaves as mulch and added fertiliser. On his small area of land he was able to produce enough vegetables for his family with excess to sell.

The program provided the participants with training, tools and storage facilities; seeds were supplied in the form of a 'seed loan' that had to be repaid at the end of harvest. Part of the group therapy involved nutritional education and technical gardening skills to maximise productivity. Traditionally, rural Zambian diets have little variety: they are limited to maize, meat, potatoes, tomatoes and onions. This being a semi-arid region, these people would normally have a precarious food security situation: between January and March many would have to live on one meal a day. By learning to grow and prepare a range of fresh produce, they could eat well all year round, and general health and immunities improved markedly. Along with all the above-mentioned vegetables, the moringa tree that we first came across in the Sahel region had been introduced. Powdered

A better diet has reduced some dependence on anti-retroviral drugs

moringa leaves are like a 'super food,' full of antioxidants and immunity-boosting properties.

This project had been so successful that some of the group were able to reduce dependence and even live without their anti-retroviral drugs (ARVs). While it is not a complete answer, this initiative had certainly resulted in a happier, healthier, more productive community.

One of the questions I asked of the group was 'What are your their biggest concerns?' Participants universally agreed that their worst nightmare would be for their supply of ARVs to end: this would be akin to a death sentence. According to a number of people I spoke to and articles I have subsequently read, there was real cause for some concern, if not for this specific group then for other communities of southern and central Africa. Overall, the number of new HIV infections remains high and is

John and Benjamin wait for the group

not yet on the decline, and therefore the number of people requiring treatment continues to rise, even if at a slowing rate. About two-thirds of AIDS funding in Africa for both prevention and treatment comes from non-African sources. In 2009 and 2010, funding to end AIDS decreased by 13 per cent, due partly to the global economic crisis and partly because other major donors started to focus on more easily treatable diseases. ARVs need to be supplied for life and are expensive. It now costs about $US100 to treat a patient for a year (down from almost $US10,000 a decade ago) whereas treating tuberculosis costs between $US16 and $US35, and treating malaria costs $US2 a dose, with bed nets to prevent infection about $US10 each. More lives can be saved by treating these other diseases than treating HIV/AIDS. So for some who are alive and well today due to the ARV treatment they receive, a Damoclean sword hangs over their heads. In addition, those who stop the combination of treatments face the danger that the virus will become resistant to the drugs they are on.

As long as the ARV drugs remain available, AIDS is no longer a death sentence. These people are now able to have a productive, healthy life as normal citizens in their community

In Namibia and Botswana, richer countries with low populations (two million people each), and in Rwanda, a country that has made the most of the higher levels of international assistance it has received, ARV treatment is now available to all those who qualify for it. In Zambia, about two-thirds of the HIV-positive population receive the ARV treatment they need as the country strives for universal access to the drugs.

As with other highly-burdened nations, Zambia's epidemic was exacerbated because, when the first case was discovered in 1984, the authorities swept the issue under the carpet. There were no preventative measures taken, no ABC education (Abstinence, Be faithful, careful use of Condoms), blood banks were not made safe and there was no testing or treatment available. The bushfire raged so out of control that when an aggressive publicity campaign finally kicked in, it did little to douse the flames. Back in 2003, Stephen Lewis, the UN Secretary General's Special Envoy for HIV/AIDS, clamied that Zambia's second president, Frederick Chiluba, '... spent his time disavowing the reality of AIDS and throwing obstacles in the way of those keen to confront the disease'. Towards the end of his presidency (1991-2002), Chiluba discouraged the use of condoms, claiming 'I don't believe in condoms myself because it is a sign of weak morals on the part of the user'. At that time, Zambia was losing 2000 teachers a year to AIDS and drought became famine because the pandemic had weakened the agricultural community's resilience. With the election of the next leader, President Levy Mwanawasa, came a positive change in willingness to combat HIV/AIDS. His government took on greater ownership of the AIDS response, devising Zambian solutions for Zambia. The National HIV/AIDS/STI/TB Council (NAC) was set up to coordinate the actions of all segments of government and society in the fight against HIV/AIDS. Three-quarters of

Zambia's HIV and AIDS tab is currently picked up by international organisations. Donors such as the Global Fund to Fight AIDS, Tuberculosis and Malaria and the United States President's Emergency Plan for AIDS Relief (PEPFAR) contribute the most to HIV prevention and AIDS treatment.

Half of Zambia's 13.5 million people are under fourteen years of age. One of the NAC's critical strategies to meet the UNAIDS's (United Nations Joint Program on HIV/AIDS) vision of zero new HIV infections, zero discrimination and zero AIDS-related deaths is to focus on youth. The aim is to change attitudes towards stigma, gender inequality and condom use by providing young people with access to HIV testing, condoms, male circumcision and sexuality education. One outcome is that AIDS education is becoming better integrated into the school curriculum. As a result of these and other measures, the last decade has seen a 25 per cent decrease in the rate of HIV infection amongst Zambian youth and overall the incidence of HIV/AIDS has dropped from around 20 per cent to 13.5 per cent. Giving young people opportunities for meaningful involvement in HIV policy and program design and implementation is making a difference. The signs are positive for the future.

There are hopeful signs too in the area of mother-to-child-transmission. Zambia is one of the twenty-two countries identified as having the highest burden of AIDS, made more complex by ingrained cultural fears. The virtual elimination of mother-to-child transmission of HIV by 2015 is a priority for UNAIDS in its quest for an HIV-free generation. More sophisticated treatment regimens now make it possible to prevent mother-to-child-transmission of HIV by 98 per cent.

After sharing a specially prepared lunch of *nshima* (a cornmeal staple food similar to Italian polenta) and chicken, we said our goodbyes. On the return journey, our learning continued. Benjamin told us that the effectiveness of ARV treatments had led to a change in the way HIV is viewed – from a death sentence to a chronic illness. This has reduced some of the fear associated with the virus but, unfortunately, now that people know they can live a productive life by managing HIV, a degree of complacency towards prevention has evolved.

The issue of corruption was the elephant in the room in our conversations with Benjamin. He was reluctant to discuss details because the government had the power to revoke an NGO's licence to operate if damning information was disclosed. Other sources were more forthcoming. In 2009, several donors, including Sweden, the Netherlands and the Global Fund to Fight AIDS, Tuberculosis and Malaria, suspended millions of dollars worth of aid for health programs after it was revealed that aid was embezzled from the Ministry of Health. The funds were reimbursed by the Zambian government but the Swedish and Dutch governments would not resume funding until certain audits and reforms were made. The Global Fund channelled its aid through the UN Development Program to ensure it would be directed to where it was needed. Many people with whom I spoke were still angry that Chiluba had stolen millions from his people, was found guilty in the British High Court but was then acquitted in his Zambian trial in 2009. A huge dent was made in the country's health budget and, as usual, it is the people who suffer from his greed. Benjamin explained that the European Union was set to pave the road between Chipata and Chadiza but that due to the level of corruption, it pulled out of the project.

Between discussions in the car we listened to the local radio. Chat shows and advertisements constantly educated the public about their human rights, health and safety, AIDS prevention, fighting corruption, the need to vote and major community issues. In every town, outside every school and along

Typical school motto

major thoroughfares, murals and billboards sent similar messages. Nearing Chipata just on dark, we passed people pushing carts and herding cattle with radios strung around their necks. Messages were reaching the target audience.

Zambia is a beautiful country with enough natural wealth in minerals and rich agricultural land to take care of its own health and education issues. The economy is undergoing massive growth (about 6 per cent) and Zambian citizens are starting to benefit. I thought of the bright faces of the people of the Naviruli support group, jubilant at their new lease of life. They *should* have no need to worry.

❋

I left Chipata early, climbing steadily for 20 kilometres through the misty rain to the Malawi border. The crossing into country number fourteen was blissfully uncomplicated. It was immediately evident why Malawi is often nicknamed the 'Warm Heart of Africa'. Even the immigration officers were friendly and accommodating. I exchanged a few US dollars for a wad of Malawi kwachas and pushed on through the hilly countryside. I was soon mixing it with another steady procession of cyclists lugging substantial loads. One fellow with whom I rode for about half an hour explained that he and his compatriots would cycle down to Chipata loaded with sacks of maize or groundnuts to sell or trade for manufactured goods. This time his back carrier was piled high with bags of shoes that he was going to sell in his village market. It was certainly a laborious way to make a living.

Not knowing many specifics about Malawi, I expected little to change across the border from Zambia. The two countries share a similar recent history. Both were former British protectorates that achieved independence in 1964, and both were governed under single party 'democracy' led by autocratic leaders for roughly three decades before they were ousted in multiparty elections. They are two of the world's poorest countries, lumbered with comparable levels of HIV/AIDS. Yet heading towards the capital, Lilongwe, I noted a few standout differences. Initially I was struck by the numbers of people everywhere, especially children. The land looked better set up for agriculture but there seemed to be more evidence of poverty. Delving deeper, these observations proved to be pertinent.

The rate of population growth is a critical problem for Malawi. Compared with Zambia, Malawi covers only one-seventh of the land area and squeezes in a couple more million people. The average age here is seventeen, so no wonder I was a constant attraction for hoards of children. When I paused for a break in the middle of the bush, kids would appear from nowhere; some were just inquisitive, others would ask for food or gifts. Over the first 150 kilometres to Lilongwe, I noticed several billboards erected by the Ministry of Health and Population, the UN Population Fund and other organisations bearing messages about family planning, HIV/AIDS and maternal health. Malawi's population explosion took hold when Dr Hastings K Banda, Malawi's first president, banned family planning: the population trebled during his thirty-three-year reign. Only after he was removed from power was the new government able to make policy changes. In just over forty years, Malawi's population went from four million in 1966 to 13 million in 2008 to more than 15 million as I write. The government has an enormous job to stem the tide.

Dr Banda had visions of reviving the original Maravi Empire after which the country was named. Prior to independence, Banda had lived outside Malawi for forty years, studying medicine in the US and practising as a doctor in the UK and Ghana. On his return, the independence movement built him up as a messianic leader. He capitalised on this image by developing a personality cult to maintain power after his appointment. Banda saw himself as the *Kalonga* (King) and changed his middle name to *Kamuzu* meaning 'the little root' and referring to the primary source of most traditional Malawi medicines. He always carried a fly whisk, a traditional symbol of the witch doctor.

In 1971 Dr Banda declared himself 'president-for-life'. In his ruthless quest to obtain and maintain absolute power he detained without trial those who spoke critically of him. Some were jailed for merely discussing the president's age or his past relationships, and such prisoners were underfed and often tortured. Political opponents were rubbed out by security police or were the victims of 'unfortunate' accidents. Under Dr Banda Malawi essentially became a police state: mail was opened, phones tapped and calls disconnected if a bad word was said about the president. All media was censored; television was banned, pages were torn out of magazine articles, films were edited. Propaganda went as far as burning books about pre-Banda history. Ultra-conservative ideals were imposed: women were not allowed to bare their thighs or wear trousers and men could not have long hair or beards. Kissing in public was forbidden as were movies that contained kissing scenes. Foreigners were not exempted – they were deported for transgressing the rules. Perhaps the most ridiculous edict was the banning of the Simon and Garfunkel song 'Cecilia' because the lyrics were too much for the president at a difficult time in a relationship. *Kamuzu* was certainly an appropriate middle name for Dr Banda, although not for the reasons he intended. His quixotic leadership was a root cause of many of Malawi's present-day issues.

Malawi is not endowed with the obvious mineral wealth of Zambia's Copperbelt. Banda's flawed nation-building scheme revolved around developing agriculture – in fact, 85 per cent of Malawians live rurally. As the population grew, there wasn't enough land for all and eking a living from it became increasingly difficult. Once Banda was gone in 1994, the new government started to diversify to stimulate the economy. In Lilongwe, another sponsor, Globe Metals and Mining, arranged for me to meet with the Deputy Director for Mines, Mr Wona, and his small delegation. With more sophisticated explorative techniques and an increased demand for rarer minerals, the Malawi government now sees mining as

Buying papaya from kids near Rumphi (JD)

an important source of revenue. Mr Wona explained that it was focusing on attracting international expertise and investments to kick start the embryonic industry. Globe Metals, for example, had several different projects in Malawi. At Zomba, 300 kilometres south of Lilongwe, it is involved in a rare earth metals joint venture. Michael from Globe Metals told us that rare earth oxides have 'super conductor' properties, one of their many uses being to improve the efficiency of some renewable energy resource technologies such as wind turbines. At Kanyika, where we were heading next, niobium had been found; it is used to make high strength steel alloys for gas pipelines, jet engines and rockets.

A small-time tobacco producer carrying his produce to market

The day out of the saddle in Lilongwe passed quickly. Off again, I pushed north out of the city along the main road. My goal for the first day was to reach the turn-off to Globe's Kanyika exploration camp, 166 kilometres from its Lilongwe headquarters. I cycled alone for virtually the whole day as John had a few chores still to do before leaving the city. Initially the road climbed up about 200 metres and then levelled out over the high fertile plains, roughly 1200 metres above sea level. The vast fields I passed between were part of the large agricultural estates that Dr Banda had set up to drive Malawi's economic engine. The rich red-brown soils of this region supported cash crops of tobacco and cotton as well as the staple, maize. In between the estates were pockets of smaller subsistence holdings. Being the end of the Rainy season it was harvest time for all. Small-time tobacco farmers carried their produce to depots either on foot, or by bicycle. Large, precariously loaded trucks transported the tobacco to market: with the wind at my back, the distinctive tobacco scent often hit me before the vehicles passed. Cotton production was on a significant scale too – village cooperatives had stacks of bales at their depots ready to be weighed and loaded for transportation.

About 45 kilometres north of Kasungu, the regional centre, I reached Chataloma village and the turn-off to Kanyika. The bike was loaded onto the Land Rover and John navigated through a labyrinth of tracks and small communities. Arriving at the Kanyika Niobium Project site at dusk we were greeted by Lucas, the on-site manager and Cosmos, the cook. The bush camp was quiet as there was no exploration going on.

At Kanyika, I was particularly interested to visit the local Kanyika Secondary School. So far on the journey the focus had been on the importance of primary school education, so this was a good opportunity to look at the next stage – a level of education that we in the West take for granted. Globe Metals had financed the production of one hundred new desks for the school, employing local artisans to make them. Dominic Majamanda, a Globe Metals representative, took us to meet Veronica, the deputy head teacher, and Joshua Katete, a new teacher at the school. Kanyika Secondary had four teachers, who were expected to teach the ninety-six students. To cover all the classes, each teacher had to be versatile enough to tutor in four different subjects. Veronica explained that she and her colleagues needed to be extremely organised to manage each day, juggling home life, lesson preparation and marking with classes aimed at giving the students the best chance of reaching their goals. They'd had one student qualify for university the previous year while many others had succeeded in entering their chosen career paths. John and I met with a study class of four senior students who were preparing for their final exams; one aspired to be a doctor, one a nurse, one was aiming for the military and the fourth wanted to be a driver.

Aware that educating girls is of key importance in helping alleviate poverty in the long term, I asked Veronica how many girls were enrolled. She replied that only about 30 per cent of students were female. The main reason for the differential was because of early marriages – typically, girls in rural Malawi get married at around fifteen years of age and therefore do not have the opportunity for secondary and further education. As I learned in Burkina Faso, women with higher education tend to have smaller, healthier families. In Malawi, women with little or no education have an average of more than three times as many children as women who have continued their education beyond secondary level (6.9 versus 2.1 children per woman). Staying in school delays marriage and ensures girls and boys are better informed about health-related issues. Given the problem Malawi has with the rising population, keeping girls and boys in school for longer is helping address one of their biggest issues.

Girls take a break from studying for their end-of-term exams at Kanyika Secondary School

Veronica told us that in Malawi, boys and girls are considered of equal importance (unlike other cultures I had come across in the Sahel). It is a family's wealth that generally determines whether a child receives secondary schooling, Joshua adding that the annual school fee of $US70 is high for poorer families. Only 3 per cent of low income families sent their children to secondary school, whereas almost one-third of students from the richest families made it past primary level. The population is growing at a decreasing rate in the wealthier regions around Lilongwe and the south (now about 2 per cent), where there is better access to education, while in the central and northern regions it is more like 4 per cent.

We farewelled Lucas and Cosmos early the following morning, winding our way some 35 kilometres back to the highway through small settlements and fields of maize, tobacco, sunflowers and cotton. There was plenty of evidence of the old British colonial days, when the tobacco industry really thrived. Some of the colonial buildings, now mostly

Remnants of the British colonial tobacco industry

dishevelled, were obviously quite grand. The morning light gave a romantic tint to the rural scenes – people going about their daily tasks of digging vegetable plots, threshing and pounding maize, riding to work. Everyone paused to acknowledge us with great enthusiasm as we passed.

✳

Back on the road, the distant hills and high plains evolved into a series of challenging climbs. I ascended to about 2000 metres into some spectacular rugged highlands. The mountain slopes were partially tamed by a patchwork of pine plantations. According to Joseph, the elderly manager at the cheap government-run lodge where we had stayed the first night out of Kanyika, these were Mexican pines, introduced by the British to kick-start the forestry industry. Being so high, we were suddenly in an alpine climate where that night we enjoyed the warmth of a log fire – quite a contrast to the heat and humidity experienced during most of the journey to that point. Malawi's natural forest reserves are under massive pressure due to the growing need for fuel wood. As the country has no other significant natural energy resources, wood is used for nearly all household energy requirements.

Forestry plantations and industries dominated the scenes most of the way to Mzuzu. Aside from the larger sawmills, I noted makeshift camps set up along the roadside and randomly spread through the forests. Locals were harvesting wood to sell as fuel, and for their own use. About 15 kilometres out of Mzuzu we passed two men who were transporting enormous loads of firewood on their bicycles. I could not work out, firstly, how they stacked their bikes so high, and secondly, just how they mounted and manoeuvred them. The men had turned what was an onerous way to make a living into an art form: neatly hewn logs were stacked twenty high and three deep on the reinforced back carrier, the load angled forward so that the apex was positioned directly above the pedals for balance. I caught up with them as they laboured uphill and convinced them to take a break. They could not pull up until they reached level ground where the well-rehearsed stopping routine involved balancing the load against a purpose-cut stick and placing a small stone in front of the back wheel to prevent it rolling forward. Once satisfied that their loads were stable, George and Frank could relax and chat to us.

We quickly developed a mutual admiration for what each other was doing. The main difference was that I chose to cycle across Africa, whereas these two had no choice: they were doing what they could to survive and provide for their families. I had an easier task, setting off with my puny load, than they – I simply slipped my foot into the toe clips and was off. George and Frank flicked away the stone from under their respective back wheels, reattached the stick to their load and then, bracing themselves, leaned with their whole body weight onto the handlebars to start the forward thrust. As the fast walk broke into a jog, the artistes glided back on to their seats with a kind of feline fluidity so as not to break the momentum, meandering down the slope until they regained their sense of balance. Their lives were a fine balancing act in more ways than one.

In Mzuzu, the largest town in the north, we thought we'd treat ourselves to lunch at a restaurant – a change from preparing our own food. There I spoke with a couple of Médecins Sans Frontières (MSF) doctors. I was interested to find out what kind of crisis they were dealing with in northern Malawi. One doctor, an Australian who had been with the team for almost a month, said there was nothing specific, more that there was a complete lack of

George and Frank transporting their wood to sell in Mzuzu

medical facilities and healthcare in the villages. In these communities, he reiterated, poverty remains pervasive and malnutrition was widespread, especially amongst female-headed families. Malawi has

Everyone needs to make a living

just one doctor for every 50,000 people, one of the highest ratios on the planet. Trained medical staff often chose to leave for a better life in Western countries. Additionally, many healthcare workers have been lost to AIDS, especially early on because protective clothing such as surgical gloves was not provided to prevent them from being infected. MSF is just one organisation that supports Malawi's medical services to make up some of the shortfall of practised professionals. The recently qualified Australian doctor seemed a little overwhelmed by the enormity of the challenge. He was at the frontline of a silent war, where the MSF team was mostly vaccinating against

easily preventable diseases. He said that in a village he visited the previous week twenty children had just been lost in the latest measles epidemic! Difficult to fathom. I was treated for a bad bout of measles when I was a kid. Had I been born here the outcome may have been very different.

The old road from Rumphi to Livingstonia

※

We ventured off the highway to follow the old road from Rumphi to Livingstonia. It wasn't much extra distance as it ran parallel to the new artery, and the map showed it to be the scenic route. It was a relief to be off the busy road. I pedalled through a string of villages. Smaller tobacco producers were busy with harvest – some drinking a bit too much of their harvest profits away in celebration.

The track was indeed incredibly picturesque, but it had rained overnight and as I hit the higher mountains between the Nyika Plateau and Lake Malawi there was a succession of steep muddy slopes to contend with. On the finale of the claggy climb to Livingstonia, a small truck became bogged, blocking the Land Rover. John had to wait until the occupants had freed their truck by making a causeway of grass and sticks to give the tyres something to grip. I simply pushed my bike around the mess and up to the town.

Livingstonia, locally known as Kondowe, was founded by missionaries from the Free Church of Scotland in 1894. When David Livingstone visited the shores of Lake Nyasa (Malawi) in 1859 he was shocked by the brutality of the slave trade that thrived there. Returning to Europe, he drew public attention to the situation, which led to the establishment of the Presbyterian mission. Livingstonia was

An onlooker at the Livingstonia entrance. Her bucket was almost empty

The final push into Livingstonia (photo: J Davidson)

originally located beside the lake but due to the prevalence of malarial mosquitoes the site was relocated to its present position about 900 metres above the water. The vision of Dr Robert Laws, who led the mission for fifty-two years, was not limited to serving the people's spiritual needs, it was also to provide the best education and healthcare possible. The schools and technical college, the David Gordon Memorial Hospital and now a university, are all legacies of the original vision.

The 'scenic route' had taken a toll. Rolling along the unpaved main street I felt a little dazed, punch-drunk from the beating my body had received. Covered in mud, my alien figure garnered many bemused looks from locals. But then again, arriving at the mission enclave, with its characteristic red-brick buildings straight out of a Scottish school of architecture, I also could have been forgiven for thinking I had entered another world. At Stonehouse, Dr Laws' residence and now a museum, I hosed myself and my bike down – everything was caked with clay – and re-energised in the warm sunshine waiting for John, who remained trapped behind the bogged truck. I was on a high. Not only had my natural endorphins done their job numbing the aches, I could relax and absorb the inspiring views across Lake Malawi almost a kilometre below. The brilliant lapis waters sparkled in the early afternoon all the way across to the distant shores of Tanzania and the Livingstone Mountains beyond. Sitting on the brow of the lake signified an important personal landmark. I was entering the realms of the Great Rift Valley, a place I had dreamed of visiting since I was a child. This was an incredibly satisfying moment. Lake Malawi lies at the southern extremity of the Rift Valley that extends through East Africa and along the floor of the Red Sea to Israel. From this point we were to follow the Great Rift Valley to the Afar Triangle in Ethiopia.

A glimpse of Lake Malawi half way down from Livingstonia

Eventually John and I were reunited and started on the extremely steep descent, 18 kilometres of rocky slopes with large, loose gravel stones. Blood drained from my knuckles and my forearms cramped as I squeezed hard on the brake levers. I eased down the mountain almost as slowly as I climbed it, leaning my bodyweight back behind the seat for balance and concentrating intensely to keep control. With often sheer drops to the side of the track, I could not afford to make the slightest mistake. It was equally a stern test for John in the Land Rover. Every now and then we would catch spectacular glimpses of the lake through the trees.

Camping beside the lake's shore, listening to the waves lapping against the white sandy beach, the picture-postcard views transformed to reality. At almost 600 kilometres long and up to 700 metres deep, Africa's third-largest lake generates its own microclimate. Unpredictable and violent storms regularly sweep through, channelled by the mountains either side. It was easy to see why the lake is so integral to the people of Malawi – it's the country's backbone, not just geographically but spiritually, culturally and as a source of food. Its tropical waters are home to more species of fish than any other body of freshwater on Earth.

The design of Malawi's flag consists of a horizontal tricolour of black, red and green with a red rising sun centred on the black band. The black stripe represents the indigenous population, the red is for the blood from the struggle for independence

Sunrise over Lake Malawi. The lake and country are named after the first Maravi Empire, Maravi meaning 'rays of light'

and the green is for Malawi's ever-green nature. The red rising sun symbolises the dawn of freedom and hope for Africa. On our final morning in the country I watched a moody sunrise ascend over the jagged peaks on the eastern shoreline. The first delicate rays of the day broke through the ominous swirling dark clouds, fanning over the water. Maravi (the name of the first empire after which the lake and country are named) means 'rays of light'. There could not have been a more appropriate scene to symbolise the Warm Heart of Africa and its potential for the future. But my impression was that the 'warm heart' was really referring to the universally gentle, friendly nature of the people. It dawned on me that in all my interactions with Malawians, from Mr Wona to Cosmos and Lucas, the teachers and students to people in the streets, they had been placid and reserved, kind and reassuring.

After sitting out a brief downpour, I set off from the tranquil cove at Sangilo Sanctuary Lodge (where we camped), retracing the sandy track through the village and back to the main drag. From there it was a simple day's ride, passing small villages and fields of rice and sugar cane along the coast to Karonga and finally to the Tanzanian border on the Songwe River.

Total distance: 14,266 kilometres

UGANDA

N

Lake
Victoria

RWANDA

KENYA

Rusumo

Mwanza

MOUNT
KILIMANJARO

BURUNDI

Kahama ● Igusule

Nzega

Kigoma

Tabora

TANZANIA

Sikonge

Itigi

Dodoma

Zanzibar

Dar es Salaam

Lake
Tanganyika

Kitunda

DEMOCRATIC
REPUBLIC
OF CONGO

Kipembawe

Chunya

LOLEZA
MOUNTAIN

MOUNT RUNGWE

Mbeya

Tukuyu

Songwe

ZAMBIA

MALAWI Lake
Malawi

MOZAMBIQUE

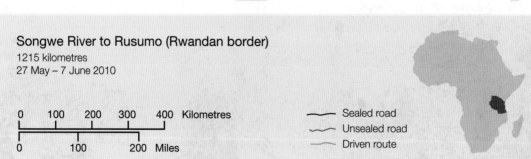

Songwe River to Rusumo (Rwandan border)
1215 kilometres
27 May – 7 June 2010

| 0 | 100 | 200 | 300 | 400 | Kilometres |

| 0 | 100 | 200 | Miles |

—— Sealed road
〜〜 Unsealed road
—— Driven route

13

A ROAD LESS TRAVELLED – THROUGH THE TANZANIAN OUTBACK

Songwe River to Rusumo (Tanzania)

Feeling claustrophobic, but ready for action in
my tsetse fly-proof clothing (photo: J Davidson)

Crossing the Songwe River and on in to Tanzania, we entered a new time zone and a new culture. The clocks advanced an hour, giving us longer afternoons. On first impression, the people were more forward too. Tanzanians seemed to be more boisterous; sparkier than the shy, unimposing Malawians, though still friendly and eager to please. Staying in the bustling border town that relied on passing trade, the traits I observed may have been slightly magnified, but as I pushed further into Tanzania's interior, I found them to generally hold true.

The first day in Tanzania was all about sucking in as much air as possible and absorbing the new culture as I cycled from about 500 metres near Lake Malawi to 2300 metres before dropping back to 1700 metres at Mbeya. Initially the road ascended away from the lake, through some wild jungle-like terrain and into the low-level clouds. About an hour out of Songwe I was entertained by two troops of monkeys in dense vegetation beside the road. I attempted to film some of them but no matter how casual and inconspicuous I tried to look, my subjects always managed to hide behind the branches. As I circled the trees, they moved to keep a branch between me and their line of view. They played games with me, peeping out from behind their cover and then pulling back before I could capture a decent shot. As the

223

fine drizzle began to set in as solid rain, I had to admit defeat and pushed on minus my wildlife scoop.

I was soon riding up through extensive tea plantations. The rain did not faze the tea pickers who worked the manicured rows in their dozens. Their colourful attire brightened the scene, contrasting with the murky sky and hills of verdant green. They toiled together in small groups; the women chatting away animatedly as their nimble fingers worked over the bushes. Snapping off selected flushes, they would fling the tips over their shoulders into the enormous baskets strapped to their backs. At times, the tossing of the leaves was a little haphazard, especially when the pickers started exchanging banter across the rows of hedges. Then, I noted, some of the carefully selected tea petals would miss their target and fall to ground, although at least the fallen tips would return to earth as mulch to enhance next season's harvest. Many of the pickers would erect their equally colourful umbrellas as the rain showers swept through so

that it appeared like a chain reaction across the hillside. Like the tea picking and the chitchat, this routine was second nature so I guessed they must be accustomed to the regular rains. John, who seemed to be relishing his new role as chief camera operator, stayed to film as I continued up the slopes.

Land use from then on became intensive, a variety of vegetables and fruit being grown on terraced plots and available for sale beside the road. I was sodden by lunchtime and so John made soup to warm me up – and to go with the 'Obama buns' he had found in a small bakery in Tukuyu. The baker had proudly

Some fertile volcanic slopes on the way to Tukuyu

told him that these were his special recipe. President Obama was a very popular man across Africa but seemed to be even more so as we neared Kenya, the birthplace of his father. I'd noted children wearing Obama t-shirts in most countries and we saw Obama posters and billboards everywhere. The president would be pleased to know that the buns were excellent – very sustaining.

And they needed to be. North of Tukuyu, the road steepened for several kilometres. Some of the local lorries struggled even more than I did as the route bowed around the western perimeter of Mt Rungwe, a volcano. I edged ahead of some of them as engines groaned in first gear and clouds of black smoke bellowed from their exhausts. At almost 3000 metres, Mt Rungwe is the highest peak in the southern Tanzanian highlands and sits at the junction of the eastern and western arms of the Great Rift Valley. As the tectonic plates gradually stretch apart, Rungwe is potentially active and earthquakes are a common occurrence. The mountain effectively seals in Lake Malawi's wetter climate and its nutrient-rich volcanic soils are the reason for the extreme fertility I had noted on the climb. The south-eastern slopes of Mt Rungwe receive up to three metres of rainfall annually, the highest rainfall in Tanzania – no wonder the tea pickers looked unperturbed by the downpours. Gradually the gradient eased as I ascended above the tree line and to the crest of the Poroto Mountain chain. Here the road snaked in the opposite direction around the eastern side of the peaks that surround Ngozi Crater Lake, another jewel of the southern realms of the Rift Valley.

By the time I started the spectacular descent into Mbeya, John was already in town trying to source information about our planned route out of the city. Mbeya is the centre of commerce for south-west Tanzania as it is an important junction for road and rail. The main thoroughfares from Malawi and Zambia intersect at Mbeya and continue east towards Dodoma, Tanzania's administrative capital, or more usually to Dar es Salaam, the country's economic and business capital on the coast. Most travellers tend to follow this principal route, also a part of the Great North Road connecting Cape Town to Alexandria on the Mediterranean. But we wanted to take a road less travelled to Tabora, almost 600 kilometres due north of Mbeya, as this would lop about 500 kilometres off our journey to Rwanda. The alternative was to follow the paved road through Dodoma. Our maps showed the connection between Mbeya and Tabora as a minor road with a long section marked as impassable in the Wet. With the Rainy season not long gone, there was a chance that water still flooded the road. The rains we had encountered around the Lake Malawi environs had given us a greater cause for concern: we could not afford to get 350 kilometres into what was obviously going to be a testing section only to find the road impenetrable. It was already a tight schedule to reach Kigali by 9 June, in time for Zdenek's return and to keep planned dates farther down the track. John headed straight for the truck depot and quizzed drivers who had recently travelled or knew about the route we wanted to take to Tabora. The consensus was that it should be passable for a Land Rover but not a two-wheel drive vehicle due to patches of sand. We decided to go for it.

❊

Although Mbeya started as a gold-mining town in the 1920s the fertile district has now developed into Tanzania's major food bowl. Maize, rice, wheat, potatoes, soya nuts, bananas and beans, along with cash crops such as tea, coffee, cocoa and spices, are railed to other parts of the country and beyond via the TAZARA Railway, which has a major depot in Mbeya. The town forms an elongated sprawl along a narrow valley surrounded by high mountains. Loleza Mountain, which forms the northern lip of the basin, loomed as the imposing gateway to our 'road less travelled' to Tabora. As we knew little of what to expect on the other side of the mountain and we had no contacts or projects to visit, this section promised to be one of pure, uncomplicated adventure travel. We just had to make the promised date in Kigali.

There was no warm-up climb – it was simply straight up out of the town – and immediately I dropped into the lowest range of gears. The path was extremely steep and stony so it was a matter of focusing just ahead of the front wheel to keep upright. When I did have the opportunity to look up, the views were exceptional. One of Tanzania's largest towns, Mbeya gradually contracted into an insignificant mark within the immense scale of the valley, set against the backdrop of the Poroto Mountains.

About one-third of the way up Lolezo, in a lather of perspiration and straining just to turn the pedals, I was concentrating intensely on the task at hand when a fellow shouted from the verge while performing an animated double-handed wave, 'Hey...hey, whitey, good morning, whitey...' I was getting used to being called *muzungu*, the Swahili term for a white person, but the direct English translation sounded so wrong. However, the unrestrained enthusiasm and genuine sincerity of the well-wisher more than counter-balanced the political incorrectness of his comment. He was honouring me by converting to my language. Imagine if I had responded with the opposite? He wouldn't have cared; in his eyes, there would have been nothing awry. Still, being brought up in a culture where such terms are deemed racist, I could not say it. 'G'day, my friend' seemed appropriate. I was so tickled by our interaction that I momentarily melted with the hilarity. Weak at the knees, I nearly came off the bike as I returned a single-handed wave, hoping he perceived my cheerful response was as genuine as his. Regaining my composure, I wondered what surprises awaited around the next hairpin.

The summit

I did take a tumble farther up the mountain, where the road had been reinforced with loose, coarse railway ballast and, annoyingly, I skinned the same elbow I first damaged in Cameroon – for the third time. A sign at the summit confirmed that I had just conquered the country's highest trunk road. Whoever wrote the sign was 450 metres too generous with the altitude though. While it sure felt like I had pushed up to 2916 metres, and I wanted to believe so, the GPS recorded the actual altitude as 2466 metres. I arrived at the pass alone as John needed more time in town to prepare for the remote journey ahead. Wirri, a young fellow who worked at the nearby weather station, led me to the best vantage point. The views to the plains almost a kilometre below and across to the distant mountains were jaw-dropping. It was difficult to portray a sense of the scale through my camera lenses. From there, the road wound a convoluted path back down through the forest and along a ridge, staying above 2000 metres for at

A view from the north side of Loleza Mountain

least 20 kilometres. Eventually, I dropped down through some treacherous patches of bulldust and on to Chunya, an old gold-mining centre. The high plateau region we'd entered was noticeably drier, being in the rain shadow of the mountain system.

Out of Chunya, population density was sparse with the result that the land suffered from little of the pressures of human settlement. Pushing along the undulating gravel road through untamed *miombo* bushland, I felt released – similar to the freedom I experienced cycling through the Australian outback. I paused to watch three kudus amble across the road as if it wasn't there at all, and wander deep into the grassy woodland, nibbling away at the vegetation without a care in the world. Normally they are quite nervous animals but here there were no immediate threats.

✳

The third day out of Mbeya started all right and I enjoyed passing through a series of small villages, none of which was marked on our map. Then it all began to become heavy going on the legs as the path became sandy, especially along the low points. That wasn't the worst of it, though – just as I was struggling through deep sand I was bitten again and again by tsetse flies. Pretty soon I had become the main attraction for a large, angry swarm of tsetse that hovered around and behind me. My clothes gave no protection: they could bite through my cycle shorts, shirt, gloves and socks. Sharp, painful pinpricks, some bites left spots of blood on my skin. Via its syringe-like proboscis a tsetse can draw its own weight in one blood meal – give me the good ol' Aussie fly any day! Like sweat bees, Australian bush flies are just annoying. During my Australian expedition, once I had generated some speed and brushed my shirt a few times, I could lose them. But tsetses are the streamlined athletes of the fly world. Even at 40 kilometres an hour, they would easily keep up – I could not shake them off. The attacks were most severe in the moments after I stopped pedalling, when I was engulfed in the cloud of frenzied insects. In desperation, I would fling my bike to the side of the road and crouch in a foetal position to reduce my surface area and thus minimise the number of bites sustained. The flies seemed to be attracted to movement so if I kept completely motionless they would soon lose interest and disappear back into the bush. The trouble was that I had

to cycle eight hours a day. I found myself pedalling faster and faster to try to escape them – to no avail. Villages seemed to be void of tsetse, so passing through them did give respite. Preferring to rest on the trunks of trees, they tend to stay away from totally cleared areas. Villagers could also control numbers by trapping or spraying them.

Apart from starting to feel like a pincushion from incurring hundreds of tsetse bites, I did have a greater cause for concern. Diseases transmitted by tsetses are responsible for killing approximately

Tsetse flies rest on my bar bag

one-quarter of a million Africans annually and can wipe out rural livelihoods by destroying their cattle, horses and pigs. In humans, the parasites injected most commonly cause sleeping sickness; in animals, they transmit *nagana* (animal sleeping sickness), among other diseases. In its most acute form, sleeping sickness first attacks the lymph nodes and gradually progresses to the central nervous system where

John explores the ruins

swelling on the brain leads to extreme lethargy and eventually death if not treated. Tanzania and Angola, where I encountered the tsetse, are two of the most severely affected countries but tsetses are also found in pockets throughout sub-Saharan Africa.

At Kipembawe, one of the few villages shown on our map, we had expected to find the usual string of shops with little to buy and people milling around, chatting, selling from roadside stalls. But Kipembawe was different: it was completely deserted – a ghost town. Its single overgrown street was lined by a row of houses; and although they had solid, well-made brick walls, the roofs and woodwork were down, slowly returning to nature. The abandonment seemed strange. In other similar places on our journey, locals had either moved into the empty houses or at least reused the materials.

It turns out that our 'road less travelled' was once of far greater importance. In pre-automobile times Kipembawe was a junction town on the Tabora to Mbeya caravan route. During the German occupation of Tanganyika (German East Africa included what is now Rwanda, Burundi and Tanganyika – mainland Tanzania), Kipembawe was an important halfway town on another trade route between Itigi, a railway town on the Central Line, and Mbeya. The Central Railway Line, the most important legacy built during the German occupation (pre-1919), shadows the old slave and ivory trade route from Dar es Salaam through Tabora to Kigoma on Lake Tanganyika. The buildings we saw were obviously not of that era: the date 1945 was painted on one

facade. Serial numbers branded each house, suggesting a Second World War military association when Tanganyika was under British control. The reason for Kipembawe's abandonment, however, remains a mystery that I have been unable to solve.

The tsetse problem worsened. The following day I started off wearing a thick cotton long-sleeved shirt which also protected my backside a little. The flies bit straight through that so I added a cycle jersey under it. While the double layer of clothing worked for the areas covered, the flies just concentrated on other body parts,

A building in Kipembawe returning to nature

especially my hands and the backs of my legs. Next, I added a waterproof jacket and wrapped the shirt around my waist – a little better. Heading north from the remote village and mission of Kitunda, the problem intensified. I was travelling under a cloud of thousands of aggressive insects. My bar bag was coated with a thick mass of flies, their wings neatly folded one on top of the other as is characteristic of the species. It was a scene I thought I must photograph but in opening the bar bag to retrieve my camera, I tipped most of them off and incurred even more retaliatory bites on my hands. John noted that they would sit on the spare wheel of the Land Rover, some lingering in his vehicle's slipstream as he drove, so that he had to keep the windows closed.

After lunch I resorted to desperate measures. My full suit of armour included: thick socks, double-lined track bottoms with a pair of cycle shorts over the top, cycle jersey and waterproof jacket, winter gloves, tape around my wrists because the flies kept finding the gap between glove and jacket, scarf and an insect net for my head. All this was extremely hot to wear but did bring relief.

Kitunda to Sikonge was the section marked as impassable in the Wet. The road was in the process of being improved and had been built up over some of the swampy areas. There were a few sections that remained as sand and loose boulders. Negotiating these, my tsetse-proof gear

My full suit of armour to keep out the tsetse flies (photo: J Davidson)

was soon saturated with perspiration but this was much better than being bitten. I could relax a little.

Despite the discomfort, we were travelling through a beautiful wild place. In the forest I caught glimpses of troops of baboons and monkeys. The wetlands chirped with birdlife, and wading birds

Everyone came to look at Kitunda village

Girls in Kitunda

patrolled the waters in the late afternoon. I felt like Darth Vader cycling along in my veiled tsetse-proof costume but I was inspired by my surroundings and on a high on coming through a tumultuous eight-hour day. There were no people around; not even a car passed during the night. The region is part of a protected wildlife corridor that links a number of game reserves and national parks, allowing animals to roam freely between them. The band of protected zones runs from the north-west corner diagonally across the country.

A Tanzanian Monet

About a kilometre from our campsite, John noticed some lion footprints on the road. I was pleased to have missed these setting off earlier from our idyllic campsite. My focus was on when the next tsetse blitz would start and this time I was fully prepared from top to toe with wrists taped up and the insect net at the ready, should I need it. But although a few flies hovered threateningly over my head or nestled on my panniers, the battle never resumed. Just as unexpectedly as they had descended upon us, they disappeared. I was soon out of the wildlife preserve and for the final 120 kilometres through Ipole, Sikonge and on to Tabora, I passed regular villages and fields of maize intermingled with pockets of dense woodland. A series of road works increased my level of difficulty because here the gravel was simply dumped over the sand and traffic was expected to find a way around: there were no temporary slip roads. Most of the way to Sikonge I had to struggle with either the soft roadworks or the original sand and corrugations.

After Sikonge, John headed straight for Tabora to find a place to stay, as he usually did. Then, to stretch his legs, he cycled a few kilometres back out to meet and guide me in. This time he caught up with me as I was passing through Kwihara, just out of Tabora. The town is remarkable only for its history. Formerly known as Kazeh, Kwihara was founded by Omani traders in about 1825 as a caravan depot. It eventually became the hub of the slave and ivory routes that spread north to Lake Victoria, west to Lake Tanganyika and south to Lake Malawi (along the route we had just travelled). In the 1860s, an estimated half a million porters and countless slaves passed through Kazeh and Tabora each year, heading east to the coast. Early explorers David Livingstone and Henry Morton Stanley famously stopped in Kazeh after their legendary 'Dr Livingstone, I presume' meeting in Ujiji. To me, Kwihara was simply a dusty, standard African town. The unpaved main road was potholed and busy with the usual donkey carts, motorbikes, cyclists and pedestrians. The last few rolling hills just about finished me as we finally hit the bitumen of Tabora.

✤

Riding with local traffic on a lesser road from Nzega to Kahama

Location was also Tabora's raison d'être. The Germans had capitalised on its position on the main caravan trade route by building the Central Railway Line through the town and making it their administrative centre for the region. Apart from the railway station and Fort Boma, there wasn't much left of the German era. The mature mango trees that adorn the leafy streets and the high prevalence of Islam in the town are the main legacies of the Arab traders before them. Tabora, the largest town in German East Africa, impressed us with its friendly, relaxed ambience; there wasn't the usual pressure associated with more tourist-oriented centres. Earmarked for a new wave of development, it was now luring investors through its untapped potential for agricultural enterprises. The region is renowned for the production of world-class honey, and the government is seeking investment to develop edible oils, bio fuels and dairy as well as tourism. The road improvements that we encountered are part of a grand plan to improve infrastructure for economic development. Our 'road less travelled' will soon be no longer so.

We'd been led to believe that was the end of the rough unsealed road but once over the railway line and back into the rolling hills, within six kilometres I was again on the dirt. This was disheartening because I had expectations of an easier time. The road to Nzega was much busier, with traffic generally heading towards Mwanza, Tanzania's major city on Lake Victoria. Tanzanian bus drivers take the prize for the whole of Africa for being the most aggressive. Literally flying along over the washboard surface, like rudderless ships they would snake over the whole road as their tyres barely touched the tops of the corrugations. At high speeds, there was little control and brakes would have been relatively ineffectual. The drivers just appeared to plant their foot and expect everyone else to give way. I was driven off the road several times. Not surprisingly, the road toll here is horrific.

After Nzega, I followed a lesser dirt road that connected with the new tarmac about 70 kilometres farther on, near to Kahama. I was now travelling through open plains covered with low scrub interspersed by salt flats, directly to the south of Lake Victoria. There was little shade and the sun's rays were piercing through the heat of the day. I left John trying to send emails in Nzega and travelled alone for the morning. Passing through a small village called Igusule, I decided to take a look at the village bazaar that was in full swing. Sellers had spread mats over the ground to display their wares – everything from shoes and clothing to household items. But I had my sights firmly affixed on a stall of sweet, juicy mangoes and bananas. The moment I parked my bike

Women on a short break from hand-threshing grain in a field near Kah

against a tree, I drew a crowd – it felt as though everyone in the village had stopped to watch my every move, see what I bought. Robert, the most proficient English-speaker, stepped forward and we struck up a conversation about what I was doing, where I came from and what they thought about the road ahead. After filling my bags with the fruit I'd bought, Robert asked if he could have my address to keep in touch. By this stage a large group of friendly, curious locals encircled me, eager to see what I was carrying in my bags. I scrounged around in my bar bag for a piece of paper and by mistake pulled out a sachet of

Easing my way through more traffic along the main road just after Igusule

rehydration salts. 'Ah,' an anonymous voice called out, 'she's got a condom'. I made a joke about being well-prepared and the whole group roared with laughter.

The tone became more serious when I enquired about the road ahead. The region near the Rwandan border, John and I were told, was still full of refugees who had fled from Burundi and Rwanda during and after the 1994 genocide. I'd heard stories of bandits robbing buses, ambushing travellers and worse. Robert was very concerned. He was afraid to travel through that zone himself and insisted that I should take a bus between Kahama and Rusumo on the Rwandan border. John rejoined me just after Igusule and we decided to seek the advice of the truck drivers in Kahama, now just a few kilometres away. John quizzed a few farmers and truckies and learned that the real danger of being ambushed and robbed was after dark. We decided to proceed with caution, ensuring that we reached the safety of a village by nightfall. This meant lopping off a couple of hours at day's end to guarantee we were set up well before sundown.

Nearing Rwanda we were also approaching the western periphery of the Rift Valley. The landscape crumpled into a series of north-to-south folds, becoming higher and steeper as we neared the frontier. Advancing west, the dry scrubland was replaced by lush forest, the greenery becoming incrementally more verdant as I crossed from valley to valley. Rwanda is often dubbed 'Land of a Thousand Hills'. Pausing after another seven-kilometre climb at the summit of the last 'hill' before descending to Rusumo, it was easy to understand why. An ocean of enormous mounds extended to the horizon. To a cyclist with heart pounding and legs already working overtime, the sight was an indication of stormy seas ahead.

Most people travel to Tanzania to climb the peaks of Kilimanjaro and Meru, see the big game of the Serengeti and Ngorongoro Crater, relax on Zanzibar's beaches and experience the throng of Dar es Salaam. I had missed all of these but valued a journey off the well-beaten track where there were still spectacular mountains and corridors of *miombo* bush in its untouched state. Mbeya and Tabora were smaller cities brimming with optimism, earmarked by Tanzania's stable government for a bright economic future.

Despite all the uncertainties of travelling along a little-used trail over Tanzania's high Central Plateau, John and I made it to Kigali a day early. Zdenek rejoined the expedition the following day in time to take a closer look at Rwanda and how it is moving forward.

Total distance: 16,898 kilometres

UGANDA

DEMOCRATIC
REPUBLIC
OF CONGO

N

Lake
Bunyonyi

Kabale

RWANDA

Lake Kivu

Kigali

Ntarama

Mayange
Millennium Village

BUGESERA DISTRICT

Rusumo

TANZANIA

DEMOCRATIC
REPUBLIC
OF CONGO

BURUNDI

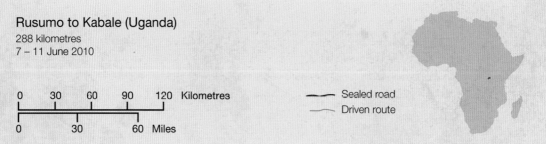

Rusumo to Kabale (Uganda)
288 kilometres
7 – 11 June 2010

| 0 | 30 | 60 | 90 | 120 | Kilometres |

| 0 | 30 | 60 | Miles |

——— Sealed road
——— Driven route

14
GHOSTS OF THE PAST, SPIRIT OF THE FUTURE

Rusumo to Lake Bunyonyi (Rwanda)

A sincere welcome to the 'Land of a Thousand Hills'

Arriving in Rwanda, I didn't know what to expect. I mainly knew of the horrors of the 1994 genocide when at least two-thirds of the population was displaced and an estimated one million people were killed. I had been warned of the dangers and heard stories of hardship. Initial impressions were completely different.

After crossing over a spectacular waterfall at Rusumo, and dealing with immigration and customs formalities, we encountered a dramatically changed landscape and culture. On the Tanzanian side of the border, much of the land was still in a reasonably natural condition, but on the Rwandan side just about every square metre was being used for intensive cultivation or for pasture. The valleys mostly

Intensive land use. Almost every square metre is accounted for

supported rice or sugar-cane production, the slopes were terraced to grow maize, vegetables, bananas and other fruits, and some of the steeper sections were grazed by milking cows. There were people everywhere. From what I could see, homesteads tended to be fairly evenly spread amongst the hills, more like a continuous 'rural conurbation' with the occasional larger town. Rather than one cyclist joining me at a time, now it was more like a whole peleton. Whenever I stopped I would be set upon by a swarm of inquisitive kids to the point where I found it claustrophobic. The Rwandan tourist bureau markets the country as 'The Land of a Thousand Smiles' and on my day-and-a-half ride to Kigali, the locals certainly lived up to this claim. Finding a spot secluded enough to take a nature break was virtually impossible without a beaming face popping out from behind a wall or materialising in the midst of a banana plantation!

Rwanda is a tiny landlocked country, less than half the size of Tasmania, with a population of 11 million. Despite the high density of people, villages were clean and tidy. The government has banned the use of plastic bags, which in the rest of Africa can be seen clogging up the waterways and sewers and becoming entwined with thorn trees and fence lines. In Rwandan towns that I rode through along the highway, the main streets were lined with rubbish bins. Many shops were freshly painted and houses had neatly-kept gardens.

Following the main route to Kigali I was constantly being passed by a steady stream of trucks carrying loads of imported goods. This was a country on the move. The leaders and citizens of Rwanda, it seemed, were on a mission to airbrush the unimaginable horrors of sixteen years ago from memory and rebuild the proud nation.

✻

Waiting for Zdenek to rejoin us, John and I visited the Kigali Genocide Memorial Centre. This explains why those horrors happened, the events leading to the one hundred days of frenzied killing and torture, the lack of response from the international community and the aftermath. Before German colonisation in the late 1800s and early 1900s, there were eighteen different clans living in Rwanda. The clanspeople were categorised as Hutu (84 per cent), Tutsi (15 per cent) or Twa (1 per cent) depending on their socio-economic circumstances, and they lived together in harmony: there is no evidence of any conflict. Under German rule, these distinctions were made racial. The Germans considered the Tutsis, the minority group, to be of higher intelligence and began to favour them for all the positions of importance and responsibility. Rwandans were classified by the colonists as a Tutsi if they owned more than ten cows and also by anthropometric measurements. A person was deemed a Tutsi if they had a longer, thinner nose than other indigenous populations. During the First World War, Belgium took over as the colonial power and continued the same 'divide and rule' regime. In 1932 it introduced identity cards, formalising the ethnic classification. Amongst the Hutu majority, this move naturally bred dissent, which incubated over the next few decades into racial hatred. Towards the end of their rule, the Belgians, along with the Catholic Church, reversed their historic position of favour, giving considerable support to Hutu demands for political dominance.

Tension erupted into the first large-scale conflict in 1959, just before independence, which left 20,000 Tutsis dead. Between then and 1973, about 700,000 Tutsis were exiled. Racial hatred was incited by the ruling Hutus, who used media propaganda to powerful effect. For example, in 1990 *Kangura,* a widely read Hutu journal, published the infamous 'Hutu Ten Commandments' that branded any Hutu who had interacted with a Tutsi a traitor. The tension spring coiled tighter. The Rwandan Patriotic Front (RPF), comprising of exiled Tutsis including Paul Kagame (Rwanda's current president), invaded from Uganda in an attempt to reclaim their homeland. President Juvenal Habyarimana's armed Hutu forces, with the assistance of France, were able to repel the attack and used the conflict to administer appalling human rights abuses as reprisal. A peace agreement brokered in Arusha, Tanzania, did little to calm the situation, and hatred and mistrust continued to prevail. The architects of the genocide made ready their plans. More than half a million machetes were imported from China, AK-47s were acquired from a variety of sources, and mortar bombs, rocket launchers, ammunition and grenades were supplied courtesy of an Egyptian arms deal. The Rwandan Armed Forces and killing squads such as the *Interahamwe* were organised, primed and provided with death lists.

There were many warnings given that were not heeded by the international community. UN commander Lieutenant General Romeo Dallaire estimated that as few as 5000 troops with authority to enforce peace could have stopped the genocide. Instead, the UN mission was recalled after ten soldiers were shot. This deliberate tactic cleared the way for the anarchy to commence – the exact outcome the Hutu regime wanted. The shooting down of a plane carrying President Habyarimana and President Cyprien Ntaryamira of Burundi (both Hutus) provided the spark. Within an hour, roadblocks were set up in Kigali and shooting began. Much could have been done to prevent or at least reduce what occurred during the one hundred days of madness when the Hutus attempted to eliminate the Tutsis – along with moderate Hutus who did not want to participate in the ethnic cleansing – from the face of the planet. The killings only ceased when the Rwandan Patriotic Front, led by Kagame, captured Kigali and the Hutu government collapsed, declaring a ceasefire. By then, approximately one million people, including three-quarters of the Tutsi population, were dead and at least half-a-million women had been raped, many deliberately infected with HIV/AIDS. About two million Hutus, fearing Tutsi retaliation, fled to neighbouring Uganda, Burundi, Tanzania and Zaire (as the Democratic Republic of Congo was then called). Although the killing in Rwanda was over, the presence of Hutu militias in the DRC has led to the deadliest conflicts since the Second World War – the First and Second Congo Wars – resulting in more than five million deaths and two million refugees. But that is another complex story.

The upstairs gallery of the memorial centre was dedicated to the child victims of the genocide. The room was lined with photographs of beautiful children, some just toddlers, with text recounting their favourite foods, friends, activities and toys, and how they were brutally clubbed to death. I couldn't imagine how anyone could view this exhibition with a dry eye. I left the memorial with a clearer understanding of the complex genocide events and a numbing sadness in my heart, disappointed and

and angry with humanity. Adjacent to the museum, a flame flickered defiantly in the gentle afternoon breeze, as it does every year to commemorate the hundred days of massacre. Pausing beside the flame, I gazed across the beautiful terraced memorial gardens where one-quarter of a million people are buried in mass graves. Just as the flame burns on and on so does life go on outside the memorial grounds. Several cranes were working late into the afternoon, transforming the city skyline. Children were playing in the street – just as kids normally do.

✾

We had hurried to reach Kigali in time to make a scheduled project visit to the Mayange Millennium Village. Like Potou in Senegal and Tiby/Ségou in Mali, Mayange is located in a vulnerable socio-economic hotspot. As each of these Millennium Villages has an individual set of circumstances, I was interested to see how the Mayange roadmap to achieving the Millennium Development Goals by 2015 compared. Potou and Tiby are both located in the Sahel region where the marginal, drought-prone climates are a major cause of their precarious circumstances. The terrain around Mayange, about 40 kilometres south of Kigali, is flatter and drier than most of Rwanda. As the climate is classified as temperate, I was surprised to learn, looking at the grassy hills and high plains, that lack of water is still a problem – it needs to be piped from a reservoir about 40 kilometres away. But erratic climatic conditions are only a part of Mayange's challenges. Community vulnerability here is also exacerbated by the events of the genocide and its aftermath.

Donald Ndahiro, the team leader of the Mayange Millennium Village cluster, explained that the project is focusing on 'economic development as a means of unity and reconciliation'. Mayange is located in the Bugesera District, widely regarded as the epicentre of the genocide. It is estimated that about 60 per cent of Bugesera's largely Tutsi population were killed, hacked and bludgeoned to death by their own neighbours. Other residents were internally displaced or fled to Burundi, devastating many lives. Human remains are still found in the fields, especially when released prisoners return to the community and reveal the scene of their crimes. Now perpetrators and victims live side by side, working on reconciliation and improving their living conditions. They refuse to let the past stand in the way of a better future.

As with Potou and Tiby, Mayange was conceived in 2006. At that time the four principal villages had no facilities, not even any electricity, so the headquarters were set up in a larger town several kilometres away. There Donald outlined what his departments were doing to improve infrastructure and communications, education, farming and agriculture, health and trade/business. The plan was to see at least one example of each of the main projects. From the head offices, we drove to Mayange where we met Jeanette Mukabalisa, who showed us around for the rest of the day. Mayange has several *umudugudus*, or settlements of closely-spaced dwellings, which the government built to house returnees after the genocide. Essentially, it is the villagers who decide on the initiatives they would like to adopt. Jeanette's job involved liaising with the village committees and then reporting their ideas and needs to Donald and the team. The Millennium Village staff assessed how a certain directive could fit in to the overall scheme – to assist in realising the MDGs. Once a plan was approved, Jeanette would present a proposal to the village leaders.

The Millennium Village Project began on the back of a drought in 2005 when the team worked in conjunction with UNICEF and the World Food Program to establish emergency feeding centres for malnourished mothers and children. Donald explained that by applying targeted, science-based interventions and maximising community leadership and participation, the circumstances of the Mayange community were transformed from chronic hunger to a bumper harvest in one year. Since then they have been working on drought protection by increasing crop diversity, improving agricultural techniques and by developing opportunities for small businesses. Agriculture-based programs, including the artificial insemination of cattle, honey production, fishing, poultry and a cassava-processing plant, had been introduced with a focus on skills transfer.

Jeanette took us to meet one of the most successful farmers. He had really embraced everything he had been taught and proudly showed us his field of pineapples, mango and avocado trees laden with fruit, as well as his bananas, sugar cane, maize, capsicums, onions, beans and tomatoes. He'd learned how to intercrop, had introduced nitrogen-fixing plants to improve soil fertility, dug drainage channels and spread mulch around plants to reduce moisture loss and increase fertility. Everything looked amazingly healthy, including the dairy cows: one nuzzled John with her sloppy wet snout as he gave it a vigorous pat. The farmer could afford to extend his house with the money he had made from selling his excess crops, and was in the process of reinforcing the original mud brick walls. He was obviously a showcase for the farming initiative but his enthusiasm and optimism were infectious.

Mayange farmer shows off his field of pineapples, mobile phone in hand

I still found the whole experience a little overwhelming. It was difficult to comprehend the transformation – from killing fields sixteen years ago to drought-ravaged infertile lands just four years previously and now thriving vegetable gardens oozing with prosperity. Hunger and land property issues had contributed to the build-up of pressure that led to the society imploding in 1994. Jeanette explained that people now having enough to eat and being better off economically helps with fostering unity.

One of the most effective interventions has been the introduction and use of information and communication technologies. Integrating mobile technology has helped advance business development, education and health. Initially, Ericsson installed mobile phone towers, bringing mobile connectivity to the whole region. As a result, farmers used their mobile phones to check prices at local markets and schools acquired internet and computer labs. The technology has transformed access to medical care, management and training.

Prior to the commencement of the Millennium Village Project, primary schools were overcrowded, with as many as eighty students in a class. At Kagenge, where the project first began, more classrooms had been built and extra teachers provided to improve the teacher-to-pupil ratio, regular training keeping teachers up to date. The computer laboratory had Wi-Fi, and information technology had become a standard subject in the school curriculum.

As of 2009, schoolchildren in Rwanda started to learn in English rather than French. John thought he would test the students' English knowledge and took an impromptu

John giving an English lesson

lesson in a Year 4 class. I doubt whether they had heard a Scottish accent before but they seemed to get the gist of it: 'My name is John, I live in Scotland'. 'Where is Scotland?' The students loved it.

Adjacent to the school was the health centre, built in 1999. Until 2006, it had been the only centre servicing the 25,000 people who live in the district. At that time, there was virtually no service at all: barely any medicines or equipment, no running water and no electricity. The inadequate numbers of nursing staff often did not show up to work. In partnership with the Access Project, all the basics were now shored up – infrastructure, medical training and payment of staff, provision of adequate basic medicines. Access to health services throughout the district had improved dramatically. Health posts were being set up as satellite services to take care of easily treatable maladies, nurses using their mobile phones to record data and the internet as reference. Everyone in the community now had a mobile phone and with universal coverage across the district, people could easily summon assistance. In case of medical emergency, there was a free number to dial and an ambulance would arrive to transport the ill to hospital at no cost.

Jeanette and a doctor took us through the new maternity wing. It was far from state of the art, but it was clean and functional. There were three newborns, too recently arrived to have names yet, defenceless, cradled in their exhausted mothers' arms. The infants were entering a world very different from the one their parents were born into. For a start, they were born in a clinic with a nurse in attendance whereas their mothers were most likely born on the floor of a mud hut. In Mayange, maternal deaths have virtually been eliminated, diarrhoea is minimal, new cases of malaria are rare and universal measles vaccinations have been achieved.

One of the most effective strategies introduced by the Rwandan government was the implementation of 'financial accessibility to health services for all'. The government initiated a community-based health insurance program, Mutuelle de Sante, to cover the basic expenses of primary healthcare. The insurance plan costs individuals roughly $US2 a year, making it accessible for most people. In Mayange, many had been reluctant to take up the insurance plan; they were still too poor to afford it. Others could not understand why they would not be reimbursed at the end of the year if they did not require treatment. The MVP made it more accessible for the poorest citizens by allowing them to take out loans against the anticipated harvest, in cash or in kind with farm produce (such as maize or beans). Jeanette explained that uptake increased with some simple education and promotion.

Finally we were taken to see two of the many business cooperatives that are transforming lives financially and socially. At the new cassava processing plant, a cross-section of the community was involved. Outside, men, women and their children sat together, working hand in hand to prepare the cassava roots, chatting, laughing, sharing thoughts, regardless of ethnicity. The root from the cassava plant provides the staple food in their diet. Cassava is a wonder-plant in these parts because it can grow in just about any conditions, even drought. The starchy tuber is peeled, washed, chopped in a machine not unlike a wood chipper, fermented, dried and ground into fine flour. The cooperative produced high-quality cassava flour which meant better returns for the families. A women's basket-weaving business had similar benefits. Many of the women were widowed with large families to provide for and the business provided them with extra income which allowed them to get ahead, send their children to school, buy a cow or goat and save money in a new bank account. Their work is of a high standard and an international market was being developed. The camaraderie and social inclusion that went with working together were just as important to participants as the financial gains.

Preparing cassava for processing is a community affair

Washing the cassava

I wondered what would become of these Millennium Villages in five years time, once the project is complete. How sustainable will the interventions we saw be? What will their contribution be to alleviating extreme poverty on a national scale? Although the interventions were innovative and relatively low-cost, the injection of money is much greater than was previously available. The model was designed on the assumption that Western governments of the G8 would honour their promise to increase aid to 0.7 per cent of GDP. With the global financial crisis, some of these pledges have been put on hold. If these commitments are not met and local governments cannot afford to match such investments, where will this leave the Millennium Village communities? Outside these tight-knit communities, social harmony was altering because equally poor families were missing out on the life-changing opportunities. Some critics argue that it is a more effective use of aid money to focus on the eradication of one issue at a time, such as a major illness like malaria, polio or HIV/AIDS, rather than creating integrated cells.

Unlike past failed attempts of creating model communities, the MVPs have a greater emphasis on nurturing management, problem-solving, business skills and networking and communications. Fertilisers and seeds are provided in the form of loans, which prevents the goods being traded for short-term gain. The loans are not a handout, so the recipients have a better sense of their value. In Mayange I could see a great emphasis on community development and socialisation, more likely to keep people together in the future. I hoped that this sense of community would extend beyond the boundaries of the MVP rather than the other way around, as some suggest. Donald had explained that the Rwandan government recognised the scalability of the MVP and had taken steps to include some of the strategies as a national priority. Under its Vision 2020-Umurenge initiative, it plans to expand the Millennium Villages Project to all thirty of Rwanda's districts, with each district identifying its neediest sector for MV interventions. That can only be a positive development.

Operating the cassava chopper is a messy job

*

On the way back to Kigali we made a short diversion to see the Ntarama Memorial Site to the Rwandan genocide. For me (and I think the others too), Ntarama was without doubt the most disturbing, horrific, emotive display I have ever experienced. Ntarama is a monument to humanity at its most evil. Many people fled to Catholic churches such as at Ntarama to hide and seek sanctuary from the carnage, believing that they would be safe there. But some of the priests betrayed their trusting congregation by turning them over to the Hutu murderers. At Ntarama over 5000 people – men, women and children – were slain. The aim was not just to kill but to inflict as much pain and indignity as possible. As we walked in to the rear of the church, victims' bones were laid out on shelves as a macabre, orderly exhibit. Hundreds of skulls were arranged on the higher shelves, some with spikes and other instruments of murder still embedded. The lower shelf was stacked with limb bones: femur, tibia, humerus and radius bones all sorted into separate caches. Victims' bloodstained clothes hung on the rafters and covered the side walls. A certain 'musty slaughterhouse' stench which I will never forget pervaded everything.

To the right of the altar, there was a collection of the victims' most prized possessions; pendants, crosses, glasses, jewellery, personal belongings. In front of the altar women were raped, their wombs removed before they were shot. Our guide, himself a survivor of the genocide, pointed to where bullets had scarred the concrete. We were taken to the Sunday school classroom behind the church. The atrocities committed here stretched the depths of my imagination to a new low. Children and toddlers would have sat terrified and crying on the tiny pews, watching as their friends were tortured and killed, their heads smashed against the back wall. The bloodstains were still there. Finally we were led to an adjacent building where people had been wrapped in mattresses, doused with fire accelerant and set alight. The room had been left untouched; amongst the charred remains on the floor were fragments of teeth, a jawbone and clumps of singed hair. I paused for a few moments after the others left. The smell of burnt mattress foam and kerosene will forever haunt me as the odour of Hell.

I took a few photos from outside the church (we were not permitted to photograph inside without paying a licence fee). The three of us were deeply affected and barely a word was spoken on our return trip to Kigali. John was upset with me for taking the pictures because he thought it was an undignified act. We were all in shock but had reacted in different ways. I considered it important to record all parts of the journey, including the most shocking. But these images were firmly engraved in my mind anyway – I didn't need to see them again. I understood John's point of view and deleted all bar one that I missed, which showed people's prized possessions. Memorials such as Ntarama are widely documented in the media for all to see if they wish.

Some of Ntarama victims' most treasured personal belongings displayed in the church

I seriously deliberated as to whether I should even write about what we saw. One of the main purposes of the Ntarama and Kigali memorials is to educate people about the genocide in the hope that the world will learn. To Rwandans, the memorials are preserved to acknowledge the painful past, to promote healing and help them move on; to outsiders they are a reminder of why the world should never turn its back on humanity. To everyone it is testimony to just how far the nation has come in the sixteen years since. With even more recent events of ethnic cleansing in Bosnia and Serbia, I am not sure how much has been learned but these monuments send powerful messages and there is always hope.

✳

In Kigali we stayed at the One Love Guesthouse, part of a self-funding effort for the Mulindi Japan One Love Project. Profits from the guesthouse, restaurant and bar go towards developing and maintaining orthopaedic workshops in Kigali and Bujumbura (Burundi) that have so far supplied over 8000

prostheses, orthotics, sticks or wheelchairs to those disabled during the 1994 genocide. Gatera Rudasingwa (Emmanuel to us), the founder and driver of the project along with his Japanese wife Mami and son, spent time showing us around. Gatera had himself been physically impaired as a youngster after an injection during a medical procedure went wrong. He experienced all the difficulties of being disabled in a society with no facilities or

With Gatera Rudasingwa, co-founder of the Mulindi Japan One Love Project (ZK)

support to accommodate his disability – he is a survivor who had to struggle physically and mentally to be independent.

The rather long-winded name reflects the project's history and Gatera's vision. Clearly of a kindred spirit with the late Bob Marley, 'One Love' signifies Gatera's hope for a unified, peaceful future, mirroring the pre-colonial days where Tutsis, Hutus and Twa shared one language and one culture. In 1989 Gatera, a Tutsi, fled to Nairobi to escape the violence. He met Mami there, two years later travelling with her to Japan. There, after visiting an orthopaedic

Shaping a cast for a prosthetic leg (ZK)

workshop, the germ of what would become the couple's lifework evolved. The idea to help disabled Rwandans was first hatched in 1991 when hiding out with Paul Kagame's Rwandan Patriotic Front (RPF) at Mulindi near Rwanda's border with Uganda. After the genocide, Gatera returned to Kigali and, with government support, established the Mulindi Japan One Love Project with Mami in 1996.

The project supports people with physical and/or psychological disabilities to become independent in society at several levels. The workshops were opened in Kigali in 1997 and Burundi in 2007. One Love is now diversifying, with warehouses in Miami and Kenya, where handicrafts made by artisans with disabilities are sold; profits help to fund the workshops so that beneficiaries receive

Land of a thousand hills

their artificial limbs free of charge. The organisation also trains technicians, rehabilitates people with a disability to rejoin society, has set up a vocational training school to teach all sorts of skills in business and handicrafts, encourages sports participation for those with a disability, runs the guesthouse and restaurant (which provides employment to the impaired) and many other activities which give support.

Gatera's workshop sources materials and equipment from all over the world – Japan, Switzerland, Germany, the US and the UK, for example. I found it a moving experience watching new prostheses being carefully measured and shaped, knowing that each artificial limb was going to transform the life of someone who could not afford it. The next challenge for the recipient would be to learn how to use it and then reintegrate into the society in which they had previously been marginalised.

✳

I moved on from the One Love Guesthouse, pedalling out of Kigali and up a beautiful terraced valley, over a high pass and into Uganda. The Rwandan hills were a hive of activity. They were alive – not with the ghosts of the past but with the spirit of the future. I encountered the customary smiling faces and many men cycled alongside me for a few kilometres at a time. They had moved on too, or at the very least, they got on with life. To see Rwanda now it was hard to believe what happened just a few years before – the government is doing a remarkable job, and Rwanda is now often referred to as 'Africa's Singapore'. There is little crime and women can walk around Kigali safely at night – contrary to what I had heard prior to arriving in the country. Rwanda is the first country in the world where women are in the majority in parliament and everyone, even the president, participates in community service on the

A spirit of the future

last Saturday of every month. From the Rwandans I met at the One Love Project, in Mayange, at the memorials and in the street, I sensed an incredible fortitude and self-determination to rebuild their own society. Ethnicity is a banned topic. Officially citizens are no longer able to be categorised as Hutus or Tutsis – they are simply Rwandans moving on to a better life.

Total distance: 17,186 kilometres

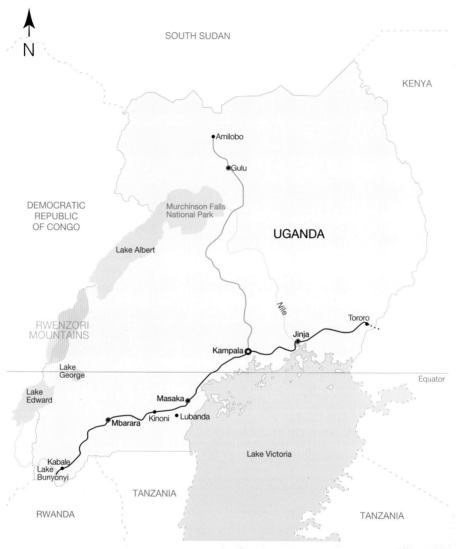

SOUTH SUDAN

KENYA

•Amilobo

•Gulu

DEMOCRATIC
REPUBLIC
OF CONGO

Murchinson Falls
National Park

UGANDA

Lake Albert

RWENZORI
MOUNTAINS

Nile

Tororo

Jinja

Kampala

Lake
George

Equator

Lake
Edward

Masaka

Kinoni •Lubanda

•Mbarara

Lake Victoria

Kabale
Lake
Bunyonyi

TANZANIA

RWANDA

TANZANIA

Kabale to Tororo (Uganda)

645 kilometres
12 – 23 June 2010

0	60	120	180	240	Kilometres

0	60	120	Miles

——— Sealed road
——— Driven route

15

THE PEARL OF AFRICA: RESTORING THE LUSTRE

Kabale to Tororo (Uganda)

Lake Bunyonyi

Everyone has the desire and capability to improve their own living standard,
but perhaps not the opportunity.

David Ssemwogerere

Tucked away in Uganda's extreme south-west corner is Lake Bunyonyi. The crater lake, featured on the Ugandan 5000-shilling note, is regarded as one of the country's most stunning natural wonders. Its convoluted shoreline and calm, crystal-clear waters are revered as an environment to inspire and re-energise.

Seeking a spot to chill out for a night, we set off from the bustling market town of Kabale along the Kisoro Road on a short, end-of-day excursion to the lake. But the ride was anything but relaxing. The four-kilometre climb to the lip of the ancient volcano started off sedately and I enthusiastically smiled and waved to the locals as I coasted by. But after rounding a hairpin corner, the path rose dramatically out of the dense forest; the wriggling ascent assumed the form of an angry serpent set to strike. The sight of the challenge transformed my mood from open and buoyant to one of blinkered focus as I attempted to summon the energy to make the summit. I overtook two men, straining as they pushed their single-geared bikes up the slope on foot.

About 500 metres into the steep section, I fell into a state of severe oxygen debt – an 'energy bonk' – when lactic acid flushes through the body, the heart pounds in order to pump as much oxygen to the extremities as possible and sweat pores open their floodgates. In an effort to keep the pedals turning, I combed the recesses of my mind for some positive inspiration. But this time the inspiration found me. I caught and passed a young man lugging a part-filled yellow water container on his shoulder. To my amazement he picked up his pace to a half walk, half jog, to draw back level with me. 'Jambo,' he said, his greeting snapping me out of my tunnel-visioned trance. His bright breezy disposition and pearly ear-to-ear grin was so earnest, his sentiment contagious; 'Jambo,' I echoed back. From there it was mainly a conversation of gestures rather than words as we both struggled for breath. I found it a little off-putting to my rhythm that the young fellow could keep pace with me on foot, carry a load – and maintain such a cheerful outlook. He served to distract my attention for a few hundred metres until he peeled off, stirring my competitive instincts. He forced me to dig deeper to find the resolve to complete the climb without being defeated by it – or by him.

The view of the lake from the village at the brow of the crater was indeed spectacular, well worth the effort. A series of emerald islands bejewelled Africa's second deepest lake. The intensively terraced hillsides rose almost sheer from the contorted shoreline. Bunyonyi translates as 'place of many little birds' but, taking a pause, as far as I could see it was a place of many little people. Children flocked to see what the *muzungu* had in her bags and whether I would give them anything useful such as water bottles, pencils or food.

The climb had been an exhausting bookend to a long day that had begun in Kigali. The effort had whittled away my patience and I quickly moved on towards the lakeside a few hundred metres below, still almost 2000 metres above sea level. We camped on the garden terraces beside the water's edge at Kalebas Camp. When I awoke at dawn, it was clear why the place was steeped in local mythology – and a popular tourist attraction. The mystical, dewy morning was so placid that the lake surface doubled as a canvas, perfectly reflecting its surroundings: the reeds that delineated its shallow edges, the nearby jetty and the tapestry of textured greens that carpeted the hilly backdrop. The glassy waters were occasionally broken by a lone canoeist heading out across the lake, carrying produce or fishing. As the sun gradually illuminated the western slopes and burned away the surface mist, I watched locals swim in the warmish waters. Although we only stayed by the lake for a night, I left invigorated.

Returning down the mountain, a harsh contrasting reality struck – quite literally, with the rhythmical resonating blows of steel on rock. In my effort to get to the lake I had barely noticed the bluestone quarry that scarred the verdant wild side of the mountain. It formed a rough amphitheatre where Pharaonic-type real-life scenes were being played out. Here, rather than cutting the building blocks for the pyramids, people were cracking the blue metal aggregate used to surface Uganda's roads. All generations and both sexes were represented. Men broke rocks with sledge hammers and crow bars, boys swung pick axes, grandmothers, mothers and children smashed smaller shards of scree. There were certainly no safety

Pharaonic-type scenes at a bluestone quarry near Lake Bunyonyi

precautions in place. I watched one woman raking gravel over the cliff face, perched in a precarious position – no harness, no shoes, no protection. Only the boss wore shoes. I had just read in a Ugandan newspaper that the wages earned by women who picked flowers at a nursery were usually about $1.20 a day, rising to $1.50 after a year of service. I doubt these quarry workers were even getting that. We had paid almost $US50 for three of us for camping, dinner and breakfast on the other side of the hill, considering it to be a good deal, yet here it would take a labourer more than a month to earn that amount. Life isn't fair. John handed the foreman/boss/master a little cash for his trouble. He was assured the tip would be divided amongst the workers. I hoped so.

❊

Resuming the journey out of Kabale was another strenuous affair. To the west and north, the enigmatic Rwenzori Mountains, or 'Mountains of the Moon', the highest and most permanent sources of the Nile River, rise over 5000 metres. From there, like a seismic wave, the land ripples down to Lake Victoria which lies at about 1100 metres above sea level. My route, the main road, bisected these folds. Out of Kabale I pedalled over some huge hills, a high plain and then more rolling hills and on through the busy centre of Mbarara to reach the small market town of Kinoni, 20 kilometres from Masaka. At Kinoni we diverted to a small village called Lubanda to meet Helen Brown and learn about her HUG Project.

Helen first contacted me in response to an article in *The Age* newspaper in Melbourne and we quickly realised that we shared a common passion with regard to the theme and purpose of our initiatives. She invited me to visit her project in southern Uganda, HUG, which stands for Help Us Grow. Helen set up the not-for-profit organisation with David Ssemwogerere after their paths crossed when she and her husband Adrian first visited Uganda to take part in a program to rebuild and refurbish primary schools. Helen felt that there was a division between the organisation that she was working for and the local people to whom she instantly became endeared. David, along with like-minded Ugandans, had established an in-country NGO, Development Plus, that focused on creating organic gardens in schools. HUG was conceived to develop relationships between community members and volunteers so that both cultures learnt from each other in a mutually rewarding way. By connecting people on a direct and equal level, Helen and David were endeavouring to foster lasting partnerships between individuals, families, businesses and schools

Planning ahead. On the road, just out of Mbarara (photo: Z Kratky)

249

from two different societies. Sharing ideas and knowledge, the benefits go both ways to build community spirit and resilience.

As we arrived, Helen and David had just returned from Kampala with a family of volunteers from Melbourne – the Tomaino family. It was their first experience of Africa and some of the cultural contrasts had left them rather wide-eyed. Our group was honoured with a traditional welcome dance by about twenty women from the Lubanda

In discussion with Helen Brown (photo: Z Kratky)

community. Helen explained that when they started the project eighteen months earlier, these women did not have the self-confidence to give such a special performance. Helen and David were reviving self-esteem by encouraging the women to reconnect with their own traditions.

David's philosophy, that 'everyone has the desire and capability to improve their own living standard, but perhaps not the opportunity', is at the heart of HUG. His vision was to create a focal point in his community where people could come to learn new life skills, interact, support each other and be inspired. David's dream was realised with the building of the Suubi Education and Community Centre on family land donated by his mother, with funds provided by HUG. ('Suubi' means 'hope' in the local Luganda language.) The Centre was only about a year old when we visited but already, under David's

David Ssemwogerere with one of the youngest students at the Bright Light Primary School

direction and with the group's passion and enthusiasm, it had become the envisaged beacon of promise, empowering the surrounding communities.

There were no huge budgets here. This was a small grassroots organisation where initiatives were based on knowledge and skills transfer, community needs, simplicity and positive encouragement at a pace that suits the lifestyle. Volunteers like the Tomaino family became part of the community and learned just as much from the locals. It was refreshing to watch the reactions of the teenagers – straight out of comfortable Melbourne into rural Uganda. Here there were no PlayStations or televisions. Instead Lucynda and Christian fully engaged with the local kids and became a part of what was going on. Helen's idea is to harness volunteers' skills and put them to use in the various programs such as sewing and handicrafts, cooking, gardening, construction, computer skills, sport, drama, music and dance. Each person gains something different from HUG: the motivation comes from within.

At the local Bright Light Primary School David explained how he had teamed up with the head teacher to develop the school vegetable garden using Permaculture techniques, the core work of his Development Plus organisation. Initially the head teacher was sent on a training course where he learned about fertilising, mulching and cultivating different types of vegetables and fruit – many of which were not normally grown in the limited traditional vegetable gardens. He appeared to be very proud of the resultant diverse school garden. Some of the produce was used for the children's meals while the rest was sold to create an income to buy in maize and beans, the staple foods. While the garden wasn't big enough to provide the 600-odd students with food all year round it was obviously making a significant contribution to their wellbeing. The plot also served as an outdoor laboratory, providing a medium for learning across a number of subjects from mathematics to health, agriculture and science. Children were taking what they learned at school to apply at home.

Sprinkled throughout the village was evidence of more successful ventures. There was the mushroom project and a pig-breeding program and many were benefiting from improved agricultural practices. Seeds, mushroom spores and animals were provided as loans to be repaid, with various commitments required to secure the loans.

Getting to know some of the students at the Bright Light Primary School (photo: H Brown)

Uganda has had a turbulent recent history. In 1979, nearby towns such as Masaka and Mbarara were trashed by the Tanzanian army during the war that ousted the country's most cruel and oppressive dictator, Idi Amin Dada. Times of fear and extreme hardship were not that long gone, but the people of Lubanda and surrounding communities did not appear to be suffering from abject poverty. HUG is giving them the opportunity to lift themselves out of the vulnerable zone, to become more resilient and better able to cope with the hard times.

In a country of 35 million people, of whom about one-third are illiterate, where each woman bears 6.65 children and 6.5 per cent of the population have HIV/AIDS (down from about 30 per cent in the early 1990s, a Ugandan success story), Suubi is more than a beacon of hope for the people of Lubanda. As the projects catch on and grow, the hope is that a ripple effect spreads back over the hills from where we had just come, to reach people like the quarry workers beside Lake Bunyonyi. It was 'HUGs' all-round as we

Mushroom-producing initiative. Women from Lubanda who wish to participate must build their own dark room in readiness to receive their mushroom spores

farewelled the team and volunteers. I returned to Kinoni and restarted the journey from where I stopped cycling – the beginning of a marathon day to Kampala.

✳

I continued to cut across the undulations until I reached Masaka and then headed north-east, through the flat, swampy environs of Lake Victoria. Although the main road closely tracked the shoreline, I did not catch a glimpse of the great lake all day. The apparently perennial roadworks turned long sections of the busy highway in to a dustbowl. Powdery entrails left in the wake of each vehicle lingered in the still atmosphere, gradually dispersing in to the otherwise clear sky.

I was constantly being enshrouded with the pale dust so I pulled my manky neck scarf – the same tea towel that I had started wearing out of St Louis, Senegal – over my mouth and nose to crudely filter out the worst of it. Its dark blue stripes had become so sun-bleached they were barely distinguishable from the once white, now dirty beige, background. Over the last eight months, this perspiration-soaked rag had protected my neck from frying under the African sun, had prevented me from inhaling too much alluvial Saharan sand and had been used to wipe Congolese mud from the corners of my eyes.

Crossing back over the Equator put another important motivational notch in the journey. With roughly two months to go, it really felt as though I was getting there. I paused to contemplate the moment.

Beside the monument marking the Equator were two billboards joined to form a V-shape so that the angled signs could be seen by on-coming traffic from the north and south. The messages were part of a media campaign to 'end corruption'. On the north-facing mural the artist had painted caricatures of a

Crossing back over the dusty Equator – another important motivational notch in the journey

politician and his wife receiving funds from the global community on one side; on the other, medical staff explained to the sick that they had no medicine. The adjoining billboard portrayed local government leaders dreaming of material gains while the community went without. Magnifying the poignancy of the message was the fact the artwork was rusting and the paint peeling off. The artist's expression was slowly corroding, just as a society decays when the cancer of corruption takes hold. The signs were an indicator that corruption in Uganda is pervasive across the many layers of bureaucracy, from the highest level down.

Back in 1909, Winston Churchill dubbed Uganda 'the Pearl of Africa' due to its wealth of natural beauty, diversity of wildlife and cultures and the fertility of the soil that supported profitable cash crops such as cotton and coffee. By the time Yoweri Museveni took over the reins in 1986, the 'Pearl' had lost its lustre. Uganda's development had already been stifled in the extreme by the chaos and corrupt actions of post-independence quixotic leaders, Dr Milton Obote (1966-71, 1980-85) and General Idi Amin

Enough said – a billboard positioned beside the Equator

(1971-79). One of my first impressions of Africa was seeing news stories of Amin dressed in full military regalia addressing a crowd; he wore his medals as would an obnoxious child, showing off the full set of bling collected from inside cereal packets. As a primary school student, images of Amin tainted my perception of the African continent as a dangerous place. The 'butcher of Africa' instilled fear in Uganda's people for a generation. As many as half a million Ugandans were killed and many more suffered gross human rights abuses under Amin and Obote. Uganda was banished to the economic wilderness and spiralled into social disintegration. Kampala was a battered, paralysed capital city, an empty shell gutted by looters.

The ride into Kampala was a white-knuckle affair. The main road was certainly not built to withstand the heavy traffic that developed into a constant barrage as I neared the city limits. I had to remain extremely alert and aware of traffic coming from both directions – usually very fast. I'd become adept at picking the line of a vehicle coming from behind just from sound. At times, where the surface was reduced to potholes or the edge had crumbled away completely, I was squeezed out and forced onto the gravel. At speed this was like skating without blades and I fought to prevent myself from crashing into pedestrians or oncoming cyclists, or from sliding off the slope completely. Sticking at it, I reached the city after 150 kilometres, just in time for peak hour. Right as I was tiring, awareness needed to be most acute. Roadworks blocked our planned route and the diverted traffic gridlocked any alternatives. The city, now undergoing unprecedented economic growth, was literally bursting at the seams. We were soon lost. Kampala is known as the city of seven hills, and by the time we found our way to the city centre, I had inadvertently toured a good number of them – in the dark.

Reaching the Queen's Clock Tower, the gateway to the Kampala city centre 20 kilometres later, my heightened state of awareness had been numbed with exhaustion. Traffic was still congested but starting to flow in a kind of orderly chaos. To negotiate the roundabout, vehicles and motorbikes were segregated; four-wheeled types queued on the outside left lane while the two-wheelers flocked to the inside right. I gravitated to the right and was quickly enveloped into a mob of about fifty motorbikes. Here, my trusty scarf did little to protect my lungs. Fumes contaminating the night air smelt so volatile that, had someone struck a match, we may all have spontaneously combusted in a huge fireball. Packed in like sardines as we were, I was accidentally nudged off balance by a rider next to me. With my foot firmly attached to my pedal, I had nowhere to go except over, onto the lap of the next rider who caught me before I ended up on the road. As the lights switched to amber and engines revved like a swarm of frenzied bees, he gestured to me to stay beside him; 'I protect you', he reassured. Go! The group surged in unison, cutting off the circle in a race to get ahead of the cars. I just managed to keep up with my friend, spinning my pedals furiously. Once safely on to Entebbe Road, bikes and cars re-merged, forming a confetti of red tail-lights that gradually dissipated into the dark. It was just a few hundred metres up to the junction with the Jinja Road and we were there.

✱

We'd reached Kampala two days ahead of schedule. There were dates to keep here and in the northern city of Gulu, so to make use of the time I continued for a day-and-a-half towards the Kenyan border. The traffic situation did not improve until the other side of Jinja, about 80 kilometres east of Kampala. The highway is Uganda's principal connection with Kenya and the Indian Ocean ports and is the main artery linking Rwanda, Burundi, the DRC and South Sudan. For much of the way, dense rainforest constricted the route to just a single lane in each direction. I felt more nervous on this section of road than on any other on my whole journey, especially of being rammed from behind or flattened from head-on by overtaking juggernauts. Once across the Victoria Nile at Owen Falls Dam wall (the Nalubaale Power Station supplies Uganda's power) and through Jinja, I could relax somewhat on the wider refurbished roads and even take in views of the lake. I passed through vast tea, sugar and rice plantations for much of the way around the northern perimeter of Lake Victoria to near Tororo and the border, mostly long-established concerns with roots going back to pre-independence days. Great Britain ran Uganda as a protectorate rather than as a rigidly-controlled colony as in Kenya. From 1894 to 1962 the British administration worked within a loose federation of tribally-based kingdoms, the favoured and most prominent being the central kingdom of Buganda. Ugandans were encouraged to produce cash crops for export and a greater level of self-determination was harnessed for the benefit of both sides.

We returned to Entebbe airport at Kampala just in time for John to meet up with his girlfriend, MaryJane Johnson. MaryJane had been following and supporting our expedition from Scotland, so this was an opportunity for her to take part in a two-week section from Kampala to Nairobi.

✱

Throughout the expedition I had been wearing organic cotton t-shirts provided by a sustainable trade company called Edun Live, a sister brand of EDUN Apparel. EDUN was founded by Bono and his wife, Ali Hewson. Garments are made in sub-Saharan Africa from grower to sewer, and I wanted to follow this chain of processes from the growing of the cotton through to the finished t-shirts. The reason for our

370-kilometre diversion to Gulu in northern Uganda was to see where the cotton is produced, meet the farmers and learn how growing organic cotton as a cash crop is transforming many communities.

It took the best part of a day to reach Gulu, Uganda's second city. Once free from Kampala's congested urban sprawl, it seemed that the best of Uganda was on display. The lush countryside was punctuated by regular villages and colourful roadside markets brimming with fresh fruits and vegetables. We paused at the spectacular crossing of the Victoria Nile. The river was only about 300 kilometres into its 6000-kilometre course to the Mediterranean Sea yet the volume of water crashing over the cataracts was already awe-inspiring. Between us and the river, perched on the highest branches, a regal-looking black-and-white Colobus monkey posed as king of the jungle, its white-masked face easy to spot against the blizzard of brilliant greens. For the stunningly attired monkey, constant surveillance was essential for survival. On a closer study through the binoculars, it didn't seem too concerned about us although other humans have posed a serious threat in recent years. Soldiers have hunted them for bushmeat or used them as target practice, loggers have destroyed their habitats and poachers have prized their striking black-and-white-fringed coat as trophies of fashion. Just over the bridge, a troop of baboons, another member of the old world monkey clan, and perhaps the most adaptable, had humans all worked out. The gang formed a highway patrol; their toll to dallying drivers was mangoes, bananas and any other fruit people cared to fling them. If only that was the most serious charge around here.

The Victoria Nile

Uganda is considered a crossroads of Africa, where the eastern savannah meets the jungles of the central west. It is also a cultural melting pot where sometimes cultures have collided, particularly between the north and south. Crossing the Nile River we entered Uganda's north, specifically Acholiland. People here are of a different ethnic background; the languages spoken are derived from the Nilo-Saharan family, unlike the Bantu languages of the south. The Acholi people have not only had to deal with the evil antics of Obote and Amin: in the 1980s, when the wealthier, more politically entrenched tribes of the south assumed control over the disenfranchised Acholis, tensions erupted into civil war. The region where we were heading had been a productive cotton-growing area but the conflicts brought an end to the industry during this time.

The acute poverty that ensued 'parted the waters' for messianic Christian warlord, Joseph Kony, and his guerrilla group, the Lord's Resistance Army (LRA). Himself an Acholi from the Gulu district, Kony wanted to create a theocratic state based on the Ten Commandments and Acholi traditions. He believed his role was to purify the Acholi. Often preaching in tongues, he claimed he received direct instruction from the Holy Spirit and used biblical references to justify his actions – to kidnap, rape, mutilate and kill his own people, specifically those who would not support his movement.

Kony's followers believed he could see the future and them wherever they were. At the height of his power, children abducted by Kony made up 80 per cent of his troops, and child soldiers were forced to kill their parents or bite their friends to death in punishment. Fearing that their children would be abducted, villagers in the bush would send their young ones, even toddlers, on long commutes every evening to the relative safety of a larger town to sleep together in hospital grounds, on playing fields or wherever they felt they would be more protected. At dawn, thousands would begin their long march home to do all their usual chores and go to school, then repeat the night commute again for months, even years, on end. Kony's nineteen-year reign of terror ended in Uganda in 2006 when government forces finally drove the LRA out of the country and a desperate Kony agreed to peace talks. During the two years of negotiations, the LRA, by then set up in north-eastern Democratic Republic of Congo, were provided with food, clothing and medicine as a gesture of goodwill. In the end Kony refused to sign and fled with his revitalised forces. A much-diminished regime remains on the run, fleeing between the dense jungles of the DRC, Southern Sudan and the Central African Republic, continuing to kill, maim, abuse and terrorise those in their path. Left in Kony's wake, tens of thousands are physically and emotionally traumatised, struggling to piece their lives back together.

I wanted to see how some of these people were faring and learn how the revitalisation of the cotton-growing industry was benefiting and empowering communities. In Gulu, we were met by John Tembo, project manager and agronomist for the Cotton Conservation Initiative of Uganda (CCIU), which was established by EDUN and the US-based not-for-profit organisation, Invisible Children. CCIU started under an initiative of Invisible Children, and profits from Edun Live's t-shirt sales fund the project. CCIU's aim was to contribute to the economic development and resettlement of the Gulu and Amuru districts in northern Uganda. It provides a financially viable farming alternative to people returning to their villages of origin after the war.

Over dinner, John Tembo gave us some background to the circumstances of the farmers and how CCIU was working to improve their lives for the long term. Originally from Zimbabwe, John was a quietly spoken man whose passion for the cause and his expertise in organic agriculture shone through brightly. In 1996, unable to stop the LRA, the government forced around 1.7 million villagers into Internally Displaced People's (IDP) camps, ostensibly to protect them and to smoke out Kony's collaborators. These refugee camps, virtually unsupervised, were rife with disease and violence. Kidnappings continued and atrocities were committed by both the LRA and corrupt Ugandan army soldiers. Civilians lived in fear: they didn't know who to trust and there was no chance of making a living. Since the start of the 2006 peace talks, northern Uganda has enjoyed increasing harmony, which has enabled people to return to their villages and ancestral land, and begin to rebuild their lives. Yet they are returning to fields that have not been tilled for fifteen years and more, to places that have no economic activity or opportunities. A large percentage of the returnees are below the age of twenty (the median age of the Ugandan population is fifteen) and, having been recipients of food aid and other handouts, have never engaged in agriculture before. John explained that with the demise of the cotton industry and with it the whole cooperative movement and unions, the smallholder farmers had no voice, and thus were no competition for the larger firms that control the fully privatised agricultural commodities sector. Unscrupulous agents and middlemen leeched off the system, leaving the farmers with only a fraction of the value of their cash crops. Under these conditions, small-time farmers were kept on the edge, susceptible to the increasingly unreliable seasons. CCIU was working to change all this, John told us, by cutting out the middlemen and by finding ways to add value throughout the production process so that maximum benefits were returned to the small producers.

Our day began in the office, CCIU's nerve centre that also happened to be John's home. John lived alone – his family were all still based in Zimbabwe. Although it was a Saturday morning the seven dedicated staff were still hard at work. The shelves were stacked with files containing all the farmers' completed forms detailing the various crops they grew and the sprays they may have used in the past. Typically, they owned up to eight acres each on which they grew their staple foods (maize, cassava, vegetables) and a cash crop – organic cotton. To be certified as 100 per cent organic there were stringent standards, rules and procedures to be observed. The data the farmers provided was tabled to be presented to the international governing bodies; as these bodies regularly checked a random selection of producers for authenticity, everything had to be accurate and up to date.

The way the program works is that CCIU distributes government-supplied organic cotton seed to its farm collectives and provides oxen to plough their land. All farmers receive training, farm leaders being responsible for teaching, on average, a group of about thirty of their farmer peers. Members are given a calendar detailing planting dates and information about farm management, fertility enhancement, pest control and crop rotation. As well, CCIU provides training and basic equipment to ensure every group knows how to run committee meetings, appoint office-bearers, and record decisions. Group leaders communicate with field officers who in turn answer to two area coordinators who then report to John and Claude Auberson (Project Director). CCIU is also responsible for sourcing local buyers to guarantee the farmers' income, providing opportunities for economic stability, a situation that had never been experienced by the younger farmers. The initiative is expanding rapidly, starting in 2009 with 1000 farmers signing agreements; at the time of our visit in 2010, 3500 farmers were involved and John told us that the plan is for 8000 members recruited and committed in the next two years.

※

From Gulu we set off along the rough unsealed Juba Road, towards the South Sudanese border (100 kilometres from Gulu). CCIU had set up demonstration plots at secondary schools so that students could learn how to produce organic cotton. The first school we visited, Sacred Heart Secondary School – which had a reputation as one of the best boarding schools for girls in the region – was also where the first girls were abducted by the Lord's Resistance Army. By targeting this school, the LRA were intending to maximise their statement of intent, inciting shock and fear in the society. Girls were raped, given to soldiers as wives, desensitised and forced to live in the bush as child soldiers.

We were shown around by Jonno, the charismatic head groundsman, whose role was to teach the girls new skills in cotton farming. The plots had been sown four days previously with the optimum seed variety and already the seedlings had sprouted. With a combination of high soil fertility and optimal growing conditions new shoots could virtually be seen developing before our eyes, as if they were being studied through the lens of a time-lapse camera. As a decoy to attract insects that would normally feast off the young cotton plants, around the perimeter of each plot the girls had planted sorghum prior to sowing the cotton, an organic farming practice that meant spraying plants with insecticides could be avoided. Jonno hoped that the success of this pilot project would result in many members of the local community adopting organic

One of several positive sculptures at Sacred Heart Secondary School

cotton as their cash crop. His expertise he offered for a minimal salary, his prime motivation being 'to make a difference to tomorrow's leaders'. As we returned through the school, Jonno explained that a substantial wall – he called it their 'Roman wall' – was being built around the school grounds to protect the girls. Even though the war was well and truly over, a feeling of insecurity was still pervasive. In front of the main school buildings were sculptures with positive captions such as: 'Never give up', 'Fly away from evil' and 'Aim higher to achieve something'.

A little further along the road at Keyo Secondary School, the head teacher, Calistus Nyeko, along with the agriculture teacher talked about the conditions they faced in improving education. Keyo employed thirty teachers; twenty were paid by the government and the salaries of the other ten came from the school fees paid by the families. For those children who had no family support, the head teacher said he encouraged them to earn their way by doing physical work to help maintain the school grounds. Invisible Children provided mentorships for twelve of the most gifted disadvantaged students, and had also set up a teacher-exchange program and given funds to improve infrastructure. There was a specific focus on supporting girls to stay in school: of the 790 students, only 255 were girls, the excessive dropout rate being mostly due to early pregnancies, marriages or lack of support. Calistus pointed to where more accommodation was being built to house female students; if the girls

Calistus, the head teacher of Keyo Secondary School, discusses the problems many of his students have readjusting to life post-LRA (with John Tembo, Calistus Nyeko, the agriculture teacher and MaryJane) (photo: Z Kratky)

lived at school, staff could more easily detect and deal with their problems as they arose.

Many of the students were psychologically distressed and received counselling. The majority had grown up in Internally Displaced Person (IDP) camps where they had lived in each others' pockets with nothing to do and with poorly educated parents as role models. Kony's army had conscripted between 25,000 and 66,000 children over the two decades of his occupation. By addicting them to a mixture of cocaine, heroin and gunpowder and incarcerating them by the fear of reprisals, the LRA made it virtually impossible for child soldiers to escape. For the Keyo students who had been abducted, readjustment to normal life was particularly difficult. The head teacher explained that some of the boys still wanted to treat girls as they had learned in the bush – 'as their wives'. I found it near-impossible to comprehend the enormous challenge of reintegrating these students back into society. The teaching staff had more than Jonno's 'Roman wall' to climb; more than the Great Wall of China, in my opinion. I thought back to the plight of the Sisyphus beetle I had watched conquer the sand dune near Timbuktu in the Sahara. It had evolved to be perfectly adapted to the harshest of environments; protected by its 'suit of armour' exoskeleton and hardwired to never give up. These committed teachers, mentors and community members had taken on similar qualities of resilience. They were doing the hard yards, adapting to the changing circumstances. They worked not just to survive but for the community to flourish and thrive. Educating the students and the wider community on how to grow organic cotton here was just one important strand weaving a more prosperous, peaceful future.

After about an hour's drive from Gulu, we turned off the dusty main road, winding and bumping our way along a potholed track towards Amilobo village. The only comfort I took out of the ride in John Tembo's beaten-up old Toyota was that CCIU's money wasn't being wasted in providing its staff with shiny new vehicles. Operating costs were being kept to a minimum. Fields were being worked over in readiness for planting, so the landscape was a collage of freshly ploughed chocolate soils and newly sprouted lime-green tips that appeared fluorescent when the sun broke through. Our tight schedule for the day had given way to what around here was called 'Uganda time', meaning we were a little late. The farmers had been waiting patiently for us. As we pulled up, the women broke into their traditional welcome as if it were second nature; dancing, singing, ululating, some with unrestrained fervour. In turn they stepped forward to greet me. All were immaculately dressed, their smiles complementing as a must-have fashion accessory. I felt honoured and slightly overwhelmed by the reception and, after eight months on the road with minimal attention to my appearance, quite scruffy by comparison. As the festivities died down, Joska Aweko, the 2010 lead farmer, introduced herself and led our group to their prepared meeting place under a shady tree. The men, who appeared equally accepting but were more reserved, mostly took the peripheral seats whereas the women sat on mats on the ground before us.

Joska Aweko, farm leader of Amilobo village

John Tembo initiated the discussion, ably interpreted by the Acholi area coordinator. When he explained that the t-shirt that I was wearing had been produced from last year's crop, I could see their eyes light up. They connected. I added that my t-shirt had come home. The farmers probably didn't get to see the end product too often. The raw cotton balls they had grown had been transformed into a high-quality garment appreciated by someone who came from the other side of the world. I wanted them to feel proud that they had grown the cotton to make a t-shirt that could go the distance across their continent, for 18,000 kilometres to that point. It was a priceless moment where the group appeared universally inspired.

I asked group members if they would share with us their stories of life before and after the introduction of the cotton-growing initiative. Joska led the conversation. She, like the whole group – a mix of fifty-six extended family and neighbours – had returned over the last three years from living in an IDP camp. The previous year, 2009, was her first growing organic cotton. Fields that had previously been treated with chemical fertilisers and sprays had to be 'clean' for three seasons before produce could qualify for the 100 per cent organic tag. In Joska's first season, she churned out 628 kilograms of cotton from one-and-a-half acres. In 2010, she planned to double her cotton production. The thirty-seven-year-old had never had the opportunity to go to school but with the $US351 made from growing and selling the cash crop she was able to educate two of her children. Other group members had similar accounts. As farm leader, Joska's role was also to encourage other producers to take up organic cotton farming, which in the circumstances should have been an easy sell. All of those who spoke said they were increasing production the next season. Group members (refreshingly, men and women had an equal voice) asked John when the collective would receive more oxen so that the workload could be eased. There were also plans to diversify and grow other organic cash crops such as chillies and sesame oil.

In the past, these farmers would have just produced enough food to eat, perhaps selling any excess at a local market. It was very much a hand-to-mouth existence: if there was a crop failure, children would miss out on school (if they could afford it in the first place) and/or they would go hungry. In villages like Amilobo the people were learning how to put money away and plan for the future. John Tembo explained that the sole purpose of growing organic products was to attract the 25 per cent premium above the market price. There were plans in hand to add further value along the production chain. From the collectives, the raw cotton was sent to a ginnery where the fibre is separated from the seed. Cotton

Lead farmer, 2009   Committee treasurer   Farmer and lead singer (of our exuberant welcome)   Joshua, a visiting retired farmer, encouraged people to take up farming organic cotton

seeds have a lot of value, normally exploited by the ginnery. By introducing mini-gins that could be operated by the farmers, profits from seed products such as oil, soap and animal fodder would go to the growers. The whole program aims to become self-sustaining in a few years, after which the CCIU's work will be done.

Armed rangers keep watch over the rhinos every hour of every day

❋

The final link in the chain was to see how the t-shirts were manufactured, and for that we had to return to Kampala. We broke the long drive back by stopping off at the Ziwa Rhino Sanctuary located just south of the Nile River crossing and Murchison Falls National Park. In the 1960s there were still 400 black rhinos and 300 white rhinos in the region's national parks. Due to the civil unrest in the 1970s and early 1980s, rhinos were poached to extinction – the last wild rhino was seen in Uganda in 1983. Rhino horns are worth more than gold. Mostly they are sold to be made into ineffectual remedies – for traditional Chinese medicines and as a cure for cancer. In Yemen they are sometimes carved into ceremonial dagger handles.

As the 69-square-kilometre sanctuary has no other dangerous animals, a guide and group of rangers – armed in case of an unexpected encounter with a poacher – were able to lead us to see the rhinos on foot. As the rhinos were protected around the clock, it didn't take long for us to locate some of them. A huge male wandered to a point about ten metres away: ears twitching, it barely took time off grazing to acknowledge its audience. An animal this size consumes up to 200 kilograms of grass a day. I felt insignificant standing just a few steps away from a wild beast that was about forty times my weight and powerful enough to flip me up in the air like a rag doll. Thankfully, white rhinos, the larger of the two species, are not aggressive, though they will defend their ground if challenged. Our guide whispered that the rhino, Taleo, was one of four donated from Kenya in 2005. The other two founding white rhinos were donated by Disney Animal Kingdom in Florida. The three males and three females had produced three calves in 2009.

Nandi with baby Obama. Born in 2009, Obama was the first rhino calf born in Uganda for at least twenty-eight years

Once Taleo had wandered past, we delved a little deeper into the bush. Another head popped up out of the tall grass. This time it was a female, Nandi, with her calf. Since she was born of a Kenyan father and an American mother, the guide explained with a cheeky smile that they had no choice but to name the calf, Ziwa's firstborn, Obama. Once the sanctuary breeds a viable population of thirty white and black rhinos they will, provided that it is safe for the animals, reintroduce them back into their original habitat, most likely in Murchison Falls National Park. Ziwa Sanctuary was a sustainable business where the profits made from accommodation, souvenir sales and the rhino treks were ploughed straight back into protecting the animals and supporting the local community.

❋

Back in Kampala we drove straight to Phenix Logistics, the factory that produced organic cotton garments for Edun Live as well as a number of other companies. According to Innocent Mwesigye, the Phenix project manager, it was the only organic cotton factory in Africa, processing the 8 per cent of northern Uganda's cotton harvest that qualifies as organic. Uganda, like Africa in general, has historically been a primary producer, exporting raw materials such as agricultural products and minerals. Manufacturing

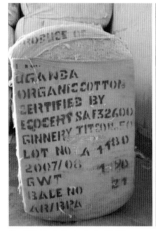 

A cotton bale branded with its production pedigree

Knitting machine transforms the yarn into fabric (photo: Z Kratky)

Phenix, a fair trade employer, looks after more than 300 staff

processes add considerable value but, for a number of reasons, many African countries have tended to be uncompetitive. Innocent explained that in Uganda it was difficult to compete with other countries, especially in Asia, because of poor infrastructure, much inefficiency and a lack of trained technicians.

By converting the organic cotton into garments, Phenix had tapped into a niche market that China could not supply. With this smart business strategy and benefiting from an improved government policy, Phenix was showing the world that it is possible for Ugandans to produce high-quality products competitively. Being certified as a fair-trade company, not only did the 300-odd employees gain from better than average working conditions, the fair trade and organic certifications appeal to the same niche market. Innocent added that this was an example of how trade and commerce is the tonic Ugandans need for a real and sustainable economic future. No-one wants to rely on development assistance, he stressed. That should only be a stop-gap. People want to make it on their own terms.

Innocent Mwesigye, project manager, guides us through the manufacturing process (photo: Z Kratky)

Phenix bought the organic cotton from the CCIU compressed in bales. Branded on the butt were the details of exactly who produced the cotton and when and where it was ginned. Cotton from the CCIU's farmers was only used for Edun Live t-shirts and the traceable pedigree proved it. It had to be that way to receive the 100 per cent organic label. Cotton produced before the three-season qualifying period was up was labelled as 'organic cotton in conversion'. Innocent took us right through the process, from where the cotton is manually relaxed from being compacted in bales to the final garments. There were many processes involved in making the yarn, right through to knitting the material, dying, cutting, sewing and screen printing.

We drove back to where I had stopped cycling just before Tororo and the Kenyan border. As I set off wearing a freshly rinsed t-shirt, I became acutely aware that the cotton on my back was symbolic of a story much bigger than I ever could have imagined. The journey through Acholiland to Kampala was not simply one of 'I've been there, got the t-shirt', it was much more. The t-shirt signified realistic hope (Suubi) for continued peace and a more prosperous future. Hope for a pearl in perfect condition.

Total distance: 17,851 kilometres

SOUTH SUDAN

ETHIOPIA

Lake
Turkana

Moyale

Sololo

DIDA GALGALU DESERT

UGANDA

Marsabit

KAISUT DESERT

Laisamis

KENYA

Sereolipi

Archer's Post

Tororo
Turbo

Eldoret

Isiolo

Nyahururu
Nanyuki

MOUNT
KENYA

MOUNT
MERU

Equator

Nakuru

Lake
Victoria

Lake Nakuru

Lake Navaisha

SOMALIA

Narok

Hell's Gate
National Park

Nairobi

Maasai Mara
National Reserve

Serengeti
National Park

MOUNT
KILIMANJARO

Indian Ocean

TANZANIA

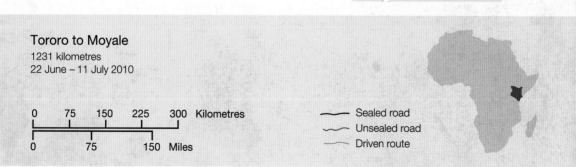

Tororo to Moyale
1231 kilometres
22 June – 11 July 2010

| 0 | 75 | 150 | 225 | 300 | Kilometres |

| 0 | 75 | | 150 | Miles |

——— Sealed road
- - - - Unsealed road
——— Driven route

16

RHYTHM AND BLUES: KENYA'S TWO FACES

Tororo to Moyale (Kenya)

One of the Maasai Mara's happy couples – happier once the tourists had left for the night

As I approached Kenya, I rarely rode alone. Local cyclists, always men, would join me for several kilometres at a time before peeling off to their destination, mostly to trade goods or on family errands. My little band of followers would total four or five at times. Some were inquisitive about who I was and where I came from, others just listened, perhaps a little shy. Nearing the border, I finally had some time to myself. The mountains ahead signified a new country. As the main road meandered around some spectacular craggy foothills I contemplated what Kenya, country number eighteen, might offer. For me Kenya conjured up classic images of the African savannah speckled by flat-topped acacias and alive with all the big game – elephants, giraffes, a pride of lions resting out the heat of the day, a lone leopard stalking a gazelle, the wildebeest migration. I also associated Kenya with being the home of world-class distance runners and the highlands that are their training grounds. But I knew it was a country far more diverse than this stereotypical image, and I intended to sample that variety.

A band of followers on the way to the Kenyan border

The plan over the first two-and-a-half days was simple – straight down, or more accurately, straight up the main highway, through Eldoret and back across the Equator to Nakuru where we were to base ourselves. Entering Kenya's western uplands, there was an awful lot of climbing to do over the first day-and-a-half to reach 2800 metres before dropping down towards Nakuru at 1800 metres. I rode through tea-garden-green landscapes supporting a range of staple and cash crops; large and small agricultural concerns. I noted dairy cows, and for the first time on the journey, sheep being produced for their wool. In warmer, drier African climates the sheep looked more like goats, with short hair instead of wool and fatty tails to help sustain them in times of drought. It was easy to see why the British colonists felt at home in the milder climate and fertile rain-soaked hills of Kenya's highlands, no doubt attracted by their incredible productivity and potential.

As I neared an altitude of 2000 metres towards the end of a long day, the moody skies gradually darkened. All around, a symphony of grumbling thunderclouds bubbled up until, one by one, they burst in a dramatic crescendo with the sounds of thunder claps and forked lightning whipping across the hills. The tempestuous conditions kept me on edge. I felt totally insignificant against the forces of nature. All I could do was keep moving forward at a steady pace, and stay focused on the road … passing drivers are easily distracted in such conditions. Narrowly avoiding a couple of localised downpours, just catching a sprinkle as I rode through the periphery, I hoped I would remain lucky and miss the violent cloudbursts but I slipped on my rain jacket and safety vest just in case. Soon after, the cloud directly in my path darkened to gunmetal grey, eclipsing any light from above. Cars coming from the opposite direction flashed their lights to warn me. Then, an eerie, momentary pause before the heavens opened: freezing cold rain turned to sleet, drops pelted the road so hard that the splashes formed a misty film over the tarmac. When hailstones started to lash my bare legs it was time to take cover.

Set back from the road amongst a field of tall maize was someone's mud-walled home and, alongside, a tiny dollshouse-sized church with a sheltered porch. I made a dash for it. A grandmother, sitting out the storm from under cover next door, watched my every move in bemusement as I parked my bike against the wall and scrambled around in my bags for something warmer to put on. Then two schoolgirls, aged about eight and ten, peered out from behind the old woman. Feeling numbly cold, my forced, chattering smile and friendly wave was enough encouragement for the girls. With an approving nod from their grandmother, the sisters, still in school uniform and one barefoot, sprinted around the fence line, splashing through the puddles and straight to me, giggling, laughing. Their luminous smiles warmed my heart and melted away the discomfort of the cold. The older girl waved back to the house, and two more sisters braved the downpour to join us. It was difficult to hear much at all as the hailstones hammered the tin roof of the United Pentecostal Church of Msembe. The girls spoke good English and were intrigued with my cameras and bike. I had been recording the situation as a diary cam entry but as we played around with the flip-screen, the moment was transformed into compelling viewing. We waited out the worst of the storm together, making simple conversation, but as soon as the rain eased, the girls skipped off again and I continued for another hour or so to the village of Turbo where the team had found some accommodation. John, MaryJane and Zdenek had missed the storm, but had been worried about how I was getting on.

＊

John arranged for us to stay at a campsite at Kembu, a highlands farm about 30 kilometres south of Nakuru. The 900-acre property, cottages and campsite was owned by the Nightingales, a long-established white Kenyan family. They grew wheat and maize, produced milk, bred race horses and ran the camping and accommodation, employing over 200 local staff. Aside

The Msembe schoolgirls who shared my shelter during the thunderstorm

from these businesses, Patricia Nightingale had set up Kenana Knitters, a grassroots program to support and empower the local women to 'take charge of their lives through dignified work.'

Patricia took time out to explain how the venture evolved and the kind of impact it was having on the women and their families. 'It's all about helping with stability in the family,' she told me. The seeds of the idea had germinated roughly twenty years earlier, and the business grew, very slowly at first, out of the trust, empathy and deep understanding that only someone of the area could possess. For Patricia, developing Kenana Knitters was a steep learning curve, as her only prior experience had been in sewing soft toys. When she was charged with taking on the project she had to dig out her mother's old knitting patterns to teach the women the craft. Since many of the participants possessed limited numeracy skills, patterns often had to be learned by heart.

Kenana Knitters, which at the time had 300 registered spinners and 240 knitters on its books, purchases fleeces from local farmers and sells the wool to spinners at a subsidised rate. The spinners wash, card and spin the wool using homemade spinning wheels constructed out of wood and old bicycle wheel rims, and they then sell the skeins of wool back to Kenana Knitters for a profit. Everything has to be organic, from the fleece to the natural dyes extracted from dahlia flowers, red cabbage and native trees to the rain-water harvested from the roof for washing the end products. As with the Edun Live t-shirts, Patricia was attracting higher premiums for Kenana Knitters' organic, fair-trade products. In this case garments and toys bear the signature of the woman who created it, adding yet more value.

Women from the local community elect to sign up with the grassroots business to earn extra income for the family. Once the quality of their knitting is of a high standard they nominate to produce as much or as little as they can guarantee to complete on time. A very practical craft, knitting can be done at home, fitted in around the women's usual farming chores and family commitments.

Patricia and her small local management team had developed markets around the world for their output, however they were careful to only take on orders that they knew they could fulfil at the right quality and on time. As village life in Kenya is laid-back there was no drama if something was not completed by a certain day as it could always be finished the next. It was therefore difficult for the knitters to comprehend that if an order was not ready on time, they would lose the customer as is standard in the trade in Europe and the US. The key to making the business work was the clever design of the system: it was culturally sensitive and served the women's needs so that they could deliver to the satisfaction of Western cultures which are defined by rigid trade rules and time constraints.

The knitting workshop on Kembu farm had become a centre of the community, a place where camaraderie with other women outside of their usual hardworking home environment developed and social support and medical services could be accessed (including a health clinic and free HIV/AIDS testing service, which was discreet for the women to use, and provided free counselling and support). Most of the knitters we met as we walked around the workshop were finishing off their toys and garments. They sat in groups with their friends, chatting away while their children were free to play. The women generally earned a little more than their husbands – a fact they daren't broadcast as their husbands usually demanded that they hand over all their earnings, which would then be spent rather than saved. Patricia has provided a facility for women to save small amounts of money, ensuring that there was something in the kitty if a child was sick, or extra was needed to pay school fees. The women are the heartbeat of the community, she said, so to look after them, empower them with dignified work and education (literacy and IT classes are also offered), was to strengthen the whole community.

A Kenana knitter with one of her finished products

✣

We used Kembu as a base while we were in central Kenya. From there, we drove for seven hours to Kenya's most renowned attraction, the Maasai Mara National Reserve. While it wasn't that far the scenic shortcut, ascending to over 3000 metres through the highlands, was very rough. Once we dropped down to Narok, the vegetation changed dramatically, from lush fertile, 'grow anything' pastures to dry, semi-arid scrubland. On a short break, I wandered into this new world. Studded through the wispy grasses and dull sclerophyllous sage-green woodlands were all sorts of surprises; some eye-catchingly beautiful, some spiny and torturous and yet others had features that seemed downright strange, even out of this world. I noticed a chameleon making out that it was part of a dead stump. It noticed me too. One bulging eye tracked my every move while the rest of the creature's body remained perfectly motionless. Yet here I felt that I was the alien. All around were splashes of vibrant colours; flame-red cactus flowers, delicate sprays of purple, white and yellow brightened the backdrop of monotonous greens and browns.

Entwined through the same bush were all sorts of flora and fauna that scratch and bite and sting. A stunted whistling thorn tree caught my attention, its spiky prongs protruded from bulbous nodes looking like some kind of medieval weapon. Or at least that is how I would have perceived this tree had I been skewered by its enormous spikes. But on my journey through this wondrous continent, I was learning to see beauty even in some of these 'nasties' of the bush. Mother Nature can be an incredible artiste, in this case, an architect, a sculptor and a musician. The whistling thorn was born out of a mutual dependence for survival between the tree and four species of tiny ants. The ants make their home by boring minute holes into the hollow bulbs called domatia and feeding off sweet nectar produced near the base of the leaves. In return, the acacia is protected by the ants that aggressively defend it against hostile invasion by other insect species, even warding off herbivorous megafauna such as elephants and giraffes. When the wind blows through the domatia, it turns old and abandoned hollow spines into tiny whistling flutes. The result is a kind of lamenting concerto that can be anything from a barely noticeable background murmur to haunting, quavering songlines, depending on the number of domatia and the strength of the wind.

A tall, slender Maasai fellow loped through the bush sporting his traditional red plaid *shúkà* and holding his spear as a woman carries her handbag. Moving with fluidity and poise, he somehow managed to avoid snagging his flowing toga in the thorns. This was his domain and his presence graced the landscape. Vanity is important to many twenty-first century Maasai men. Although they may still choose to wear traditional dress and maintain their semi-nomadic cattle-herding lifestyle many are also successful businessmen, partial to a night out on the town. Perhaps that was where this young buck, clad in beaded jewellery, had been – living the good life in downtown Narok. Nevertheless, he completed what to me was a harmonious scene. Even his favoured red attire matched the flame-coloured cactus flowers I had just photographed. In contrast, I moved through the bush and back to the Land Rover with the same type of cautious, jerky steps as the chameleon adopted in my presence. Not so cool.

A stunted whistling-thorn acacia tree. Tiny ants bore holes into the hollow domatia (bulbs) to make their nests

On the recommendation of Andrew Nightingale from Kembu farm, we stayed at the Riverside Campsite near the Talek Gate entrance; it was basic but perfectly adequate. The campsite was run by a group of Maasai fellows who kept watch around the clock; warding off dangerous animals during the night and preventing baboons from raiding our gear during the day. We employed one of the Maasai, Amos, as our guide. Dressed to the nines in traditional kit (except for the white tennis shoes), Amos rode in the middle of the back seat of the Land Rover, binoculars in one hand,

Amos, our Maasai guide, surveys the savannah from a hilltop

mobile phone in the other. He spoke excellent English and constantly communicated with other guides by text to learn of any big game sightings. Sitting beside him, I had to take care not to sit on the knife that was strapped to his side. At about 40 centimetres long, this was the dagger he would use to defend us from a lion should one attack.

We had visited the park for a couple of hours the previous evening and had seen a leopard's kill hanging in a tree, but no leopard. Re-entering the park at first light the next morning we decided to return to the site in the hope it might still be there. And it was. The leopard was gnawing on the young wildebeest for breakfast. I had to remind myself this wasn't a dream: a scene straight out of a *National Geographic* documentary and we were privy to it for about half an hour. What strength and balance the leopard must have had to haul such a large animal up a tree.

The famous wildebeest migration had started early as the 2010 season was drier than usual. The migration was not yet in full swing but the western plains of the Maasai Mara were still densely populated with tens of thousands of wildebeest and their entourage of herbivores – zebras, giraffes, topi, Thompson's gazelles and antelope. Over 1.5 million wildebeests migrate annually from the neighbouring Serengeti Plains to the Maasai Mara in search of rich pastures. Amos explained that the zebras made good partners for the wildebeests. The beasts have poor eyesight and benefit from being guided by the zebras and the zebras are attracted by the safety of numbers.

Wildebeests had begun their migration from the Serengeti early due to the unseasonal dry conditions

After the early morning rush was over, Amos directed us to a vantage point high above the plains. The hilltop provided a 360-degree view. From our position, the lines of wildebeest below appeared like an army of invading ants as they wandered into new pastures. Behind the herds, the Mara River – the obstacle they would eventually need to cross at their peril – carved its meandering course. And beyond, the horizon, defined by the Esoit Siria Escarpment, a chiselled edge of the Rift Valley.

The word *mara* means 'spotted' in Maa (Maasai) language. From our position, this description of their savannah homelands was particularly apt. Before us, the shadows of moving clouds mottled the landscape; the rolling plains were dotted with lone umbrella acacia trees and clumps of scrub and, of course, there were the animals. Amos surveyed the land to plan our next move. On the far side of the Mara River he noted a few cars gathering. So we descended, passed by a patched giraffe, a spotted hyena and a committee of vultures cleaning up a dead wildebeest carcass, crossed the river and into the western pocket of the park to find ... more spots! A family of cheetahs was resting under a cotton tree. Wow – the cheetah was the animal I most wanted to see in the wild and here were two adults and two teenage cubs lounging about 15 metres away. Cheetahs are very sensitive animals, so I was relieved to see a warden directing the traffic, ensuring people remained a respectful distance. He would allow one vehicle at a time to get a good look for five minutes then move on. We'd already seen several vehicles doing the wrong thing – cutting through a herd of zebras, driving off the tracks, putting unnecessary pressure on the wildlife. A few of the Kenyans I spoke to said that the Maasai Mara was under threat because of overuse. People pressure has created similar problems in the Serengeti next door.

Throughout the day we continued to tick off our bucket list of wild animals. The highest concentration was in the west and along the tree-lined watercourses, ribbons of green that segmented the undulations into vast natural paddocks. Elephants wallowed in mud, hippos surfaced nostril-first from the depths of the Mara River, crocodiles basked on the rocks, buffaloes grazed the savannah and ostriches strode out. As a dazzle of zebras turned away from us their rumps resembled a row of black and white humbug sweets – I was starting to become blasé, except we hadn't seen any lions. Finally, near the end of the day, Amos received a text message and we headed towards a dry creek bed in the east on the park.

A part of the dazzle of zebras

There were two pairs of lions – and about fifteen vehicles, mostly mini-buses queued up! Amos knew the lions were brothers and that both pairs were courting. This time there were no wardens to control the traffic but the lions just ignored the chaos in any case. We watched and waited patiently. Slowly the vehicles disappeared, speeding off to their lodges for the evening; in the end, there were just two left. We observed one pair of lions from just five metres. On one hand, I couldn't believe our luck in seeing them but on the other hand I felt a little sad that these regal beasts had to tolerate such a circus every day. They were totally chilled, maybe a bit bored. The males barely stirred from their slumber. Certainly Amos did not need to use his dagger to protect us.

There was plenty to talk about around the campfire that evening with our Maasai friends. For them, conserving their culture and the Maasi Mara National Reserve was one and the same thing. As with the whistling thorn and the ants, there was a mutual dependence. While Amos and his colleague John didn't care for the hoards of mini-buses that swarm through the park each day, agreeing they were too much, they understood the need to earn a living and the importance of the Maasai Mara. Sustainable tourism was their business. The Maasai seemed to have found a balance between their proud culture and adapting to modern ways, tapping into both their cultural roots and the new information age to find their path forward. John (Maasai) claimed that life is both bad and good but if they can listen to the 'mouth of Maa', they cannot die.

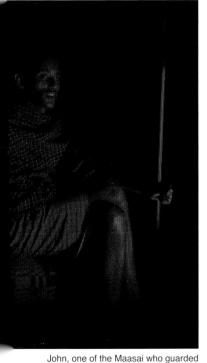

John, one of the Maasai who guarded our camp. If they can listen to the 'mouth of Maa', they cannot die

We returned to Kembu and then, to save time, drove from Nakuru to Nairobi for the next project visit and to sort out our

Ethiopian visas. We would to return to Nakuru to resume the cycle journey (so not to break the line of the route) once we had done everything in Kenya's capital. MaryJane was to leave us in Nairobi.

✻

To break up the long drive we stopped off at Hell's Gate National Park, near Lake Navaisha. Hell's Gate is one of the few national parks that allows cyclists, as it has no man-eating wildlife. This was an opportunity to cycle amongst some of the great herbivores without being cooped up in a vehicle. I also thought that doing so would be a good team-building exercise for the four of us. We hired two very inadequate bikes for Zdenek and MaryJane, and John and I used our own, the idea being that we would take a couple of hours to cycle as a team around a 22-kilometre course. Assuming that the whole park would be suitable for the average cyclist we set off along the Buffalo Circuit around the southern perimeter only to find that our path rapidly degraded into a rough 4WD track and that we were soon pushing through sand and bulldust, climbing steeply for several kilometres. MaryJane dubbed this section 'Hell's Track' – it was a baptism of fire for her. She joked that participating in Breaking the Cycle was 'breaking her will to cycle'. But the team toughed it out and the reward for effort was the spectacular views from the summit overlooking Lake Naivasha, a freshwater crater lake, and the surrounding mountains of the Rift Valley.

Just to the west, steam bellowed from the Olkaria geothermal power stations. Boreholes about a kilometre deep have been drilled into the bowels of the Earth's crust, eggshell thin and fragile in this section of the rift (compared to other parts of the Earth's surface), to tap the natural energy reserves. Steam rises out of the ground at about 300 degrees Celsius. Eventually, with all features symbolic of Hell behind us, we turned on to the main track that bisects Hell's Gate Gorge – the track that was recommended for cyclists! Here we ambled at a leisurely pace along the floor of the broad sandstone ravine, passing zebras, gazelles, giraffes and warthogs. Scattered amongst the savannah grasses, they blissfully chomped away, unchallenged by predators in their own version of Heaven. If only more of Africa (or anywhere else for that matter) could be this uncomplicated and idyllic to cycle through.

Hell's Gate Gorge (photo: Z Kratky)

✻

Nairobi is a city of two faces. The compact city centre is a glossy conurbation of office blocks, restaurants and hotels. We stayed at Karen Camp on the southern periphery, Karen being one of Nairobi's more affluent leafy villa suburbs, home to expats and the urban middle classes. These areas are the face of Nairobi, marketed as the 'Green City in the Sun'. But more than 60 per cent of Nairobi's four million residents live in rusting corrugated iron shacks amongst mud and open sewers, with not a blade of grass in sight. They occupy just 1 per cent of the city's land area. This is the other face of Nairobi, never mentioned in the tourist brochures of the 'Safari City'.

One of the main reasons for diverting to the city was to visit the Ruben Centre located in the

Mukuru kwa Ruben area – the Mukuru Slum. The shanty town developed on unclaimed land at the back of Nairobi's industrial district in the 1970s when people began to build makeshift homes near the factories they worked in. Located less than 10 kilometres from the city centre, Kenya's hub of business and culture, Mukuru is Nairobi's second largest slum. It is now home to an estimated 600,000 people who live in its twenty villages, packed together on 2000 acres of land.

Turning off the paved road behind the factories and onto a rough, partially dried mud track, we instantly entered another world. Lining the street, vendors were crammed close together, competing to sell just about anything – at a good price. Though the circumstances were very different, I again felt like I was the alien as kids peered through the windows of the minibus, inquisitive to see who we were. Zdenek and I were guests of The 500 Supporters' Group, an expedition partner, and travelled with a few visiting members and friends of the organisation. The Ruben Centre is just one of the projects the Group assists.

Within the compound's heavily protected walls lay a sanctuary of hope and opportunity – even some greenery. Brother Barry, the centre manager, explained that the Ruben Centre offered a diverse range of services to improve education, health, financial and social needs. The centre began in 1986 with the establishment of a primary school founded by Sister Mary Killeen, an Irish nun known as 'The Mother of Mukuru'. In 2000, the Christian Brothers responded to Sister Mary's request to administer the centre which by then also had a fledgling medical clinic. The principal sponsor for the daily operations is the Edmund Rice Foundation (Australia). While the Christian Brothers take care of the centre's day-to-day running, they have several partners contributing to the many departments. We concentrated on those relating to health, education and micro-finance.

The health centre, the only facility of its kind in the slum, was a real eye-opener. The Christian Brothers built it in 2003 to replace the original tin shed that had sufficed as the Ruben Health Clinic since 1992. The central courtyard was crowded with outpatients waiting for their appointments or to receive their pharmaceuticals. Brother Barry said that the staff typically treated about 200 cases every day but that so many more people needed attention. The clinic offers general outpatient and curative services, immunisations, HIV testing and counselling, and dental services. Mary-Jane, the nutritionist, explained that malnutrition was an acute and ongoing problem in the community. She frequently had to put chronically underweight children on a course of 'Plumpy'nut', a kind a fortified peanut paste used in famine situations, to bring about rapid weight gain. I learned from Sarah, the HIV/AIDS counsellor, that due to the high incidence of prostitution and forced sex and poor levels of education, the Mukuru communities suffered from extreme rates of HIV infection. Sarah had become a counsellor after watching her uncle die of AIDS. There were so many stigmas and myths associated with his illness, she explained, that he was outcast by society and not even family members were permitted to touch him for fear of contracting the disease. She spoke with immense passion about her work – to educate and dispel the myths, encourage testing and counsel those who were HIV-positive.

With a name like Scholastica Opiyo, the head teacher of the Ruben Primary School must have been destined for the job. Scholastica had been running the school for twelve years and had watched numbers grow until the place was bursting at the seams. The primary school now had 1700 students: eighty children squeezed into each class. Scholastica told us that they were always eager to learn and make the most of their opportunity. In many cases, the lunch provided at school, usually maize or beans, was their only meal of the day. The kitchen was simply four huge vats of maize which were being steamed and were almost ready for lunch when we looked in. Parents were not required to pay school fees but as a token gesture they had to compensate for the charcoal used to cook the food, and even this small charge was a challenge some found difficult to meet. According to Scholastica, the children were often reluctant to leave at the end of the day as the school environment was so much better than their home situations. She and seven of the twenty-eight teachers were paid by the Ministry of Education, the rest were funded by the Christian Brothers organisation. It was often difficult to entice teachers to work at the Ruben School, but once they were employed there, the spirit and enthusiasm of the students was a great motivator. Most teachers committed for long periods of time.

Phaustine and Rose, social workers at Ruben

Having learned about many of the services provided at the Ruben Centre, it was time to venture in to the slum. Brother Barry and community workers Rose Mbithe and Phaustine Ambaisi led the way with a security person following just in case there was an issue. Brother Barry said that during daylight hours there should be no problem but at night the streets were unsafe. The first thing that struck me was the stench. The place smelt like a septic tank. Open drains channelled sewage down the streets and often the ditches were blocked by rubbish forming stagnant pools. Underfoot, the surface – a composite of layers of rubbish, mud and dust – was spongy. The word *mukuru* means 'garbage site', as the villages were originally built on a rubbish dump. Judging by the condition of the streets, the name is still apt. It was a case of treading very carefully much of the time, with extra motivation to keep balance on the planks that bridged the sewers.

Small corrugated-iron dwellings and shops lined the streets and laneways. Most homes were embedded a step or two below the level of the street which meant that when it rained, water often flowed into them and into the shops – water that had washed over the open sewers – making living rooms a health hazard. In the slum, clean water was one of the most precious commodities. Those who could afford it paid local water vendors for potable water and for the use of the free-standing sanitary bathroom facilities they managed.

Conditions may have appeared squalid but people seemed to be getting on with their daily lives as if the rubbish wasn't there. There were kids everywhere, playing in the streets, following us around. The thoroughfares were active with small businesses standard to any village; tailors, hair salons, bars, mini-markets stacked with a bespoke assortment of items – it was the shanty architecture and lack of sanitation that were superficially different. Barry explained that unemployment was one of the biggest issues and that the young men we saw hanging around the street corners and playing pool were the cause of many problems at night.

Treading carefully – a typical Mukuru laneway

We were led through the narrow back lanes to a tiny shack belonging to Mary Makhwana, a resident who had recently been diagnosed with tuberculosis and AIDS. She had sought medical help for respiratory difficulties associated with TB, and as is commonly the case, she discovered she had AIDS as well. AIDS weakens the immune system and therefore increases susceptibility to TB and other diseases. Mary's home, a typical slum dwelling, would have measured about three by four metres, inclusive of the bedroom that was divided off by a curtain. The living space was dank and dark. I found it extremely claustrophobic. Zdenek, at 1.95 metres tall, had to stoop to fit in the space. There were no windows

Kids followed us everywhere; most don't have the opportunity to go to school

and no ventilation; the only light was produced by a dim bulb and through opening the door. Then the stark white midday sun pierced the room and turned the tin shanty into a hotbox.

Mary pointed to the blemishes on her legs – scars from the sores caused by her condition. She described how she had endured debilitating pain but that financial pressure meant she had to work until she could no longer do so. The cost of food and rent in the slum was very high relative to what she could earn, and now lacking an income to pay the rent, she feared that she would be evicted from her humble shack. The cost of medical treatment had been beyond her reach, so she was fortunate to have been found by Rose and Phaustine. Compounding the situation, Mary was a single mother with five children, the youngest of whom sat with me on the couch while the older ones were out fending for themselves. The uniformed students we saw at Ruben Primary were the fortunate ones in Mukuru: most children do not have the opportunity of going to school and are forced to work to supplement the family income. Child labour in Mukuru includes hawking, carrying items for other traders and commuters and doing menial household chores. Some children look to other means of survival such as drug peddling, prostitution, begging and criminal activities. Mary's older children had flown the nest and she said that she didn't receive financial support from them.

For Mary, Rose and Phaustine were like her guardian angels. When they had spotted her, she had hit rock bottom – she could see no future. Like many slum dwellers, Mary had been attracted to the potential opportunities of the big city from the countryside. Sick and with no significant income, she ended up trapped in a downward spiral. Now that she had access to the right medication, she was feeling better and Rose and Phaustine were organising for her to return to her village near to Kisumu beside Lake Victoria where she would have family support and her children would have a better future too.

There was a much brighter side to Mukuru. In another corner of the slum, businesses were thriving; resourceful entrepreneurs were more than making ends meet. We met Wilson, a young businessman who had benefited from a micro-loan system set up in the Ruben

With Mary Makhwana (photo: Z Kratky)

Centre. Initially, with a group of friends as guarantors, he took out a small, $US200 (15,000 Kenyan shillings) loan. With this he started up a shop and paid the loan off within three months. With a second, larger loan he developed a small hotel beside it. With the profits – he made $US75 (6000 Kenyan shillings) a week – he had taken out a third loan to buy a vehicle to start a courier business. A vibrant, hardworking character who stood tall, Wilson was immensely proud of what he had achieved. When

I asked whether with all his success he planned to leave the slum, he replied that Mukuru was his home. He was happy there and did not want to move away from his friends or the strong community he valued.

The future of Mukuru and other slum communities around Nairobi is in limbo. Committed community members like Wilson are fighting to prevent their homes from being bulldozed by developers. Provincial administration privatised slum lands after they were occupied by slum communities (Mukuru had been a rubbish dump). Even though it was home to interdependent communities, 'unclaimed' land in the slums was allotted to ministers, civil servants and businessmen. This has become extremely valuable due to the central location of Mukuru and Nairobi's many other slums, and because of a fast-improving economy. Developers want to claim the slum land they illegally attained (according to Mukuru citizens) and, as a result, thousands are being made homeless.

Wilson, a Mukuru entrepreneur, optimistic for the future

✳

Back in the relaxed Karen Camp, I took the opportunity to catch up on writing and worked to coordinate the final stages of the expedition. There was a huge grey, threatening cloud looming ahead that could compel me to break the continuous line of the journey. When I set off from Senegal, obtaining an Ethiopian visa was possible at the border with Kenya, but for some reason and without warning, the rules were changed. Back in Uganda we'd heard that they weren't issuing visas in the Ethiopian Embassy in Nairobi and we'd tried unsuccessfully to apply for them in Kampala. On Kembu Farm I had been stressed out trying to find a solution and now in Nairobi, we really had to sort out the problem. I managed to organise a letter of invitation from an Ethiopian travel company and had written a letter to the Ministry of Tourism but all to no avail. The day we spent at the embassy in Nairobi was wasted. No reason was given for the refusal and the consular official had little empathy for our cause. I thought the change of rules may have been due to security issues related to the recent election, however there were no problems for people travelling overland from Sudan or flying in. Travellers were able to cross the same border from Ethiopia to Kenya but not the other way around. Ethiopia and Kenya don't share the best of relations, so I thought it may have been to do with that. At Karen Camp, we heard that a tour group had sent a representative down to the Ethiopian embassy in Harare, Zimbabwe, and had successfully collected twenty visas. Our only option seemed to be to send Zdenek there too to apply for visas while John and I restarted the journey from Nakuru. The only party who benefited from this farcical inconvenience was the airline. It was a ridiculous waste of time and money but it was the only way, otherwise not having the visas would totally mess up the schedule.

I may have only had about 4000 kilometres to go, but this situation I found extremely worrying – we'd come all this way yet some consular technicality that we could not have foreseen may have prevented me from completing the journey in one line. So near, yet so far. I was feeling a bit down but then a response posted on my blog about the Maasai Mara really spurred me on. It was from Austin, my very switched-on three-and-a-half-year-old nephew and godson, who had been inspired by the images I'd uploaded (his message recorded word for word by Megan, his mother):

> *Dear Aunty Kate,*
>
> *We love the animals. I love lions, all locked up in the grass, so you're safe. It looks windy and sunny. Sometimes when it is sunny it is cold still. I love monkeys, zebras and lions and crocodiles and tigers. I like the colours of the special clothes, my favourite colour is red. And blue and yellow and green. I would like to see you Aunty Kate, now.*
>
> *Bye Aunty Kate*

Austin's response brought a tear to my eye. It was another unexpected regrounding that reminded me why I was doing this expedition. His message urged me on to complete the mission and return home safely. Resuming the journey from Nakuru, I had a sense that this was the beginning of the end. Between Kigali and Nairobi, the ride had been very stop-start with so many diversions and project visits. From here it would be a return to intensive cycling pretty much to the finish. Back on the bike, I felt excited to be on the homeward run but, at the same time, fingers were crossed behind my back. John and I had to hope that Zdenek would be successful in obtaining the visas and then catch up with us on the road somewhere in northern Kenya. I knew that ahead were hundreds of kilometres of appalling roads and a vast desert that is the realm of bandits.

✳

The new phase began with a long, taxing climb – across the Equator once more at Subukia – to Nyahururu, Kenya's highest major town (2350 metres above sea level). This was Rift Valley heartland where lush forests interlocked with plantations of coffee, tea, sugarcane and maize. As I switched back and forth, around every prosperous corner there was a hive of activity or a new view worth savouring. At Nyahururu I turned east, heading around Mount Kenya, Africa's second highest mountain, to Isiolo. For much of that route, the road tracked Mt Kenya's foothills; a rolling transition zone between the verdant highlands and the golden savannah plains that stretched to the northern horizon. As the afternoon wore on, the open spaces and the dusty scents of the wheat harvest that was in progress had

North of the Equator once more at Subukia

me reminiscing about home. I had been constantly concerned about the Ethiopian visa situation and how Zdenek was going in Harare but here I began to feel more at ease.

Not too much though. Gastro number four was under incubation and my system fizzed away all afternoon. I'll never know whether it was because I was feeling ill, or whether I was totally engrossed in the scenery, but I missed a turn-off – there were no obvious signs – and ended up way off-course on a road that veered on a southerly tangent to the one we were looking for. Not what I needed when I couldn't keep my food down. John found a safe spot to camp beside a lonely police outpost. The following morning the officers directed us to a shortcut, a 34-kilometre trek on bumpy gravel roads around a wildlife conservancy and back to Naro Moru on the main road north, the A2. A little further on out of Nanyuki I ascended again steadily for about 40 kilometres up to 2800 metres. For most of the way there were large farms growing cereal crops such as barley, still green, and horticultural tunnels of fresh-cut flowers, grapevines and other produce. I never got to see any of Mt Kenya's dramatic peaks, not even from the top of the climb. For the whole time I was there the ancient volcano was enshrouded in a swirling mist that revealed only thumbnail images of the igneous slopes.

The downhill, a blissful 1300-metre drop over 50 kilometres, was literally like sliding off the mountain face and into another world. Behind me was the Kenya I had come to know – green, fertile, productive with mild alpine climates – and before me a parched, dusty, rugged landscape with spectacular jagged ranges as far as I could see. The people were different too. A cosmopolitan town of mosques and churches at the geographic centre of the country, Isiolo is where the people of the desert and pastoral country mix with those from the mountains. Compared to other parts of Kenya that I had experienced, rolling into Isiolo was akin to entering the Wild West. I felt very conspicuous as I searched the broad street for an open cafe to wait for John. Many of the townsfolk were descended from Somali soldiers who settled there after the Second World War. Others, like the Samburu, Turkana and Borana from the north and the Ameru from nearby Mt Meru, add to the ethnic melange. The main street was even more of a dustbowl than usual as it was being upgraded. Because of its potential for tourism, Isiolo had been earmarked as a part of the Kenyan government's Vision 2030, a twenty-two-year economic plan to elevate Kenya to a middle-income country by 2030.

Until recently, Isiolo was the end of the paved road. The next 500 kilometres to Moyale on the Ethiopian border was notoriously corrugated and stony. I was pleased to learn that brand-new tarmac had been laid at least to Archer's Post, our destination 40 kilometres to the north. On Isiolo's outskirts and for several kilometres towards Archer's Post, makeshift dwellings constructed out of whatever materials were available – sticks, animal skins, rolled out tins, bags – had been built within close proximity of the road. Children, and occasionally their mothers, waited at the roadside, holding their hands out as I rode past. I felt terrible: these people, mostly Somali refugees, were desperate and there was nothing I could do. It didn't matter how many times I was confronted by this kind of situation, I could never get used to it. I had most definitely arrived in the other Kenya.

Gradually, the transient population petered out and I rode alone. I glided over the smooth bitumen, fanned by a tailwind, appreciating the good surface while I still had it. The route tracked a spectacular chain of mountains that I could just see above the level of the acacia-speckled plain. About midway to Archer's Post, John caught up to me to deliver great news. Zdenek had messaged him to say mission accomplished – he had the Ethiopian visas. What a relief! The whole episode had been absurd and expensive but at least we had found a way. He was able to apply for and receive our visas within a day in Harare. Zdenek was to fly back to Nairobi that evening. He would then take a bus to Isiolo and another to catch us wherever we were the next night.

At Archer's Post, a small town built beside a military base and sandwiched between the Samburu and Shaba Nature Reserves, we stayed under the protection of a group of Samburu families. Nomadic herders with language and customs similar to the Maasai and Turkana peoples, the Samburu wear their colourful traditional dress with pride and not simply as a means of impressing tourists. They are pastoralists whose diet is based around the products of the animals they care for: meat, blood, milk.

A member of the Meagari Early Childhood Group, formed to ensure the next generation has access to a decent education

The women at Archer's Post had formed the Meagari Early Childhood Group to ensure their children's education and to empower each other. The money we paid for camping and filming was divided amongst the group. John also gave them some pencils and notebooks that MaryJane had left with us, donated by her mother who worked at a school in Scotland.

It seemed that, as they were becoming a part of a better-connected world, the traditional Samburu lifestyle was at a crossroads. The pastoral way of life that has developed over thousands of years was rapidly changing to face the challenges of the twenty-first century. A young fellow named Robin took charge of convening our stay and explaining Samburu customs. One of the next generation – better educated and wanting to break away from the nomadic existence – he spoke of his plans to build a guesthouse right beside the Ewaso Nyiro River, near to where we pitched our tents. Now that the road was paved, he said it could be a great avenue for progress and he dreamt of making a thriving business from passing travellers. Robin, his father and a couple of others kept watch over us all night beside a campfire, spear at the ready, to ensure our safety. Only months earlier, people had to travel through there in a convoy because of the threat of bandits. We'd heard about a motorcyclist who'd had his spokes shot out not long before we passed through, somewhere between Archer's Post and Marsabit.

I had fully expected the tarmac strip to end abruptly in the first few kilometres north of Archer's Post, but the brand-new surface kept luring me toward the horizon. On and on, kilometre after kilometre, I delved deeper into a fairytale landscape, working my way up and then coasting over the long, slow undulations. It was a Big landscape – Big sky, Big mountains, Big open expanses. The scrub may have flashed by as a monoscape to many passing drivers but at my pace I was constantly exposed to the finer details. I marvelled at small dik-dik deer darting through the bushes and ostriches striding out across the road. Occasionally, elegant, brightly clad Samburu moved their herds parallel to the new avenue.

Kenya's north was proving to be a land of contrasts and never more so than 65 kilometres later where the new road finally did end. There, at Sereolipi village, the scene read more like a horror story for the Samburu. As I arrived, many nomads were milling around. There were no more cute 'Bambis' lolloping through the bushes – they were replaced by mules being loaded with sacks of maize. The World Food Program was distributing a monthly supply of food aid. The region had been hit by successive

Rugged, parched, often spectacular northern Kenya

seasons of drought and many of the Samburu had lost most, if not all, of their animals – stock that they depend on for their livelihood. The atmosphere was tense: people were on the edge. While receiving food aid was necessary, in their eyes it was undignified. I wanted to know more, but I didn't want to pry.

One of the village leaders, Mark Rosket, stepped forward to welcome me. He explained that about 85 per cent of the aid came from the United States, about 5 per cent from Japan and the rest came from elsewhere, including Australia. Although receiving aid was much better than nothing, Mark said, the people needed more than just maize: they required protein to sustain pregnant and lactating women and growing children. Maize was so different from their traditional milk-blood-meat diet. While obtaining

enough sustenance was the emergency – to get the nomads back on their feet – acquiring more breeding animals to replenish their stock numbers so they could resume their traditional existence was a main concern.

The long-term goal of the Samburu group was to develop their education program. Educating nomadic children was a challenge because few non-Samburu teachers would embrace the idea of transient bush classrooms. Behind us was the Sereolipi Primary School where some children could board. It was one of only two schools in an area of 10,000 square kilometres. With the assistance of some international organisations, Mark told us, many more Samburu children now received a primary education, but illiteracy was still high. He

A tense atmosphere at the Sereolipi food aid distribution point

affirmed that when his people were better educated they were more able to adapt to the rapidly changing world, they had far fewer, but much healthier, children and they were better able to cope when faced with drought and other crises.

After Sereolipi, the road was in the process of being upgraded, but gradually the bulldozers, graders and piles of gravel phased out. By the time I reached the boundary of Losai National Reserve, I was bouncing and rattling over a shocking surface, a mixture of extremely deep corrugations and large, loose stones that slowed me to an average of only 12 or 13 kilometres an hour. With my whole body taking a hammering, in desperation I tried trailblazing through the bush. I found some animal tracks and dry clay pans to follow, but overall this was no quicker. And while the ride may have been more comfortable and interesting it would have only been a matter of time before thorns penetrated my tyres. Eventually, after landing in a thorn bush I decided to return to the main road. Arriving in Laisamis at last light, my sitting bones were chafed so raw I could barely touch the saddle.

Zdenek arrived by bus in the middle of the night, visas in hand: we welcomed him as a hero. He rarely gave much emotion away but this time he looked very proud of himself. It was great to have the A-team reunited. Out of Laisamis, most tree-cover soon dissipated as we entered the Kaisut Desert. I had not regained full strength since the last bout of gastro and the penetrating heat, abominable rocky road surface and dust showers from passing vehicles really tested my resolve. I just needed to get to Marsabit that day, about 100 kilometres from Laisamis. It was a case of head down and fighting the handlebars to pick the best path between the stones. Slow and steady wins the race.

The town of Marsabit sits atop an extinct volcano, Mount Marsabit, almost 1000 metres above the desert. From a distance, the mountains appeared as a pimple on the horizon. Inching my way closer, when I could afford to look up from the shocking road, Marsabit loomed, 'floating' above the heat haze, as an ever-more-imposing forested wall. At Log-Logo, a substantial village at the base of the mountains, I kept pace with a water truck fully loaded. Over the rough, dusty softer surfaces at the base of the climb, we jostled for front position. Marsabit was short of water and hoteliers and other businesses paid 2000 Kenyan shillings

Attempting to ride along a camel track, but the large stones of the Dida Galgalu Desert were too hard on the bike and body (photo: Z Kratky)

($US25) to have a tank-load brought up from wells in Log-Logo. As the gravel road improved, the truck left me in its dust trail and I continued the 50-kilometre, seemingly never-ending uphill slog.

The next morning in Marsabit John came down with a bout of giardia and was feeling very ill. Being such a tough, well-travelled person, it took a fair amount to knock him around. John had been a rock, who always got on with it without complaint, so this time I knew he really was sick. As soon as the pharmacist opened, I bought the appropriate medication and he recovered very quickly. In fact he claimed it was the best dose of giardia he had ever had! In the past he had suffered for much longer.

Zdenek and I spent the day exploring the town, markets and spectacular 600-metre-deep volcanic crater just a few kilometres away. During our trek, Duba our guide showed us to the Marsabit War Cemetery – something I wasn't expecting to see here. The Second World War brought Kenya into conflict against the Italians in Somalia and Ethiopia in the north and the Germans in Tankanyika in the south. The Marsabit region was defended from the Italians who controlled Moyale on the border. The cemetery was the resting place for twenty-four East African soldiers.

Descending from Marsabit's green oasis, the struggle resumed. John and Zdenek took time to prepare for the journey ahead and did not catch up with me until mid-afternoon. By then I was well into the stark landscapes of the Dida Galgalu Desert, with its endless black shattered lava fields melting into

A typical scene in the Dida Galgalu Desert, here about 70 kilometres north of Marsabit

the mirages. The ground was so inhospitable that even the occasional thorn tree looked as though it had battled to push through the stony ground – so constructing any half-decent road in these parts was obviously going to be a very slow and costly process.

Without doubt this was the worst continuously rocky surface I had ever had to endure. The main drag consisted of two pairs of wheel ruts up to half a metre deep that over time had been gouged out by heavy trucks, creating a roadface guaranteed to reduce anything but the sturdiest of machines to a pile of scrap metal. Nuts and bolts that had shaken loose were strewn over the path. John drove very cautiously in the hope that the Land Rover would remain intact. And there were no alternatives: I did try to follow some camel tracks but it was hopeless.

Despite the inhospitable environment, pastoralists managed to survive out here. We'd regularly sight a distant camel train or a family droving their cattle, sheep or goats across gibber plains. The women were always colourfully dressed. The men usually carried guns – out here it truly was like the Wild West: disagreements over grazing rights and altercations with cattle rustlers were common. Once these problems

Give and take. Trying to stay upwind of the dust is difficult when truck and bike are following the same wheel rut (photo: Z Kratky)

would have been settled using tribal laws and a system of compensation but now, as guns were easily acquired from conflict zones in neighbouring countries, violence was the more than likely outcome. The pressures had escalated with the recent string of droughts. Protecting and managing their herds and flocks had become a matter of life and death for these pastoralists, not just because of the scarcity of water.

Thankfully, nearing Sololo the surface improved, but was still heavy going, sandy and washed out in places. From Sololo the path ran parallel with the Mega Escarpment which defines the frontier. I was back in dense woodland that fed from run-off from the range. The path also served as a stock route where pastoralists watered their animals in clay-bottomed pools that collected at the base of the escarpment,

Pastoralists driving their fatty-tailed sheep to Sololo to trade

however all but the larger pools beside the road were bone dry. Some nomads were driving their herds to market to try to sell them for a fair price before they lost them to the drought. The pressure was definitely on.

As the sun disappeared behind the hills and myriads of dik-dik deer darted through the bushes, I still had a way to go. It is never wise to camp anywhere near the border as these areas are the realm of smugglers and bandits. I had to push on to Moyale. By the time I reached Moyale Odda, the village at the base of the escarpment, I was cycling by the light of the moon. The police at the village checkpoint estimated Moyale to be a further six kilometres uphill. It was probably a good thing that it was dark and I was unable to see the scale of the task before me. The Mega Escarpment lived up to its name and John drove close to my tail to provide light. An hour later I was still going. The evening chill seeped through to my core – my lower back and knees felt brittle with cold and exhaustion. I was totally spent but on a mission, willing myself towards the border town … I kept reassuring myself that it couldn't be much further. Finally up ahead I could make out some faint lights scattered amongst the hills, twinkling like distant stars as I passed through the silhouettes of the bush. The diffused glow became brighter until I reached lit streets and came out of the tunnel. I'd done at least an extra 15 kilometres, climbing 500 metres in the final seven kilometres.

Tunnel vision. My final push up the Mega Escarpment to Moyale (photo: Z Kratky)

From the bustling centre of town we were directed to the prize – a swish hotel complete with a cold drink and a television on which to watch Spain win the World Cup final.

Total distance: 18,960 kilometres

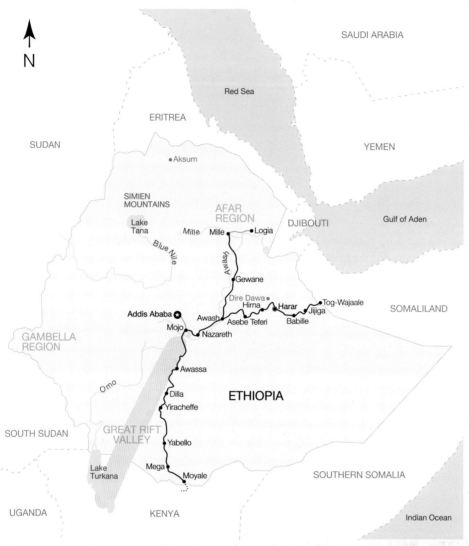

Moyale to Tog-Wajaale

1708 kilometres
12 – 31 July 2010

| 0 | 170 | 340 | 510 | 680 | Kilometres |

| 0 | 170 | | 340 | Miles |

——— Sealed road

----- Driven route

17
ETHIOPIA – CHALLENGING HERITAGE

Moyale to Tog-Wajaale (Ethiopia)

Young Afar men perform a traditional story-telling dance on the final evening of their inaugural youth conference

On crossing the border, there were immediate changes in the climate, landscape and people. Although it was the Wet season in Ethiopia I couldn't have imagined such a remarkable transition from parched desert to drizzly, sometimes heavy rain. Vast grassy vistas melded with cultivated plains all the way to the horizon and beyond to the hills of Mega. People, mostly children, shouted 'You, you, you' at every opportunity, running towards and alongside me as I rode by. At first I was perplexed as to the meaning until a university student explained that 'you, you, you' had been taken from English, learned from missionaries. It was simply their way of saying 'white person,' especially in the southern regions. The novelty wore off before I left the streets of Moyale.

Ethiopia is different. It is the oldest independent country in Africa and one of the oldest in the world. History here runs as deep as the Great Rift Valley which divides and defines the country's landscapes, from the highest of the Simien Mountains to Africa's lowest point in the Dallol Depression in the Afar desert of the east, from Lake Tana, the source of the Blue Nile, to the swampy lowlands of the Gambella region in the west. Writing in the fifth century BC, Herodotus described Ethiopia, its peoples and its customs. Along with Armenia and Georgia, Ethiopia was one of the first countries to adopt Christianity as its religion (in the first century AD). Its monarchical bloodlines can be traced from Emperor Haile Selassie, who was deposed in 1974, directly back to King Menelik, the son of the Queen of Sheba and King Solomon.

Our first night in the country was spent camping behind the ruins of an old fort, three kilometres north of Mega; it was the only place John could find that shielded us from view of the road and all but a handful of children. The ruined fort, a legacy of Italy's two unsuccessful attempts to take possession of Ethiopia, was built in 1897 by Emperor Menelik II's army in order to repel the first Italian invasion. Known as the 'Father of modern Ethiopia', Menelik II first consolidated his power by unifying traditionally discontiguous regions, mostly by force. During 'the Scramble for Africa', he fended off the encroachment of colonial powers, famously defeating Italy in the Battle of Adwa. In 1935, the Italians under Mussolini again tried to colonise Ethiopia. Mussolini's plan was to extend Italian East Africa, taking Ethiopia to unite Italian Eritrea and Italian Somaliland. Using their superior artillery, including chemical weapons, his troops invaded Ethiopia and forced Emperor Haile Selassie into exile. The brutal Italian military occupation lasted for five years. In 1941, at the end of their East African Campaign, the Allied Forces assisted Abyssinia (as they called Ethiopia) to regain its independence. The Mega Fort, which had been

Mega Fort in Italian possession, just prior to the attack by the South African 1st Infantry Division, 1941 (Source: Lt-Col Harry Klein,1946)

Mega Fort, 2010

in Italian possession, was ransacked by the South African 1st Infantry Division after prolonged fighting.

The fort looked as though it had barely been touched since, left to be slowly incorporated back into the hillside. The crumbling walls were overgrown and huge cactus plants thrived amongst the rubble. Some boys showed John and Zdenek the gravestone of an Italian who died in 1940, just before his comrades would have been ousted. Anything of value had long been picked over.

The following morning the hillside and derelict ramparts were enshrouded in thick fog. As I struggled to focus through my puffed up, bleary eyes it was hard to tell whether I was still in a dream or whether the atmospheric scene was a reality. The same boys as yesterday had returned. Appearing like spirits out of the mist, they kept an eye on our every move. But although inquisitive, they remained a polite distance, watching from atop of a pile of stones. My pulling out my satellite phone must have been a mystifying act. With our arrival in Somalia due in less than three weeks, I was using it to try to coordinate exact dates and finalise details of our arrival and departure.

Communications in Ethiopia away from the main centres proved to be near-impossible. The one mobile phone company, Ethio Telecom, is controlled by the state and only Ethiopian nationals are permitted to own a handset. In every other country we had been able to buy a SIM card for our phones as soon as we arrived but here we had to manage without until we reached Addis Ababa, where a friend who was an Ethiopian resident secured an account for us. Only about 15 per cent of Ethiopians have access to a mobile phone in any case, whereas the average across the continent is in excess of 50 per cent. Internet availability in Ethiopia is even worse, and non-existent outside of the main cities. (Fewer than half a per cent of people have access to the internet.) I learned from several sources that monopolising communications and the media is one of the government's methods of controlling the burgeoning population, depriving ordinary citizens of a voice by keeping them uninformed and in the shadows. Both television and radio are run by the state. Since over half of the population is illiterate, newspapers are not a very effective means of communication outside the cities. So to the boys from Mega watching me from a distance on the first dank, misty morning in Ethiopia, I must have looked like a Martian as I shouted down my satellite phone, its thick antenna pointing to the sky, trying to make myself understood.

✳

Mega was the point where the climbing started, the road winding a path through an ancient volcanic field. Fifteen kilometres north of Mega we made a short diversion to the village of El Sod (the 'House of Salt') to see a saline crater lake that the indigenous Borana people call Chew Bet. The villagers were obviously used to tourists – on arrival we were immediately swamped by locals eager to be our guides, and as I wandered off to find a good vantage point there was no chance of quietly taking in the awe-inspiring scene. The crater was an enormous 600-metre-deep divot in the Earth's crust, and positioned on its floor the inky Chew Bet looked like a black eye staring back from the underworld. Given the scale of the crater the lake didn't look that big, though its surface is actually several hundred metres in diameter. We watched as a couple of parties of boys and young men set off, donkeys obediently in tow, to zig-zag their way down the steep two-kilometre trail to the murky waters. These artisanal miners immerse themselves in the briny cocktail and then dive down to extract the black salty mud, mostly with their bare hands. The 'culinary gold' is then lugged up by mule and stored in rickety wood and thatch warehouses at the lip of the crater. All ages are involved in the work, with skills and knowledge passed on from father to son.

Four types of salt are produced from the lake: black salt used for animals, fine white salt, crystallised salt and rock salt, the most valuable. Traders come from far and wide, once by camel train but now by truck, to buy the salts. These days the inhabitants of El Sod supplement their incomes with the profits of tourism. On the way out, I noted that the village was well-equipped with the basics: electricity, a health centre and a new school.

It may have been the Wet season but we were back in the latitudes of the Sahel. Around Yabello and smaller villages, people were busy harvesting their fields of maize and millet. Most of the land in between was characterised by scraggy acacia woodlands punctuated by some alarming bare patches of red dirt where the trees had been taken for fuel wood and the topsoil had washed away. It was a cathedral landscape: conical anthills, some three or four metres high, protruded above the scrubline, mirroring the spectacular granite spires that defined the mountainous backdrop. The long, raking

Salt miners begin their two-kilometre trek down to Chew Bet, 600 metres below

undulations gradually increased in severity and altitude until I reached the summit at just over 2500 metres, about 140 kilometres from Yabello. It was testing work, though not unexpected. I entered into a milder, wetter alpine zone full of lush forests and grasslands with conifers growing on the highest points. This area, the highlands around the Great Rift Valley, is also famous for being the home of coffee.

Another puncture back in the latitudes of the spiky, thorny Sahel region (photo: Z Kratky)

The coffee plant, *coffea Arabica*, is indigenous to the Kaffa Region (from which the word coffee was derived) just across the Rift Valley to the west. There are several legends as to how coffee was discovered but almost certainly it was the Oromo people of this area who first recognised the energising effects of the red coffee berries, which in Amharic are called *bunn*. Chewed as a stimulant by travellers and slaves, coffee berries reached the shores of Yemen (575 AD is the earliest date claimed). It was most likely the Yemenis who first cultivated the coffee plant, refined the brewing process and marketed *coffea Arabica* beyond their borders, initially to Mecca and the Arabian Peninsula, and centuries later, back across the Red Sea to Egypt and Europe via the Yemeni port of Mocha. These days coffee is Ethiopia's biggest export commodity.

After a long, exhilarating downhill into Yirgacheffe, we paused for a proper coffee break. Some claim that Yirgacheffe, not Kaffa, is the real home of coffee. The plants grow wild amid the forested slopes and the town is a centre for modern production. As Yirgacheffe coffee is one of the world's most sought-after varieties we could not pass through without sampling a traditional brew. No lattes or macchiatos here, this was the real thing: freshly roasted beans coarsely crushed with a pestle and mortar and brewed in a *jibuna*, a traditional slender-necked earthen pot. The aromas and flavours were distinctive, an essence of the surrounding hills – earthy and citrussy clean. The brew was so concentrated I could almost stand a spoon in it. Many would add sugar but I could see no need. After consuming two pots, my heart was already pounding at quite a pace and I was suitably primed to take on the next sequence of challenges.

✳

Just beyond Yirgacheffe the road joined the basin of the Great Rift Valley, which is characterised by a string of lakes. By Dilla, capital of the Gedeo Zone and a major centre for the coffee export industry, I had dropped 1200 metres from where I was the previous night. Beyond the busy trading town, things started to get lumpy again although the going was more manageable. I didn't mind the climbing too much as I expected it in this part of the world: the real problem for me was the constant hassle I received from children. The adults could not have been more friendly and accommodating, and I always welcomed enthusiasm, but my days cycling up the Ethiopian Rift Valley, all the way to Addis Ababa and then later to Harar, were perhaps the most stressful and unpleasant of the whole journey. At every opportunity children would run at me, often in mobs, shouting 'You, you, you' and demanding 'Money, money, money'. They would grab onto my bike, throw stones and manure, swipe at me with sticks, try to strike me with whips, they would spit and beg. It was non-stop. Of course, struggling up the steepest of inclines, I could only manage about eight kilometres an hour and so could not outpace them. I had heard from other cyclists that this would be the norm in parts of Ethiopia but the situation was much worse than I had imagined. These were not a few isolated incidents: the responses were constant, like a relay from one hill to the next, around every corner and through every village.

I did two nine-hour days taking this abuse, trying to get through this part of the journey as fast as possible. The harassment really clouded my enjoyment, which was disappointing as I had really been looking forward to travelling through this country where the scenery was much of the time stunning. Although the Rainy season was not very conducive to photography, the main reason why I took almost no images was because of the kids. I was unable to stop even for a nature break for hours on end.

Nowhere else in Africa had I received such a reception. There were a couple of reasons as to why I believed I had such a problem. Firstly, Ethiopia's population has exploded from 30 million to 91 million in just thirty-five years. The Rift Valley is one of the most populous regions, and children away from the main centres have limited access to education: many of them are expected to tend the cattle and work rather than go to school. I met a German woman who had spent the last eleven years living in Ethiopia deciphering unwritten languages so that students could learn in their native tongues. She explained that both the Christian Orthodox and Muslim ministries taught their children to beg, drilling them to demand 'What is your name?' and 'Give me money' as soon as they see a white person. It didn't matter to them if, like me, that person was cycling up a mountain or was sitting in a vehicle or was doing something else. Another problem is that Ethiopia has been the victim of a cycle of devastating drought and famine and generations of Ethiopians, especially since the droughts of the 1970s and onwards, had grown up receiving stop-gap aid designed to treat the emergency. The cause – lack of community development, skills transfer and empowerment – has often (though not always) gone unaddressed and money has frequently been poured into a bottomless pit.

I felt angry and frustrated – not at the children but at the systems that have perpetuated the problem. This is a country steeped in history. The people are proud. Nobility courses through their veins as the majestic rivers – the Blue Nile, the Omo and the Awash – flow across the land. And now, as I cycled through the Great Rift Valley I got 'You, you, you' and 'Give me money' and 'Give me bicycle' because that is what the poorly educated think white people do.

I could also see signs that times were changing for the better. In major towns like Awassa and the capital, Addis Ababa, I was amazed at the amount of construction going on. New hotels and industries seemed to be sprouting along the roadside from Mojo and over much of the way to Addis Ababa. It would be easy to criticise the government's human rights record, or its smokescreen of a democracy, but relative stability has meant that it has been able to develop the economy, attract investment and move many out of extreme poverty.

Addis Ababa was a pit stop where we finally had an opportunity to organise our communications and put plans in place for the journey ahead. It was also a chance to catch up with and thank Suzie, Misgane and Gebre, friends from the tourism industry who had worked hard to help secure our Ethiopian visas while we were in Nairobi. Dinner was an opportunity to try some traditional Ethiopian fare: lamb tibbs, chicken, Nile perch and various condiments served on an *injera*, a large spongy, sour-tasting pancake made from the flour of fermented teff seeds grown in the highlands. As we tore off pieces of the *injera* and used it to wrap around each mouthful, Misgane spoke with passion about his views on development in Ethiopia. He said he found most of the Western aid responses patronising and reiterated that Ethiopians most of all need education; they want to be in control of their own development. Foreigners, even with the best of intentions, driving around in Land Cruisers and staying in expensive hotels when they are meant to be directing aid to where it is needed most – the people – sent all the wrong messages. I told

Misgane about the responses I was receiving from the children and he seemed to think that throwing stones at cyclists was a normal sport – it came with the territory. There was nothing I could do that would alter this behaviour. Misgane had his own very successful travel business and, having lived in Europe for ten years, could see both sides of the story.

It had been good to have a couple of days off the bike. I needed time to recover from another bout of severe gastro (number five) and the energy-sapping days through the mountains, toiling in the rain for hours on end. I rejoined the line of my journey at Mojo with more of my mojo intact, cycling east towards Awash, direction Somaliland. As I continued through the heavy rains out of Nazareth, I noted that hassles with the kids had dissipated, firstly due to the weather but then probably because I was heading into a less populous region. I felt a sense of relief.

❋

Before pushing for the border, there was one very important project to visit in the Afar Region, Ethiopia's desert lowlands. From Awash, I made a big diversion 320 kilometres north to Mille and Logia in order to meet Valerie Browning and her husband Ismael Ali Gardo, and learn about the NGO they had set up called the Afar Pastoralist Development Association.

Turning away from Awash, a sensitive military region, I headed north towards the desert, a tailwind enabling me to zip along the smooth tarmac. The modern, busy highway is Ethiopia's economic lifeline, the constant flow of cargo trucks circulating between Addis Ababa and Djibouti, the main port accessible to landlocked Ethiopia, symbolic of the capital's developing economic prosperity. The scrubby acacia bushland gradually dissipated into vast open plains

Another wet start leaving Nazareth (photo: Z Kratky)

and beyond, flanking horizons in the west and in the east, two prominent mountain chains. We were travelling up the eastern perimeter of the Afar Triangle, a part of the Rift Valley where the Earth's crust is constantly diverging. Here three tectonic plates, the Arabian, Nubian and Somali plates, are tearing apart, forming a depression that will eventually become an extension of the Red Sea (also a part of the same rift) and break off the Horn of Africa.

The route loosely tracked the course of the Awash River, the desert's main artery. In contrast with the fast-paced highway, the river is literally a slow, meandering timeline of human evolution. Here, in the realms of the Awash River valley, the oldest fossils of our hominid ancestors Australopithecus Afarensis were discovered: 'Lucy' in 1974 and 'Selam' in 2000. 'Selam', which means 'peace' in Ethiopian, was the name given to a three-year-old child who lived 3.3 million years ago. The fully-fledged versions of modern human beings, Homo sapien sapiens, arrived here from the central Rift Valley region (around Olduvai and Laetoli gorges) about 200,000 years ago. It was a small band of these people that first ventured from the Djibouti coastline about 300 kilometres to the east of Mille, crossed an archipelago in the

Bab-el-Mandab Strait to reach the Arabian Peninsula and eventually inhabited the world. As a human being, in theory, I could say that after thousands of generations, I was coming home. In reality, it didn't feel like I was arriving at the front gate of my home farm in Australia but I did feel a strong sense of place. I was at ease, relaxed in the wide open spaces.

A few kilometres after Gewane, half-way to Mille, I clocked my 20,000th kilometre. The scene was rather different from the 10,000th kilometre and the shooting incident in the steamy, muddy,

20,000 kilometres completed

claustrophobic rainforest of the Republic of Congo. There were still guns around though. We camped after 190 kilometres at a communications tower which was protected by armed police. As the highway is Ethiopia's main avenue of trade, communications towers and bridges over the Awash River are strategic targets for insurgents to sabotage.

Nearer to Mille, the land became stony and desolate. Normally at this time of year temperatures soar into the mid-40s, even higher, but the rains over the preceding few days had kept conditions unseasonably cooler. The second day on the road to Mille, however, was a taste of what the Afar people typically endure. The sticky black tarmac snaked through the gently undulating terrain, disappearing beneath an endless mirage, a river of false hope. The molten atmosphere clung to me like a thick, heavy cloak; just sucking in enough oxygen was a laborious effort. My water didn't stay refreshing for long, even with the wet socks over the drinking bottles. Any moisture evaporated in minutes.

Finding satisfactory shade for a lunch break was a challenge. Eventually we settled for some thorn bushes that lined a dry creek bed, its patchwork of brittle, dried mud tiles, fragments curling at the edges, looking as parched as my throat felt. Materialising out of the scrub, a herd of pot-bellied goats grazed their

way from bush to bush. They didn't seem too perturbed by our presence and nibbled their way around us, focused on extracting every last nutrient from the fine leaves while avoiding the thorny booby-traps. Some of the goats flopped down to share our shade, exhausted and panting furiously in an effort to cool down. Three young goat herders were ambling along at the rear. Initially, they were shy and cautious. This was a normal day at the office for them. They seemed to cope with the heat better than us or their charges, always moving around the herd to keep the group together. Eventually, they wandered close enough so I could see just how young they were – no more than primary school age, not that these angelic-faced kids would ever have the opportunity to go to school. John replenished their

Young Afar goat herders

plastic water bottles and the trio rounded up the stray goats and moved on in their ragged clothes and broken plastic sandals. This was the way of life for most Afar children but as we were about to learn, the future is looking brighter for many.

Constantly during the two-day ride to Mille we would see Afar nomads, often children, tend to their herds of sheep, goats, camels and/or cattle. Adults, even some of the women, carried guns as a normal part of life. They needed to protect their livestock from Somali animal rustlers and hyenas mostly. I found the number of guns around a bit unnerving.

❀

Although I had been emailing Valerie Browning, as communications in this region were unreliable I was unsure whether she would be in Mille, where she was building a hospital, or at Logia about 60 kilometres further on, where she and her family live. We were just about to give up on Mille and head for Logia when she appeared, looking for us. Diminutive in physical stature but with an enormous presence, Valerie martialled all who were with her, shooed away those who were standing and staring at us (we were used to attracting a crowd at this stage), and took us to a cafe for a welcome drink.

I particularly wanted to see the hospital that Valerie and the Afar Pastoralist Development Association (APDA) were building, to learn about the mobile health units and mobile classrooms they had pioneered, and find out about their other community work that benefits the Afar. Sitting together in an old APDA vehicle on the way to Logia, Valerie and I got to know each other as we talked about development, poverty, various projects and organisations. I did most of the listening and learning. The Afar, she told me, are very much a minority group: they number approximately 2.2 million among 91 million Ethiopians, and their rights and needs are generally overlooked by the government.

An Australian nurse, Valerie has been living in the Horn of Africa for more than thirty years. In that time she has nursed famine victims in Ethiopia, helped independence fighters in Eritrea, supported guerrilla soldiers in Djibouti and reported undercover on human rights abuses in Ethiopia and Somalia, risking her life on many occasions for her belief in justice. Valerie has been married to Ismael, a clan leader of the Afar, for more than twenty years, and they have two children, Aisha, who was studying in Australia, and eight-year-old Rammidos, who was determined to cycle with me through to Somalia! Together Valerie and Ismael have created the APDA which brings education, life-saving medical aid and community empowerment to the nomads. The organisation started in 1993 with thirty-four committed staff and by 2010 had expanded to 750 workers. The Afar people regard Valerie so highly they call her 'Maalika', which means 'Queen'.

With Valerie in the Afar Pastoralist Development Association office, Logia (JD)

We drove directly to the Logia office so I could meet Ismael – a gentle character who also works tirelessly for his people –

and clean up. It had been two long days on the road and even a cold shower was particularly welcome.

In a mostly one-way conversation, Valerie explained that evening that she believed poverty is not simply about living on less than one or two dollars a day:

'Poverty is disempowerment. You have no ability to speak for yourself. You are utterly frustrated. Your heart is burning you. You know where to go, you want to go, you know what to do, you want to be, you want to do something…but you can't. Your government and the international community are cutting you off. Poverty is being upset, very upset. Poverty is nothing to do with lack of money or lack of food. Those are consequences. If you disempower somebody they will not be able to feed themselves. If you take away work, they will lose the incentive to work.

'Illiteracy is the crucial issue of poverty. Literacy is the absolute living right of humanity…Illiterate traditional people (like illiterate people everywhere) are living in abject hell. Illiteracy, if you want to put it into spiritual terms, it is actually of the devil. It will lead you into a hole to kill yourself – from illiteracy. You will not know what to eat when you are pregnant. You will not know how to look after your child when she is burning with fever. You will not know how to use the economy. The Afar don't have bank accounts in the year 2010. It's crazy. All around the resources are being ripped out of the Afar hand when it's the resources that could have developed the people. It's just crazy. Illiteracy is the devil itself.

'The Ethiopian constitution says that every nationality has the right to develop through its language and culture, but they're not doing it. And so "we" are dominated by another nationality that has all the jobs, all the work, all the wealth and are taking it out of the region and into another place. We're left here to die. It's literally like that. So we (the APDA) are running a race against time to get the language going.' *

Before the ADPA set up the mobile bush classrooms only about 2 per cent of the Afar population were literate. In any case the education previously available was geared towards non-Afar town dwellers, with lessons given in Amharic, a foreign language to the Afar. It wasn't until the early 1970s that the Afar language, which belongs to the Cushitic family of languages spoken primarily throughout the Horn of Africa, was first deciphered by Dr Enid Parker of the Red Sea Mission. Often known as the 'Mother of the Afar language,' Dr Parker unlocked the words phonetically using the Latin script and wrote five primer books which taught students to read and write in six months. In a pilot programme for UNESCO, Valerie, Ismael and the APDA created an 'emergency teachers' package' using these primers. They also wrote a teaching manual and assembled a portable resources kit that could be easily packed up and carried in a backpack or on a camel.

Candidates for APDA teacher training are selected by each clan; usually they are people of high standing in their community. Literacy and teaching methods are taught before they are sent back to their people, and their skills and knowledge later upgraded so that they can teach a broader range of subjects. The APDA now has almost 250 teachers in the field, reaching about 85,000 children, with support from many other NGOs and agencies. Students are educated up to Year 4 level, learning in their own language.

---

* Transcribed word for word from the video of our conversation

I thought these numbers were impressive but Valerie said that she could not feel content while there were so many other children who needed an education.

That evening we attended a youth dance performance to celebrate the end of the inaugural Afar Youth Conference. Young people from all over the vast Afar territories had congregated for a week to exchange ideas and discuss their direction, interact and make friends. The dance performance, an uplifting celebration of Afar identity, was supported by at least a couple of hundred locals in the audience. Within the performances were snippets of where the Afar have come from and where they are going to. Some say they are descended from the Pharaohs and here it was possible to see the connection. The young men looked the part in their traditional attire with slender physiques and broad foreheads, some framed by ancient Egyptian-style haircuts. The young women, bejewelled and glamorous, wore loose-flowing, electric

The APDA aims to educate all children to at least Year 4 level

blue veils draped over the sparkling colours of the rainbow. They could have been royalty (except for their lack of shoes).

The event encapsulated the Afar cultural juxtaposition between ancient tradition and an eclectic array of modern influences, overarched by an atmosphere of optimism for the future. Time-honoured dances told stories and new compositions generally educated about good health practices and the importance of education. The Afar are very poetic: Valerie explained that they are naturally gifted improvisers and love to create verses and stories on the spot. A particular highlight was the girls' performance, which would not have taken place prior to the arrival of the APDA: these now-literate young women had the self-confidence to sing and dance in front of a crowd. After they had finished, the group gathered together and I was introduced and invited to say a few words (Ismael translating).

Young Afar women revel in their performance of a modern dance

I continued the education theme, with the message of the importance of going to school and learning new skills.

We returned to Mille the next day to see the Barbara May Maternity Hospital. Named after Valerie's mother, the building had taken shape and only needed internal furnishings before it could be equipped. The large central section was to become a twenty-bed ward. One end would house all the operating and technical equipment while the other would have rooms for teaching Afar nurses, birth assistants and medical professionals.

Improving maternal health amongst the Afar women is a major priority

But at the core of the APDA health plan are the mobile health units, the most practical way of administering healthcare, particularly vaccinations, to the nomads. To reach communities where there are no roads, Valerie and the team must carry a generator by camel to make ice to keep the vaccines cold. Once they reach an accessible distance, they carry the vaccines packed in ice and walk with the heavy packs for anything up to fourteen hours. Over a week Valerie and her small band of healthcare workers may walk about 300 kilometres. The purpose of the centrally located hospital in Mille is to service those who cannot be treated by the mobile health units (as well as train Afar medical staff).

Valerie made particular mention of the major problems of the Afar in relation to women's reproductive health. About one in twelve Afar women dies in pregnancy and 35 per cent of children do not survive past the age of five years. Improving maternal health (Millennium Development Goal 5) is made more difficult because of the traditional practice of female genital mutilation (FGM). All Afar women traditionally undergo the most severe form of FGM, often called the Pharaonic technique, which involves the removal of both the labia and clitoris and then the stitching together of the skin. This causes dreadful complications during child bearing, and often severely affects the kidneys.

Our plan had been to visit one of the mobile classrooms but overnight storms had caused local flooding; three people had died and many were fleeing to higher ground. The Awash and Mille rivers had swollen to become brown, silty torrents cascading across the floodplain, so school was off. Instead, we drove the long way round from Mille, back down the Awash Road and across the floodplain to Gahla village where a large group of people was seeking refuge. The waters had risen quickly and many of the men had had to guide and swim their families across the tempestuous currents to safety away from the flood zone. Valerie was on the job immediately, talking with the community leaders, men and women, to find out the extent of the emergency and what was needed; about 165

Valerie consults women who have escaped the rising waters to find out the severity of the situation

families were displaced at that stage. The people seemed in reasonable condition, but without food and supplies their health would deteriorate after a few days. Valerie's first priority was to report the crisis to the relevant authorities and await their response before taking further action.

She explained that floods were becoming more of a regular occurrence for a couple of reasons. Firstly, over the previous twenty years, the region had experienced greater extremes of climate. Secondly, the flow of the Awash River has been altered since the government built a dam just west of Logia. The reservoir extends for over 30 kilometres upstream, making the waters behind it susceptible to flooding. The purpose of the dam is to supply 60,000 hectares of prime riverside land with water to irrigate a sugar-cane plantation for ethanol production. For the Afar, this development was having devastating consequences: apart from the increased susceptibility to flooding, their

Some of the children who had fled to safety

most fertile land, normally reserved for grazing during the driest part of the year, had disappeared. As a result, their livelihood was threatened as there was nowhere to graze livestock. Given that Ethiopia often struggles to feed its people, and the country has untapped oil reserves, it seems a very strange decision to produce ethanol from sugar-cane.

The Afar territories extend across some of the world's most desolate landscapes in Ethiopia, Djibouti and Eritrea. In order to survive amid barren hills of volcanic rubble and sparse vegetation lining the river floodplains, the Afar have evolved a pastoralist way of life in harmony with the environment.

The contents of a traditional Afar home, a *deboita*, can be easily packed onto a camel when the pastoralists have to move their herds to new grazing grounds

Nomadic life, Valerie explained, is the most beautiful because it is in perfect balance with the ecology; between water, land and other natural resources. The Afar, she said, have rules and regulations about 'how long their herds can drink from a water source, which routes they can take with their animals and which routes they can take on foot. These are all worked out in the tradition of the Afar. If they break the rules and regulations, the clan will punish them in a traditional court of law.' Unlike in Western judicial systems where hearings in a court of law are transcribed word for word, the Afar clans arbitrate using an oral system whereby a skilled orator memorises the last phrase of each sentence in order to recite every word spoken.

However, in order to survive as a culture, the Afar must adapt to be more than just herders. The APDA was training the community to set up cooperatives to increase their incomes and improve economic resilience overall. The men were looking further afield to market their animals and the women were learning how to diversify their income by selling handicrafts and butter. Ecotourism was another largely untapped industry that would help to sustain the communities in times of hardship.

Before leaving, I asked Valerie what advice she would give to people of the Western world who wanted to know how best to help the Afar and those subject to poverty. On a philanthropic level, she said it was about choosing to support organisations such as the APDA which have community development as a focus. She stressed that the only worthwhile, sustainable type of development is community-based, where local leaders make decisions about their direction and cultural development. Every community has its own genetic fingerprint: needs are different from village to village, region to region and culture to culture and are dictated by ever-changing environmental, socio-economic and political conditions. Empowering communities with an emphasis on skills transfer is the best possible leg-up organisations can give.

Afar women, always beautifully dressed, must learn to diversify their income to survive through increasingly difficult times

Her broader message was a more radical concept for Westerners to digest – about the unsustainable level of consumerism and the negative effects of globalisation. One-fifth of the world's population assumes a lifestyle of excess as a right at the expense of the remaining 80 per cent. If people took only what they

In the shadow of the water tank at Gahla village that, according to Valerie, is a legacy of a largely ineffective development program

needed in respect for the other seven billion people who share the planet, there would be plenty of food and resources to go around. The Afar are severely affected by what happens beyond their borders, global situations that are totally out of their control. While their ability to feed themselves is regularly challenged by increasingly erratic climatic events, the global financial crisis, beginning in 2008, quadrupled their food prices, rendering their staples unaffordable.

Valerie chose to become an Afar person because she believes 'it is real'. By this, she meant the Afar people, their sense of community and the sustainable relationship they have with their environment. As she farewelled us, her call to action to myself, John, Zdenek and anyone who follows our story was, 'If you see it and you do nothing about it, then you are the biggest liar on the face of the Earth'.

The fertile Ahmar Mountains, the southern edge of the Afar Triangle

Sitting in the Land Rover on the return trip to Awash to rejoin the line of my journey, there was plenty to think about. I could not see myself giving up my life in Australia or Europe to serve as Valerie does for the Afar. My role here was to use my skills to tell the story, be the messenger, educate. My time with the Afar would always remind me of my position as a global citizen and to carefully consider my actions in respect to others.

✿

The two-and-a-half-day ride from Awash to the ancient walled city of Harar was always going to be physically testing. The road crosses the scenic Ahmar Mountains at the southern periphery of the Afar Triangle, wriggling its way up and over numerous folds. From Asebe Teferi, I had a tough day, climbing up to 2500 metres then down, up and down several times more. The fertile soils were intensively cultivated most of the way, with the population being largely concentrated along the roadsides. Once over the first significant climb, the problems with the children returned. It was even worse than before: stones, manure, sticks... On the outskirts of the town of Hirna, I was having such an issue with a particularly aggressive bunch of youths that a helpful tuk-tuk driver offered protection. As I pedalled down the centre of the road, he traced the kerb so that his small three-wheeled vehicle shielded me.

Then when I pushed up the massive climb out of the town, a man with a scythe grabbed onto my bike. He was high from chewing chat leaves – a very strong stimulant which many men of the region chew for

Shoa Gate, one of six main entrances thr[ough] the 500-year-old *Jugol* (city walls)

hours every day. At first I politely asked him to let go, then less politely, then very assertively. This not working, I slammed on the brakes so that he fell into my bike. I confronted the man and he ran off, but this incident stressed me out. In despair, I found a small green stick, stripped off the leaves, and kept it

with me to help ward off anyone who looked threatening. Desperate measures. It was totally against what I normally would do but I did have the right to defend myself. Just holding the stick reduced the problem and I never used it.

During the afternoon thunderstorms bubbled up and 'exploded'; I continued pushing through lightning and torrential rain. I endured the storms too. By the end of the day I had covered just 130 kilometres in eight-and-a-half hours and was absolutely freezing. John found us a building site to camp beside. A museum and a hotel were being constructed on an historic battleground: here, along with Menelik II's forces, locals had fought off the Italians in 1895.

Women about to unload charcoal outside our guesthouse, set amongst a labyrinth of alleyways inside the walled city

❊

Harar developed more than one thousand years ago as one of the most important cities on the Muslim map and as a vital trading town. It was administered by its own people until Emperor Menelik finally conquered it. Islamic Harar and Christian Orthodox Aksum (in Ethiopia's north) were the last two cities to be incorporated into the diverse country Menelik unified (kind of). In more recent times, Harar with

its distinctive culture had been an elusive city to reach for all but a handful of intrepid travellers, mostly because of the threat of insurgents in the surrounding mountains.

We set up base in a traditional Harari guesthouse, tucked away within the old city walls, using the day off the bike as an opportunity to explore while catching up with all the usual administration. The 368 alleyways within the city walls were originally made of natural stone and rendering but now most have received a colourful facelift. I noted numerous mosques scattered amongst the streets; the

One of many private houses of worship. According to UNESCO, Harar is considered the fourth holiest city of Islam after Mecca, Medina and Jerusalem

majority were private houses of worship incorporated into the family homes. These family mosques were used during the week, with people generally attending the main mosque on Fridays. I had heard that non-Muslims had historically been unwelcome in Harar because of its religious significance but our guide, Abdul, assured us that this was not the case. Religious tolerance, he explained, had always been an integral part of devout Harari culture.

Just about anything and everything could be traded in Harar's string of markets. We ambled through the Smugglers' Market where a seemingly endless array of cloth from all over the world was on display. Much of the material had been imported from nearby Somaliland and I successfully bargained for a beautiful piece of Somali cloth coloured with traditional red, purple and orange dyes. The Smugglers' Market backed on to the Recycling Market: Abdul told us that anything that was lost in the town ended up there. John was like a kid in a candy store looking at all the spare parts and tools. The Recycling Market merged into the Christian Market, an older section where people could buy spices, grains, vegetables, fruit, chickens and other types of food.

As night fell, we were led to the back of the abattoir, just outside the city's eastern wall, to experience the feeding of wild spotted hyenas. There are several theories as to the origin of this century-old Harar ritual. Some say Hararis began feeding wild hyenas in times of famine to prevent attacks on local people; others say the hyenas were fed porridge as part of a Muslim tradition.

Harar, a city of religious tolerance – passing through Recycling Market

Over the last fifty years, hyenas have been fed daily, whether there is an audience or not. The job of Abbas, the hyena man, is an inherited vocation. As he started calling out, a group of about eight wild animals

A gentle encounter – feeding a wild hyena (JD)

emerged from the shadows, some cautious, others drooling with expectation as they waited to be fed leftovers from the day's butchery. Once he had primed the creatures, Abbas invited people from the small audience to participate in feeding them. Somehow I was selected as first up. Kneeling beside the hyena handler with a short stick balanced in my teeth and a piece of suspect offal draped over the other end, I looked into the eyes of a wild predator. There was a fair amount of faith involved – its jaws and forequarters were so powerfully built it could have mauled my face off in an instant. Yet when a mature hyena came to accept the meat off the stick, it was as gentle as a well-trained puppy.

Zdenek was able to get right in close to film, so close that a young hyena snapped at the fluffy microphone, mistaking it for someone offering a tidbit!

Until very recently, travelling to the Somaliland border by bicycle or vehicle would have been fraught with danger due to the presence of Somali bandits. The local advice was that things had quietened down but that we should employ some sort of protection to be sure. Abdul, our Harari guide, arranged for Mahammad, a Somali, to travel with us. Born in Harar with duel Ethiopian/Somaliland citizenship, he was very well-connected and knew the region.

Friendly, enthusiastic followers near Babille

To add to the drama, the Land Rover had developed a major problem with the transmission. Back in Awash, John had pulled a fragment of a gear cog out of the gearbox. The vehicle consequently lost the ability to change gears: sometimes the top gear wouldn't be available, then it would return for no apparent reason, and sometimes it was the second and third gears that were the issue. The major worry was that there were likely to be more pieces of shrapnel floating in the oil which could become jammed and strip more cogs – then again, we could be lucky and nothing happen at all. It was rather like playing Russian roulette and extremely stressful for John who drained and checked the gearbox twice a day. Finding Land Rover parts or, better still, a reconditioned gearbox is difficult in Ethiopia. John had to deliver Zdenek and me to the border (where we were due to meet Omer Jama, who was to look after us in Somaliland) and then drive all the way back to Kenya on his own.

The road from Harar to Jijiga was one of the most picturesque of my whole journey. The first 30 kilometres continued with the same kind of problems I'd had before Harar, with stone throwers and even more men sitting around chewing chat. But after the first decent climb to Babille, I could draw a

East of Babille, an avenue of stunning granite rock formations made a perfect hideout for insurgents

With Mahammad at our lunch stop on the way to Tog-Wajaale (photo: Z Kratky)

line. From that point on the people, including children, were friendly and the hassles ceased, a most welcome transformation.

East of Babille, I climbed up a small hill and then descended through a stunning valley strewn with spectacular granite rock formations on both flanks. According to Mahammad, this was one of the most hazardous regions where, until recently, ambush and robbery would have almost been a certainty. Then the land opened out into more vast mountains and green valleys, maize and chat being the main crops cultivated. Livestock herders worked the green slopes, also home to roaming herds of camels and large troops of baboons. In the past, this region was the most treacherous because of armed conflict: land-mines had been laid and the road blown up. Once I was over the final long, steady climb, the vast Somali Plain stretched to the horizon, with the town of Jijiga 10 kilometres below. During the day, the Land Rover had lost third and fourth gears for a couple of hours but then they returned and behaved as normal. Mahammad took John and Zdenek to meet the best mechanic in Jijiga but he didn't have any parts which could fix the problem. The team drove on.

The road over the vast grassy plains to Tog-Wajaale at the border had just about been completely

The road forty kilometres from Tog-Wajaale – too new for cars but not for bicycles or Somali camels (photo: Z Kratky)

sealed; the Chinese were about 40 kilometres short of finishing the job, which was funded by the European Union. Eventually this road would connect to the Somaliland port of Berbera and give Ethiopia a second avenue of trade. The better surface made my ride much easier than expected and we arrived at Tog-Wajaale a day early. I had been coordinating our transfer into Somaliland for about three months with Omer Jama. He had organised our visas, the support vehicle, the security car and two security guards and had committed to accompanying Zdenek and me for the ten days we planned to be in Somaliland. Our unexpected arrival was no big deal for Omer, who simply adapted his plans and drove out from Hargeisa to meet us the next day.

This was the end of the road for John, who had to return to the UK for harvest. It was strange and sad saying goodbye after so many months on the road and I felt quite emotional. John had done such a brilliant job driving and coordinating the expedition support – I could not have asked for a better person. He had embraced the spirit of the expedition, not only driving safely and maintaining the vehicle but also adapting to changing conditions, getting involved in the visits to projects and enjoying cycling a few kilometres just about every day. With the Land Rover in such bad shape, I was pleased that Mahammad was with John at least to Harar but I worried about his long solo drive back over the appalling roads of northern Kenya where there was a high probability that the transmission would rattle to pieces.

We emptied the vehicle and sorted all the gear at our very average hotel in Tog-Wajaale. As John could not drive over the border and Omer was unable to cross into Ethiopia, Omer arranged to load all of Zdenek's and my belongings onto a couple of wheel barrows. Some of the more valuable items were carried across the muddy border by a little entourage of well-wishers. Immigration was straightforward: getting stamped out of Ethiopia and into Somaliland.

I set off towards Hargeisa in the early afternoon with one vehicle in front, the other behind. For the first 20 kilometres we followed a maze of rough, unmarked tracks but once I hit the bitumen it was relatively simple cycling. I reached the Somaliland capital at last light, just as the evening call to prayer floated over the city. It was as if the curtain was being drawn on the penultimate stanza of the expedition. The night served as an expectant pause, a hesitant pause. A new country, a new culture, a new team. And an atmosphere of uncertainty as to how we would cross the disputed buffer zone between the Somali territories of Somaliland and Puntland coupled with a precarious security situation brewing in Puntland: the stage was being set for a whole new adventure. There were less than three weeks to go if all went to plan. This really was the beginning of the end.

Total distance: 20,668 kilometres

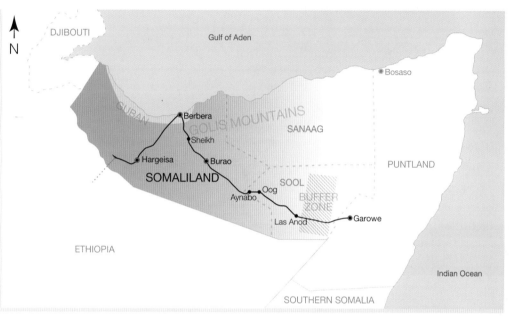

Hargeisa to Garowe (Puntland)
697 kilometres
2 – 10 August 2010

0   90   180   270   360   Kilometres

0   90   180   Miles

——— Sealed road
~~~ Unsealed road

18
TWO STEPS FORWARD...

Hargeisa to Garowe (Somaliland)

A young model of Somaliland pride,
Berbera markets

When I first conceived the expedition route, I thought it unlikely that I would be able to pass through Somalia and that I'd probably have to be content with reaching the coast of Djibouti as the most accessible easterly point in Africa. I knew just what I'd heard in the news – that Somalia was one of the most dangerous countries in the world with an on-going civil war, the presence of pirates and religious extremists. It was only after meeting with Peter Landau and Range Resources, a resource company that had been exploring in the state of Puntland, that I started to believe it was possible to make it to Cape Hafun, the most easterly tip of the continent.

I was put in touch with Issa Farah, a minister in the Puntland government in charge of Petroleum and Minerals. I had met Issa while he was visiting Melbourne prior to the expedition and we had devised a plan for me to cycle across northern Somalia to Hafun. Throughout the expedition we remained in touch, keeping abreast of the constantly changing security situations. Issa began to organise my safe passage through to the finish when I was still in Zambia, about three months before I was due to reach Somalia. By the time I arrived at the Somaliland border, a day ahead of schedule, he had mobilised the Puntland government, while his friend, Omer Jama-Farah, a Somaliland politician and chairperson of a local charity, had volunteered to host Zdenek and myself in Somaliland. In Issa and Omer I had two trustworthy and well-connected colleagues who were my best chance of reaching Africa's most easterly landmark. In fact, without these two I would not have been given permission to travel further than Hargeisa.

While Somalia is officially recognised as one country, I learned that I needed to consider it as three separate states: southern Somalia, Somaliland and Puntland. Southern Somalia, where the federal government is seated in the capital, Mogadishu, is the most troubled area. The region had had no effective government administration since the overthrow of socialist President Barre in 1991. Decades of inter-clan warfare had resulted in a rudderless state incapable of coping with natural disasters such as drought, or repelling the threat of al-Shabaab, an extreme Islamist insurgency that took control over much of the south from 2006. Although not internationally recognised, Somaliland, formerly British Somaliland, has its own peacefully elected government and had been effectively run as a separate country since the advent of the 1991 civil war. Puntland is administered independently by its own government as an autonomous state of Somalia.

The safest and indeed only option for me to reach Cape Hafun was to follow a route across Somaliland, through a buffer zone in the disputed state of Sool and finally through Puntland with the permission and assistance of both governments.

When Issa and I originally sat down to plan the journey, our main security concern in Puntland was the chance of being kidnapped by pirates. Since then, the situation with al-Shabaab had worsened: the Islamists had almost total control of southern Somalia and had started to infiltrate some remote regions in Puntland. Training camps had been set up west of Bosaso and the Puntland government needed to act decisively to prevent al-Shabaab gaining a stronghold over its people and land. When Omer and I phoned Issa on our first day in Somaliland, he warned that some sort of military operation was imminent and that I needed to prepare myself for the idea that I may not be permitted to cycle all the way to Cape Hafun.

*

The two days in Hargeisa were jam-packed, learning about some of the many projects Omer's non-government organisation, the Taakulo Somaliland Community, was undertaking and ensuring that appropriate security plan was put in place for our journey through Somaliland. While it may be the most stable territory and the most advanced country economically, it was still rough around the edges.

On the security side, the process was set in motion when we consulted the National Security Advisor for NGOs. Yusef, the director, agreed in turn to consult all traditional leaders in the sensitive areas from Burao to Las Anod and then the Somaliland side of the disputed buffer zone. After gaining clan permissions the following day, he set up a meeting with the chief of police. We

Omer discusses a clean water and sanitation project at a school on the way in to Hargeisa. This was one of twenty-four initiatives the TSC was implementing in partnership with Caritas (ZK)

306

again received the all-clear and the police commissioner wrote an official letter for us to present at all checkpoints en route. Somaliland may be at peace but al-Shabaab was present and in recent times had blown up three key sites in Hargeisa. Ever since insurgents killed two NGO representatives on the main road between Hargeisa and Berbera (in 2007), the Somaliland government had vowed to safeguard visitors. Omer was taking no chances and arranged for us to be protected around the clock by two security guards, Abdul and Karim, both trained by the British army.

'Taakulo' in Somali means 'to help.' Omer's Taakulo Somaliland Community (TSC) was

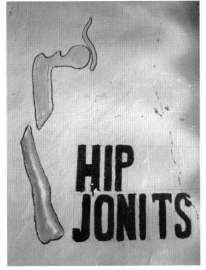

Radiology department at Hargeisa Hospital

certainly making a difference to many in need in Somaliland. In particular, the TSC focuses on clean water, hygiene and sanitation, education, health issues, disability and empowering women. Somaliland is almost totally reliant on international development assistance, making the TSC's role in coordinating aid vitally important. The TSC partners with many global organisations – working with all major religious denominations, government and private organisations, professionals and individuals – to ensure their expertise and funds are directed to those who most need it.

The Hargeisa Group Hospital we visited was an eye-opener. The 450-bed public hospital was the only one serving Hargeisa, a city with a population of almost one million. It was built by the British in 1952 when Hargeisa was a town of about 10,000 people and by now the city was crying out for more hospitals equipped with better facilities. Structurally, the old hospital was in urgent need of repair – walls and ceilings were leaking while there were still bullet holes and shrapnel damage from the civil war more than twenty years earlier – and most equipment was worn out and needed updating. There were limited numbers of teaching professionals at the hospital to train Somali medical students and healthcare workers. The TSC was working with Australian Doctors for Africa (ADFA), a Perth-based organisation

that sends small teams of orthopaedic surgeons and medical professionals to Hargeisa to perform stints of much-needed surgery and provide medical training, supplies and equipment. Still, those who had access to Hargeisa Group Hospital were more fortunate than many others who live beyond the capital city and regional towns where there were virtually no opportunities for medical assistance.

In Hargeisa, Omer introduced us to several of the organisations his Taakulo Somaliland Community works with: the Hargeisa School for the Deaf, the Disability Action Network, the Somaliland Association for Special Education and Caritas. Of the estimated 3.5 million people in Somaliland, around one-tenth are dealing with disability in some way. These organisations are responsible for

A radiologist shows the outdated X-ray machine

307

enabling those with disabilities to integrate and contribute to society, and lead better quality lives.

Yasmin Abdirahman, director of the Hargeisa School for the Deaf (HSD), explained that her organisation was set up by a group of proactive parents of hearing-impaired children – before the school was built, deaf children did not have an opportunity to go to school. Yasmin introduced us to a class of teenage girls. Communicating by Somali sign language was, of course, foreign to me – well, almost. As I was being presented, I noticed the girls starting to smile as they made a sign that looked like charades for 'kangaroo.' In fact, this was Somali sign language for 'Australia.' I thought they were having me on, but no, making like a kangaroo's front paws really did mean Australia! The students seemed a happy, out-going bunch as they took it in turns to write questions for me on the blackboard. We didn't spend as much time with the

Somaliland Association for Special Education School: a special teacher

boys but they too impressed as a very bright, though much larger, group. The School for the Deaf was also special in that it offered equal opportunities for girls' and boys' education in a country where only 25 per cent of women and 55 per cent of men can read and write.

Ali Jama at the Disability Action Network, a physical rehabilitation centre, explained how it treated a wide range of conditions from growth and development issues in children to movement-impaired adults. Every year the centre cared for about 1500 day patients, getting people up and mobile and providing equipment such as wheelchairs, crutches and prostheses. With limited resources, staff often improvised by using whatever materials were available to fabricate such mobility aids. They still very occasionally received patients affected by poliomyelitis, Ali told us; those cases usually came from remote regions and across the Ethiopian border. This matched with Valerie Browning's information that in 2010 there were pockets in the Afar Region where people had not yet been vaccinated against polio.

Though Somaliland has many issues as a result of civil war, as well as difficulties associated with not being recognised as an independent country, some systems work incredibly efficiently – its remittance or money transfer system and communications, for example. In Hargeisa I needed to arrange to receive $US2000 cash to cover expenses for the final two weeks. Nearly everywhere else in Africa money transfers had been difficult to organise and so I had mostly relied on team members coming and going from the expedition to bring cash with them. Here,

Somali sign language for Australia, Hargeisa School for the Deaf

Omer simply made a phone call to a remittance company and my sister in Australia was able to transfer the amount to an agent in Melbourne. Within half an hour Omer collected the cash. It was a totally seamless procedure and there was virtually no transfer fee. International phone calls from Somaliland and Puntland cost around eight cents a minute, cheaper than anywhere, and the internet was surprisingly accessible compared to other parts of Africa.

These systems had evolved as a matter of necessity to cope with the fledgling economy. The Somaliland shilling is virtually worthless and since Somaliland is not officially recognised as a nation, it does not qualify for much support from financial institutions such as the World Bank and the International Monetary Fund. Other international aid donors also find it difficult to provide assistance. Remittance companies like Dahabshiil have been set up so that the large Somali diaspora community – Somalis earning a living in foreign countries – can send money back for their relatives, for development aid and for business investments. In 2010, it was estimated that approximately $US400 million was injected into Somaliland's economy from the diaspora community via this process. The system has become integral to each Somali state, a lifeline to development and investment in the communities where the banking system does not work, opportunities to make a reasonable living do not exist and development aid does not reach.

When I met with returned members of the diaspora while walking through the markets, and in restaurants and offices, I learned of a deep-rooted national pride. Somaliland's citizens are typically patriotic and hungry for success. They desperately want to make it on their own – individually and as an emerging nation. The Somalis I met tended to be switched-on, spirited and business-orientated. They are survivors of hard times.

Money changers trade the virtually worthless Somaliland shilling

I was almost totally out of bicycle tyre patches and glue so Abdul and Karim led me through Hargeisa's undercover markets in search of new mountain bike tubes or puncture repair kits. This was most likely my last chance to find such specialist items. The alleyways were a jumble of colourful stalls, selling everything from incense, shoes, cloth, household utensils and tools to street food. Traders were keen to show their wares without being too overbearing, though having two armed and uniformed guards keeping watch may have dulled the enthusiasm somewhat. Eventually, Abdul tracked down a tyre tube but it had the wrong type of valve and I was unable to use it. If only we could find some vulcanising glue – that was really all I needed. We had no luck anywhere in town. As a result, I couldn't afford to have more than three punctures in the next 1600 kilometres.

Omer invited us to his home for lunch – actually a feast! His family showed us true Somali hospitality. Omer's wife, Hibo Ismail Muse, produced an enormous quantity of food: goat meat, rice, salads, watermelon juice and fruit. Afterwards I was presented with a *dirac* and *gabarsar* (a Somali dress and scarf) to use when I was off the bike in the more conservative villages away from Hargeisa and Berbera. The *dirac* is like a colourful sack with two slits cut at the shoulder for the arms and an opening

The streets outside Hargeisa market

for the head. I was curious to experience what it was like to wear these clothes as they were so different from what I was used to. I wanted to honour local custom but I did struggle somewhat wearing them as it felt like I was covering up who I am.

About two months before I had arrived in Somaliland, the country had held a peaceful democratic election. Omer's United Peoples' Democratic Party was ousted from government by the Peace, Unity and Development Party. Just prior to our setting off from Hargeisa, Omer arranged a breakfast meeting with Said Mohamed Jama, the secretary to the new president of Somaliland. Though they had some opposing political views, Said and Omer remained good friends. Omer was happy to work with the new government for the greater good of the country and Said supported Omer's philanthropic work. Having lived and studied in the UK for many years, Said was one of the many Somalis from the diaspora who had returned to serve his country. With a limited tertiary education system, Somaliland relies on the return of some members of its diaspora, educated abroad, to provide not only a cash injection but also the know-how to help lead their homeland out of the economic wilderness.

Lacking official nationhood status the people of Somaliland are up against it, according to Said. Not only are they unable to access the development assistance and international credit they need, they are also hit by international trade rules that hinder private ventures. Potential partners, for example, cannot obtain insurance to secure their investments so in order to lure the foreign investment it requires to develop greater self-reliance Somaliland has to prove to the world that it is a safe, stable, democratic country. The new government was in the process of producing its five-year plan for sustainable development and poverty reduction. If it was unsuccessful in improving the living conditions of the general population and Somaliland remained economically challenged, there was a danger that the country would revert to some of the problems of the past. Inertia could mean that a poverty-stricken next generation might be lost, susceptible to extremist persuasion where education beyond fundamentalist ideology is forbidden and where women have no future. This was a sobering thought but the messages from Said and Omer were overwhelmingly upbeat and optimistic.

Just prior to setting off from Hargeisa, I was interviewed by a Somaliland satellite television network. I understood why this was an important public relations exercise: I was, as a Western woman cycling across their land, embracing their country in an amiable, trusting and respectful manner. The authorities of Somaliland were giving a complementary response – caring, accepting, courteous. The interview was an opportunity to show their people and the outside world that Somaliland was safe enough for me to cycle through, yet when I was quizzed about my intended route, I could only say that we were going to complete the journey in Berbera. From the beginning of our time in Somaliland I was advised, for security reasons, not to publicise our planned route to Las Anod and across to Puntland. As a result, I always felt a modicum of uncertainty about our security situation in the back of my mind.

It would have been a much shorter distance to cycle from Hargeisa directly to Burao rather than venture down to Berbera on the coast and then back up through Burao on the way to Las Anod but we were told that we could only be effectively protected if we followed the main road. Off the beaten track, we were more likely to be subjected to an ambush. Out of Hargeisa, I resumed my journey across the tinder-dry Somali plateau. The sparse tree-cover offered little shelter from the sun's piercing rays. About midway through the 166-kilometre-day to Berbera, just as I approached a rugged mountain range, I passed by an old battleground. Whatever could be salvaged for scrap metal had been taken so only the cast iron bodies of the armoured tanks remained, some now decorated in graffiti. In 1988, as President Barre's regime was crumbling, his forces had committed massacres against the people of Somaliland who wanted to break away from the Republic of Somalia. This was one of the events that led to the civil war. The Somali National Movement (SNM) declared independence three years later, after the collapse of the federal government.

Abdul inspects the wreckage of a tank battle from the civil war

Once through the mountains I descended to the Guban, the arid littoral plains that extend from Djibouti along the coastal strip to just east of Berbera. Down at sea level, I hit a tsunami of hot air, an Arabian furnace; the temperature spiked dramatically, into the high forties, fanned by swirling north-westerlies. The average maximum for June, July and August here is 42 degrees Celsius, though temperatures regularly crack 50 Celsius. Berbera receives a mere 50 millimetres of rain annually, spread over just six days. Arriving in the dilapidated, quiet streets weakened and heat stressed from the day's effort, I totally understood why many residents migrate to the cooler inland cities during the summer.

✱

Berbera has been fought over, destroyed and rebuilt several times. Located at the head of the Red Sea, it is the principal port along the southern shore of the Gulf of Aden, and has been strategically important since antiquity. In the first century BC Berbera was known to Greek merchants as Malao and Chinese scholars from the Tang Dynasty wrote about it in AD 863 as a port where slaves, ivory and ambergris were traded. The Moroccan explorer Ibn Batutta (whose West African exploits are featured in chapters 2 and 3), recorded his visit in the thirteenth century. The Portuguese, at the height of their powers, ransacked it in 1518 and the Ottomans rebuilt and occupied the same port a few decades later. Over the next 300 years, Berbera was home to one of the most important trade fairs on the east African coast, where local clanspeople traded with caravans from Harar and Haud in Ethiopia and merchant ships from Arabia and India. To protect their businesses from competition, the Somali, Arabian and Indian merchants sought to keep the trade fair secret, and in later times made it off-limits to Europeans. But when British explorer Richard Burton in 1855 identified Berbera as the 'true key to the Red Sea and the centre for East African traffic...', he kindled his country's interest in the strategic port with its significant economic potential. In 1875 the Egyptian Ottomans briefly re-established control of Berbera before it was made a part of the British Somaliland protectorate (between 1884 and 1960). During the Second World War, the first Australian prisoners of war were taken hostage from Berbera in 1940.

Still ahead of schedule, I could afford to spend a day exploring. Zdenek was struck by yet another bout of gastro, so Omer, his cousin Jama and I toured the small city. Knowing a little of Berbera's history, I was expecting a bustling port with energetic markets but in the main I found a broken-down town. Goats foraged through the rubble of ancient Ottoman buildings that had not been touched since they were shelled and destroyed by Barre's forces more than two decades earlier. Still, beneath the dust and derelict tree-lined avenues and within some of the high-ceilinged colonial buildings, I found clues to its colourful past – along with a flickering flame primed to ignite Berbera's and Somaliland's economy should opportunities for trade and investment blow in off the Gulf of Aden.

President Barre's socialist affiliations saw the Soviet Union build a deep water harbour and an extra-long runway at Berbera's airport in the mid-1970s. A decade later, the US used both facilities, NASA designating the runway as an emergency landing strip for the Space Shuttle. The harbour may have been littered with the wrecks of vessels blown off-course at low tide but it was fully functional. Somaliland's government has a vision – that with the right investment, Berbera's port can again be a regional trading hub between Africa and the Middle

Colonial past, Islamic future in Berbera

East. However, as I gazed across the harbour from the lone waterside restaurant, which was encircled by a barbed wire fence, the only docked ship I saw was an empty livestock vessel. Livestock – sheep, goats and camels – account for 65 per cent of Somaliland's trade. In the past, the British used Somaliland to provide meat for their British Indian trading post in Aden on the northern side of the Gulf. These

Jama, Omer's cousin, shows some 'fruits de mer' caught in the Gulf of Aden

days, animals are exported live to the countries of the Arabian Peninsula and Egypt. The docked ship was empty because the cargo had just been rejected by the Saudi Arabian authorities. Later that afternoon, Omer, Jama and I visited the holding yards just outside the city. The situation here was dire, with two thousand animals in limbo; the camels appeared in reasonable health but the goats and sheep were sick, some dying of thirst and hunger. The livestock trader we met afterwards requested that I did not show the images I took of the distressed beasts. He told us that one of Somaliland's main problems is that it has to compete with countries such as Australia which are able to supply superior quality meat at a comparatively low price, undercutting Somali sales.

As the age rings of an ancient tree forever record the climate and its growing conditions, the decaying and damaged remnants of Berbera's architecture reveal evidence of its multicultural history. Early Ottoman and more recent Arabic structures were built on the trade of frankincense, myrrh and gum arabic while the colonial buildings generally stand as a result of the livestock trade. Future developments in basic amenities (schools, hospitals, water and sanitation), port facilities, housing and industries will most likely be built from revenues gained from untapped oil and gas reserves and the port itself – considered the jewel in Somaliland's economic crown. Most significantly, since the Eritrean-Ethiopian War, Berbera is being developed as landlocked Ethiopia's second avenue for sea trade after Djibouti. Every year, despite the threat of pirates, about 30,000 ships pass by the port of Berbera en route through the Gulf of Aden, the Red Sea and the Suez Canal. Somaliland's leaders envisage Berbera as a future Singapore, replete with container terminals, industry and oil refineries.

✻

Berbera had barely woken up as our convoy set off early in a vain attempt to beat the heat; rush-hour traffic certainly wasn't an issue. Pushing out along the Burao road, passing a few ramshackle street stalls, I got the feeling that it would be some time before the town would have to worry too much about traffic congestion. I passed the airport and livestock holding yards, Berbera's historic urban landscape with its leafy avenues soon well behind me and ahead the stark, waterless plains of the Guban. Stunted thorny shrubs did little to impede the gale-force crosswinds. The first 70 kilometres to the base of the Golis Mountains looked flat, but there must have been a very steady slope away from the ocean. I felt so much resistance due to this and the relentless winds that I may as well have been towing Omer's vehicle. I could not build any momentum at all and battled along so slowly it was embarrassing. Glancing down at my odometer which registered that I was struggling to manage 12 kilometres an hour was depressing so I opted not to look and concentrated on keeping the pedals turning.

By midday, the mountains, which from Berbera had appeared as a few molehills on the horizon, now made for an imposing wall. The Golis Mountains are a part of a steep limestone escarpment that extends virtually the length of the coast of northern Somaliland and Puntland. The scarp forms a barrier rising around 2000 metres above the coastal plains and is the stairway to the Somali Plateau. Known as Cal Madow further to the east towards Bosaso, the mountains are honeycombed with limestone caves, which served in the past as perfect hideouts for smugglers and pirates and in the present-day for

insurgents. The upper part of the escarpment is the wettest, greenest area in Somaliland; frankincense trees and myrrh have been harvested there for centuries.

The village at the base of the mountains revolved around passing trade. The restaurant was a Somaliland version of a roadhouse though it could not have been more different to the Western equivalent. At a European services stop, for example, patrons expect a pristine, rubbish-free premises where they can choose from a long menu of sterile convenience food balanced by a selection of perfectly formed fresh fruit that has done more road and air miles than the average driver: bananas

One of many dry wadis that carve the desertous Guban Plain near the c

from Costa Rica, oranges from Turkey, maybe even pineapples from Cameroon! Armed with a suitable dose of caffeine to go, they dump excessive waste – packaging, plastics, papers – in the appropriate recycling bins on the way out.

What was lacking in amenities here was certainly compensated for in character. The moment I grounded my feet on the gravel, a woman rushed over with a tray of lemons and oranges she had grown herself, eager to sell. I was too exhausted to raise any more than a grimaced smile before Omer and Abdul ushered me to the water trough outside the restaurant to wash. The noisy, busy open-air restaurant seemed to be men only; women and children stayed on the periphery. Omer negotiated a space on a table and I was seated with no fuss. Goats roamed freely through the dining area, under the tables, everywhere. They appeared untroubled by all the commotion though they should have been nervous: boiled goat was the main option on the menu. Knowing my first task after the break was to climb an enormous mountain pass, one that my Somali friends thought I would not make, I skipped the rubbery-looking meat and kept to plain rice and watermelon. Food was simply slopped on to wet plastic plates, and most patrons ate it with their hands. Puny cats padded around at our feet, cleaning up any morsel virtually before it spilt on to the floor.

I was treated with respect and given plenty of space, though there were a few bemused stares as I prepared to depart – a Western woman dressed in cycling gear, applying sunscreen, filling water bottles and covering them with wet socks. As I pushed my bike back out to the road, the person I had encountered on arrival persisted with her tray of citrus fruit, still hopeful of a sale. It was impossible for me to explain that I couldn't carry her lemons up the mountain. A trail of women and children followed me as far as the tarmac, intrigued as I slipped my feet into the toe clips and pushed off.

A cooler environment near the summit of Sheikh Pass

This section of the Golis Chain is known as the Sheikh Mountains. From the village, I began almost immediately on the long ascent above the plains. The first couple of kilometres weren't too severe and I tried to establish some sort of rhythm and hone my focus. In the intense midday heat, the steep section, characterised by a series of switchbacks etched into the face of the escarpment, proved brutal. It was a case of putting my head down and not stopping, no matter how slowly I was going or how bad I felt. It wasn't long before I was glad that I had refused the boiled goat at lunch! As I approached the top of Sheikh Pass, the gradient levelled off and I was able to appreciate spectacular views of the mountains cascading towards the horizon.

At around 1600 metres above the Guban Plain, it was noticeably cooler. The milder climate and evergreen surroundings had been recognised early on by the British as the best place for agricultural production and as a suitable location for learning. Along with the mountain range, the town of Sheikh a few kilometres after the summit took its name from a Sheikh, recognised as a father of Somaliland education, who lived in the region in early colonial times. Sheikh School, built in 1937, was the first intermediate school in Somaliland. Twenty years later the British built a boarding school for Somali boys and girls with academic potential with the intention that some would become the country's leaders after independence in 1960.

At the summit of the Sheikh Pass, 70 kilometres from Berbera, my average speed was just 11.3 kilometres an hour. After a short tea-break in Sheikh, I felt re-energised and, in the comparatively temperate conditions, knocked off the last 70 kilometres to Burao at normal pace, arriving in the dark after almost ten hours in the saddle.

❈

Cycling through the town of Sheikh (photo: Z Kratky)

Burao was where Somaliland's clan elders met to declare their independence from the federal republic. The town of about 120,000 had been largely rebuilt by the diaspora community after it was badly damaged by Barre's forces. Burao was a very different beast to Berbera. Omer and particularly our security guards were much more on edge here. Now we were in the more conservative Togdheer region, Omer insisted that I wear the *dirac* and *gabarsar* his wife had given me when I changed for dinner. In the morning, Abdul was very concerned that I wasn't ready to set off at first light. By the time I'd been served breakfast, changed out of the traditional clothes and had a long phone conversation with Issa, who was trying to organise our safe path through the buffer zone to Garowe in Puntland, it was about 8.30 am. Abdul had hoped we would be out of there at daybreak, before too many people saw me cycling. He seemed anxious and some of that apprehension rubbed off. As I was escorted through the streets, past the markets and back to the main road, it felt like every person had stopped in their tracks to stare. I tried not to make eye contact, concentrating on looking strong and capable.

Just as I was easing up to pass by some busy street stalls a man grabbed at me. I easily shrugged him off – assuming that he intended no harm and probably only wanted to invite me to his stall for a tea – but Abdul was very upset about the incident. He took it personally, considering it a blight on his professional charter to protect me. 'There are some people around here that are not so friendly', he claimed. Travelling on a bike, I am used to putting my trust in the local people, believing that this attitude will bring the best out in them, but a security guard who has been exposed to the threat of insurgents and conflict must consider the worst-case scenario. The protocol was to keep a distance from the locals in most situations. Working as a team, I had to respect that, even though it was against what I would normally do.

Lying in the rain shadow of the prosperous Sheikh Mountains, Togdheer is a semi-arid region. Where the land was devoid of any significant vegetation cover, I was severely hampered by the relentless crosswind. In the most barren areas, sand had collected beside and over the built-up road and the worst gusts gave my bare lower legs a sandblasting. Occasionally, I could see pastoralists tending to their herds, battling the conditions as they do day after day, their traditional attire providing much more protection than mine from the elements. A patchwork of spiky vegetation prevented the sand from blowing away altogether. I relied on passing through these

A desert tortoise has the ultimate protection from the elements

Omer steadies my bike as I close my bags after a break, sheltered by some thorn bushes near Aynabo (photo: Z Kratky)

filtering acacia thickets for some sanctuary from the prevailing winds. Inside, I could hear the streams of air whistle eerily, like a dying shrill as the energy was dissipated, absorbed by the thorny masses.

Around Aynabo, a small regional centre, there had obviously been heavy fighting at some stage. I passed several abandoned tanks before arriving at the first security checkpoint that required the police commissioner's letter. The town was an assortment of newer residences, homes that were still either damaged or undergoing renovations, and many buildings that remained as unsalvageable piles of rubble. Aynabo lies just within the jurisdiction of Sool, a state with a long history of disputes. In the late 1800s and early 1900s, the region was the seat of the anti-colonial Dervish movement. Led by religious leader Muhammad Hussan, the spirited Dervish army resisted attempted conquests from the ground forces of Somali Sultans, the Ethiopians, British and Italians. Eventually the army was defeated by the British, who used air strikes to bomb Taleh, the Dervish capital in 1920. Both Somaliland and Puntland lay claim to Sool and the neighbouring state of Sanaag to the north.

Aynabo evolved because it had a plentiful underground water supply for pastoralists to water their stock. As much of Omer's regional work involved trying to improve the supplies of clean water and sanitation, he diverted into the town to investigate. Aynabo's natural waterhole was in dire need of restoration. An impressive hand-carved open aqueduct, about 30 metres long, led to a limestone cave with steps leading down to the water's edge, however the supply was reduced to a puddle of stagnant, stinking polluted water. Another emergency.

Aynabo would have been an interesting place to spend more time. When I had set off from Burao that morning I had intended to stay there but, while we were devouring a mound of spaghetti and sauce for lunch, Abdul announced that we had to continue for an extra 30 kilometres to Oog to meet with the chief of police. I pushed on through dusk, arriving in Oog by the light of the vehicles once again. Now travelling through Sool's western periphery, the security situation escalated another notch. Circumstances in this part of the world can change rapidly and the regional commander had the final say as to whether we needed increased security or whether we could even proceed. Like many of the leading military commanders, Mohammed, the district chief, was an impressive character; educated at the Sheikh boarding school, he spoke perfect English. Thankfully, he gave us permission to pass through with no need for extra security.

Oog definitely felt like part of a rough frontier. I didn't sleep well: my door in the very basic Sool Hotel did not lock and there were a lot of strange noises outside. I was glad that Abdul and Karim were guarding the building throughout the night but I became most concerned when at about 3.00 a.m. I heard gunshots. Apparently some nomads had appeared from the bush and were shining torches at our vehicles, which they viewed with suspicion. Abdul said that when they did not heed his cautions he fired two warning shots above their heads and they fled back in to the darkness.

The stack of Somali pancakes served for breakfast looked to be the perfect energy food to sustain me for the 100-odd kilometres to Las Anod. But when I tried them I got a shock – they were doused in goats' ghee that tasted to me like rancid fatty goat's milk. That was definitely an acquired taste. Battling a severe crosswind and the repeating taste of the ghee, I knocked over the distance by noon. We were in a hurry because my sister, Jane, was due to fly in to Berbera the next morning to join the final leg of the expedition. Our security guards had to drive the 400 kilometres back to collect her and bring her to join us.

Arid plains near Las Anod

✳

At the checkpoint we were held up for some time while the chief of police and a clan leader were consulted for permission to proceed. Entering the town, Abdul shoved Zdenek to the back seat of Omer's vehicle and stood up through the sunroof, on guard, surveying all with rifle at the ready. I followed, tucking myself closely behind. The security car tailed me, with Karim sitting out of the side window, also armed and alert. This was not a place for us to spend time.

Some of the townsfolk were welcoming while others were not too pleased by our presence. We were whisked straight to the Hamdi Hotel, a quiet, secure sanctuary built on the edge of town with diaspora money. The local press followed us there and I was interviewed once more for Somaliland television. Again, I was very careful not to reveal our intention of crossing into Puntland. The story was aired on the news that night.

A tense security situation cycling through Las Anod (photo: Z Kratky)

Las Anod is the capital of Sool and was an early centre for the Dervish resistance. At the outbreak of the civil war, Somaliland laid claim to Las Anod and the Sool province. With the consent of the residents, in 2002 Puntland, with its more similar clan composition, took over administration of the town and region. Due to delays in development spending in Sool, some locals felt disenfranchised and sided with Somaliland when their military reoccupied Las Anod in 2007. Many civilians moved away from the Sool capital after Somaliland regained control, and it remains at the centre of the dispute for jurisdiction of the region. Surrounded by an outcrop of bare weathering hills, Las Anod exists because of its subterranean water resources and its location on an important Somali trade route. Reinforcing the incentives for controlling Sool and Sanaag is the desire of both Somaliland and Puntland to exploit the more recently discovered underground resources, especially oil and gas.

Confined within the secure walls of the hotel, I had an anxious wait. I was very concerned because if, for some reason, Jane missed her connecting flight from Dubai to Berbera, or the flight was cancelled, I didn't know what we would do. We had to pass through the buffer zone the next day as it was a major security operation. From the Puntland side, Issa and the Puntland government had been working for a week consulting all the clans and sub-clans within the lawless region, informing and gaining permission from them for our safe passage. Omer had been working on the Somaliland side. I was only going to have one shot at cycling through the 135-kilometre buffer zone, the most uncertain section within it being a narrow no man's land, about 10 kilometres wide. Jane phoned early in the morning to say she had made the flight to Berbera, which relieved a little of the stress, but I was not going to relax until she was safely with us. The day passed slowly as I hung on for the regular updates from our security guards, who finally arrived with Jane in the early evening.

It was great to see my sister, and I was relieved that everything had gone right for her to reach us on time. Even though it was her choice to come in support of the finish of the expedition, I felt totally responsible for bringing her there. Our reunion was a little emotional; I had not seen a member of my family for about eleven months and I felt strengthened by her care and commitment.

All of that strength was needed the next day. With the buffer zone in front of us it was like D-Day. I felt slightly apprehensive but ready to confront the journey head on, believing that to have the best chance of success, these kinds of situations must be approached with an air of positivity and perceived inner confidence. On the whole, I saw the likely challenges of the day ahead as an opportunity for an adventure rather than a potential minefield of disasters. This was the end of the road for Adbul, Karim and their driver. They had done a very professional job but no Somaliland security personnel or hire vehicles were allowed beyond Las Anod. Omer arranged for a local vehicle and driver who was willing to support us as far as no man's land – about 40 kilometres from Las Anod. From there, the plan was to rendezvous with a vehicle from Puntland and security reinforcements. The driver who was initially recommended to Omer refused to accompany me cycling – he wanted to put my bike in the car – but Omer, knowing how important it was for me to complete the journey in a continuous line, persisted until he found another driver willing to do the job.

✱

After a few final checks, we bid farewell to our Somaliland security team and friends who put us up at the Hamdi Hotel and set off at around 7.30 a.m. I was followed through the compound barrier and back onto the main road by a white estate car containing the local driver and a security guard in the front seats and Jane, Omer and Zdenek in the back. Omer kept in constant contact with Issa and his entourage who had already started driving from Garowe. The president of Puntland would not permit Issa or any member of his cabinet to pass through no man's land as they were targets and there was very real fear that they could be shot.

With the wind at my back and adrenalin pumping through my body, I took off out of the gate like the hare in a greyhound race. I literally flew along the road, pushing in my top gear at almost 40 kilometres an hour on the flat. The support vehicle followed at a constant 50 metres behind. As I approached each checkpoint I would ease up to allow the car to draw level. At the barrier I waited calmly and let Omer and the guard do the talking. The police commissioner's letter organised in Hargeisa proved to be very useful, and the first few stations were friendly. Some of the guards on patrol were genuinely interested about what I was doing and where I had been. When they asked where I was going to finish the journey, I would reply that we were just going to Garowe and that we would stop there. I'd always smile and shake hands with each of the clan's representatives. I was kept busy – there were at least six checkpoints in the first 40 kilometres.

The 'technical' military escort vehicle sent from Garowe met us – exactly as planned – just past a village 43 kilometres from Las Anod. Technicals are old anti-aircraft units. The technical usually carries eleven men: a driver, captain, gunner and eight regular soldiers, though the group that arrived to protect us didn't look to be army elite. The technical was sent specifically to escort us through no man's land where the reception was not so friendly – at either the entrance or exit of the zone. Entering, the soldiers passed through first then, after some heated discussion, the clansmen replaced the barrier in front of me and our vehicle, preventing us from following. Our security soldiers then stopped and reopened the barrier and after more threats and some push and shove, I was let through. There were further arguments before the support vehicle was allowed to pass. Our Somaliland driver and security guard would not be welcome to enter the Puntland side of no man's land, so again, precisely as planned, another driver whom Issa had arranged to collect my support team, Abdirizak Shole, Director of the Garowe Teachers' Education College, rendezvoused in the middle of no man's land. Omer, Jane and Zdenek moved to the four-wheel drive vehicle, transferring all our gear. The Somaliland local driver and security guard then turned back to Las Anod.

Leaving no man's land involved a much more spiteful confrontation. There were many armed people around and the clan had set up a customs post to collect large fees from travellers. Again, the technical was allowed through but the barrier was quickly replaced. I sat calmly on my bike, hoping I appeared confident and in control. There were threats, physical bravado and intense arguments between the commander and the clansmen. I was asked to move my bike over to a tent away from the road, but thinking it was unwise to become separated from our group, I nodded in acknowledgement to their request and moved just a little to the side of the road. The situation escalated until eventually the technical driver reversed back over the bollards to clear a path. The soldiers would wave me through but then the clan guards would stop me. Forward, back, forward and back. Eventually, our soldiers insisted I cycle through while they protected me, physically holding the locals back. I moved on alone and stopped about 300 metres further along to wait for the others. We'd congregated away from the blockade when one of the clanspeople called the main negotiator and abused us to him saying they did not want whites on their territory. The negotiator was personally offended as he considered us as a part of his team. He revved up the engine and started on his way back, threatening to 'shoot the bastard'. Fortunately for all of us, his colleagues stopped him and we moved on. It was a reminder of just how easily tempers can fray in the volatile buffer zone.

About three kilometres into the Puntland side of the zone, in the middle of a vast Nullarbor-like plain, I spotted an official-looking convoy approaching. In any other circumstance I would have been worried but I realised this must be the government entourage. There was Issa's car with his security team followed by the Minister for Civil Aviation and his security team that included another white technical vehicle. We were very pleased and relieved to see them and ecstatic to make it through no man's land.

For the remaining 80 kilometres to Garowe, Puntland's administrative capital, I cycled with the protection of a five-vehicle procession involving three government ministers travelling in their bulletproof vehicles, a car driven by a university academic containing Omer, my sister and cameraman, and two military

Breaking through – meeting our security who had been sent through no man's land to protect us (photo: Z Kratky)

technicals. The level of security seemed excessive but I felt honoured by the effort the government had made to take care of me and my team. The Minister for Civil Aviation was a member of the main clan in the region and it was he who had helped negotiate our safe passage.

The whole day was surreal. It was virtually non-stop apart from one tea-break and pauses for checkpoints and the various meetings. The plan essentially worked without a hitch but it is an experience I wouldn't care to repeat. This was Jane's first day travelling with me – the beginning of her adventure.

Meeting Issa and the Puntland entourage in the middle of nowhere (photo: Z Kratky)

Total distance: 21,455 kilometres

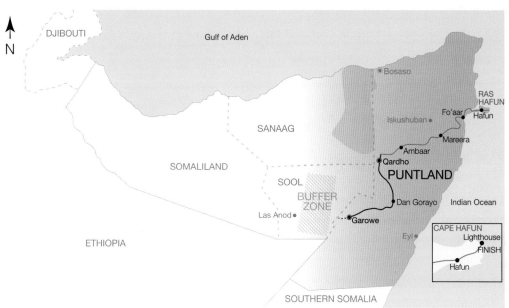

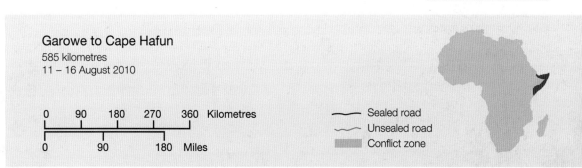

Garowe to Cape Hafun
585 kilometres
11 – 16 August 2010

| 0 | 90 | 180 | 270 | 360 | Kilometres |

| 0 | 90 | 180 | Miles |

Sealed road
Unsealed road
Conflict zone

19
KATE'S ROAD

Garowe to Cape Hafun (Puntland)

Leaning in to gale-force crosswinds in an effort to stay on the road
(photo: Z Kratky)

Halfway across the Puntland side of the buffer zone we decided to take a break. Two of the vehicles travelled ahead to a tiny roadside village to check that it was safe and to organise for some women to boil water for tea. When my sister arrived in advance of me, she noted a proud-looking young pastoralist, about eighteen years of age, who was obviously suspicious of her presence. Being a product of his isolated secular environment, Jane's and then my appearance would have challenged his perception of how women should look and act. Just by being there we were pushing the boundaries of his world. He would not trust what he didn't know. The young man settled under the bush shelter, curious, his eyes fixated on us, observing our every move and how we integrated with and were accepted by our Somali team. Over the course of our time in the village, he gradually relaxed, probably realising that we were friendly and harmless. We knew he had been won over when he asked Issa how many camels Jane was worth. The ultimate compliment.

As I prepared to move on, quite a crowd gathered around me, intrigued, as I refilled my water bottles, re-applied sunscreen and donned my sunglasses, gloves and helmet. Setting off again, I happened to overtake the lead technical vehicle as it negotiated the bumps and potholes in the road. A group of local women, impressed as I pushed ahead of the cavalcade, clapped and cheered, finally waving me off. I had not expected this kind of genuinely enthusiastic reaction out here.

The last person who attempted to cycle across Puntland four years previously, a Chinese man, was deported from Garowe by the government. When I first met Issa before the journey he had explained that one of the main reasons the Puntland government would support the expedition was because it understood the value of the project – it viewed what we were doing as an opportunity to promote cultural understanding about Somalis around the world. As I regained my rhythm and the convoy settled back to the right order, I was struck by a sense of how our actions could help improve ethnic awareness both within Somalia and internationally. Here in Puntland, simple interactions were assisting to dissolve some misconceptions about my culture. But by successfully reaching the finish and reporting experiences of acceptance, I hoped we would be helping to dispel some of the ignorance equally as rife in some Australian and other Western communities.

Taking a tea-break with the Minister for Civil Aviation, Jane and a local warlord (photo: Z Kratky)

On reaching Garowe, security was incredibly tight: we were accompanied by armed guards twenty-four hours a day. While we may have perceived this experience as very restrictive, all of the government officials and their families had to live under these conditions all the time. Virtually imprisoned in their own homes and offices, they could not venture down the street or wander off for a walk. Issa's Australian wife, Anne-Marie, and their two children, Bishaaro and Bilan, had just moved to Garowe in the previous month. It was a huge commitment to relocate the family there and for them to adapt to such a confined environment.

In the late afternoon after it had cooled down a little, everyone (except me) was in need of some exercise. But going for a walk was a major excursion. It involved rounding up the security guards and bulletproof vehicles and driving to the tabletop plateau above the town. From that vantage point, Garowe's townscape of freshly painted blue and red corrugated iron roofs contrasted against the bare stony hills. Puntland's administrative capital was much smaller than I had imagined. Prior to the setting up of the state government in 1998, it was just a village. The town of now roughly 50,000 people was fundamentally a collection of new buildings and high security compounds with satellite dishes, the occasional communications mast and mosque protruding skywards. After a short stretch of the legs and just enough time to appreciate a spectacular orange sunset, we returned via an alternative route. Our movements had to remain unpredictable in case someone was plotting to ensnare our group.

Puntland state took its name from the 'Land of Punt,' a coveted trading partner of ancient Egypt. As far back as 2500 BC, the Land of Punt provided the Egyptian elite

Issa with his eldest daughter, Bishaaro, during our sunset walk

with exotic riches. Expeditions sailing down the Red Sea to Punt were the equivalent to modern-day space travel. After Queen Hatshepsut's famous voyage to the Land of Punt in 1493 BC, no more was written about Punt in a factual way. It held, though, a strange fascination for Egyptian people as a 'land of plenty' – a land where the gods lived. Punt became so elevated in the minds of Egyptians that it was lost in legend and folklore, and ever since, it's exact location has been hypothesised and debated. In actuality, the Land of Punt most likely encompassed the northern Somali coast, including some of Puntland, as well as parts of Ethiopia, Djibouti, Eritrea and Sudan.

Plans for the last stage were constantly evolving. Even as we arrived in Garowe there was no certainty that I would be allowed to cycle through to Cape Hafun as major security concerns remained regarding the al-Shabaab extremists and the pirates. The government had initiated its proposed military intervention on 7 August, three days before we arrived in the capital, and the conflict zone was just west of Bosaso and to the north of Qardho, very close to where we needed to pass through. Although the government forces were winning, having stormed the principal training camp during our time in Garowe, a major concern was that splinter groups of al-Shabaab soldiers had fled to hide and reorganise themselves in villages near our planned route. This was perceived to be our main danger. As the frontline was not static, the government was relying on hourly intelligence reports that would essentially determine whether we could go on.

There were a couple of route options. The original suggestion was to travel along the main road to within 60 kilometres of Bosaso before turning east via Iskushuban to Hafun. This would have taken us dangerously close to the combat zone. The alternative was a more direct line from Qardho to Hafun, a shorter distance but obtaining reliable information about the state of the rough tracks was proving problematic. The land is very remote so if we did get into trouble, it would have been difficult to rescue us.

The pirates were known to be operating along the coast to the north and south of Hafun at this time of year, sheltering from the dominant north-westerly winds. The principal pirate cells were being monitored by government and international intelligence and at the time of our stay were deemed to be inactive. The following day I met with Ali Yusuf Ali, Deputy Minister for the Interior, Local Government and Rural Development. After a long discussion about the various options and perceived associated risks, he in effect gave us the all-clear to travel to Qardho and then on the more direct, least travelled route to Hafun, though this was pending the final word from the president, whom we were to meet that evening.

It was an honour to be received by the President of Puntland State, Dr Abdirahman Mohamud Farole, especially as he was on-call day and night. He was under intense pressure due to the on-going conflict and his mind was always busy. When following official greetings we sat down to discuss the plan, he warned of the potential dangers ahead in relation to al-Shabaab and the pirates. I replied that I fully respected his advice, but once the risks had been assessed, if it was deemed feasible to reach Cape

With Ali Yusuf Ali, Deputy Minister for the Interior, Local Government and Rural Development on a school visit in Garowe (JL)

Discussing Puntland's situation with President Farole (photo: Z Kratky)

Hafun safely, I was prepared for the challenge. It would have been extremely disappointing if I had made it this far in a continuous line but could not complete the ultimate goal. At the same time, if the threats were too great I would never have wished to endanger any of the team.

Dinner was a Somali smorgasbord of dry camel and goat meat, spaghetti, rice, salad and watermelon. Jane and I were seated at the head of the table, either side of the president. This was a chance to learn more about the Puntland government, what kind of international assistance it required and what action was needed to improve the situation there and in southern Somalia.

The Puntland state government was formed in 1998, largely of representatives of the sixty-six different clans, to stabilise and govern their homelands that since the start of the civil war had no effective administration. Puntland has an embryonic democracy where parliamentary candidates are nominated by their clan elders and are expected to make a financial contribution. The members of government then elect the president and office bearers. This way every clan is represented, though there is always some opposition to whoever has the balance of power. This electoral process is transitional, the first stepping stone towards a full democracy. Unlike Somaliland, the Puntland government has no desire to secede from the Republic of Somalia, rather it aims to work with the federal government while improving the social, economic and political conditions of its state.

Most of the ministers grew up in Puntland but then left Somalia before or during the civil war to live and study in Western countries such as Australia, UK, Canada, USA and New Zealand. They had all chosen to return, foregoing a peaceful, comfortable lifestyle to serve in the government in order to improve the lives of their Somali brothers and sisters. I found their commitment inspirational.

The development of the Puntland region had been stunted for many decades before the civil war. The Italian colonists applied economic policies to the north-eastern territories that destroyed the political,

The Somali and Puntland flags outside the president's residence. The five-pointed white star represents the Somali ethnic group found across Djibouti, the Ogaden region of Ethiopia, north-east Kenya and the former Italian and British Somaliland territories. The blue colour represents the role of the United Nations in Somalia's transition to independence

economic and commercial structures of the Somali Sultanates whom they conquered. Italian trade companies forcibly replaced traditional markets along the coastline, channelling the bulk of Somali exports, such as salt, frankincense, hides and cash crops, through Mogadishu and importing consumer goods from Italy. With few opportunities to earn secure incomes and with increased susceptibility to drought and famine, many pastoralists, fishermen and merchants moved to southern Somalia. In the 1920s, the Italian fascists exiled royalty and traditional elders to Mogadishu and some nearby Arab states to maintain control. After independence in 1960, with the balance of power in the south, the Puntland region was essentially excluded from development plans.

Before the fall of the Barre regime and the onset of civil war in 1991, Mogadishu, as the capital of the Republic of Somalia, had become the centre of everything: government, the education system, health, communications and development. For students from Puntland to receive a higher education, for example, they had travel to Mogadishu to study. During and after the war, anyone not from southern Somalia was expelled back to their homeland. Those returning to Puntland had no access to healthcare and education and little opportunity to generate a reasonable living.

The war and ongoing conflicts has pared development still further. Without travelling to Puntland to see it for myself I could not have imagined how little they had to work with. The government had an immense mountain to climb. Where do they start? That was my first question. President Farole's plans to achieve a more stable and sustainable future seemed logical. He said that nothing could work without peace and justice, so eliminating al-Shabaab and piracy was first priority. He began his presidency by ensuring all civil servants, including the dwindling armed forces, were paid: none of them had received any wages for many months preceding his election to the top job. Educating the next generation of leaders and professionals was also a major focus. Since Puntland had too few teachers and inadequate facilities, the education minister was procuring scholarships in neighbouring countries such as Sudan, Ethiopia and Kenya so that the most gifted students could be educated to a higher level. The government was also planning to develop trade and encourage investment to kick-start the economy. Livestock was the traditional primary industry but now the government was looking to tap into the country's known oil and mineral reserves to inject funds into the state. The ministers were negotiating for a fair return for the state's natural resources to build new roads, transport systems, hospitals, schools...

Several of the government ministers, including the president, Issa, Abdiwali Hersi Nur (Deputy Minister for Livestock and Animal Husbandry) and Dr Farah Ali Jama (Finance Minister), were Australian Somalis. They were appreciative of the opportunities Australia had given them and considered us as family. This was the initial reason why I trusted working with them when so many, whose opinions were shaped by the negative stories about Somalia, questioned my judgement. These people looked after Jane, Zdenek and myself as their own. Unified in its support of us and the expedition, the Puntland government ensured that we had the protection we needed. The president gave us his blessing and we were told to prepare to leave as soon as possible the next day – the longer we hung around Garowe and the longer I took to complete the journey, the greater the security risk. From this point until the finish there was a total embargo on all publicity and communications – I was not even able to write of our intentions in emails in case they were hacked.

✻

The following morning, 12 August, I was given the green light. President Farole farewelled the team from the Puntland State House and the final push was on. His personal red beret Special Forces led us through the barriers and along Garowe's busy streets. I tucked myself in closely behind the soldiers with the two bulletproof vehicles following. Every time the route was impeded by traffic, the driver of the technical sounded a siren to clear the way as he would normally do to when parading official dignitaries. This was an honour but I was more concerned about how much attention they were drawing. Then again, we were travelling as such a distinctive convoy that the sound of a siren probably would have made little difference.

A few kilometres clear of the town we paused to reorganise. This was the end of the expedition for Omer who had to return to Somaliland via the buffer zone. He had a tear in his eye as we parted. An integral part of the team for two weeks, Omer had hosted us safely through his country, embraced the ethos of the project and fought for our cause wherever necessary. I was always amazed at how the expedition provided common ground, a neutral platform to bring people together. In Garowe I had found it particularly inspiring to see the goodwill between Omer and President Farole. Omer had been welcomed into Puntland as a friend of the government despite the recent history of poor relations between the two states.

At this point Issa also had to leave us to deliver intelligence materials to the frontline. He would rejoin us in Qardho the next evening. Abdiwali Hersi Nur, who had committed to accompanying the team to the finish, took charge for the 210-kilometre journey along the main road to Qardho.

Ready to set off with the president's Special Forces, just outside of Garowe (photo: Z Kratky)

A raging tailwind made my task much easier. I sat high in my saddle as I sailed along the only paved road. Built by the Chinese in the mid-1970s when they first took an interest in Somalia's resource potential, the road forms Puntland's spine, connecting its administrative capital with Bosaso, its main port and economic capital. I carved a path across a fairly featureless landscape where sparse low vegetation supported a few hardy grazing animals. The wind constantly whipped eddies of dust and debris into an atmospheric haze, causing me to ride for long periods with a scarf – still the trusty tea towel I had first started wearing out of St Louis, now a faded rag – covering my mouth and nose. I watched as these small packets of energy merged to become powerful forces spiralling skywards from the powdery plains. As one twisted out of energy and fizzled into thin air, others would form, stirring up a different part of the horizon.

I wondered how people made ends meet out here. The occasional roadside village was an assortment of makeshift shelters and homes in disrepair intermingled with new, well-built residences and whitewashed mosques. The temporary dwellings either belonged to nomads or internally displaced people (IDP) who had fled to Puntland from southern Somalia. Immediately after the commencement of the civil war, Puntland clans were expelled from southern Somalia but now those from the south were fleeing as refugees to escape the violence, seeking a new start in relatively peaceful Puntland. This was just one more economic burden that the state and its four million Puntlanders had to cope with. The new houses and shops, often with decorative painted walls and coloured corrugated iron roofs, were most commonly funded by the diaspora community. Abdiwali explained that almost all families in Puntland rely on cash injections from their diaspora relations, via the remittance companies, to survive. The livestock industry remained under-developed and there were few other economic means.

On the outskirts of Dan Gorayo village, about half way to Qardho, we ventured in to an IDP camp. Already poor, these woman-headed families had been temporarily displaced by an environmental double-whammy. Many who lived beside the coast had had their homes destroyed during the 2004 Indian Ocean tsunami. Then the bulk of their stock had been killed during fierce hail-storms that occurred at around the same time. Abdiwali spoke to one woman who explained that she had lost more than 90 per cent of her goats and sheep. Though it was taking several years, she was gradually rebuilding her stock numbers. Her flock had increased to thirty and she hoped to have eighty animals before too long: that, she claimed, would be enough for her to move on. In the meantime, life was hard in the IDP camps. The shelters provided by the UNHCR were helpful but not sufficient for this woman and her family of six children, so she had manufactured a larger, sturdier home from whatever she could find to use for building material: sticks and brush grasses, empty aid bags, cardboard, plastic and rolled oil drums.

Leaning in to gale-force crosswinds in an effort to stay on the road (photo: Z Kratky)

Between the hills of Dan Gorayo and Qardho, the road direction dog-legged ninety degrees and I was battered by the strongest crosswind I have ever had to deal with. Tossed around like a rag doll, I often had to lean aggressively into the gusts just to stay on the road. Stopping in a small village for a tea-break was the only respite I had from the conditions. Here I noted another of the economic problems the locals were dealing with – inflation. I had given my sister the task of controlling the petty cash in order to pay the women who boiled our water, but as there were 3.2 million Somali shillings to one US dollar, Jane soon grew frustrated counting out great wads of notes and passed the responsibility on to Abdiwali.

I valued the downtime as a rare opportunity to learn about some of the situations facing the people of Puntland in more depth. In a little shack halfway between Dan Gorayo and Qardho, Abdiwali explained why al-Shabaab was evolving as such a formidable force. Somali soldiers were trained at a great cost to the government but it was difficult to prevent some from defecting because al-Shabaab offered to pay them more. Al-Shabaab is funded by al-Qaida and its sympathisers, who include some powerful Arab businessmen and organisations. Abdiwali told us that it was often difficult to know where some soldiers' allegiances lay: the extremists prey on the vulnerable, the illiterate, poor and young, who are brainwashed into believing that they will be better Muslims if they adopt the fanatical mandates. In some cases this has resulted in soldiers swapping sides. The purpose of the government-initiated conflict was to prevent these ideologies spreading like a cancer through communities and taking a strong hold.

❋

Arriving in Qardho, I was ushered straight through town and inside the secure gates of the hotel compound. Now, near the edge of the conflict zone, there was no pausing to photograph the streets and no chance to visit the market. That evening, Issa arrived back from the frontline, exhausted but ready to travel with us for the remainder of the journey. He said that the president had been very nervous about allowing me to cycle on. Had I not been travelling accompanied by the two bulletproof vehicles and the technical unit, I would not have been permitted any further and the

Abdiwali counts out a bundle of Somali shill to pay the women who boiled water for our t

expedition would have ended in Qardho. That evening the president's guards were called to the frontline and were replaced by a new military unit which had returned from its tour of duty. We were sad to later learn that three of the president's Special Forces who had protected us between Garowe and Qardho were killed in an ambush.

No-one in our group had travelled along the route we proposed to take; although the commander of the military unit and one of the drivers had spent time in the region they had not taken the exact path. In Qardho we attempted to access the best local knowledge, and after much consultation, the mayor was able to provide a list of approximate distances, village locations and information about the terrain and road conditions. I had several maps but none showed all the settlements or tracks and there was a lot of conflicting information. I switched to my off-road tyres in anticipation of the sand and rough breakaways.

If the security situation heightened, Issa told us that we should expect to be moved to a new location every few hours during the night so it would be more difficult to trace us. Following the new technical unit out of the gates the next morning, I was ready for every kind of condition and prepared to face whatever it took to make it to the finish, now no more than 400 kilometres away.

Sixteen kilometres out of Qardho we turned off the main tarmac road, heading east, weaving a path through a complex network of tyre

Three of the president's guards (pictured) were killed in an ambush on the frontline, three days after they left us, the gunner and driver were targeted first

tracks. Initially the terrain was flat, easy-going claypan. The powerful north-westerlies swept our trails of dust into the otherwise pristine sky. I hoped our dust stream didn't act as a smoke signal for any stray insurgents who could possibly be lurking in villages or in rocky breakaways along our path.

❧

The plan for the first day was simply to slog it out and cover as much territory as possible. Small settlements were generally about 30–50 kilometres apart, and after 67 kilometres we stopped for the first break in Ambaar village. The reception was typically friendly at an open-sided shack – a kind of outdoor living room made from sticks, brushwood and whatever second-hand building materials were available – where we rested up. The women, especially, were intrigued. The fact that I looked very different from them in my cycle kit was not an issue. Aisha, a matriarchal figure with the most welcoming smiling eyes, boiled water for our tea. Even though we must have appeared like aliens, she and her friends treated Jane and myself as long-lost sisters.

In this temporary, remote sanctuary it was easy to forget that we were travelling through a war zone. But the mood quickly changed when Issa explained what to do if we heard a gunshot. The drill was for me to fall to the ground immediately while the drivers of the two bulletproof vehicles provided an arrowhead protection. They were instructed to drive either side of me, forming a V-shape so that one of the guards could then drag me in. I had been making good time, so this discussion was sobering. Though the chance of the gunshot scenario occurring was not very likely, it was essential to know the plan. As I set off, the villagers lined the path, forming a loose guard of honour, singing and clapping the group on our way, creating an ambience more suited to the Tour de France than a tour of duty.

Donkeys seek shade in the heat of the day at Rako village   Aisha, Ambaar village

By mid-afternoon it was obvious that I was going to exceed expectations for the day and we altered plans to now aim for a village about 40 kilometres further on. As I 'flew' across the Somali plains, my mind was a jumble of thoughts and emotions. Ever since I had planned the expedition and seen images of the Somali Plains I had dreamed of these final days. I had wondered how I would feel in the twilight of such an epic journey. I could only imagine how my views of Africa might have been affected. The pendulum swung from experiencing a euphoric sense of achievement to feeling extremely humbled by the effort, energy and enthusiasm so many had invested to make the dream a reality.

The African continent had been an incredible canvas for an expedition. My journey had flowed from one country to the next and from one issue to another, encountering a continuum of different cultures and crossing diverse landscapes. I had seen and experienced so much but at this point it was all still so raw. Now, nearing the finish, it felt like I was only at the dawn of my voyage of understanding. How would I arrange all these dimensions into some sort of perspective and articulate it for others to comprehend? At this moment, the challenge seemed overwhelming. I had seen examples of humanity at its best and worst. I found Africa to be complex, confusing and frustrating, yet also inspiring, magical, alive and brimful of promise. Mostly, I was in awe of what Bob Geldof calls the 'luminous continent' and felt extremely privileged to have the opportunity to cycle across this part of the world.

Without warning, my front wheel struck a bulldust-concealed dip in the track and I tumbled head first over the handlebars, landing with a spectacular face-plant into the ground. Fortunately, the only damage was a slight scrape on my nose and a dent in my pride. It was no more than an embarrassing slap in the face and a reminder to remain vigilant all the way to the finish. There were still at least 250 kilometres to go and I was aware that most expeditions fail on the homeward run.

By the early evening I began to wonder just when we might make it to the finish. During the course of the day the commander had been trying to avoid villages wherever possible – the fewer people who knew our position the better for security. While attempting to divert around significant settlements we lost our way more than once. At night we sought the opposite situation – it was preferable to be within the protection of a community rather than out in the open.

Standard group formation travelling across the Somali plains (photo: Z Kratky)

After obtaining security advice, Issa had arranged for us to stay in a small village called Hiriiro. The local mayor reported by phone that his community was ready to welcome us and had slaughtered two goats in our honour. But about three kilometres before Hiriiro, our security guards suddenly halted the convoy. The commander had just received fresh intelligence information that a group of twenty-two al-Shabaab militants was hiding in the village; the insurgents had arrived the previous day having fled the conflict. At a cost of offending the Hiriiro mayor and community, Issa decided that we give the village a wide berth. We veered off the main track, following a faint trail away from the settlement and behind a large hill that shielded us from view of the village. The new plan was to continue to the next known village, Mareera, in search of cover. But now off the main route, it was impossible to know which course to take. There were faint, unmarked wheel ruts peeling off in every direction, most dissipating in the bushes. We could find no obvious path leading to Mareera.

As the sun set I was still going strong. I continued for another hour in the dark until finally Issa and the other Somali group leaders conceded that we were lost. By this stage nothing fazed me. I had done 190 kilometres and was well into overdrive, numb to just about everything. In the preceding hours I'd tipped over several times, jagged myself on thorn bushes and my knees complained from the constant jarring. Pain and negative emotions such as fear and frustration had been blocked out as a matter of course. Now, focused on the moment, I was most acutely aware of the evening chill as it started to seep through my saturated clothing, but I didn't care. The headlights provided me with a tunnel vision where I just concentrated on the ground in front in an effort to stay upright. I found a pace that I could maintain for as long as it took. All I wanted was to get to a place – a landmark, a village, or a nomad encampment – any place where we could identify our location. After unsuccessful attempts to pinpoint some nomads, it was decided that we should camp in the open, near the best groundcover we could find. Not ideal.

Discussing what to do, lost after a 190-kilometre day (photo: Z Kratky)

My Somali colleagues could not believe that I was able to keep going after nearly ten hours of bad roads; they thought I might be overcome with exhaustion and not able to continue the next day. I was fine, having done it all before, although I was a little tired. I was more worried about them. Two days earlier, the soldiers accompanying us had survived a vicious battle on the frontline and their nerves were frayed. To make matters worse, it was the middle of Ramadan and the entire Somali support crew were fasting during daylight hours. As soon as the sun had set they immediately stopped to drink and pray but they were famished. The soldiers were supposed to organise their own supplies, however having joined us directly from the conflict, they were not carrying any food. We gave what we could although it was not enough to sustain them while they guarded the camp that night and then through to the following sundown. I refuelled on spaghetti and a tin of tuna. Not fancy but it did the trick. Despite all the work Issa had been doing – travelling to the frontline and leading our journey – he insisted on doing a shift with the soldiers and as a result had minimal sleep. Very much a team man, Issa led by example. He showed great empathy with the troops, who were so exhausted that some of them fell asleep directly on the ground as soon as we stopped.

At daybreak, Issa, Abdiwali and the commander were able to locate the nearest group of pastoralists and ask directions. I was relieved to learn that we had strayed only about five kilometres from where we were meant to turn off. Abdiwali bought two goats from the nomads to feed the soldiers who had decided to break their fast to keep their energy up for the next couple of days. I had been concerned about causing the soldiers to alter their tradition, though it was made clear that whether they were fighting in the conflict or protecting us, they were always going to have to break their fast: a provision in the regulations of Ramadan allows participants in extenuating circumstances to break their fast so long as they make it up later. These soldiers were happier accompanying the expedition to Hafun than fighting in the conflict because it was far less risky – and much more exciting. The goats were loaded on to the back of the technical and we returned to the junction where we had gone wrong. I continued the line, cycling to Mareera village only six kilometres away. There we had a long wait while the goats were slaughtered and cooked.

❋

Having covered so much ground the previous day, I was now in a position to reach Hafun a day earlier than planned. Initially, being holed up in Mareera for the morning frustrated me. It felt like I was undoing some of the hard work of the day before and it meant I would have to pedal non-stop through the heat of the afternoon and into the night to reach the next destination. But this was a team effort and the soldiers' welfare was of equal priority. Time spent waiting in Mareera turned out to be an important break in the hectic push to the finish; time to consider where we were, what life was like for these villagers, what was being achieved and how fortunate I was to be with such a collection of team-mates.

Young women in Mareera village

During the downtime, as with the whole operation, Issa was regularly on his mobile phone trying to obtain directions and information from local sources. I found it surprising that even out here he regularly had mobile reception. He also carried a satellite phone as backup in case of an emergency when he would need to contact the NATO warships stationed just off the coast. Travelling with us from Qardho as well was Yassin Musa Boqor, security advisor to the president of Somalia and grandson of the last king of this region – the locality of Iskushuban.

Nothing seemed to be cultivated in this tiny isolated community. Mareera was a local livestock trade depot where goats and sheep were loaded to be transported to market in Bosaso. There were a few fishing

Soldiers holding a traditional milk container locally known as a *doobi*

nets around so I presumed that, with the coast not far away, the locals would sometimes travel there to fish and trade. That got me wondering about the pirates. With a couple of hours to fill in, this was a perfect opportunity to find out more about the situation from Issa, Abdiwali and Yassin.

From our discussions and subsequent research I learned that modern piracy stems from sustained economic hardship of Somalis in the Horn of Africa. Territorial waters, particularly around the state of Puntland, once contained a vast supply of fish and provided another lucrative income stream for their economy. According to testimonies from captured pirates, the practice began in around 1994, not long after the commencement of the civil war. With no coastguard to regulate the waters, fishermen from neighbouring countries, especially Yemen, began to help themselves to the Somali bounty, emptying and stealing Somali nets to bolster their own catch. In retaliation, some

Somali fishermen used small boats and basic weapons to attack and extract fines from trespassing sailors. Early on, these encounters were reactionary and uncoordinated responses by Somalis who were simply protecting their livelihoods.

Over the next decade, the seas around the Horn of Africa were gradually fished out. Perpetrators not only came from across the Gulf of Aden but also from the Mediterranean and the Far East with their long dragnets, cleaning out what was left from the unprotected waters. Somali fishermen could not catch enough to sustain a living. Then the 2004 Indian Ocean tsunami struck, causing 289 deaths and destroying more than 600 fishing boats and hundreds of buildings. Compounding the hardships, illegally dumped harmful waste began washing up on local shores, raising health concerns and further affecting the fish stocks. Due to the anarchic political situation in Mogadishu, international assistance was limited and precious little support trickled down to ordinary Somali communities to help with the recovery after the tsunami.

Pastoralists, fishermen and other Somalis who were affected by the depleted fishing areas turned to hijacking foreign vessels in sheer desperation. Piracy escalated from simple ad hoc hijackings of foreign fishing vessels to complicated manoeuvres to take cargo ships, oil tankers and luxury cruise liners. By 2008, when the severity of the problem magnified tenfold in one year, the piracy problem had developed into a sophisticated alliance of international financiers and insurance companies, mother ships, pirates and the financial distribution networks. The pirates required significant start-up capital from a financier to buy boats, weapons, supplies and fuel. Local financiers received funds from investors in Iran, Syria, Libya and Egypt and from terrorist organisations. Funds were also collected from some diaspora communities via the efficient money transfer system. Somali remittance companies are an avenue for channelling money to organised crime syndicates as well as for supporting development. Investors usually expected to receive about half of the profit from the ransom.

The arrival of a hijacked ship at port sets off a complex web of interactions, the benefits and negative effects pervasive throughout the local communities. The pirates pay a docking fee – about 10 per cent of the profit of the bounty – and arrange for the ransom negotiations. These funds are filtered back through a broad spectrum of the society from officials and clan leaders to primary producers and merchants. The money can be used for anything, from covering daily living expenses to paying off debts and even for community development. Those who threaten to cross paths with the pirate business live in fear of their lives. For the average person who does not benefit from the pirates' spoils, the arrival of a hijacked ship at port also signals mass inflation of the price of everyday goods, making them unaffordable and thus increasing hardship.

Given the all-encompassing nature of the problem, piracy cannot simply be stamped out by isolating perpetrators one by one in the wake of their hijacking a ship somewhere in the Indian Ocean. And an expensive international military presence in the Gulf of Aden will not fix the problem long term. Sheltering from the ferocious weather conditions in an empty room in Mareera, my colleagues, now vigorously gnawing their way through rubbery portions of boiled goat, discussed some of the reforms the government had initiated and what they still needed to do. According to them (and the Minister for Ports and Counter Piracy, whom we met in Bosaso after the expedition), eliminating land and sea piracy called for a multifaceted strategy, locally coordinated but assisted by international cooperation. There were three main requirements, as they saw it. In the shorter term, the Puntland government, which was strengthening its navy, needed a small fleet of agile, fast boats that could be used to more easily apprehend pirates out to sea, by force if necessary. This would complement the partnership just secured with the NATO alliance. Secondly, the government needed assistance to police piracy at its sources on land and to bring offenders to justice once they were captured. At present, officials and judges who apprehend and sentence land and sea pirates live in danger of assassination. One of the pre-emptive initiatives undertaken by the government was to convene a social campaign led by Islamic scholars and community activists aimed at discrediting piracy and highlighting its negative effects. And finally, the long-term solution to breaking the cycle of piracy is to deal with the root causes. Improve economic conditions by developing the natural resources and the primary industries, and improve education, health and living standards and the need to adopt a precarious existence as a pirate will no longer prevail.

✳

Restarting prior to midday, it was more of the same nondescript, arid Somali plateau for another 90 kilometres before our convoy began to gradually descend. Over the millennia, the forces of erosion had sculpted natural terraces into the rugged landscape; each level defined by a rocky breakaway. To me, every step was a step closer to attaining my dream. But to Issa's bodyguard, Osman, who grew up in the region, each drop-off had significance. While I saw the land as parched semi-desert, Osman's people have every contour and every detail mapped in their minds. As nomadic pastoralists they have developed an intricate relationship with it, and know where best to graze their stock and how to effectively manage its limited resources.

Approaching the coast, I could smell and feel the cooler salty sea air before I caught a glimpse of it. The chalky plains ended dramatically with cliffs dropping 100 metres or more to the Indian Ocean. Descending to sea level involved a spectacular two-hour ride along and then winding down the face of

a steep, stony escarpment before tracking a broad valley out to the coastline. The prevailing wind switched to the south-west as I pushed along a dry riverbed in the dark. These conditions, combined with the exertions of the previous three days, suddenly hit as if I had slammed into a wall. By the time I struggled into the road builders' camp at Fo'aar, I was shaky, saturated with perspiration and wrestling with reality. As welcoming locals materialised like colourful ghosts in front of the headlights, all I was focused on was finding and opening the last tin of pineapple chunks. Once I had downed those, the instant sugar rush perked me up and I was ready to greet our hosts.

The brains trust – (clockwise from myself top left) Issa, Abdiwali, Yassin and the commander – trying to determine the distance to the lighthouse (photo: Z Kratky)

The Fo'aar road builders didn't appear to have anything much at all; theirs was an isolated existence in makeshift camps in the bush. The women prepared a site for our group, laying woven mats down on the sand beside a brush barrier, erected to protect us from the sea breeze. As we pored endlessly over the maps trying to accurately determine the distance to the lighthouse at Cape Hafun, the villagers slaughtered

The Fo'aar road builders honour us with a special dance performance

and cooked a goat and served it along with the usual spaghetti and sauce. After we'd had our fill, they put on a special performance to welcome us and to celebrate the occasion. With no formal musical instruments, their dance performance, like everything else they did, was very much a triumph of improvisation. They created their own beat using yellow plastic water containers and spoons and by clapping, singing and ululating. It was the rhythm of their lives.

The people of Fo'aar lived there by choice, their calling to build a road to Hafun, 50 kilometres away on the end of a sandy, limestone-based isthmus. No one paid them – they were not employed by anyone and they received no outside help. They were simply there to build their legacy, a better road to the historic and ancient port. They possessed minimal effective road-building equipment, and although they would definitely benefit from some sort of development assistance, they weren't asking for it as it had never been an option. They just did their best in the circumstances. These people had a great sense of purpose and a strong desire to make it on their own terms.

On the final morning the air of excitement was palpable. The ambience was created not only by me but by the whole team and the villagers: in fact, Issa, Abdiwali and the soldiers seemed more animated than even I was. The women cooked a huge stack of Somali pancakes to sustain me throughout the morning. Remembering my previous experience in Oog, I gave special instruction to cut the goat's ghee. I couldn't bear to have the taste of rancid goat's milk repeating all the way to the finish!

Until our visit, no officials from the current government had been out this way. Now that Issa, Abdiwali and Yassin had travelled there and seen what the Fo'aar road builders had achieved with strong motivation and virtually working with their bare hands, they promised to provide some support. The village leader, in his response to our 'thank you' speeches, decided to name the road to Hafun 'Kate's Road' – a great honour I replied, in total admiration of their spirit.

✳

As I prepared to set off on my final day from the junction at the start of Kate's Road, some of the soldiers could now barely contain their excitement. In trying to help, they kept getting in my way. Our group was also joined by the mayor of Hafun and a

Setting off on the final day

highly respected elder who had driven from the ancient port town to officially welcome us and to escort us through the region to the finish. Hafun is virtually cut off from the mainland, except for the sandy four-wheel-drive track the people from Fo'aar were trying to improve. By all reports my final day was likely to be tough physically and I reminded myself to remain focused until I had safely reached the lighthouse.

For the first few kilometres, the road quality was quite fair. My only battle was with the strong crosswind that lifted beach sand directly off the huge sandy ergs. The surface soon deteriorated into periodic sand drifts and then to deep sand where cycling became akin to pushing along Bondi Beach. Where sand drifts accumulated, the road builders had laid a loose pavement of bowling-ball-sized stones in an attempt to stabilise the track. Unfortunately the sand between the stones had blown away, leaving gaping crevasses which were treacherous to cycle over. Within a couple of kilometres, the surface

Bogged on the edge of a stony hand-built causeway

transitioned to just deep sand. With the wind constantly eroding their work, I could see that the Fo'aar road builders, lacking proper equipment and investment, had taken on a Sisyphean task to build Kate's Road.

I managed to find slightly firmer ground away from the churned-up track. All three vehicles became bogged, but I thought that, since I would be the slowest in the group most of the day, I should continue on to save time. All I wanted to do was reach Cape Hafun as quickly as possible. In their efforts to protect me, some of the soldiers tried to keep up, running alongside me. Eventually, the commander caught up and I was asked to wait for the vehicles: I was a worry because all the soldiers could see was me disappearing off the track and through the bush. I was experienced at cycling in such conditions and was confident that I knew what I was doing, but they didn't know that. When a local nomad told them that he had recently lost a number of his livestock from hyena and leopard attacks, Issa decided to loan me his 9-millimetre pistol so that I could protect myself from the wild animals and to attract attention if I became lost. Having never used a pistol before, I was a little hesitant and thought I'd be more likely to shoot myself in the foot or something! Issa and the commander gave some instruction and I practised squeezing the trigger before the pistol was loaded and the safety catch set. The weapon sat in my bar bag for the rest of the journey.

At the beginning of the final leg, my back tyre contracted a slow puncture. Now out of glue, I was unable to fix it but as it only needed to be inflated about every 10 kilometres or so, it wasn't too much of a problem. Mid-morning, when I went to pump up the tyre, I noticed a split down the rear wheel rim. About 10 centimetres long and running towards the valve hole, this was a serious

Learning how to use Issa's 9 millimetre pistol (ZK)

Working hard over the tidal flat (photo: Z Kratky)

injury for my bike, probably sustained while hitting the road builders' loosely laid boulders. I had been carrying my spare bike all the way across Africa but unfortunately had decided to leave it in Berbera. The wheels of the bike I was using had been hand built and I was impressed that up to then I had not even popped a spoke. I again checked the rims in Berbera and since they remained perfectly true and there was little room in the vehicles, I decided to carry only essential tools and spares, and left the other bike behind. Now with just 50 kilometres to go, I was afraid the wheel would not last, and removed the bags to help my chances. I approached any stony section with great caution, gently negotiating bumps and obstacles by leaning as far forward as possible to take the weight off the back wheel.

Now led by the mayoral car, we soon traversed the neck of the isthmus and turned onto the tidal flat: according to the mayor this was a much better surface than the track. Although the damp surface was heavy-going at times, there was effective shelter from the wind. To avoid becoming bogged the vehicles hugged the more solid shoreline. It was a race against the rising tide – at one stage, not long before we turned away from the beach and towards Hafun, the sea was within a couple of metres of our path.

Back on the sandy track – the other end of Kate's Road – it was a struggle. Gale-force crosswinds caused sandblasting so severe I joked that it was blowing in one ear and out the other. In the vicious conditions I barely noticed some derelict Italian garrison buildings at the entrance to the old Hafun

Approaching Hafun in a sand storm (photo: Z Kratky)

The Italian-built salt works

town site and cycled straight past. Hafun was destroyed by the tsunami of 2004 when a three-metre-high wall of water washed right over the low-lying peninsula, killing nineteen local people. The villagers lost everything, and as open sewage had flushed through the buildings, they were forced to relocate. They rebuilt about two kilometres away on slightly higher ground nearer to the base of Ras Hafun.

Adjacent to the old town and dominating the scene were the ruins of the Italian-built salt works. Due to Hafun's strategic location, the colonists chose it as a satellite port to Mogadishu. In the 1920s they bombed the sultan's fort and forcibly took control, renaming their new port Dante. Only the skeletal remains of what were once some mighty concrete structures stood high over the old town, a somewhat fitting, decaying memory of the fascist era that was characterised by cruelty and forced labour. Salt was stockpiled before it was loaded on to ships via a large-scale cableway. Only the rotting stumps of what

once were the enormous pylons of that system remained, extending for several hundred metres out to sea. The salt works was only operational for about fifteen years and had been disused since the Second World War when poor old Hafun was bombed again, this time by the British who seized the town from Mussolini's forces.

None of these sinister monuments gave any inkling about Hafun's vibrant past as an ancient trading post; this evidence lies

The buildings and cableway jetty have been disused since the Second World War. Old Hafun, destroyed by the 2004 tsunami, is to the right

under the ground. Archaeologists have identified Hafun as the site of the historic port of Opone. Some pottery found in the tombs of Opone dates back to the Greek Kingdom of Mycenae. In antiquity, the tip of the Horn of Africa was known as the Cape of Spices: merchants came from Phoenicia, Egypt, Greece, Yemen, Persia, India and from as far away as what is now the Indonesian archipelago to trade cinnamon, cloves, ivory, frankincense, animal hides and cloth. Had there not been such a tight security situation we would have relished the opportunity to explore some of the underground sites such as an ancient necropolis and a seventeenth-century mosque.

We paused outside new Hafun for one final breather. It was time to pull out the Australian flag I had carried right across the continent to fly at the finish. In response, the mayor tied the Somali flag to his vehicle's antenna. Issa arranged for me to be interviewed by the BBC World Service, the program to be aired just as I finished. We were ready for the final stage: a 22-kilometre ride up Ras Hafun and across the table-top mountain – well, almost ready. The mayor wanted to make the most out of the moment and led me up and down the main street of new Hafun to parade the event to his people. I obliged, smiling and waving to enthusiastic townsfolk.

The beginning of the ascent up Ras Hafun (photo: Z Kratky)

❀

As I ascended the unprotected slopes away from the town, conditions worsened. I was constantly blown off the track, the challenge made more difficult by the surface of large, loose gravel stones and steep inclines. The path I navigated up through a narrow gorge and dry wadi would have been suitable as a BMX racing circuit but then, as I scaled the side of the 210-metre Ras Hafun, it degraded to a path fit only for billy goats. The limestone plateau was completely exposed: nothing grew more than 30-40 centimetres off the ground in this desolate place. Our trail across the island gradually deteriorated. Protruding stones had weathered into sharp edges so I had to nurse my broken wheel while avoiding further punctures from the thorns.

The final two kilometres. The climate is so bleak, vegetation grows flat over the stony ground (photo: Z Kratky)

Finally, Issa and the mayor pointed out a speck in the distance – the lighthouse! Now I was becoming excited. When the overgrown path petered out completely about two-and-a-half kilometres from this landmark, we continued on foot. No one had been out there for a long while. The mayor and village elder confirmed that no cyclist had ever been to Cape Hafun. They should be good authorities because for anyone to reach Hafun town, they would first have to travel down the sandy isthmus, only one kilometre wide at its narrowest, near the town. Then they would need to take a local guide or at least ask for directions to find their way up Ras Hafun and across the land mass – the route was far from obvious. Some of the party raced ahead to the lighthouse while I led the main group, pushing my broken bicycle over the stones and slaloming around the splayed-out vegetation. The Somalis cheered as I arrived at the derelict lighthouse and crumbling buildings at Africa's most easterly landmark.

A team effort (photo: I Farah)

I leant the bike against the lighthouse and wandered as near to the edge of the continent as I dared. The breeze was so strong that a gust could have swept me off my feet and over the cliff face that fell away 200 metres sheer to the Indian Ocean. I was tingling with so many emotions I didn't know what I was feeling: proud, elated, relieved, satisfied, a little reflective and thrilled to share the occasion with Jane, Zdenek and the Somali team. I was on such a high that I did not experience any fatigue whatsoever. I had arrived four days ahead of schedule after ten months. The vision was complete: I had pedalled from Pointe des Almadies, Dakar, Senegal to Cape Hafun, Puntland, Somalia in a continuous line. As expected, the route was adapted at times to make way for new opportunities and the ever-changing conditions but with the exception of river crossings, not a kilometre had been missed in 22,040 kilometres.

I may have been the only cyclist but successfully reaching the finish and achieving the mission on time, on budget and without incurring any significant injuries or illnesses, was testimony to the committed efforts of my whole team and band of supporters. Throughout the expedition, John, Zdenek, Daniel, Simon, Paddy, Stuart and Jane had played significant roles, as had all of the partners and sponsors – a list too long to mention here. I would never have had the opportunity to reach Africa's most easterly point without the support of the state government and the people of Puntland. Issa, Abdiwali, Yassin, the mayor, the elder from Hafun and the security guards were ecstatic. The soldiers fired a few rounds into the air to signal the finish.

I would have liked to stay around longer to absorb the moment but the sun would soon set and we had to get back to Hafun.

Holding the bike aloft with the lighthouse behind (ZK)

Total distance: 22,040 kilometres

Crossing the Dida Galgalu Desert, northern Kenya (photo: Z Kratky)

AFTERWORD

Three years on

Cramped in the back of a bulletproof vehicle on the fourteen-hour drive from Hafun to Bosaso, I felt on a high; proud, immensely satisfied and jubilant. I had managed to successfully traverse the continent from west to east and I couldn't wait to share my extraordinary story.

Travelling by bike had certainly given an honest and grounded perspective and a great snapshot of Africa in 2009-10. But I could not have imagined how lengthy and complex would be the task of telling the story in a book and a film.

In the three years it has taken to produce both, Africa has been constantly changing, struggling in some places and thriving in others, adapting, evolving, emerging.

If I attempted the same journey three years on, some of my experiences would be different and parts of the route would have to be altered. Extreme ideologies and extreme climatic conditions continue to test the resilience and, in some cases, the very existence of communities across the Sahel. It would now be difficult to make the same diversions to Oualata in Mauritania, Timbuktu in Mali and Termit in Niger due to the increasing threats imposed by al-Qaida in the Maghreb (AQIM) and its affiliates. Boko Haram has resumed its campaign of terror in the Borno region in north-east Nigeria, so I would most likely have had to choose another path to reach Cameroon.

But if I was to visit the same projects and initiatives being developed and run by my expedition partners now, I would find one good-news story after another. All of the organisations I worked with, large and small, have continued to develop, many initiatives having an increasingly significant impact in the communities and countries where they are active. For example, thousands of lives were saved and livelihoods protected because of the added resilience the Farmer Managed Natural Regeneration (FMNR) movement provided during the West African drought of 2012. The movement continues to expand across the continent, from Niger through the Sahel and now to the Horn of Africa.

I would still be able to wear the same Edun Live t-shirts as I did in 2010. The Cotton Conservation Initiative in Uganda has gone from strength to strength. Once the number of participating farmers stabilised at 8000 (the number CCIU ascertained was sustainable), the focus shifted to include cultivating other rotational crops. As a result, farmers' fortunes been revived, and they can look forward to a secure and more prosperous future. While there have been some changes to the manufacturing side of the project, the t-shirts are still 'grow-to-sew' products of Africa.

The Millennium Villages Project has been scaled up to include initiatives in twenty countries across sub-Saharan Africa. Communities are taking charge of their own development and many partnering governments are adopting Millennium Village-like policies in their national agendas. This ensures that as international financial support phases out and the Millennium Development Goals are redefined to become the Sustainable Development Goals after 2015 the economic, social, technological and environmental benefits will endure.

Plan International maintains its multi-faceted child-centred development work throughout Africa. In Burkina Faso, the second phase of the BRIGHT (Burkinabe Response to Improve Girls' Chances to Succeed) project is underway with the building of six more schools in the region we visited. In eastern Cameroon, the fight for the rights of the Baka people goes on; many more are being forced to resettle as 2000 square kilometres of the country's forests are lost to logging every year. Plan Zambia's HIV/AIDS education program has adopted a greater emphasis on preventing mother-to-child transmission (MTCT).

World Bicycle Relief has expanded to include much of southern and eastern Africa where almost a thousand mechanics have been trained to service more than 170,000 bicycles used to benefit the education, healthcare and microfinance programs I learned about and more.

Valerie Browning's twenty-bed Barbara May Maternity Hospital, under construction when I visited, opened on 24 October 2011. Valerie and her nephew, Dr Andrew Browning, a gynaecologist who works in Ethiopia and Tanzania as a fistula surgeon, have set up the Barbara May Foundation, primarily to support their maternal healthcare projects. Valerie, her husband Ismael and the Afar Pastoralist Development Association continue to serve their people, improving literacy, primary health, income diversification and drought support (much needed in 2011-12).

Help Us Grow (HUG) is proving to be an appropriate title for Helen Brown's and David Ssemwogerere's organisation. A health clinic has been added to the Suubi Centre, and several more community and income-building ventures and cross-cultural interactions developed.

In Nairobi, the projects run at the Ruben Centre in Mukuru slum have grown in size and scope. In 2013 extensions were completed to the medical clinic to meet needs ranging from neonatal classes to the treatment of AIDS and other infectious diseases. Twenty-four new classrooms were added in 2014 to the primary school and a framework for a secondary education service has been initiated.

Omer Jama remains as busy as ever procuring donors and implementing projects through his Taakulo Somaliland Community organisation to benefit education, health, disability, clean water and sanitation and, in 2011-12, drought relief.

Three years on and the final days of my journey across Puntland to Cape Hafun would have been slightly less restrictive in that there is no military offensive taking place against al-Shabaab and the state government and its allies have managed to kerb some of the pirate activity. It is all relative though, and both threats remain significant. The Puntland government's transition towards a full democracy took another step forward, with a peaceful presidential election held on 8 January 2014. Dr Abdirahman Farole lost by one vote to the former prime minister of Somalia, Dr Adbiweli Gaas, and by all reports Farole stepped down with grace and dignity.

The Breaking the Cycle Expedition has given me, and I hope those who have followed the story, a strong sense of place – a perspective of how the African continent fits together. In 2012, when I heard that a group of religious extremists had seized Timbuktu for ten months, destroyed some of its ancient monuments and burned some of its irreplaceable manuscripts in an attempt to obliterate Timbuktu's time-honoured traditions of piety, tolerance, wisdom and justice, it felt like a personal loss. Like every place I visited on my journey, the ancient city is etched in my heart; connected to the rest of my world so that now Timbuktu no longer seems so far away.